This *Companion* offers students crucial guidance on virtually every aspect of the work of this complex and controversial writer, bringing together the contrasting views of major critics and active practitioners.

The opening essays place Brecht's creative work in its historical and biographical context and are followed by chapters on single texts, from *The Threepenny Opera* to *The Caucasian Chalk Circle*, on some early plays, on the *Lehrstücke* and on the neglected contribution of Elisabeth Hauptmann to the Brecht canon. The third group of essays analyses Brecht's directing, his theatrical theories, his poetry, his interest in music, his significant collaboration with stage designers and his work with actors, concluding with an assessment of Brecht's continuing influence on theatre practice.

A detailed calendar of Brecht's life and work and a selective bibliography of English criticism complete this provocative overview of a writer who constantly aimed to provoke.

THE CAMBRIDGE
COMPANION TO
BRECHT

CAMBRIDGE COMPANIONS TO LITERATURE

THE CAMBRIDGE
COMPANION TO
BRECHT

EDITED BY
PETER THOMSON
Professor of Drama, University of Exeter

AND
GLENDYR SACKS
formerly Department of Drama, University of Exeter

CAMBRIDGE
UNIVERSITY PRESS

Published by the Press Syndicate of the University of Cambridge
The Pitt Building, Trumpington Street, Cambridge CB2 1RP
40 West 20th Street, New York, NY 10011–4211, USA
10 Stamford Road, Oakleigh, Melbourne 3166, Australia

First published 1994
Reprinted 1995, 1997, 1998

Printed in the United Kingdom at the University Press, Cambridge

A catalogue record for this book is available from the British Library

Library of Congress cataloguing in publication data
The Cambridge companion to Brecht / edited by Peter Thomson and
Glendyr Sacks.
p.   cm. – (Cambridge companions to literature)
Includes bibliographical references and index.
ISBN 0 521 41446 6 (hardback) 0 521 42485 2 (paperback)
1. Brecht, Bertolt, 1898–1956 – Criticism and interpretation.
I. Thomson, Peter, 1938–   . II. Sacks, Glendyr, 1955–   . III. Series.
PT2603.R397Z58187 1993
832'.912 – dc20   93–18181   CIP

ISBN 0 521 41446 6 hardback
ISBN 0 521 42485 2 paperback

This book is dedicated to
Rhoda Sacks
and to the memory of
Lily Thomson

CONTENTS

CONTENTS

ILLUSTRATIONS

Acknowledgement is made to those people and institutions named.

NOTES ON CONTRIBUTORS

Christopher Baugh is Senior Lecturer in Drama and Theatre Arts at Goldsmiths' College, London University. He has worked in England and Ireland as a professional designer, and at Humboldt State University, California, as Visiting Professor of scenography. He is a regular scenographer for the Mecklenburgh Opera. Author of *Garrick and Loutherbourg* (1990), co-editor of *The Play of Personality in Restoration Theatre* (1992), he has also written articles on eighteenth-century scenography, Inigo Jones, William Capon and Edward Gordon Craig.

Peter Brooker is Reader in modern literary and cultural studies at the University of Greenwich. He helped found and edit the journal *Literature and History*, has published *A Student's Guide to the Selected Poems of Ezra Pound* (1979) and *Bertolt Brecht: Dialectics, Poetry, Politics* (1988). He has also co-edited the volume *Dialogue and Difference: English into the Nineties* (1989) and completed a Critical Reader titled *Modernism/Postmodernism* (1992). He is currently working on a book on modernism and the American city.

Margaret Eddershaw is Senior Lecturer in the Department of Theatre Studies at Lancaster University. Her publications include various essays on Brecht in performance, on Stanislavsky and Brecht, and her book entitled *Performing Brecht* is scheduled for publication in 1993.

John Fuegi is Professor of German at the University of Maryland. He has served as editor of fourteen volumes of the Proceedings of the International Brecht Society. He is the author of *The Essential Brecht* (1972), *Bertolt Brecht: Chaos, According to Plan* (1986) and the forthcoming *Brecht & Co.: An Archeology of Voices* (1993). He co-directed and scripted the 1992 film on Ruth Berlau, *That Deadly Longing*.

Kim H. Kowalke is Professor of Musicology at the Eastman School of Music, University of Rochester and President of the Kurt Weill Foundation for Music. He is the author of *Kurt Weill in Europe* (1979) and the editor of *A New Orpheus: Essays on Kurt Weill* (1986) and *A Stranger Here Myself: Kurt Weill Studien* (1992). Currently editing and translating the Weill–Lenya correspondence (forthcoming 1994).

Robert Leach is Senior Lecturer in Drama and Theatre Arts at the University of Birmingham. He has written poetry and plays, and was for two years Artistic Director of Cannon Hill Community Theatre, Birmingham. His books include *How to Make a Documentary Play* (1975), *The Punch and Judy Show: History, Tradition and Meaning* (1985) and *Vsevolod Meyerhold* (1989).

Christopher McCullough is Lecturer in Drama at the University of Exeter. He has published widely on the dissemination of Shakespeare's plays on the English stage and on the English stage deconstruction of Brecht's plays. He is one of the editors of *Studies in Theatre Production*.

Stephen McNeff is a composer and conductor who has worked extensively in the field of music-theatre. He co-founded South West Music Theatre and spent seven years in Canada as Associate Director and Composer in Residence of the Music Theatre Programme at the Banff Centre School of Fine Arts.

Tony Meech is Lecturer in the Drama Department of the University of Hull. His publications include articles on the theatre of the GDR, and he has translated plays by Lessing, Büchner, Brecht, Christoph Hein and Botho Strauss.

Roswitha Mueller is Associate Professor of German and Film Studies at the University of Wisconsin. She is co-editor and founding member of *Discourse: Journal for Theoretical Studies in Media and Culture*. Her book on *Bertolt Brecht and the Theory of Media* appeared in 1989 and another on Austrian film-maker Valie Export is forthcoming in 1993.

Michael Patterson is Reader in Theatre Studies at the University of Ulster, Coleraine. He has published several books and articles on German theatre, including *German Theatre Today* (1976), *The Revolution in German Theatre 19000–1933* (1981), and *Peter Stein* (1981).

Eve Rosenhaft is Senior Lecturer in the Department of German, University of Liverpool. She is the author of *Beating the Fascists? The German Communists and Political Violence 1929–1933* (1983) and *The State and Social Change in Germany 1880–1980* (1990), as well as numerous articles on the history of the communist movement, youth and women in modern Germany.

Glendyr Sacks was, until 1992, Lecturer in the Drama Department at the University of Exeter. She was Visiting Lecturer at Humboldt State University, California, and Ewha University (Korea); has co-edited the journal *Studies in Theatre Production*; has been involved in Trade Union activities, Equal Opportunities, Anti-Apartheid, and has made theatre for these campaigns.

Joel Schechter was, until 1992, editor of *Theater* magazine, and dramaturg at the Yale Repertory Theatre. His book, *Durov's Pig: Clowns, Politics and Theatre* (1985) includes several chapters on Brecht. He has also campaigned as a Green Party candidate for the Senate in Connecticut. In 1992, he was appointed Professor of Theatre Arts at San Francisco State University.

Maria Shevtsova's main field of research and publication is the sociology of the theatre. She is Reader in French Studies at the University of Sydney. Her publications include sociocultural studies of productions and cultural theory, and she is at present researching theatre audiences.

Darko Suvin is Professor of English at McGill University. His books include *To Brecht and Beyond* (1984), works on science fiction and two volumes of poetry. He edits, for the International Comparative Literature Association, *Literary Research / Recherche littéraire*. He is currently working on Brecht and Japanese theatre.

Peter Thomson is Professor of Drama at the University of Exeter. He is the author, with Jan Needle, of *Brecht* (1981). He is co-editor of *Studies in Theatre Production* and the author of two books on Shakespeare's theatrical practice.

Philip Thomson is Professor of German Studies at Monash University, Melbourne. He is the author of *The Poetry of Brecht: Seven Studies* (1989) and numerous articles on Brecht's work.

Carl Weber became directing assistant to Bertolt Brecht in 1952, as well as a dramaturg and actor with the Berliner Ensemble, where, after Brecht's death, he remained a director of the company. Since 1957 he has directed in major theatres in Germany and elsewhere and for GDR television. From 1984, he has been Professor at Stanford University, and has directed extensively throughout America and Canada. He has translated and edited contemporary German theatre, including the work of Müller, Handke and Kroetz.

Elizabeth Wright is Lecturer and Fellow in German at Girton College, Cambridge. Among her publications are *Psychoanalytic Criticism: Theory in Practice* (1984), *Postmodern Brecht* (1989) and, as editor, *Feminism and Psychoanalysis: A Critical Dictionary* (1992).

A Brecht calendar

As a visual aid to the following of Brecht's sometimes complex movements, cities and countries in which he was present at the time indicated are highlighted.

1898   **10 February:** Brecht born in AUGSBURG.

1917   Enrols at University of MUNICH.

1918   Writes 'The Legend of the Dead Soldier'. Writes first version of *Baal*.
October: military service as a medical orderly in AUGSBURG.

1919   **9 January:** Brecht demobilised.
13 February: 'Spartakus' (later *Drums in the Night*) completed.
Takes small part in Karl Valentin's political cabaret, MUNICH.
July: Brecht and Paula Banholzer's son, Frank, born.
October: works as theatre critic for *Volkswillen*.
During 1919, probably wrote several one-act plays, including *The Beggar or the Dead Dog*, *The Wedding*, *Driving out the Devil*, *Lux in Tenebris*, *A Humble Wedding*.

1920   **21 February:** first visit to BERLIN. Leaves on 13 March, the same day as the Kapp Putsch. Returns to AUGSBURG.

1921   **September:** short story, 'Bargan Lets It Happen (Be)', is published in *Der neue Merkur*, MUNICH.
7 November: second trip to BERLIN. Attends Max Reinhardt's rehearsals of Strindberg's *A Dream Play*, along with other major directors' rehearsals.

1922   **Spring:** begins directing Arnolt Bronnen's *Vatermord* in BERLIN. Arguments lead to his withdrawing from the production.
29 September: *Drums in the Night* opens at the Kammerspiele, MUNICH. (Directed by Otto Falckenberg; Brecht attends rehearsals.) *Baal* and *Drums in the Night* are published.
October: signs contract to work as dramaturg at Kammerspiele, MUNICH.

13 November: awarded the 1922 Kleist Prize for *Drums*. BERLIN.

20 December: Deutsches Theater production of *Drums*. (Directed by Falckenberg; Brecht attends many rehearsals; Alexander Granach (Kragler).) BERLIN. Brecht returns to MUNICH soon afterwards.

1923   **March:** Marianne Zoff and Brecht's daughter, Hanne, born.

9 May: première of *In The Jungle* at the Residenz-Theater, MUNICH. (Directed by Erich Engel; Brecht involved in all stages of production; designed by Caspar Neher.)

August: co-directs, with Arnolt Bronnen, the première of a condensed version of Hans Henny Jahnn's play, *Pastor Ephraim Magnus*. BERLIN.

8 December: première of *Baal* in Altes Theater, LEIPZIG. (Directed by Alwin Kronacher; Brecht participating in most rehearsals.)

1924   **19 March:** première of Brecht/Feuchtwanger's adaptation of Marlowe's *Edward II* at the Kammerspiele, MUNICH. (Brecht directs; designed by Neher; Oskar Homolka (Mortimer).)

September: moves to BERLIN, to work as assistant dramaturg at the Deutsches Theater.

BERLIN

1924   **29 October:** production of *Drums* in Deutsches Theater, BERLIN. (Directed by Engel; designed by Neher; Fritz Kortner (Shlink); Walter Frank (Garga).)

November: Helene Weigel and Brecht's son, Stefan, born.

1925   **February/March:** works on adaptation of Ferdinand Bruckner's version of *The Lady of the Camelias*. (Directed by Bernhard Reich and Elisabeth Bergner at Deutsches Theater.)

1926   **14 February:** *Baal*, revised together with Elisabeth Hauptmann, performed by the Junge Bühne, at the Deutsches Theater in BERLIN. (Directed by Brecht and Oskar Homolka, who also played Baal; designed by Neher.) A single matinée performance.

Series of short stories published, under Brecht's name, although 'written in the closest possible association' (Fuegi)[1] with Hauptmann.

25 September: première of *Man is Man* at Landestheater, DARMSTADT. Hauptmann co-worked the text. (Directed by Jacob Geis; designed by Neher.)

1927   January: *Hauspostille*, a collection of poems, published by Propyläen publishing house under Brecht's name, although some of the poems were written by Hauptmann.

18 March: Berlin Radio broadcasts *Man is Man*, directed by Alfred Braun, with Weigel as Begbick.

17 July: première of *Songspiel Mahagonny* in BADEN-BADEN. First collaboration with Kurt Weill. (Directed by Brecht; music by Weill; design and background projections by Neher; Lotte Lenya (Jessie).) During this year, Brecht involved in Piscator's directors' collective, based in the Piscator-Bühne, in Nollendorfplatz, BERLIN.

14 October: Berlin Radio broadcasts Brecht's adaptation of Shakespeare's *Macbeth*. (Directed by Alfred Braun; introduced by Brecht.)

10 December: revised version of *In the Jungle of the Cities* performed in DARMSTADT; directed by Carl Ebert.

1928   **31 August:** première of *The Threepenny Opera* by Hauptmann/Brecht/Weill/Klammer at the Theater am Schiffbauerdamm, BERLIN. (Directed by Engel with participation by Brecht; designed by Neher; conducted by Theo Mackeben with the Lewis Ruth Band; Harald Paulsen (Macheath); Roma Bahn (Polly); Lenya (Jenny).)

December: Brecht's short story, 'The Beast', wins first prize in *Berlin Illustierte* competition.[2]

1929   **March/April:** production of Marieluise Fleisser's *Die Pioniere von Ingolstadt* at the Theater am Schiffbauerdamm, BERLIN. (Directed by Brecht and Jacob Geis; designed by Neher.)

Summer: radio production of Brecht/Weill's *Berlin Requiem*, with Weigel.

28 July: directs the first *Lehrstück*, *The Flight over the Ocean* (co-written with Hauptmann and Weill) and *The Baden-Baden Cantata of Acquiescence* (co-written with Hauptmann, Dudow and Hindemith) in BADEN-BADEN.

31 August: première of Hauptmann's *Happy End*, with music by Weill and some songs by Brecht, at the Theater am Schiffbauerdamm, BERLIN. (Directed by Engel and Brecht; designed by Neher; with Peter Lorre, Weigel, Homolka and Carola Neher.)

1930   First three issues of Brecht's collected writings (*Versuche*) – including first notes on the plays – are published.

9 March: première of *The Rise and Fall of the City of Mahagonny* by Brecht/Hauptmann/Weill/Neher, in the Opera House, LEIPZIG. (Directed by Walter Brugmann; design and projections by Neher.)

23 June: *He Who Said Yes* by Hauptmann/Brecht/Weill performed at the Central Institute for Training and Teaching in BERLIN. (Directed by Brecht and Weill.) Ending later revised to create *He Who Said No.*

18 October: Weigel's and Brecht's daughter, Barbara, born.

10 December: première of *The Measures Taken*, by Brecht and Hauptmann, at the Grosses Schauspielhaus, BERLIN. (Music by Hanns Eisler; designed by Teo Otto; with Weigel, Ernst Busch, Granach and workers' choir.)

1931 **31 January:** Berlin Radio broadcasts Brecht's adaptation of Shakespeare's *Hamlet.* (Directed by Alfred Braun; with Fritz Kortner and Oskar Homolka.)

6 February: production of revised version of *Man is Man* at Staatstheater, BERLIN. (Directed by Brecht; designed by Neher; Lorre (Galy Gay); Weigel (Begbick).)

19 February: film version of *The Threepenny Opera* opens in BERLIN. (Directed by G. W. Pabst; music by Weill; with Carola Neher, Lotte Lenya, Rudolph Forster, Busch.) Brecht began collaborating on the script, but when his work was rejected, withdrew from the film and sued Nero Film Company.

4 April: *The Flight over the Ocean* performed in America, at the Philadelphia Academy of Music, under Leopold Stokowski.

August: Brecht completes collaborative filmscript, *Kuhle Wampe.* Brecht finishes *Saint Joan of the Stockyards*, written with Hauptmann, Borchardt and Burri, between 1929–31.

21 December: production of *The Rise and Fall of the City of Mahagonny* at the Kurfürstendamm Theater, BERLIN. (Initially directed by Brecht and Neher, later by Neher alone when arguments between Weill and Brecht disrupted rehearsals to the point that Brecht was given money to direct *The Mother* instead; designed by Neher; Lenya (Jenny).)

1932 **17 January:** première of *The Mother* (collaborators: Eisler, Weiseborn, Dudow) at the Theater am Schiffbauerdamm, BERLIN, and toured to working-class districts of Berlin. (Directed by Brecht and Emil Burri; designed by Neher; Weigel (Vlassova); Busch (Pavel).)

February: police ban further agitprop performances of *The Mother.*

11 April: Berlin Radio broadcasts *Saint Joan of the Stockyards.* Directed by Alfred Braun.

14 May: *Kuhle Wampe* premièred in MOSCOW. Brecht travels there to attend première.

30 May: censored version of *Kuhle Wampe*, by Brecht, Slatan

Dudow and Ernst Ottwalt, opens in BERLIN. (Directed by Dudow; music by Eisler.) Banned soon after release.

1933　28 February: Brecht and Weigel flee Berlin the morning after the Reichstag fire. Travel to PRAGUE, VIENNA, SWITZERLAND and then PARIS.

EXILE IN EUROPE

1933　13 April: *The Threepenny Opera* opens at Empire Theatre, New York. (Translated by Krimsky; Neher's designs used.)

7 June: première of Brecht/Weill ballet, *The Seven Deadly Sins*, at Théâtre des Champs-Elysées, PARIS. (Choreography by George Balanchine and Boris Kochno; Brecht involved in some rehearsals; designed by Neher; Tilly Losch and Lotte Lenya in leading roles.)

June: settles in DENMARK.

September: returns to PARIS.

December: leaves Paris and joins Weigel in SKOVBOSTRAND, DENMARK.

1934　Completes *The Threepenny Novel*. Published in Amsterdam.

Publication of second book of poems, *Lieder Gedichte Chöre*, with Eisler.

Together with Margarete Steffin, writes last *Lehrstück*, *The Horatii and the Curiatii*.

October to December: first visit to LONDON.

1935　Spring: visits MOSCOW where he meets Joseph Losey and sees the performance of the Chinese actor, Mei Lan-fang.

April: begins work with Steffin on the sketches that will form *Fear and Misery of the Third Reich*.

June: stripped of German citizenship by the Nazis.

15 June: goes to PARIS for international Writers' Conference.

7 October: *The Mother* performed in Copenhagen by Ruth Berlau and the Revolutionary Theatre Group.

15 October: in NEW YORK at the invitation of the Theatre Union to work on their production of *The Mother*, but quarrels led to Brecht and Eisler being finally removed from rehearsals on 8 November.

19 November: the Theatre Union's version in English of *The Mother* opens in New York. (Translated and adapted by Paul Peters; directed by Victor Wolfson; designed by Mordecai Gorelik; Helen Henry in title role.)

29 December: leaves New York.[3]

1936   **April to July:** in LONDON.

4 November: première of *Round Heads and Pointed Heads*, in Danish, in Knight's Hall Theatre, COPENHAGEN. (Directed by Per Knutzon; Brecht involved in some rehearsals.) Twenty-one performances.

12 November: production of *The Seven Deadly Sins* in COPENHAGEN. (Choreography by Harold Landers; involvement by Brecht.) Two performances.

1937   **28 September:** World Fair production of *The Threepenny Opera* in PARIS. (Directed by Francesco von Mendelsohn; participation by Brecht.)

16 October: première, in German, of *Señora Carrar's Rifles* (written in collaboration with Steffin) in PARIS. (Directed by Dudow; involvement by Brecht in rehearsals and casting; Weigel in title role.)

19 December: production, in Danish, of *Señora Carrar's Rifles* in COPENHAGEN. (Directed by Berlau; Brecht present at some rehearsals; performed by the Revolutionary Theatre Group with Dagmar Andreasen in lead role.)

The Exception and the Rule published in *Internationale Literatur*, no. 9 (Moscow, 1937).

1938   **14 February:** production, in German, of *Señora Carrar's Rifles* in COPENHAGEN. (Directed by Brecht and Berlau; set from 1937 Berlau production; Weigel in title role.)

21 May: German-language première of eight scenes from *Fear and Misery of the Third Reich* under title of 99% in PARIS. (Directed by Dudow; participation by Brecht; music by Paul Dessau; Weigel as the Jewish Wife.)

August:[4] première of *The Exception and The Rule*, by Brecht, Hauptmann and Burri, in Hebrew at Kibbutz Givat Chaim in Palestine. (Directed by Alfred Wolf.)

13 September: production of *Señora Carrar's Rifles* in English, at Unity Theatre, London. (Directed by John Fernald; Peggy Cochrane in title role.) Toured to other English cities.

November: Brecht and Steffin complete first version of *Life of Galileo*.

1939   **3 February:** *Señora Carrar's Rifles* produced at San Francisco Green Street Theatre.

March: begins work on *The Good Person of Szechwan*, in collaboration with Berlau and Steffin.

23 April: Brecht moves to STOCKHOLM, SWEDEN, as Nazis move closer.

August: production of *What is the Price of Iron?* in STOCKHOLM. (Directed by Brecht and Berlau; Brecht used the pseudonym John Kent as playwright; performed by students from an Adult Education school in Stockholm.)

Third book of poems, *Svendborger Gedichte*, published.

November: completes *Mother Courage and Her Children* and *The Trial of Lucullus*. Steffin collaborated on latter.

1940   **17 April:** moves to HELSINKI, FINLAND, eight days after the Nazis invade Denmark and Norway.

12 May: Radio Beromünster (Berne, Switzerland) broadcasts *The Trial of Lucullus*.

July: moves to the country home of Hella Wuolijoki in FINLAND.

September: in collaboration with Hella Wuolijoki, completes work on *Mr Puntila and his Man Matti*.

1941   **March to April:** collaborates with Steffin on *The Resistible Rise of Arturo Ui*; completes *The Good Person of Szechwan*.

19 April: première of *Mother Courage and Her Children*, at the Zurich Schauspielhaus. (Directed by Leopold Lindtberg; sets and costume by Otto; lead played by Therese Giehse.)

13 May: Brecht, Weigel, their children, Steffin and Berlau leave HELSINKI for America. They go via LENINGRAD and MOSCOW – where Steffin died of tuberculosis on 4 June. Brecht heard the news when he arrived in VLADIVOSTOK, from where he and his entourage embarked for California on 13 June – nine days before the Germans invaded Russia.

EXILE IN AMERICA

1941   **21 July:** arrives in CALIFORNIA.

1942   **May to October:** having collaborated with Fritz Lang on the story, Brecht works with John Wexley on the script for *Hangmen Also Die*. The film is shot between November and December. (Story by Brecht and Lang; directed by Lang; the credit for the script goes to Wexley; music by Eisler.)

28 May and 14 June: two performances in German of several scenes from *Fear and Misery*, translated and adapted by Eric Bentley as *The Private Life of The Master Race*. (Directed by Berthold Viertel in New York.)

October: begins collaboration with Lion Feuchtwanger on a Joan of Arc play which later forms *The Visions of Simone Machard*.

1943   **4 February:** première of *The Good Person of Szechwan* in the Schauspielhaus, Zurich. (Directed by Leonard Steckel; designed by Otto.)
8 February: Brecht goes to NEW YORK and stays with Berlau.
26 March: *Hangmen Also Die* premièred in Hollywood.
March to May: Brecht and H. R. Hays collaborate on an adaptation of Webster's *The Duchess of Malfi.*
26 May: returns to SANTA MONICA.
June: completes *Simone Machard* and continues work on *Schweyk in the Second World War* (written 1941–3).
9 September: première of *Life of Galileo* in the Zurich Schauspielhaus. (Directed by Steckel; designed by Otto; Steckel in title role.) Begins work with Berlau on *The Caucasian Chalk Circle.*
November: Brecht goes to NEW YORK to work with W. H. Auden on *The Duchess of Malfi.* In December, when Hays hears of this, he withdraws from further collaboration on the script.

1944   **March:** Brecht returns to CALIFORNIA.
June: Brecht completes first draft of *The Caucasian Chalk Circle.*
September: Berlau's and Brecht's son is born and dies a few days later.
Seventeen scenes from *Fear and Misery* published as *The Private Life of the Master Race.* (Translated by Bentley, under supervision of Brecht and Hauptmann; published in New Directions.)
December: begins work with Charles Laughton on a new version and translation of *Galileo.*

1945   **23 May:** returns to NEW YORK to oversee the production of *The Private Life of the Master Race.*
12 June: nine scenes from *The Private Life of the Master Race* are performed, in English, in the Pauline Edwards Theatre, NEW YORK. (Translated by Bentley; directed by Viertel and Brecht, after Piscator withdrew.)
July: in VERMONT, working with Bergner on *The Duchess of Malfi.*
December: completes English version of *Galileo,* in collaboration with Laughton.

1946   **February to March:** works with W. H. Auden on *Malfi* in NEW YORK.
15 October: having toured to Boston and Connecticut, adaptation of Webster's *The Duchess of Malfi* opens on Broadway, in the Ethel Barrymore Theatre, NEW YORK. (Adaptation by Brecht/Bergner/W. H. Auden/H. R. Hays; directed by George Rylands; music by Benjamin Britten; Bergner in title role; Canada Lee (Bosola). Brecht

involved in production after Rylands returned to England, but little of his adaptation was actually used.) Thirty-nine performances.

1947   31 July: première, in English, of Laughton/Brecht version of *Life of Galileo* at the Coronet Theatre in LOS ANGELES. (Directed by Joseph Losey, with participation from Charles Laughton and Brecht; title role played by Laughton.) Seventeen performances.

30 October: Brecht questioned by House UnAmerican Activities Committee in WASHINGTON. The next day, he flies to PARIS.

BACK TO EUROPE

1947   November: travels to SWITZERLAND, where he and Neher are reunited. Settles in ZURICH.

7 December: *Life of Galileo* transfers to the Maxine Elliott Theatre on Broadway.

1948   15 February: première of *Antigone*, adapted by Brecht from Hölderlin's translation of Sophocles, in CHUR, SWITZERLAND. (Directed by Brecht; designed by Neher; Weigel (Antigone); Hans Gaugler (Creon).) One matinée performance.

5 June: première of *Mr Puntila and his Man Matti*, by Brecht and Hella Wuolijoki, opens in the ZURICH Schauspielhaus. (Directed by Kurt Hirschfeld with Brecht mostly responsible for rehearsals and production; music by Dessau; designed by Otto; Steckel (Puntila).)

July to August: works on *A Short Organum*; begins work on *The Days of the Commune*.

Late October: leaves for EAST BERLIN via SALZBURG and PRAGUE, as he is refused a visa for the American zone.

BACK TO BERLIN

1949   January: Berliner Ensemble created.

11 January: *Mother Courage and Her Children* opens in Deutsches Theater, BERLIN. (Directed by Brecht and Engel; music by Dessau; sets by Heinrich Kilger, based on Otto's 1941 originals; Weigel (Courage); Angelika Hurwicz (Kattrin).)

February: Weigel appointed artistic director of Berliner Ensemble. Brecht goes to ZURICH to recruit actors for the Berliner Ensemble.

April: completes draft of *The Days of the Commune*.

May: returns to BERLIN via SALZBURG.

June to July: in BERLIN hospital with kidney trouble.

August: in SALZBURG.

September: in MUNICH and then returns to BERLIN.

12 **November:** first Berliner Ensemble production, *Mr Puntila and his Man Matti*, opens at the Deutsches Theater. (Directed by Brecht and Engel; designed by Neher; Steckel (Puntila); Geschonneck (Matti).)

1950   12 **April:** Brecht and Weigel granted Austrian citizenship.

15 **April:** *The Tutor*, adapted by Brecht (with Berlau/Benno Besson/ Egon Monk/Neher) from J. M. R. Lenz, opens at the Deutsches Theater. (Directed by Brecht and Neher; designed by Neher; Gaugler (Läuffer).)

8 **October:** *Mother Courage and Her Children* opens in the Kammerspiele, MUNICH. (Directed by Brecht; Bentley an assistant director; Giehse (Courage).)

1951   13 **January:** *The Mother* is performed by Berliner Ensemble in the Deutsches Theater, BERLIN. (Directed by Brecht; music by Eisler; designed by Neher; Weigel (Vlassova).)

17 **March:** *The Trial of Lucullus* – opera version by Dessau, later revised as *The Condemnation of Lucullus* – given a trial performance in East Berlin State Opera. (Directed by Wolf Völker; designed by Neher.)

May: Brecht begins adapting Shakespeare's *Coriolanus*.

5 **August:** *Report from Herrnburg* at the Deutsches Theater. (Directed by Monk; designed by Neher; music by Dessau.) Awarded National Prize.

11 **September:** new production of *Mother Courage* at the Berliner Ensemble.

1952   *Theaterarbeit* is published.

February: decides to buy house in Buckow. Brecht and Weigel visit WARSAW, to plan Berliner Ensemble performances there.

1953   17 **June:** workers' uprising in East Germany.

Summer: begins work on *Turandot, or the Whitewashers' Congress*, which is completed by 1954, but not revised.

Writes the *Buckow Elegies*.

1954   19 **March:** Berliner Ensemble moves to Theater am Schiffbauerdamm. Opens with Brecht's adaptation, in collaboration with Besson and Hauptmann, of Molière's *Don Juan*.

Summer: visits BRUGES, AMSTERDAM and PARIS, where the original *Mother Courage and Her Children* is on tour.

7 **October:**[5] German première of *The Caucasian Chalk Circle* at the Theater am Schiffbauerdamm, BERLIN. (Directed by Brecht; music by Dessau; designed by Karl von Appen; Hurwicz (Grusha); Busch (Azdak).)

21 December: awarded Lenin Peace Prize.[6]

1955 **March to April:** works on *Trumpets and Drums*.

May: visits MOSCOW to receive prize.

June: in PARIS for Berliner Ensemble's *Caucasian Chalk Circle*.

1956 **February:** in MILAN for Giorgio Strehler's production of *The Three-penny Opera*, in Piccolo Theatre.

May: in hospital.

10 August: attends last rehearsal. (Berliner Ensemble preparing for London season.)

14 August: Brecht dies.

NOTES

1 Fuegi, *Bertolt Brecht: Chaos, According to Plan*, p. 192.

2 See Willett, *Brecht Yearbook* 12 (1985) for claims that Hauptmann wrote most of the short story.

3 Lyon, in *Bertolt Brecht in America*, says 'The playwright did not return to Denmark immediately after *Mother* closed, but stayed until early February 1936' (p. 16). Völker, in *Brecht Chronicle*, says that Brecht left New York on 29 December 1935, and was back in Skovbostrand by the end of January 1936.

4 Hayman, in *Brecht: A Biography*, says 1 May 1938.

5 Willett, *The Theatre of Bertolt Brecht*, gives the date of this première as 15 June (see p. 20 and p. 56). While there were previews of the play, prior to the summer vacation and further rehearsal, the official first night was 7 October, as listed in the Ensemble's *Chronik* of 1961.

6 Previously known as the Stalin Peace Prize.

A NOTE ON TITLES

Full title in German	Full title in English	Short title in English
Baal	*Baal*	
Trommeln in der Nacht	*Drums in the Night*	
Im Dickicht der Städte	*In the Jungle of the Cities*	*In the Jungle*
Leben Eduards des Zweiten von England	*The Life of Edward II of England*	*Edward II*
Mann ist Mann	*Man is Man*	
Songspiel Mahagonny		
Die Dreigroschenoper	*The Threepenny Opera*	
Happy End	*Happy End*	
Aufstieg und Fall der Stadt Mahagonny	*The Rise and Fall of the City of Mahagonny*	*Mahagonny*
Der Ozeanflug	*The Flight over the Ocean*	
Badener Lehrstück vom Einverständnis	*The Baden-Baden Cantata of Acquiescence*	*The Baden-Baden Cantata*
Die Heilige Johanna der Schlachthöfe	*Saint Joan of the Stockyards*	*Saint Joan*
Der Jasager	*He Who Said Yes*	
Der Neinsager	*He Who Said No*	
Die Massnahme	*The Measures Taken*	
Die Ausnahme und die Regel	*The Exception and the Rule*	
Die Mutter	*The Mother*	
Die Horatier und die Kuriatier	*The Horatii and the Curiatii*	
Die Rundköpfe und die Spitzköpfe	*Round Heads and Pointed Heads*	
Die Sieben Todsünden der Kleinbürger	*The Seven Deadly Sins*	
Furcht und Elend des Dritten Reiches	*Fear and Misery of the Third Reich*	*Fear and Misery*
Die Gewehre der Frau Carrar	*Señora Carrar's Rifles*	*Señora Carrar*
Leben des Galilei	*Life of Galileo*	*Galileo*
Mutter Courage und ihre Kinder	*Mother Courage and Her Children*	*Mother Courage*

Full title in German	Full title in English	Short title in English
Das Verhör des Lukullus	*The Trial of Lucullus*	
Die Verurteilung des Lukullus	*The Condemnation of Lucullus*	
Der Gute Mensch von Sezuan	*The Good Person of Szechwan*	*The Good Person*
Herr Puntila und sein Knecht Matti	*Mr Puntila and his Man Matti*	*Puntila*
Der Aufhaltsame Aufstieg des Arturo Ui	*The Resistible Rise of Arturo Ui*	*Arturo Ui*
Die Gesichte der Simone Machard	*The Visions of Simone Machard*	*Simone Machard*
Schweyk im Zweiten Weltkrieg	*Schweyk in the Second World War*	*Schweyk*
Der Kaukasische Kreidekreis	*The Caucasian Chalk Circle*	
Die Antigone des Sophokles	*Antigone*	
Die Tage der Commune	*The Days of the Commune*	
Der Hofmeister	*The Tutor*	
Turandot oder der Kongress der Weisswäscher	*Turandot, or the Whitewashers' Congress*	*Turandot*
Pauken und Trompeten	*Trumpets and Drums*	

(Where full bibliographical details of works cited are not given in the endnotes, these details will be found in the bibliography.)

PREFACE

Political revaluations in Eastern Europe have placed Brecht's work and his reputation under renewed scrutiny, but nothing can alter the fact that he has been – and remains – a dominant force in the twentieth-century theatre. The essays collected in this book, written from various perspectives and towards various objectives, do not constitute a homage to Brecht. Some of them, indeed, may provide fuel for his detractors. More than most writers of equivalent status, Brecht has always divided his critics along partisan lines. Far too often, the resulting criticism has preferred advocacy to analysis. It is a meagre response to so committed a controversialist as Brecht to agree with everything he said or approve everything he did, and it is wholly inadequate to attempt merely to discredit him.

The *Companion* is divided into three parts. The first offers an account of pre-Hitler Germany and an outline of Brecht's life then and subsequently. Readers who would like to know more about the German theatre which influenced him, or against which he reacted, are referred to Max Spalter's *Brecht's Tradition* (Baltimore, 1967) and Michael Patterson's *The Revolution in German Theatre 1900–1933* (London, 1981). The second part contains chapters on a selection of plays. We regret, in particular, the absence of an essay on *Mr Puntila and his Man Matti* and on the overtly anti-Hitler plays, which have been squeezed out simply by considerations of space. There is, however, some indication of what might have been expected from Brecht's collaboration with Hella Wuolijoki on *Puntila* in John Fuegi's disputatious chapter on 'the Zelda syndrome'. The essays in the third part deal successively with Brecht's practice in the Berliner Ensemble, his theoretical writings, his poetry, his work with music and musicians, his work with design and designers, the theory and practice of acting in his work and the legacy he has left for other playwrights and practitioners.

There is no separate treatment of Brecht's prose (novels, short stories, letters, *Arbeitsjournal*, diaries) nor his work in and influence on film. However regrettable, these omissions are not an oversight. We have had to make choices, and the compelling one has been to acknowledge Brecht's theatrical eminence. The poetry is indissolubly linked with that eminence, the prose and films more readily separated from it.

We would like, finally, to acknowledge the co-operation of an incredibly helpful group of contributors, who have phoned and faxed across oceans, adjusted sentences and even accepted cuts from editors whose task has been immeasurably lightened by such willingness to accommodate. And Sarah Stanton, at the Cambridge University Press, is the best drama editor in the business.

I
CONTEXT AND LIFE

I

EVE ROSENHAFT

Brecht's Germany: 1898–1933

The only one among all of them who really *struck* me was Brecht, thanks to his proletarian costume. He was very lean, with a hungry face to which his cap gave a slightly crooked look; his words were wooden and clipped. Under his gaze you felt like a worthless heirloom, and he, the pawnbroker with his piercing eyes, was appraising you. He said little; you never learned the result of his appraisal. It seemed unbelievable that he was only thirty ... I grumbled about the advertisements with which Berlin was infested. They didn't bother him, he said; advertising had its good side. He had written a poem about Steyr cars, and got a car for it ... With this confession, produced as though it were a boast, he brought me down and silenced me ... 'He likes driving,' said Ibby, as though it were nothing. To me ... he seemed like a murderer; I was remembering 'Die Legende vom toten Soldaten', and he had taken part in a copy-writing contest for Steyr cars! 'He's still flattering his car,' said Ibby, 'he talks about it as though it were a lover. Why shouldn't he flatter it beforehand, so he can get one?'[1]

Bertolt Brecht *anno* 1928 (as encountered by Elias Canetti): the son of the provincial middle classes with the airs of a big-city proletarian, the enemy of capitalism transfixed by the best and worst of American culture, the pioneer of a revolutionary aesthetic who claimed he wrote only for money, the man who treated fast cars like women and women like cars, and yet contributed through his work to the movement for women's reproductive freedom. In his contradictory character, a character to a large extent self-created, Brecht epitomised the ambivalences of a Germany which, during his first thirty-five years, made the move from the provincial margins of European culture to become the capital of the twentieth century.

Brecht sometimes portrayed himself as a country boy, never quite at home 'in the jungle of the cities' and shocked into premature cynicism by the horrors of the First World War. In this respect, Brecht's own self-image echoed that of the respectable, middle-class Germany into which he was born, and it had as much of truth and myth in it as most self-portraits. The idyll of his childhood and schooldays in Augsburg was not a rural one, but one characteristic of the comfortable urban bourgeoisie. His parents – the daughter of civil servants and the managing director of a paper-mill – represented the two pillars of German middle-class culture, the historically privileged *Bildungsbürgertum* and the striving commercial classes. Their union was perhaps typical for a place like Augsburg. An ancient city of the Holy Roman Empire, Brecht's birthplace was also an industrial town of some significance, the site not only of paper and textile mills but also of the dynamic engineering firm MAN. From 1905 on, Augsburg officially qualified as a major city, with a population of over 100,000, including a high proportion of industrial workers migrating in from the surrounding countryside.[2] By 1900, the city's workers had their own Social Democratic daily paper.[3] The background, indeed the foundation for the bourgeois world of choral societies and chess-clubs in which the Brechts moved, was a rapidly modernising economy.

By the end of the century, Germany had become Europe's principal industrial power, in terms not only of its output but also of the leading role played by German firms in the 'second industrial revolution'. The heavy industrial giants like Krupp and the mining magnates of the Ruhr and Saar were joined by pioneers in the new technologies of electro-technical manufacturing (Bosch, Siemens, AEG) and chemicals (Hoechst, Bayer, BASF). Increasingly concentrated and organised into cartels and interest associations, German industrialists, though divided on many social and political issues, were united in their readiness to break out of the alliance with the old agrarian élite (the alliance of 'rye and iron') that had guaranteed the stability of the monarchical order between unification in 1871 and the dismissal of the old Chancellor, Bismarck, in 1890. At the same time that stability was being threatened by a growth of political self-consciousness among the population at large. The most alarming manifestation of this was the growth of the labour movement; under the system of universal manhood suffrage which Bismarck had introduced in 1871 to neutralise the middle-class Liberals, the Social Democratic Party in 1912 gained more than one-third of the popular vote and became the largest single party in the Reichstag. Other popular movements gave evidence of a simmering discontent with the old order and a growing capacity for mobilisation against it: tens of thousands of women (nearly a quarter of a million by 1914) joined organisations which, though rarely as radical in the prosecution of women's political rights as Britain's suffragettes, through their activities challenged the hegemony of men and patriarchal values in both private and public life. On the right, the politics of antisemitism and radical nationalism attracted sections of the lower middle class as well as younger members of the educated middle class, each group in its own way uncertain and unsettled by the challenge of new economic competitors and new values.

A sense of general crisis was present, too, in the realm of culture, where the rapid growth of cities made tangible all the anxieties associated with change. Augsburg's expansion was comparatively leisurely; the population of Berlin more than doubled between 1875 and 1910, while that of Munich more than trebled. The urban population, the crowd or the 'masses', presented itself as an entirely new social formation, indeed as a new kind of collective individual. In the new science of mass psychology and in the observations of philosophers and cultural critics alike, there was consensus on the view that the rise of the masses was a threat to the old order in culture and politics, and near-consensus that it was a sign of civilisation in decline. As the real income of the urban working classes rose, fear of their potential for unreflected violence gave way to anxieties about their capacity for unreflected consumption: the mass marketing through department stores of mass-produced goods, the wide circulation of pulp fiction, the spread of cinema-going with the shift from travelling picture-shows to purpose-built theatres (up to 2,500 in Germany by 1914)[4] – these spelt the end of taste and morality as the nineteenth century had known them.

From the turn of the century on, successive German governments pursued policies of international confrontation and armaments investment and encouraged patriotic and imperialist propaganda, in the hope of winning back both élite and popular support for the imperial system while avoiding genuine social and political reform. Germany thus bore a heavy responsibility for the war that broke out in 1914, and indeed the war was welcomed in many quarters as a relief from socio-political deadlock, an engine of cultural regeneration and an opportunity to reassert the manly virtues of a more austere, soldierly and genuinely German past. If these attitudes were more prevalent on the cultural and political 'right' than on the left, there was nonetheless a degree of agreement, across the political spectrum, that this was a defensive war, and that what needed defending was not only Germany itself but Western civilisation, now threatened from without by oriental barbarism in the form of the Russian autocracy. The first months of the war were characterised by a high degree of national unity born of optimism: 'All of us, all Germans fear God and nothing else on earth', wrote the schoolboy Bert Brecht two weeks after the outbreak of this 'ineluctable' conflict.[5]

In the event, this war turned into a protracted struggle which demanded the mobilisation of the energies and resources of the whole population, and its effect was to exacerbate the crisis which its outbreak had promised to solve. Like the wars of 'religion' of the seventeenth century, what all the combatant states entered into in 1914 in the spirit of a crusade revealed itself as an utterly futile and deeply venal undertaking. This was particularly the case in Germany, where the luxurious lifestyle of the old industrialists and new war profiteers stood in sharp contrast to the sacrifices of the mass of the population, unrewarded by victory even after four long years. But this was also a significantly new kind of war; in its length, its brutality and its character as 'total' war it represented at once the apotheosis and the revenge of technological modernity.

Between 1914 and 1918, 2.4 million German soldiers were killed. A million of these died on the Western front during the first five months of the war, in the trench warfare that came to represent the nightmare side of the conflict (as fighter planes and submarines provided objects for modernist fantasy). Dug in along a line that barely moved between September 1914 and the autumn of 1918, troops on both sides experienced war as an extended period of aimless waiting in a lunar landscape, punctuated by 'battles' in which each side bombarded the other with tons of metal and explosives. 'Combat' was less a matter of actively fighting the enemy than of waiting to see whether one would survive the next bombardment; and when an active assault was in prospect, man-to-man combat was routinely preceded by the use of new weapons whose purpose was to induce terror or paralysis, like gas or flame-throwers (both of which were introduced by the Germans). Those who did not survive, and many who did, suffered hideous wounds, disfigurement and the loss of limbs, so that the crippled veteran became one of the cultural icons of the 1920s.[6]

Perhaps the most characteristic victims of combat in this war, and those who received the most equivocal response from society at large, were the psychological casualties. Trench warfare induced its own psychoneurosis, shell-shock, which was registered for the first time on a large scale in the First World War. Yet both during and after the war military and medical authorities remained divided over whether the sufferers were to be regarded as genuine casualties and, if so, whether their sufferings were compensatable as 'war wounds' or were the consequence of an inherent psychological weakness. Thousands of veterans who were not certifiable as victims of shell-shock suffered from neurasthenia and lethargy for years after the end of hostilities. Another common complaint of war veterans, sexual impotence, points back to the specifically emasculating character of trench warfare and forward to the way in which the manifest gulf between the experiences of soldiers at the Front and of civilians at home in Germany was reworked in politics and culture in gendered terms: as a civil war between the sexes.

It was in the nature of this war that civilians were not safe at home, but engaged in the conflict on a 'home front'. In addition to the military casualties, it has been estimated that something like 700,000 civilian lives were lost, mainly through hunger and disease. A food shortage was enforced by the Allied naval blockade and exacerbated by poor harvests and inadequate systems for requisitioning and distributing foodstuffs. At the same time, the physical resistance of the population was weakened by long hours of work in the war industries, often under dangerous conditions. Women with families recruited into war-work to replace male workers suffered most notoriously, since they had to combine stressful work with hours of queuing for rationed goods and responsibility for running a household under increasingly anarchic conditions. Experienced and acknowledged as hardship, these conditions prompted the state to develop programmes for financial support and social provision for the families of soldiers, which, largely administered by women's voluntary organisations, constituted the beginnings of the modern welfare state. They also contributed to the generalised discontent and political mobilisation of women and young people, and thus to the success of the popular movement for an end to the war and to the old political order. In the social and political discourse of 1914–18, however, the situation on the home front was widely represented as a reversal of normal relations in which women and young men took advantage of the absence of adult males to seize power in the household and the workplace.

Images of female sexuality played a significant role in the sensationalism that permeated representations of war, in this first of popular wars to rely on mass propaganda for its legitimacy. If one feminine counterpart to the heroic warrior in the positive iconography of war was the woman raped by enemy soldiers, then the counterpart to the image of the crippled soldier as critique of wartime circumstances was that of the prostitute. Before the war, the figure of the prostitute had epitomised the evils of city life; now it was deployed to represent both the degeneracy of the occupied peoples and the dangers of self-indulgence, degeneration, and moral, political and physical infection at home. The actual use of brothels in occupied territories and even the provision by the military of mobile brothels for the troops were notorious features of a long war which enforced the separation of husbands and wives.[7] The syphilis sufferers who made up the bulk of the patients in the military infirmary where Brecht did his war service in the last weeks of the conflict (he was shielded by the fortunes of age and class from being called up any earlier) were as much casualties of war as the physical and psychological wrecks thrown up by the trenches.

One significant feature of the 1920s in Germany was thus the public preoccupation with the restoration or readjustment of relations in the private sphere, and the image of womanhood was a key term in the debate. Official policy was ambiguous; at the same time as women were forced out of the factories in order to make way for returning soldiers they were granted the vote and legal guarantees of equal rights in the Weimar Constitution. A strong pronatalist tendency in government had been reinforced by the slaughter of the war, and provided encouragement for pressure-groups engaged in promoting the image of motherhood. The campaign for a 'German Mother's Day', supported by florists' associations and by pronatal-ist groups, began in 1923, and contributed to the growth of a cult of mothers and sons which clearly bespoke the trauma of war.[8] And yet as the Mother's Day campaign peaked, in 1927, liberal, socialist and feminist activists were able to bring about a (limited) liberalisation of the law on abortion. The movement for reproductive rights, associated with a wider drive among progressive professionals and lay people for the dissemination of infor-mation and advice on sexual health and happiness, climaxed in a wave of national demonstrations and petitions against the ban on abortions (§218 of the penal code) in 1931. The movement itself reflected the increased self-awareness and aspirations to autonomy that many women undoubtedly enjoyed in the wake of the war and formal emancipation, as summed up in the ubiquitous figure of the 'new woman'. But it was fraught with ambigui-ties. For one thing, eugenic arguments were at least as important as argu-ments about individual women's freedom or health, particularly in attracting medical professionals to the campaign against §218. Similarly, the develop-ment of sexology and the practice of sexual and marriage counselling was powered by a rhetoric that emphasised the importance of sexual satisfaction to family stability and the production of healthy offspring.[9] And the pre-occupation with women as mothers was clearly not confined to the pronatal-ist right; not least (but not only) in the iconography of the reproductive rights campaign, the left systematically purveyed an image of the proletarian woman as essentially mother, simultaneously cursed and sanctified by unwanted pregnancy and childbirth. This figure haunts Brecht's own early poetry, as his first play to be produced, *Drums in the Night*, vibrates with the combined sexual and political uncertainty of 1918. In his own reflections on sexuality and its consequences, in acting out the tension between sexual liberty as an expression of individual sovereignty and the morning-after guilt of the libertine, and not least in projecting his preoccupations onto real and imagined women, Brecht was very much of his generation. The fate of *Kuhle Wampe*, Brecht and Dudow's 1932 film which treated the theme of abortion (among others), finally, illustrates the precarious political position of the new spirit of liberation; it was released by the censors only at its third review, and then only after all direct references to the fact that the central character had sought and obtained an illegal abortion had been cut.[10]

Reference to *Kuhle Wampe* and the political conflicts of 1932, when the Weimar political system was deep in its final crisis, reminds us that the First World War challenged historic class relations as it did gender relations. The prosecution of the war, demanding as it did the assent and the active participation of the whole population, required the creation of institutions of class-compromise. This began with the *Burgfrieden* of 1914, an informal civil peace in which the labour movement on the one hand and the state on the other tacitly agreed to abandon conflict in the interests of the war effort. As the war progressed, and the military authorities took power to direct the deployment of labour, the co-operation of the trade unions was purchased by building them into the administration of the system. And in October 1918, as it became apparent that Germany would have to make peace on the Allies' terms, the leaders of the Social Democratic Party (SPD) were drawn into government. In wartime, as far as the authorities were concerned, each of these moves had the character of a cynical manoeuvre designed to buy support or, in the case of the reforms of 1918, to deflect blame for the lost war from the monarchy and the military. None of them was sufficient to bridge the actual social divisions opened up by the strains of mobilisation.

The collapse of the monarchy and the declaration of a republic in November 1918 promised an access of real power to the democratic forces at large and to the labour movement in particular. A guarantee of the right to work or to be supported in times of unemployment, the declared right of both workers and employers to organise and to have a say through their organisations in the making of national economic policy, a system of state arbitration in industrial disputes, and not least the promise of a comprehensive system of social welfare – these features of the formal and informal constitution of the Weimar Republic bespoke a genuine optimism about the possibility of a better integrated and more egalitarian society. And in the first days after the collapse of the monarchy the power of this vision was such as to frighten representatives of the old order, the military and heavy industry, into accommodation with it: following the abdication of the Kaiser on 9 November, General Wilhelm Groener placed what was left of the Imperial Army at the disposal of the Social Democrat-led provisional government, on condition that no revolutionary experiments be tolerated, and on 15 November the representatives of employers and trade unions made an agreement in which the unions were recognised as full negotiating partners and granted significant improvements in their rights and working conditions in return for their continued support for existing property relations.

This compromise, and the democratic constitutional order that depended on it, provided the framework for a decade of openness and vigorous experimentation in social policy and in the arts. But it was never undisputed. Born of the emergency of war and revolution, it proved too fragile to withstand the strains of peacetime. The first direct challenge came from the political left. Only minutes after the Social Democratic leader Philipp Scheidemann publicly proclaimed the democratic republic, on 9 November 1918, Karl Liebknecht proclaimed the socialist republic. Liebknecht was leader of the left-radical and anti-war faction in the Social Democratic Party, which had crystallised into an independent movement during the war and became the German Communist Party (KPD) at the end of 1918. During the first months following the collapse of the monarchy, the Communists maintained a stance of opposition to the provisional government's plan for a popularly elected constituent assembly; they argued that real political democracy could not precede the socialisation of the economy, which should be carried out through the network of workers' and soldier's councils formed all over Germany since the beginning of November. The Communists also took a leading role in the revolutionary violence that flared up in the winter of 1918–19 and recurred periodically up to the end of 1923, fear of which drove the constituent assembly to hold its deliberations in Weimar rather than Berlin. The radicals' hope that even after the new Constitution was formally ratified in August 1919 it would be possible to carry the revolution further was fired by repeated exhortations from Moscow. But it was fuelled by evidence that sections of the working class and the labour movement were dissatisfied with the incompleteness of social reform, and in particular with the new government's failure to take the steps towards socialisation and workers' participation in economic management provided for in the Constitution.

Workers' resentment was further inflamed by the official policy of using volunteer troops (*Freikorps*), led by officers of the old army and recruited through nationalist and anti-bolshevik slogans, to put down unrest and disarm workers' militias. Repression of this kind was officially condoned even when, as in the Ruhr and Central Germany in 1920, the workers had armed themselves in defence of the Republic against a military coup, and the actions of the *Freikorps* were typically carried out with a self-indulgent brutality. Their most illustrious and best remembered victims were Karl Liebknecht and Rosa Luxemburg, clubbed to death and their bodies thrown into the Landwehr Canal in Berlin in January 1919. Closer to the young Bert Brecht, in spirit as well as geographically, was the 1918–19 revolution in Bavaria, led by artists and writers such as Kurt Eisner, Ernst Toller and Erich Mühsam. Himself a member of the Augsburg workers' and soldiers' council, Brecht made frequent rail journeys to Munich to observe what was going on and take part in meetings and demonstrations there. Eisner's assassination by a young aristocrat precipitated the desperate utopia of the Munich Soviet Republic. At the beginning of May, Munich fell, and the revolution was suppressed by the troops in a welter of random and official bloodshed; the sound of artillery could be heard as far away as Augsburg, which was already under *Freikorps* control.

The bloody conflicts of the Republic's early years lent a degree of passion to the rift between Social Democrats and Communists within the German labour movement, and resentment and disappointment at the Social Demo-crats' continued inability to improve the lot of the working class provided a constituency and a *raison d'être* for the party of the revolution long after the actual prospect of a workers' insurrection had receded. By the time Brecht encountered the Communist movement in Berlin in the late 1920s, it had very much developed a character of its own. That character was a contra-dictory one, for the KPD attracted an oddly assorted group of supporters ranging from narrow-minded Stalinist bureaucrats through militant skilled workers and idealistic intellectuals to former members of youth gangs – and did so as a matter of policy. While it continued to lay claim to the 'real' Marxist tradition and to the title of working-class vanguard, the Communist Party was increasingly isolated from the bulk of skilled and organised workers. These remained very largely faithful to the Social Democratic movement, with its associated trade union, cultural and co-operative organi-sations. Their loyalty was repaid in a flowering of social and cultural pro-jects, both party-based and sponsored by the SPD in local government, which included not only the extended activities of workers' cultural, welfare and sporting organisations but also the establishment of health clinics, the creation of non-confessional schools with parent participation and large-scale housing projects (some 66,000 new homes were built in Berlin between 1924 and 1930, to the innovative designs of world-famous architects).[11] Many of these developments benefited all working families where they were established, and together they contributed to an increase of self-confidence and a general mobilisation of social and political energies, particularly in urban neighbourhoods. But a section of the working class remained outside of these developments: there were those who were simply impoverished and desperate, and two economic crises – the hyperinflation of 1923 and the great depression after 1929 – swelled their numbers. There were also the young adults, the unskilled or semi-skilled, the unemployed or under-employed – and those who were all three. This group was becoming more significant in the mid-1920s, as German industry turned to rationalisation and de-skilling in order to weather the contraction that followed stabili-sation of the mark at the end of 1923. It was here that the Communist Party sought and found a constituency, by varying its rhetorical appeal to the revolutionary proletariat with practical efforts to organise in working-class neighbourhoods around the particular needs of workers and their families outside the workplace. This brought the Party closer to the plebeian culture of the streets. In Berlin, where the Party had its strongholds in the old working-class districts, the slums and notorious 'criminal areas', the communists rubbed shoulders with members of the much-mythologised crime bosses of the *Ringvereine* and attempted to politicise the prostitutes, and repeatedly engaged in campaigns to recruit members of the capital's youth gangs. Echoing this milieu, the KPD's revolutionary militancy frequently took the form of a cultivated *machismo* on the part of its leaders and activists, a masculine toughness which was particularly in evidence after 1929, when the organising of physical self-defence against actions by police, landlords and Nazi brownshirts began to absorb much of the Party's energy.

Against this background, the Communist Party continued to exercise a powerful attraction on intellectuals. They were drawn equally by the excitement of the revolutionary project and the commitment to Marxist education and intellectual rigour embodied in the Party's theoretical journals and in institutions like the Marxist Workers' College, where Brecht attended lectures in 1928–9. The growing influence of Stalin in the Soviet Union and of the Moscow-dominated Communist International in the KPD meant that open discussion and original thought were less and less welcome in the Party. But for many artists and writers the spur to political commitment and the concrete revolutionary utopia that the Soviet Union represented were sufficiently attractive in themselves. And for some intellectuals, for a time at least, the very dogmatism of the Comintern under Stalin represented a sought-after ideological anchor. The ideal of revolutionary discipline and manly sacrifice of oneself and others that characterises *The Measures Taken*, the humanist internationalism of the *Solidaritätslied* and the flat-capped, leather-jacketed proletarian tough of 1928 were all at home in the culture of the KPD, even if Brecht could never feel comfortable as a card-carrying party member.

In practice, moreover, the Party provided many opportunities in its everyday agitational work for the exploitation of new media and techniques; in the street theatre of its agitprop troupe 'Die roten Raketen' or the photomontages which John Heartfield published in the mass-circulation *Arbeiter-Illustrierte-Zeitung*, we can recognise Brecht's own preoccupation with the means and ends of truth-telling. As cinema established itself as the dominant form of public entertainment, the communist movement provided one (though by no means the only) forum for the discussion of the political uses of film and even for practical experimentation: *Kuhle Wampe*, the only film in which Brecht was involved at all stages, was initially sponsored by the communist Prometheus Film GmbH.

More generally, developments in cinematic taste reflected a cultural ambivalence that was almost universal in Weimar Germany: the simultaneous appeal of the Soviet Union and America. Widespread curiosity about post-revolutionary Russia, popular sympathy for the Russian people building a new society under difficult conditions, a near-consensus even among the old élites that Germany and the Soviet Union, as outcast nations, had common interests, contributed to the popularity of Soviet films, such as *Battleship Potemkin*, which were distributed by Social Democratic and Communist agencies. The appeal of American films was wider, and of a different nature. The heyday of German film-making was between 1918 and 1923, when a weak currency made it relatively easy for Germany to export films and the international market seemed open to artistic experiments of the nature of *Das Kabinett des Dr Caligari* or *Nosferatu*. With the stabilisation of the currency after the hyperinflation of 1923, German industry as a whole was less able to export and heavily dependent on United States investment. Hollywood products and Hollywood money began to invade the German film industry, edging out native products and injecting new technical and aesthetic norms into films produced in Germany.[12]

Cinema and America thus came to be closely identified with one another, with a fascination that worked on many levels. American themes had had an important place in popular literature for nearly a hundred years, and Westerns or crime stories set in New York or Chicago continued to be the staple fare of cheap novels and serial fiction, especially those read by young people. In setting his plays in actual or fictitious American cities, in an imagined underworld or on an imagined frontier, Brecht was addressing a set of emotions and associations – fear and longing, corruption and freedom, mass and individual – that were familiar to his audiences. American films appealed by their exotic content, whether in one of the familiar adventure genres, or in the portrayal of actual or idealised social conditions. The Hollywood star system contributed to this appeal; in his admiration for Charlie Chaplin, for example, Brecht was entirely typical. Chaplin was massively popular in Germany, adored by movie-goers and discussed at length by critics and intellectuals of all political persuasions. The American film industry was fascinating to left-wing intellectuals, too, as a manifestation of the sheer power of capital. This was a power to control people's imaginations, thanks to the new technology in which the American industry displayed a particular virtuosity. Contemporaries and associates of Brecht's, like Walter Benjamin and Siegfried Kracauer, saw political danger here, but also the possibility that the new technology could be used to develop a new and progressive consciousness on the part of the workers.

Part of the appeal of America, then, was closely related to the appeal of technology itself. Brecht's paean to man's power to overcome nature, *The Flight over the Ocean* (itself written for a new mass medium, the radio), echoed the general exhilaration at the first transatlantic flight. His passion for wheels was widely shared by his countrymen; the number of private cars in Germany increased sevenfold between 1921 and 1928, and after 1925 Germany led the world in motorcycle sales.[13] In architecture and design, whether in the specialist work of the Bauhaus or the new urban housing projects, the forms preferred were those that expressed the objects' practical function and made no effort to conceal their character as industrial products. This reflected not only pride in the new possibilities of mechanised production, but more broadly an attitude that sought to apply the engineering principles of rationality and streamlining to all aspects of life.[14] 'Rationalisation' became one of the central terms of public discussion. In industry, it meant the introduction of new machinery to replace human labour and the use of 'scientific management' techniques to eliminate any source of friction, waste or inefficiency in the labour process. The same principle was applied to the private sphere in the movement for the rationalisation of housework, in which the household was regarded as a workplace like any other, compactly designed to save unnecessary steps, equipped with a battery of electrical appliances and staffed by a housewife trained in 'domestic science'. In a positive inversion of the anti-industrial and pacifist critique of the dehumanising effects of mechanisation, the growing popularity of athletics for both men and women, accompanied by the emergence of sporting stars, celebrated the approximation of the human body to a perfectly functioning machine. The same message was conveyed by the precision dancing of the popular Tiller Girls, and as professional boxing became a respectable form of entertainment, Brecht was not alone in seeing the boxer as the model for the comprehensively functionalised modern man, the struggle in the ring as the original epic theatre.[15] In personal relations, as in the arts, the enthusiasm and experimentalism of the first post-war years were succeeded by a 'new objectivity' (*neue Sachlichkeit*), which eschewed sentiment in the name of clarity and utility. In the Berlin of the late 1920s, Brecht's coldly appraising gaze, like his tough-guy pose, were very much *à la mode*.

If the quest for efficiency and the fascination with new technology were essential to the dynamic and progressive spirit of the Weimar Republic, they were equally important in the thinking of its enemies on the right. The industrial and military élites had survived the war and revolution, through their own single-mindedness and the readiness of their adversaries to compromise. But after 1919 they were operating in severely straitened circumstances. The Versailles settlement which the victorious allies imposed on Germany after its defeat reduced Germany's large and heavily-armed military machine to a professional army of 100,000 men (plus a navy of 15,000), forbidden to acquire offensive weapons, aeroplanes, tanks or submarines. German industry – particularly the historically dominant iron and steel and heavy engineering sectors – was denied the right to produce armaments and rendered more exposed to the international economy by the loss of raw materials (through territorial losses). The costs of war had precipitated an inflationary spiral which was accelerated during the 1920s by Germany's response to the reparations stipulation of the Versailles Treaty. While inflation contributed in the immediate post-war period to growth and profitability, its climax in the pathological hyperinflation of 1923, the rapid stabilisation of the currency that followed, and the terms on which reparations were renegotiated in 1924 left German industry heavily dependent on foreign loans and under pressure to reduce costs. Under these circumstances, the concessions made to the rights of workers in 1918 and the tax and insurance costs associated with the welfare state were seen by many employers as an intolerable charge on profits.

The élite response to these constraints was to seek to maintain or to win a free hand, not in order to return to the nineteenth century, but in order to exploit the possibilities for effective functioning offered by the twentieth. In material and organisational terms, this meant continuing the 'modernisation' already apparent before the war: developing and acquiring the latest technologies, whether industrial or military, adopting more rational and streamlined forms of man-management ('scientific management' and paternalist social policy in the factories, a new and notionally apolitical ethos of service for a new, meritocratic officer corps), concentrating production and interest-representation through cartels like the chemical giant IG Farben. In political terms, it meant striving to break out of the post-war compromise, both through the use of extra-legal power and through direct involvement in the political process. In the early years of the republic the military notoriously exploited the first of these strategies. In the Kapp Putsch of 1920, a section of the military succeeded briefly in overturning the legitimate government, and the bulk of the army leadership refused to intervene. In 1923, the republic was challenged by a communist revolutionary movement in Central Germany and a radical right-wing mobilisation in Bavaria (which culminated in Hitler's 'Beer Hall Putsch'); civilian government's continued reliance on the army (*Reichswehr*) as a force for political order made it possible for the military command to make policy – a policy notably more tolerant of right-wing extremism than of the left. During the mid-1920s, the army leadership found ways to circumvent the Versailles provisions by creating secret divisions (the 'Black *Reichswehr*') and entering into an arms trade with the Soviet Union. By the end of the decade, the *Reichswehr* leadership had begun to develop a new conception for the militarisation of the whole of society, which required working within the political system in order not so much to destabilise it as to transform it in the military's own image.

Big business followed a similar path. The terms of the stabilisation and reparations settlements of 1923–4 gave heavy industrialists the opportunity to exploit their power as employers as well as their political influence to do away with the eight-hour day agreed in 1918, thus precipitating the end of their working relationship with the trade unions. During the period of relative economic recovery between 1924 and 1929, employers' organisations expanded their machinery for exercising influence on the political parties and engaged ever more actively in lobbying for limitations on the powers of trade unions, taxation and social provision. In 1928, employers in the Ruhr iron and steel industry mounted a direct challenge to the social constitution of the German Republic, refusing to recognise the decision of government arbitrators in a wages dispute. Their failure to get their way in this incident left heavy industrialists, too, ready to mobilise their influence to change governmental priorities from within, if necessary at the cost of the system itself, at the point at which a general crisis would make the system vulnerable.

That crisis came with the depression that began with the Wall Street Crash in 1929. As unemployment began to rise, a Social Democrat-led coalition government was faced with the problem of who was to pay the costs of supporting the jobless through increased contributions to the unemployment insurance fund; the trade unions and Social Democratic voters could not accept an increase in workers' contributions, and the party-political representatives of the business interest successfully frustrated efforts to raise employers' contributions. In order to resolve the resulting impasse, Reich President Hindenburg appointed a new Chancellor, Heinrich Brüning, in March 1930. Brüning was equipped with the powers provided for in the Weimar Constitution to govern by emergency decree (*Notverordnung*) without reference to the Reichstag. Under him and his successors, Franz von Papen and Kurt von Schleicher, democratic government was reduced to a form of presidential dictatorship; the Reichstag became increasingly irrelevant and the power of decision resided with those closest to Hindenburg himself, all of whom envisaged an authoritarian solution to the crisis rather than a return to parliamentary democracy.

The Reichstag in its turn was paralysed by a radicalisation of popular

politics. The depression years were years of unprecedented political mobilisation, not only on the left but on the right, with the result that parties
openly opposed to the Republic came to dominate the Reichstag, making a
return to government by coalition apparently impossible. Until the summer
of 1932, when unemployment reached an estimated 8 million (or roughly
one-third of the working population), government's response to the
economic crisis was to 'starve' the economy into health by cutting salaries,
wages and public spending, including welfare and unemployment benefits.[16]
The anger of the jobless was expressed in large-scale demonstrations
organised by the Communists, but also in spontaneous outbursts against
police and welfare officers. It was answered by a heightened police presence
in working-class neighbourhoods and by a series of emergency decrees
directed at the maintenance of public order, which encroached progressively
on the civil rights guaranteed by the constitution. 'Notverordnung' came to
be a catch-phrase denoting the combination of deliberate material depri-
vation and police repression. The predictable beneficiaries of this were the
Communists; after 1929 the KPD adopted a left-radical policy of openly
fomenting revolution, attacking the Social Democrats (out of government
but 'tolerating' the presidential dictatorship) as 'social fascists' and attempting with notable success to expand its membership. It was in this climate of
frenetic activity and popular outreach that the Party was most receptive to
new artistic and theatrical forms in the service of the cause. The popular
vote for the KPD rose steadily through the three Reichstag and two presidential elections held between September 1930 and November 1932 – largely
at the expense of the SPD.

More alarming was the simultaneous explosion of the Nazi movement
onto the political scene. The National Socialist German Workers' Party
(NSDAP) had been founded in Munich in 1919, and as early as 1921 Adolf
Hitler had established his dominance within the party. The Nazis first made
an impact on national politics in November 1923, when Hitler joined other
right-wing politicians in the theatrical gesture that became known as the
'Beer Hall Putsch'. Brecht's own reaction to the activities of the NSDAP at
that time, a combination of amused contempt and fascination at a movement which was already beginning to show signs of its later mastery of mass
spectacle, was characteristic and not inappropriate. In the early 1920s, the
Nazis appeared as only one of a number of competing groups within the
broad front of the anti-republican right, a melting-pot of reactionary
officers, *Freikorps* veterans, fanatical chauvinists and antisemites, and a ter-
rorist underground which through a series of political assassinations
appeared to pose the most imminent threat to the democratic order. During
the relative stability of the mid-1920s, the Nazi movement succeeded in

absorbing many of these elements, while at the same time it prepared to address a new constituency by abjuring insurrectionary tactics and shaping itself into a new kind of party. The NSDAP was thus well placed to benefit from the disappointment of the lower middle classes with the Republic. Their radicalisation, spurred by the shock of inflation, was confirmed by the failure of the traditional parties of the centre to address the needs of small business and small farmers in the post-inflation settlement. It expressed itself first in a proliferation of splinter-parties and by the late 1920s in the drift of middle-class voters to the parties of the right, though still to the respectable right rather than the more dubious Nazis. In 1929, the NSDAP took an important step towards establishing itself as a force on the national political scene, when it joined with old conservatives in a campaign against the latest scheme for settling Germany's reparations bill. It was nevertheless a shock when the NSDAP won 108 seats in the elections of September 1930, becoming the second largest party in the Reichstag; it went on to become the largest in July 1932.

Although the hard core of support for the Nazi movement came from disaffected sections of the middle class, it became apparent during the depression that its appeal was wider. In particular, the Nazis had some success in recruiting among unemployed young men, who were attracted to the radical rhetoric, violent activism, uniforms and free board and lodging that the party's brown-shirted paramilitaries, the SA, provided. In the big cities, and most vigorously in Berlin, the SA pursued a provocative strategy of 'conquering' Communist strongholds; it set up its own tavern head-quarters in working-class areas and put on a show of strength, in the form of demonstrations, casual violence against residents and passers-by, and organised assaults on Communists and Social Democrats in their meeting-places and on the streets. This was the context for Brecht's poem of January 1932, in which he appeals to Social Democrats to renounce the timidity of their leaders and join the Communist-organised movement for workers' self-defence. It climaxes in a vision of the united front in action:

> In Berlin's East, too, Social Democrats
> Greeted us with 'Red Front', and even wore the badge
> Of the Antifascist Action. The taverns
> Were packed on discussion-nights.
> And right away, the Nazis dared
> No longer go singly through our streets
> For the streets at least are ours
> When they have taken our houses.
>
> (My translation, but see *Poems*, pp. 205–6)

That vision was never realised. While both SPD and KPD recognised the present and future danger that Hitler and the Nazis represented, that was not in itself sufficient common ground; the Social Democrats were committed to defending what was left of the constitutional order, the Communists (rhetorically at least) to replacing it with a revolutionary one. More important, the political ground had so shifted by 1932 that the labour movement could not expect any help in a united campaign against fascism; there was no significant political party committed to maintaining democracy, least of all the social democracy represented by Weimar, and any suggestion of united action between Social Democrats and Communists could only provide a pretext for new authoritarian measures.

This is not to say that Hitler was the preferred candidate of those who held the power of decision in the depression crisis. The interpretation that Brecht shared with much of the left, that National Socialism was essentially a tool of or a front for the more familiar enemies, capitalism and reaction, was as partial as the image of simple gangsterism presented in *Arturo Ui*. Many Germans of all classes, responding to the Nazi rhetoric of nationhood, decency and family, identified the NSDAP as a force that would restore traditional values in politics and society. Others took seriously the Nazis' claim to be true socialists, fighting the bosses and aristocrats to build a new kind of social order in which justice and equality were grounded in a shared racial heritage. And while this 'revolutionary' language naturally provoked anxiety among the conservatives of the old élites, it was linked to a third set of claims which had a specific appeal to the new generation of leaders in industry and the military: the promise of a fully rationalised society, technologically and psychologically geared for war, in which all sources of waste, both human and material, would be forcibly eliminated and a strict hierarchy governed by the leadership principle would allow talent to rise to the top while guaranteeing every man his due place. When the NSDAP burst onto the scene in 1930, and proceeded to demonstrate an apparently unlimited capacity to mobilise mass support, while at the same time displaying an unhealthy appetite for political troublemaking and public disorder, those in power reacted with a combination of distaste and fascination. Reich President Hindenburg, a genuine conservative, consistently resisted suggestions that Hitler be brought into government. But even when the idea of a return of constitutional normality had been abandoned, it was clear that no alternative form of government would work if the popular discontent that had generated the crisis were not either contained or permanently suppressed. Hitler was the undisputed leader of the only mass movement which was both popular and anti-Marxist, and as other schemes for ending the impasse foundered, sections of industry and the military, as well as conservative politicians, began to perceive the possibility of making him, *faute de mieux*, into the kind of political leader they required. As the NSDAP itself began to lose popular support at the end of 1932, Hitler showed himself willing to abandon the demand for absolute authority that was the final bar to Hindenburg's acquiescence, and on 30 January 1933 he was appointed Chancellor at the head of a coalition government. The conservative politicians in his cabinet were convinced that they had him 'in a corner', and that he could now be expected to carry out their programme or discredit himself trying. Within two months, using the pretext of the Reichstag fire, he had effectively abrogated all civil rights and forced through a constitutional reform giving his government long-term dictatorial powers. Within seven months all political parties except the Nazi Party had been declared illegal.

Even after Hitler's appointment, both parties of the left were transfixed by a vision of what might come afterwards, rather than focussing on the present danger. Many Communists comforted themselves with the view that the Nazis in government, bringing to a climax a long-term process of 'fascisation', would hasten a revolutionary end to the crisis. And the Social Democratic leadership persisted in its unwillingness to offer an open challenge to a legal government. In this, the left was no more helplessly self-deluded than the members of the old élite who had levered Hitler into office. But the workers really had lost the initiative – long since and decisively. That the streets were not theirs became apparent within the first weeks, as the SA was given a free hand and the police came under Nazi control. And the workers' 'houses' – the taverns and party offices, trade union headquarters and print-shops, reading-rooms and social clubs, clinics and schools, welfare centres and theatres that made up the tissue of Weimar culture – became the first objects of a wave of official vandalism carried out in the name of order, public decency and economy. With many other artists and intellectuals, Brecht was quick to draw the consequences from Hitler's takeover; on 28 February, the day after the Reichstag fire, he left Germany, and did not return permanently until 1949.

NOTES

1 Elias Canetti, *Die Fackel im Ohr: Lebensgeschichte 1921–1931* (Fischer: Frankfurt, 1985), pp. 253f, 257 (author's translation).
2 Hermann Beckstein, 'München, der bayerische Städtetag und die städtischen Organisationsbestrebungen im letzten Viertel des 19. Jahrhunderts', in *Soziale Räume in der Urbanisierung*, ed. W. Hardtwig and K. Tenfelde (Oldenbourg: Munich, 1990), p. 242.
3 Dieter Frieke, *Die deutsche Arbeiterbewegung 1869 bis 1914* (Dietz: East Berlin, 1976), p. 452.

4 See David A. Welch, 'Cinema and society in Imperial Germany 1905–1918', *German History* 8 (1990), pp. 28–45.
5 Klaus Völker, *Brecht-Chronik* (Hanser: Munich, 1971), p. 7.
6 See Eric J. Leed, *No Man's Land* (Cambridge University Press, 1979); Robert W. Whelan, *Bitter Wounds: German Victims of the Great War 1914–1939* (Cornell University Press: Ithaca and London, 1984).
7 See Magnus Hirschfeld, *Sittengeschichte des 1. Weltkrieges* (Berlin, 1929; reprint edition Müller & Kiepenheuer, n.d.).
8 Karin Hausen, 'Mother's Day in the Weimar Republic', in *When Biology Became Destiny: Women in Weimar and Nazi Germany*, ed. R. Bridenthal, A. Grossmann, M. Kaplan (Monthly Review Press: New York, 1984), pp. 131–52.
9 Cornelie Usborne, *The Politics of the Body in Weimar Germany* (Macmillan: London, 1992).
10 Bertolt Brecht, *Kuhle Wampe: Protokoll des Films und Materialien*, ed. W. Gersch and W. Hecht (Suhrkamp: Frankfurt, 1978).
11 Klaus-Peter Kloss, *Siedlungen der 20er Jahre* (Haude & Spener: Berlin, 1982), p. 5.
12 Bruce Murray, *Film and the German Left in the Weimar Republic* (University of Texas Press: Austin, 1990), pp. 58f.
13 Joachim Radkau, *Technik in Deutschland* (Suhrkamp: Frankfurt, 1989), pp. 301–4.
14 See Detlev Peukert, *The Weimar Republic* (Allen Lane/The Penguin Press: London, 1991); Jeffrey Herf, *Reactionary Modernism* (Cambridge University Press, 1984); John Willett, *The New Sobriety 1917–1933: Art and Politics in the Weimar Period* (Thames & Hudson: London, 1978).
15 See David Bathrick, 'Max Schmeling on the canvas: boxing as an icon of Weimar culture', *New German Critique* 51 (Fall 1990), pp. 113–36.
16 See *The German Unemployed 1918–1933*, ed. Richard J. Evans and Dick Geary (Croom Helm: London, 1987).

2

PETER THOMSON

Brecht's lives

'The more I learned about Brecht the less I liked him', wrote the American journalist Bruce Cook, after concluding his research for *Brecht in Exile*.[1] The response is familiar. Assessments of Brecht the man continue to intervene in assessments of Brecht the writer, and they are likely to be given renewed impetus by John Fuegi's current project, of which he gives a lively summary elsewhere in this book. It may be argued that Brecht's subject-matter licenses such moral scrutiny. If you write about 'goodness' as often as he does, you are likely to have your own virtue questioned. Brecht's inclination was to measure bourgeois notions of morality against the exigencies of economic privation under capitalism. The inclination of some Western critics has been to measure Brecht's personal morality against the approved norms of the *soi-disant* democracies, and to launch attacks on his political integrity from the elevated vantage-point thus secured. My purpose, in this essay, is not to defend Brecht, but to indicate as fairly as I can the circumstances against and within which he wrote.

THE EARLY YEARS

Brecht was born in Augsburg almost exactly nine calendar months after his parents' wedding. His paternal grandfather ran a small lithographic business in the Black Forest region:

> I, Bertolt Brecht, came out of the black forests.
> My mother moved me into the cities as I lay
> Inside her body. And the coldness of the forests
> Will be inside me till my dying day.   (*Poems*, p. 107)

This opening stanza of one of Brecht's best-known poems, 'Of Poor B.B.', cannot be taken at face value. To be sure, his grandfather was linked, however approximately, with the Black Forest, but his father had been an employee of the Haindl paper mills in Augsburg since 1893 and would become managing director in 1914. Whatever his later claims, Brecht's peasant origins were remote. Nor does the shadowy figure of his mother help to authenticate the stanza's fanciful autobiography. She was the daughter of a Swabian stationmaster, protestant and conventionally devout. It was she who persuaded her catholic bridegroom to a protestant wedding and probably to her that Brecht owed his familiarity with the Bible; but he also derived from her his dangerous image of the self-denying woman. Her devotion to her elder son is well attested, and he continued to accept the devotion of women for the rest of his life. The child Brecht may have found it as hard to respond graciously to such devotion as did Brecht the adult. He confided to his diary, a year after his mother's death in 1920, that 'I didn't tell my mother that I loved her'.[2] For a middle-class boy with a comfortable home life, there is nothing uncommon about that, but Brecht knew that neither of his parents gave him much cause for complaint. His mother encouraged the artistic invention that always astonished his father. It was a cultured household a long way from the Black Forest, whose coldness, Brecht tries to persuade us, 'will be inside me till my dying day'. By the time he wrote this poem, around 1925, he had long been cultivating coldness, for reasons partly disclosed in a diary entry from 1921: 'Meier-Graefe says of Delacroix that here was a warm heart beating in a cold person. And when you come down to it that's a recipe for greatness'.[3] It was a recipe Brecht coveted.

Already in evidence during his early years were three qualities which remained with him. The first was his delighted, sometimes obsessive, engagement in collective activity. The second was his tendency to take the lead in such activity. The third was the relish with which he gave offence. His youthful contempt for bourgeois respectability informs the ironically titled 'Utterances of a Martyr':

Day after day my mother says: It's tragic
For a grown-up person to be like this.

And to say such things, when no normal person would look at things that way.
Among the washing too . . . I call it unhealthy, sheer pornography.
But how fed up I get with having to watch everything I say
And I tell my mother: That's what washing's like, why blame me?

(*Poems*, pp. 15–16)

'Martyr' was in Brecht's armoury of pejorative terms, and this is the most contemptuous reference to his mother that I have found. His belief in himself as someone special – a poet – seldom wavered. At the Augsburg Realgymnasium in 1912, he was already perceiving himself and his classmate Caspar Neher as brothers in art. The habit of preserving almost everything he wrote began then. The true writer's recognition that anything written can be refined, even contradicted, followed soon after.

THE FIRST WORLD WAR

Brecht was sixteen when Germany went to war, twenty when the war ended. Like so many survivors, he was thrust prematurely into manhood, and it would be charitable to view his early post-war misdemeanours in that light. His journalistic career began in Augsburg before the outbreak of war, which he greeted with puerile fervour:

> Our men have gone into battle calm and composed, with iron discipline but ablaze with enthusiasm, not so much exulting in victory as with clenched teeth. And the others, those who remain behind, will show themselves worthy of their brothers and sons.[4]

In the absence of young men, volunteers or conscripts, Brecht gained flattering access to young women. From then until his death, his sexual confidence rarely faltered; but his attitude to the war shifted quite quickly. One by one his classmates were swallowed by the army, but, encouraged by his father, Brecht found a loophole. Knowing that medical students were allowed deferment, he registered for an additional medical course at the University of Munich. How seriously he studied medicine is unclear. By 1917, his real interest was in literature in general and drama in particular. The classes of the celebrated 'theatre professor' Artur Kutscher captivated and provoked him. He shared Kutscher's admiration for the iconoclastic Wedekind, but found his fellow students pretentious and sycophantic and Kutscher himself inclined to the grandiose.

Brecht's preference for poetry that kept its feet on the ground left him in proud isolation in the Kutscher seminars. He was already moving towards an identity as the poet of the streets and the cities, a sworn enemy of expressionist rhetoric and fashionable cleverness. From July 1916, his newspaper articles appeared under the signature of 'Bert Brecht', a name which may have signified for him the completion of a rite of passage, away from Eugen Berthold, into his adult personality; but the parties he held in the attic flat of his parents' home were rowdily adolescent. With so many of his friends away at the front, Brecht found his habit of philandering threatened by an increasing dependence on Paula ('Bi') Banholzer. Their affair was briefly interrupted when his military service papers finally arrived in the autumn of 1918, but, after three weeks of square-bashing, he was posted back to Augsburg as medical orderly in a military VD clinic. A month later the war was over, and by the time Brecht was demobilised in January 1919, Bi was three months pregnant.

EARLY PLAYS AND FIRST PRODUCTIONS

Brecht's earliest published play (it appeared in the school magazine in 1914) was a one-act piece called *The Bible*, chiefly interesting for its questioning attitude towards self-sacrifice. A mistrust of martyrs (archetypal bourgeois heroes) was already part of Brecht's contradictory consciousness. It was again in a spirit of contradiction that he wrote his first important play, *Baal*. He had originally planned a piece based on the disorderly life of the poet, François Villon, but the plan was modified as a result of a confrontation in the Kutscher seminar. Kutscher was promoting a new play by the expressionist Hanns Johst. *Der Einsame* portrays the poet and playwright Dietrich Grabbe as a superior isolate, a man raised by aspiration and genius above the crowd. Brecht elected to portray his 'hero', the poet Baal, as an *inferior* isolate, a man sunk beneath the crowd by what might equally accurately be seen as aspiration and genius. *Baal* is an early example of Brecht's lifelong habit of allowing himself to be provoked into writing by the urge to counter another author's work. The urge is still evident in *Turandot* (1953), his last completed play. Like Baal, the central character has been coarsened, has lost the whimsical charm of Gozzi's original and has no purchase on the nobility to which Schiller's Turandot aspires. Eric Bentley records a comment of Brecht's: 'Anyone can be creative, it's rewriting other people that's a challenge.'[5] For Brecht, there was always an alternative way to read a narrative, but in 1919 he had still to discover the technique of *Verfremdung* that would allow the alternatives to be displayed simultaneously.

The early poems are sprinkled with unflattering self-portraits:

> Smokes cigars and reads the papers
> Swigs schnapps, haunts the billiard hall
> Ice-cold, with his airs and capers
> No humanity at all. (*Poems*, p. 32)

But the self-conscious delight in maverick behaviour is unmistakable. Having set himself against German high culture, Brecht spent the immediate post-war years in Augsburg and Munich, on a greedy quest for the more raucous pleasures of the fairground, the boxing-ring and the cabaret. Much of his time was shared with a close circle of friends, from whom he expected indulgence, support and loyalty. The history of Brecht's relationships could be used to illustrate the human tendency to concede to the person whose demands are fiercest. It is easy, perhaps too easy, to accuse the demanders of *using* their friends. Brecht was not above exploiting friendships to further his theatrical projects, but there is nothing inherently shameful about that. Those who helped him towards his first successes included Lion

Feuchtwanger, Arnolt Bronnen and Herbert Ihering. Already an established novelist and playwright, Feuchtwanger was also a publisher's reader and dramaturg of the Munich Kammerspiele when Brecht sought his assistance toward the staging of his second play. It was Feuchtwanger who advised a change of title, from *Spartakus* to *Drums in the Night*. Their original meeting took place in 1919, when Brecht was desperately short of money, but the première, Brecht's first, was delayed until September 1922. By then, Feuchtwanger had read and admired *Baal* as well and was collaborating with his ambitious young friend on a version of Marlowe's *Edward II*. Meanwhile, Brecht had made his initial assault on the Berlin theatre, as director of his friend Bronnen's play, *Vatermord*. An experienced cast included the monumental Heinrich George, and the challenge to a young director on his first professional assignment was, by any reckoning, formidable. And yet, as Bronnen recalls, 'at the beginning he fooled everybody':

> When Brecht appeared you found certainty and determination. This thin, pale, bespectacled man strolled about the various stages which Seeler [the producer] made available – they had to beg their way from rehearsal to rehearsal, without knowing in which theatre they would finally have the première – as though he had decades of practical theatre work behind him.[6]

Not for the last time, though, Brecht carried insistence to the point of offensiveness, and his participation ended in fiasco when George refused to continue working with him.

For several years, a reputation for being difficult impeded Brecht's progress in the theatre. Arrogance, youthful or habitual, is not uncommon in directors, but Brecht's initial failure was to appreciate, or even to recognise, the needs and vulnerabilities of actors. The immediate effect was a curbing of his influence on the Munich production of *Drums in the Night*. Bronnen had generously commended the play to the influential Berlin critic, Herbert Ihering, who travelled to Munich for the première. Brecht was to be his discovery, and Ihering was primed in advance to declare that overnight the young man had 'changed the literary face of Germany'. The annual Kleist Prize was in Ihering's gift, and in November 1922 he awarded it to Brecht. In the following month, there was a Berlin production of *Drums in the Night* and, before the end of 1923, an early version of *In the Jungle of the Cities* (in Munich) and *Baal* (in Leipzig) had been premièred. Brecht had been catapulted into the top rank of German playwrights.

Critical responses to Brecht's theatrical work were always mixed. There were usually private scandals and always a measure of public outcry. But nothing diminished Brecht's ambition. Writing short stories and poems as well as plays, he bargained with publishers and fought for territory with theatrical producers. Bernhard Reich, newly appointed Intendant of the Munich Kammerspiele, recalls him in the autumn of 1923:

> Conversations with him soon became filled with inner drama. He spoke very quietly, but he made claims, expressing these claims in paradoxical formulations. Absolutely categorical. He did not argue with the replies, but swept them away. He made it clear to his partners that he, Brecht, regarded all resistance to him as hopeless, and that he gave them, the partners, the friendly advice not to waste time but to capitulate right away.[7]

Try as they might, producers could not block Brecht's access to rehearsals of his own work. Once there, he declared war on the egotism of actors, demanding an attention to the narrative that threatened to turn *character* (the actor's cherished refuge) into a mere function of *plot*. It was as much in rehearsal as in conversations with friends that Brecht's commitment to what he later called epic theatre was nurtured. His work on *Edward II* for the Munich Kammerspiele turned out to be a major step on the road to a dramatic theory.

BRECHT'S RELATIONSHIPS WITH WOMEN

In a better world, major writers might always be models of singular virtue. Brecht was not, and it is surprising how many people are deeply shocked by that. I find little to admire in what I understand to have been Brecht's treatment of women, and I deal with it here only because it has been the subject of so much speculation. It should be made clear, though, that the women who mattered most (or mattered longest) to Brecht – Weigel, Hauptmann, Steffin, Berlau – were strong people with interests and talents that could have been developed without reference to Brecht. The extraordinary thing is that each in her own way placed those talents almost exclusively at Brecht's disposal. Was it to comfort Berlau that, in an addendum to the autobiographical *Me-Ti/Book of Changes*, he (Me-Ti) assured her (Lai-Tu) that 'an apple achieves fame by being eaten'?[8] Some comfort! On the face of it, Brecht's power over women is the first mystery. He was not, in any obvious way, prepossessing. There was, of course, immense power, not divorced from sexuality, in the unbending confidence in his own rightness to which Bernhard Reich refers. Added to that was Brecht's abnormal, and from one perspective flattering, determination to retain his interest in anyone who had genuinely commanded it. Ruth Berlau claims to have discovered him once, 'looking through a keyhole, dressed in a long nightshirt. He wanted to find out what we did in his absence.'[9] What seems clear is that Brecht enjoyed the company of women, as lovers certainly, but even more as fellow workers. Answering her own question, 'What was Brecht like?', Berlau concludes:

> All that struck me was that, even in
> the depth of a hard
> Finnish winter, he never wore gloves.
> His hands were always warm, and he loved fresh
> air on his hands and
> forehead. Then, of course, he worked
> like no other person I have ever known.
> He knew no Sundays, no
> vacations, no public holidays. But he did
> want to have a Christmas tree.[10]

As Fuegi's research is revealing, much of the work done jointly by Brecht and his lovers was claimed singly by Brecht. Like the fictional narrator of Elaine Feinstein's largely factual novel *Loving Brecht*, they had evidently conceded that 'he had earned the right to sit at the centre of his own life'.[11]

A bare outline of Brecht's significant relationships with women would necessarily include the following information. His son by Paula Banholzer was born in July 1919. Farmed out for much of his childhood, Frank would eventually die fighting for Hitler's army on the Russian front. However attenuated, the friendship with Paula endured. The Viennese opera-singer Marianne Zoff was already pregnant when she married Brecht in 1922. As Hanne Hiob, their child became a successful actress. 'Whenever I see her on the stage', wrote Carl Zuckmayer in 1966, 'I feel as if young Brecht were up there on the boards, disguised as a woman.'[12] Neither of these children had much contact with their father. Although Brecht's divorce from Zoff was postponed until 1926, the marriage was in disarray from 1924, when he was involved with both Helene Weigel and Elisabeth Hauptmann. The extent of Brecht's reliance on Hauptmann is the central theme of John Fuegi's chapter in this book, but it was Weigel who bore Brecht's children, Stefan in October 1924 and Barbara in October 1930, eighteen months after Brecht had (impulsively, even cruelly, in the view of other women with whom he was sexually involved at the time) married her. Stefan would become an American citizen in 1946 and develop an artistic career entirely independent of his father. Barbara, both before and since her marriage to Ekkehard Schall, has sustained a fierce interest in Brecht's reputation, as well as that of Helene Weigel.

Hauptmann and Weigel were more secure politically than the young Brecht, whose early readings in Marxism were supervised by Hauptmann. 'After *Man is Man* had been produced', she records in her working notes for 26 October 1926, 'Brecht obtains works on socialism and Marxism and asks

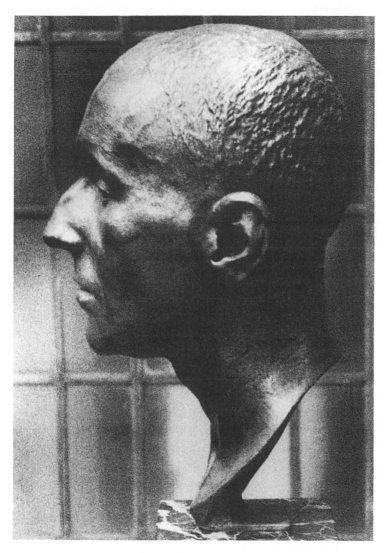

1. Bronze cast of Brecht's head, taken from a life-mask (*c.* 1927) by the sculptor Paul Hamann (1891–1973).

for lists of the basic works he should study first.'[13] But it was Margarete Steffin who most vividly authenticated for him the moral authority of the communist classics. Alone among his mistresses, she came from the working class, and she was the only one of whom he wrote like a conventional lover. Her early death from tuberculosis in 1941 shattered him. 'It is as if someone had taken my guide away on the edge of the desert', he wrote from Santa Monica.[14] Ruth Berlau's commitment to communism was more histrionic than Steffin's, and histrionics flavoured her commitment to Brecht, too. Even the notoriously patient Weigel eventually turned against her. Brecht, however, was in debt to Berlau. During his refugee years in Denmark, she did all she could to get his plays staged. It was a debt she called in during the American years, to dubious effect. Having invested so much in Brecht, Berlau lost herself. The countless photographs that were her contribution to the *Modellbuch* idea smack less of his confidence in her utility than of his recognition that she needed a purpose. Towards the end of his life, Brecht's fondness for Berlau had declined into patronage, oiled by his distaste for her public outbursts. Unsurprisingly, she was ousted by the Berliner Ensemble after his death, and her last years were lonely. She burned to death in her hospital bed in 1974. Weigel the constant had died three years earlier, Hauptmann in 1973.

THE BRECHT COLLECTIVE

In the late twenties, when the concept of literary and theatrical 'collectives' became fashionable, especially in Berlin, I once said to him: 'For you the collective is a group of intelligent people who contribute to what one person wants – that is, what you want.' He admitted, with his peculiar sly smile, that I might not be so far wrong at that.[15]

Thus Carl Zuckmayer, in old age, lends support to what is almost a commonplace assumption about Brecht's abuse of the collective ideal. We should not, however, neglect the 'peculiar sly smile'. Although he was not yet thirty when he and Zuckmayer worked together in Berlin, Brecht must often have heard himself talked about like this. Since boyhood days in Augsburg, he had taken conspicuous pleasure in group activity. Then, as in his theatre work, the original idea may have come from someone else, but it seldom became group policy until Brecht had endorsed or modified it. But it is misleading to assert that he simply overrode his colleagues. Elsewhere in this book, Christopher Baugh mounts an important argument for the significance of the creative collaboration between Brecht and the designer Caspar Neher, and Stephen McNeff explores the interaction with Kurt Weill that went to the making of *The Threepenny Opera*. The wish to collaborate was clearly there, even when the confidence to do so faltered, and that wish could only be strengthened by the readings in Marxism. It is not Brecht's sincerity but his generosity that John Fuegi's findings negate. Bernhard Reich recalls the drafting of *Man is Man*:

When a visitor came Brecht saw in this a lucky occasion for his work – he read him an especially ticklish part, testing the quality of the work on the other or reconsidering it with him. And sitting immediately down to the typewriter, he would hammer out a new version. He understood that the work profits if many take part in it.[16]

No other writer of comparable status has attempted so consistently to collaborate. It was in the aftermath of composition, in his neglect after the event of the legitimate interests of his colleagues, that Brecht was most culpable. His eagerness to challenge the control of capital over production may have motivated him in his dealings with publishers, as it did when he quarrelled or bargained with theatre and film producers, but that cannot easily excuse his preparedness to subsume the names of co-authors and to lay claim to the greater share of royalties.

The collective work undertaken in the years between 1924 and 1933 coincided with the rise of Nazism, which was most rapid in Brecht's native Bavaria. Brecht's initial response was to find Hitler risible. In the 1930s, with the Nazis in power, he would vainly attempt to expose him to universal ridicule, not only in *The Resistible Rise of Arturo Ui*, but also in his constant reference to the *Führer* as 'the housepainter', or as the opening letter of his 'Alphabet' for children:

> Adolf Hitler's facial hair
> Is a curious affair.
> It's what I'd call uncouth:
> So small a toothbrush for so big a mouth.   (*Poems*, p. 239)

It was in a spirit of angry optimism, of stubborn disbelief in the efficacy of German fascism, that the Brecht collective embarked on the *Lehrstück* project. The appropriate analogy is with laboratory practice – the testing of a theory through active experiment. In his quest for a theatre that might suit a 'scientific age', Brecht was ready to adopt the conventions of academic scientists. Like scientific papers, the plays were performed or published with the names of the contributors to the experiment listed. He need not, of course, have placed Professor Brecht's at the head.

It was in the rehearsal practices of the Berliner Ensemble, sensitively described by Carl Weber in a later chapter of this book, that Brecht's collaborative instincts found their finest expression. Not only had he mellowed, but he was also working within a political system whose ideology he supported.

THE YEARS OF EXILE IN EUROPE

We do not know whether Brecht ever joined the Communist Party, but throughout the fifteen years of his exile he was essentially part of a Marxist collective which included Weigel, Steffin, Berlau, Hanns Eisler, Walter Benjamin and, intermittently, many others. Contemptuous of martyrs and possessing very little of what is conventionally called courage, Brecht got himself (a Marxist) and Weigel (a Marxist and a Jew) out of Germany before the smoke of the Reichstag fire had dispersed. In June 1933, he was in Paris for the opening of his final collaboration with Weill, the hybrid ballet-with-libretto of *The Seven Deadly Sins*. There could be no more vivid illustration of the louche lives of Brecht's Berlin set than the backstage world of this production. Lotte Lenya had escaped from Germany with her current lover, the Austrian tenor Otto von Pasetti. She was about to file for divorce from Weill (they would remarry in 1937), and Weill, in the throes of an affair with Caspar Neher's wife Erika, was in no position to contest; but he had not abandoned hope of saving his marriage. So it was that, when the wealthy eccentric Edward James offered to finance a Weill production in Paris, Weill contacted Lenya as well as Brecht. James's offer was conditional on the provision of a part for his handsome Austrian wife, Tilly Losch, an accomplished actor and dancer. Lenya's condition was that Pasetti should have a singing part. Brecht's main concern was money, and he and Weill knocked the piece together in a hurry. Once in Paris, the bisexual Lenya embarked on a passionate affair with the lesbian Losch (her husband was homosexual, too), while Neher designed the scenery and Weill sought comfort with Neher's wife. George Balanchine, who choreographed the performance, was the chief beneficiary of what was at best a *succès d'estime*. He was spotted by the American reviewer Lincoln Kirstein and offered the directorship of the nascent New York City Ballet.[17]

The first of the many people who helped Brecht and Weigel to overcome the poverty of exile was the Danish novelist, Karin Michaelis. Through her, they found the house near Svendborg that remained their base until 1938. For a man who had been ceaselessly and pugnaciously pursuing unpopular theatrical projects for over ten years, the enforced inactivity of this Danish retreat had sometimes the unreality of coma. It was 'Red Ruth' Berlau who offered a lifeline. She took personal responsibility for Copenhagen productions of *The Mother* (1935) and *Señora Carrar's Rifles* (1937) and was an active instigator there of the première of *Round Heads and Pointed Heads* (1936) and a revival of *The Seven Deadly Sins* (1936). It was for Berlau's predominantly amateur group that Brecht wrote one of his best-known theatre poems, 'Speech to Danish working-class actors on the art of observation'. The poem commends, as an art in its own right for actors engaged in the class struggle, the cultivation of the interrogative gaze that was a disconcerting feature of Brecht's own social behaviour:

See how they walk and speak, those rulers
Who hold the threads of your fate in their white and brutal hands.
You should inspect such people exactly. And now
Imagine all that is going on around you, all those struggles
Picturing them just like historical incidents
For this is how you should go on to portray them on the stage.

(*Poems*, pp. 233–8)

Cut off from the communist workers of Berlin, who had been the pretext for the *Lehrstück* project, Brecht was evidently prepared to start again in Copenhagen. But he had no knowledge of the language, and made no attempt to learn it. It was the classic dilemma of the exile: nothing had changed and yet everything had changed. Each *Lehrstück* had been designed to open the eyes of its participants to the possibility of intervening in their own history. The programme Brecht was beginning to visualise in exile was no less dependent on Marxist dialectics. If the Danish working-class actors are to 'imagine all that is going on around' as history, might Brecht himself not imagine history as something that is going on around? *Galileo, Mother Courage, The Days of the Commune* and the parable plays from *The Good Person of Szechwan* to *Turandot* are prefigured in the 'Speech to Danish working-class actors'.

In waging his campaign against Hitler, Brecht had to bear in mind the strength of right-wing opinion in Denmark. In the spring of 1935, he visited Moscow. His reticence about a political system he would have loved to enthuse over is noteworthy. Instead, he celebrated the rapid transformation of a moribund society into an industrially productive one. Productivity was the achievement Brecht most readily recognised, in lovers as well as in politicians. It was the efficient acting of Mei Lan-fang, the Chinese dan, and the opening of the Moscow Metro that most engaged him:

Where would it ever have happened that the fruits of labour
Fell to those who had laboured? Where in all time
Were the people who had put up a building
Not always turned out of it?[18]

Ambivalent in his attitude towards Hitler's Germany, Stalin was not hospitable to German refugees. Even so, Brecht's Moscow experience was positive in comparison to his visit to New York, later in 1935, for the Theatre Union production of *The Mother*. Provoked by what he witnessed in rehearsal – a political as well as a theatrical misreading of the text – Brecht went out of his way to make trouble. At such times, he displayed all the joylessness of a Party *apparatchik*, and his removal from rehearsals, though inevitable, was a grim portent for the American years ahead.

Brecht's uncommon work-drive kept him writing plays throughout his Scandinavian exile. The rewards were slender: outside Denmark, there were Parisian premières of *Señora Carrar's Rifles*, with a nervous Weigel in the title role (1937) and of eight plays from the anti-Hitler sequence, *Fear and Misery of the Third Reich*, with Weigel as the Jewish wife (1938). But it was also during this period that *Galileo*, *Mother Courage* and *The Good Person* were first drafted. After two years in Stockholm (1938–40), Brecht responded to the Nazi invasion of Denmark by moving further away – to Finland. His hostess there was the writer Hella Wuolijoki, whose work he plundered, with inadequate acknowledgement, in *Mr Puntila and his Man Matti*. Steffin and Berlau were part of the Finnish *ménage*, and it was Steffin who assisted him with *The Good Person* and *Arturo Ui*.

In June 1940, France signed an armistice with Germany. The plan now, as the *Wehrmacht* closed over Scandinavia, was to join the refugee community in California. With a lot of help from fellow exiles, Brecht, Weigel and Berlau were granted American visas on 2 May 1941, two weeks after the Zurich première of *Mother Courage*, with Therese Giehse in the title role and the famous set and costume designs of Teo Otto. Waiting nervously in Finland, Brecht had no part in this production. Despite pressure from friends, he refused to leave until Steffin's visa arrived on 12 May. She was to be their interpreter on the trip across the Soviet Union. But she was terminally ill, and the Brecht party had to leave her to die in a Moscow hospital while they travelled on to the port of Vladivostok:

> In memory of my little teacher
> Of her eyes, of the blue sparks of her anger
> And of her old duffel coat with its deep hood
> And deep bottom hem, I christened
> Orion in the night sky the Steffin Constellation.
>
> (*Poems*, pp. 364–5)

THE AMERICAN YEARS

Brecht had every intention of making himself a good living in Hollywood, and the prospects must have seemed fair. There was an influential and mutually supportive German community, some of whom – Feuchtwanger, Oskar Homolka, Peter Lorre, Fritz Lang – had known Brecht in Germany. In the event, though he worked on more than fifty film stories, Brecht made virtually no impact in Hollywood. That failure, more than his works on plays, lies at the centre of his American experience. The period has been exhaustively documented in James K. Lyon's *Bertolt Brecht in America*, a book in which Brecht's conduct in exile is adjudged with unusual evenness.

Lyon's account reveals phenomenal productivity cancelled out by stubbornness. It is as if, having survived the isolation of his Scandinavian havens, Brecht determined to bring himself to the attention of the richest country in the world, but could never make the final compromise. His longstanding interest in films had found substantial expression in the innovative *Kuhle Wampe* (1931), but so unheroic a presentation of the lives of the dominated masses was not the stuff of Hollywood. If Brecht was looking back to the making of *Kuhle Wampe* as a model for creative collaboration in the studios around Los Angeles, he was to be sadly disappointed. Production was firmly in the hands of the producers, and there was nothing a grubby, bad-tempered writer with small command of English could do to upset the hierarchies of entrenched capitalism. It was not until years after his death that Brecht's contribution to film theory began to be recognised. Fritz Lang was too far embroiled in the system to risk incorporating Brecht's boldest innovations in *Hangmen also Die* (1942). We can only speculate on the film that might have been made if Lang's craftsmanship had been put to the service of Brecht's ideas. Disgruntled about everything except his pay-off, Brecht confirmed his view of Hollywood as a port-of-call for 'the world narcotics trade'.[19] But this was the first of two occasions on which he received a substantial financial reward from the film industry.

The second occasion began with theatre. In late 1942, Brecht and Feuchtwanger set about writing a money-spinner for Broadway. *The Visions of Simone Machard* is the most conventional of Brecht's approaches to the Joan of Arc theme. As a play, it found no American purchasers, but Feuchtwanger turned it into a novel, Goldwyn bought the film rights and Feuchtwanger gave Brecht two-fifths of the contracted $50,000. Although temporarily prosperous, Brecht had no secure income. The two major plays of the American years were written with popular actors in mind, *Schweyk in the Second World War* for Peter Lorre and *The Caucasian Chalk Circle* for Luise Rainer. Neither was performed. Instead, and in some desperation, Brecht contracted to prepare for Broadway and Elisabeth Bergner a version of *The Duchess of Malfi*. George Rylands, imported from England to direct the 1946 opening, preferred Webster's original and largely discarded Brecht's interventions. The single theatrical success of the American years was the outcome of a unique collaboration between a politically impassioned playwright and an apolitical actor. Charles Laughton and Brecht worked harmoniously on a revision of *Life of Galileo* for American consumption. It was over a decade since Laughton had last put his ferociously self-critical temperament to the test of live performance, and he found the inexorably rational Brecht a reassuring colleague. Laughton's lawyer, conscious of the hyperactivity of the House UnAmerican Activities

Committee, advised him against continuing this collaboration with a writer of known communist sympathies, but the play opened in Los Angeles at the end of July 1947, with several of the least intimidated of Hollywood's film stars in the audience. The Broadway opening was scheduled for December, but before that HUAC began its infamous interrogations of supposed subversives in the movie industry. Brecht's turn came on 30 October. Forewarned, he had laid plans for a return to Europe, but he had first to avoid the fate of his friend Hanns Eisler – forbidden to leave the United States. His device was Schweikian; to employ nothing but sly equivocation. He had, after all, been characteristically careful to conceal any hostility he felt towards the vaunted American way of life, preferring to display his hostility towards capitalism in bitter attacks on his famous compatriot Thomas Mann. Brecht's performance before the Committee was effective. The chairman called him 'a good example'. A day later, Brecht boarded a plane for Paris.

THE FINAL PHASE

Brecht returned to Europe with a number of possibilities but no secure project. Marking time in the way that suited him best, he directed his own adaptation of *Antigone* in the Swiss town of Chur. Prolifically photographed by Berlau, this production provided material for the first full-scale *Modellbuch*. Brecht may have needed this external evidence to persuade him of the importance of an event taking place in a provincial backwater. He was fifty years old, and he had to start again. 'You need a home outside Germany', he wrote to Berlau.[20] The first home was in Zurich. There he began laying the basis for a new practice by writing his *Short Organum for the Theatre*. For a man of unswerving left-wing ideals, the question of domicile in post-war Europe was a weighty one, but Brecht, the cautious professional, wished to keep his theatrical options open. It was, however, only in the eastern sector of Berlin that he was accorded the status of a pundit. His Zurich production of *Puntila* (June 1948), a play with which he hoped to initiate a revival of German comedy, had made a modest impact, but it was the performance of *Mother Courage* at the Deutsches Theater in Berlin that prepared the ground for the establishment of the Berliner Ensemble. Brecht's last years revolved around the Ensemble. They are described in this book by Carl Weber.

The enigma of Brecht's inner life under the brittle regime of Walter Ulbricht remains unresolved. He has been taxed with hypocrisy for maintaining a Swiss bank account and an Austrian passport. If he were an honest communist, the argument seems to run, he would have made sure that he couldn't afford to leave East Berlin even if he'd been permitted to. But

Brecht's honesty was never of that self-damaging kind. Though he was hungry for recognition, he had the secret of not expecting too much of himself. His response to a late reading of Homer is characteristic:

> At the time when their fall was certain –
> On the ramparts the lament for the dead had begun –
> The Trojans adjusted small pieces, small pieces
> In the triple wooden gates, small pieces.
> And began to take courage, to hope.
>
> The Trojans too, then.   (*Poems*, p. 445)

Those who looked for Brecht in the places where grand gestures are made were wasting time. He was in the Berliner Ensemble, adjusting small pieces. But was that a sufficient response to the great issues of Stalin's purges and the repressiveness of the East German government?

It is not surprising that Brecht was slow to find fault with Stalin. He wanted to believe in the Soviet system, even after hearing of the fate of Carola Neher and other friends who, having fled from Germany, had 'disappeared' into Soviet prison camps. Stalin had always the advantage of being necessary. Harold Nicolson records a conversation with Anthony Eden in December 1941: 'He has a real liking for Stalin. He says that Stalin has never broken his word once given.'[21] To form an alliance with the Soviet Union, it was shamefully convenient to forgive Stalin. Even after the signing of the Hitler–Stalin pact, Brecht remained unwilling to commit himself: 'I do not think one can say more than that the Soviet Union is saving itself at the cost of leaving the world proletariat without watchwords, hope or assistance', he wrote to the painter, Hans Tombrock.[22] He did, however, declare open opposition to the Stalinist literary policy of socialist realism, even to the point of contradicting Georg Lukács, the Party's most formidable cultural barrister.[23] When all the explanations have been made, though, we have to ask how far the Stalinist terror would have needed to go before Brecht condemned it. There is some evidence, for example in Walter Benjamin's Svendborg conversations with him as early as 1934,[24] that Brecht was more outspoken in conversation than in print, but he succumbed too often to the temptation to see Stalin's barbarity as the legacy of capitalist barbarity, and thus Stalinism as a consequence of capitalism.[25] He would say of Roosevelt in 1942 what he had said of Stalin ten years earlier: that his politics were probably the right ones in the circumstances. After Stalin's death in March 1953, Brecht contributed an obituary notice to *Sinn und Form*, electing to speak, not on his behalf, but on that of the proletariat: 'He was the embodiment of their hopes. But the spiritual and material weapons he made are there, and so also is the teaching to make new ones.'[26]

Stalin's death was an incentive for the workers' uprising in East Berlin on 17 June 1953. Brecht's defence of the government, after Russian tanks had been used to restore order, is, for forensic democrats, his greatest crime. But the case was not a straightforward one. Could he confidently advocate the dictatorship of the East German proletariat? He felt much as he had felt in August 1934, when Benjamin recorded his saying, 'In Russia there is dictatorship *over* the proletariat. We should avoid dissociating ourselves from this dictatorship for as long as it still does useful work for the proletariat.'[27] What Brecht did and wrote in June 1953 is defensible, but there were many, some of them within the Ensemble, who had hoped for more principled leadership:

> Last night in a dream I saw fingers pointing at me
> As at a leper. They were worn with toil and
> They were broken.
>
> You don't know! I shrieked
> Conscience-stricken.   (*Poems*, p. 440)

What didn't they know? That the solution, like the problem, was economic? That a false step by Brecht would lead to the closing of the Ensemble? The politics of theatre and the politics of state were at odds, certainly. Increasingly frail, Brecht spent what time he could in his country retreat in Buckow. His predominant mood is recorded in the poem '1954: First Half':

> No serious sickness, no serious enemies.
> Enough work.
> And I got my share of the new potatoes
>   . . .
> I read Voltaire's letters and Mao's essay on contradiction.
> I put on the Chalk Circle at the Berliner Ensemble. (*Poems*, p. 446)

Since the destruction of the Berlin wall, Brecht's standing has been fairly systematically threatened. There is much about him, what he did and what he failed to do, that makes him vulnerable. He was a man who lived untidily, but who combined timorousness and combativeness as few people have.

NOTES

1 Bruce Cook, *Brecht in Exile* (Holt, Rinehart & Winston: New York, 1983), p. xii.
2 Bertolt Brecht, *Diaries 1920–1922*, p. 111.
3 *Ibid.*, p. 98.

4 From *Der Erzähler*, the literary supplement to the *Augsburger Neueste Nachrichten*, 17 August 1914. Cited in Klaus Völker, *Brecht: A Biography*, p. 9.

5 Eric Bentley, *The Brecht Memoir*, p. 25.

6 Hubert Witt, ed., *Brecht As They Knew Him*, p. 33.

7 *Ibid.*, p. 39.

8 *Gesammelte Werke*, vol. XII, p. 585.

9 Ruth Berlau, *Living for Brecht*, p. 38.

10 *Ibid.*, p. 236.

11 Elaine Feinstein, *Loving Brecht* (Hutchinson: London, 1992), p. 120.

12 Carl Zuckmayer, *A Part of Myself* (Secker and Warburg: London, 1970. German edition, 1966), p. 264.

13 Witt, *Brecht As They Knew Him*, p. 53.

14 Cited in Völker, *Brecht: A Biography*, p. 283.

15 Zuckmayer, *A Part of Myself*, p. 267.

16 Reich, *Sinn und Form* (Rütten und Loening: Berlin, 1957), p. 434.

17 The information is drawn from Donald Spoto, *Lenya: A Life* (Little, Brown and Company: Boston and Toronto, 1989), pp. 109–14.

18 From 'The Moscow Workers Take Possession of the Great Metro on April 27, 1935', *Poems*, pp. 248–50.

19 Cited in James K. Lyon, *Bertolt Brecht in America*, p. 56.

20 Cited in Ronald Hayman, *Brecht: A Biography*, p. 314.

21 Harold Nicolson, *The War Years: 1939–1945*, vol. II of Nicolson's *Diaries and Letters*, ed. Nigel Nicolson (William Collins Sons & Co. Ltd: London, 1967), p. 421.

22 Cited in Völker, *Brecht: A Biography*, p. 265.

23 See David Pike, *Lukács and Brecht*.

24 Walter Benjamin, *Understanding Brecht*, pp. 105–20.

25 See David Pike's shrewd essay, 'Brecht and "inoperative thinking"', in *Critical Essays on Bertolt Brecht*, ed. Siegfried Mews, pp. 258–71.

26 Cited in Völker, *Brecht: A Biography*, p. 354.

27 Benjamin, *Understanding Brecht*, p. 121.

2
THE PLAYS

3

TONY MEECH

Brecht's early plays

The period immediately after the First World War was a time of unprecedented upheaval throughout Germany, and nowhere more so than in Bavaria. After defeat in the war (for which the German propaganda machine had failed to prepare the public), and the abdication of the Kaiser, Germany experienced its abortive revolution, which included the establishment of a Soviet State of Bavaria. When this had been brutally suppressed (ironically by a socialist government in Berlin), the country staggered from crisis to crisis during the Weimar Republic until, eventually, Bavaria became the power base of the Nazi party. So, as he was setting out on his career as a writer, Brecht experienced, albeit indirectly, both fighting in the trenches of a world war and fighting on the streets during a failed revolution.

The sacrifices demanded of his generation during this period affected the young Brecht profoundly, encouraging in him a detached view of humankind, both individually and in society, and an enduring mistrust of all forms of idealism. It is against this turbulent background, and to give expression to these developing social and aesthetic attitudes that the (sometime medical student, sometime vituperative theatre critic) son of the manager of an Augsburg paper-mill wrote his first three full-length plays: *Baal* (1918–22), *Drums in the Night* (1919) and *In the Jungle of the Cities* (1921–4), an early draft of which was produced in Munich in 1923 under the original title, *In the Jungle (Im Dickicht)*.[1]

These plays give fascinating insights into Brecht's concerns at the time of writing, as well as the way in which his means of expression as a dramatist were beginning to develop, but they repay study as texts in their own right. Their qualities have been increasingly recognised in recent years, by theatre practitioners as well as by critics. There are, however, particular difficulties which a director or reader will encounter in coming to grips, at more than a superficial level, with these plays. The first lies in the identification of a definitive text for each of them.

It is true that Brecht was given, throughout his life, to adapting his plays for each new production in a search to increase their relevance. The difficulties created by this habit are familiar to his editors and to anyone preparing his work for performance, but the peculiar problems with the early plays stem from the fact that Brecht's stimulus to rewrite them in later life was not primarily aesthetic. Largely for social and political reasons, he attempted, in maturity, to 'rewrite' the period of his life during which they were written and which they represent. We should remember that the first drafts were completed before Brecht's break with his bourgeois background in Augsburg, before his immersion in the life and theatre of Berlin, before his meeting with Helene Weigel and, crucially, before his first reading of Marx. Established in the German Democratic Republic in the 1950s, Brecht gives the impression of being embarrassed by his early plays. A first reading of the introductory essay, 'On looking through my first plays' (1954),[2] suggests an attempt to square these texts with the predominant ideology of the GDR. A reader more aware of Brecht's talent for irony might pause longer over his apparently reluctant acceptance that each play must be left more or less as it is. In general, the mature Brecht's attempts to make the younger Brecht more acceptable rob the reworked texts of their original life and intensity, for much of the vitality in these plays comes from the fact that they are the inexperienced Brecht's earliest attempts to make sense of society as he found it. Each of the early plays has a distinctive inspiration. Without this youthful drive to excuse them, the plays' inconsistencies begin to look like weaknesses. While his later revisions may be of some interest in a study of the development of Brecht's attitudes in later life, as plays for both reader and director the earliest complete text is, in each case, to be preferred.

Secondly, if readers turn to the major critics for guidance, they will find that all too often these early plays are either dismissed as juvenile, anarchic and undisciplined, or interpreted to provide a platform which can be seen to support the view the author has already formed of Brecht's later work. Critics seem all too rarely prepared to assess the plays in their own right, preferring to see them as no more than preliminary to Brecht's 'great' plays.

The three plays under consideration may seem disparate in style, form and theme. They do, however, share a number of features. They were all written before Brecht had had any practical involvement in the production of one of his own plays. He had failed spectacularly in his attempt to direct Arnolt Bronnen's *Vatermord* in 1922, and it was not until the 1924 production of his adaptation of Marlowe's *Edward II* that he took an active part in the direction of his own work. It is all the more surprising, then, that each of the early plays is, in its own way, so theatrically effective. While by no means mere exercises in style, each one is a different kind of theatrical experiment which defines itself by its rejection of a current theatrical style. No writer for the stage can ever work in a stylistic vacuum, and Brecht is inevitably influenced by current thinking and the theatre writing and practice of his day. But in these plays he does not identify himself uncritically with any pattern of thought, either of the right or the left, nor with any of the prevailing styles of theatrical presentation. On the other hand, he also avoids another route frequently followed by young writers seeking to make their mark – that of outright, negative rejection of what they find on the contemporary stage. Each of Brecht's early plays is characterised by the rejection of a style, but the rejection is both positive and constructive.

It is in this rejection that we can observe the early operation of one of Brecht's most powerful and enduring traits: that of doubt, or refusing to accept the accepted. It could indeed be argued that, throughout his life, this doubting attitude was the primary motive force behind both his writing and his theatre practice. From the much-quoted story of his unpatriotic response to the essay subject, *Dulce et decorum est pro patria mori*, to the constant rewriting of texts during rehearsal at the Berliner Ensemble, he used a questioning doubt as the primary tool with which to test the concrete nature of each truth. It is perhaps this aspect of his writing that best qualifies Brecht to comment on life in the first half of the twentieth century.

Baal was written because of Brecht's unwillingness to accept the traditional romantic view of the inspired artist, as portrayed in Johst's play *Der Einsame* (1917). Instead, he presents us with a poet's (Baal's) refusal to compromise, cost what it may in terms of personal relationships, public acclaim or physical comfort. Behind *Drums in the Night* lies Brecht's limited experience of the First World War and the abortive German revolution. Later he may have tried to tinker with the play to make it more acceptable in the GDR, but at the time of writing it was his doubting perception that led him to create the uncomfortable, but ultimately highly credible, character of Andreas Kragler – by any reckoning a profoundly sceptical revolutionary. *In the Jungle of the Cities* provides a striking early experiment in the repudiation of the dominant view of character motivation. Instead of presenting detailed psychological and social backgrounds for the characters and encouraging the audience to construct individual motivations for each, Brecht suggests that people watch the drama as they might a sporting event, as a sequence of actions, the justification for which has no more hidden psychological depths than a boxing-match might have. The interest lies in the contest, and the meaning of the drama is to be found in the outcome of the action. In the situations presented and, in particular, in the composition of the central characters, the three plays share the unmistakably cool and objective vision of Brecht in his twenties.

BAAL

While a student in Munich, Brecht neglected his medical studies in favour of attending seminars by the theatre critic Artur Kutscher. In these classes, Brecht was delighted to re-encounter Wedekind's work, less so that of Hanns Johst, the première of whose *Der Einsame* Brecht attended. It was his reaction to this play which led not only to his expulsion from the Kutscher seminar, but also to the writing of *Baal*.[3] In *Der Einsame*, Johst presents a picture of the German playwright and poet Grabbe as a man with a mission to communicate. Aware of his divine gift, he is given to ecstatic outbursts of joy such as (on completing a work), 'I am the cosmos!', but is also given to touching poetic expressions of remorse, as on the death of his lover. After this event, he goes downhill until his eventual death, serenaded by Beethoven's music. The play presents a clichéd view of the romantic poet in the style of a Hollywood biopic. Significantly, it is set indoors throughout. Johst's Grabbe is the epitome of the poet as bohemian, an image which mildly scandalises society at large, but one which it can accommodate. In the first scene of *Baal*, the poet is shown being lionised at a society soirée. In addition to praise, he is offered food, drink and publication, but he rejects an easy life in this sterile world, with its images of death and its cast of people who live by killing trees, and chooses instead a rootless existence without patronage; an altogether harder, unprotected world of first-hand experience. The patrons he respects are the lorry drivers, who will pay him for a poem if it pleases them, rather than paying him for embodying their expectations of an artist or living out for them a fantasy of the bohemian lifestyle.

The function of this first scene (so different in its grotesque style from the rest of the play) is to present Baal, as Brecht later described him, as antisocial. But Baal is antisocial in an antisocial society. In the past, the true artist had to be antisocial, since society separated art from life. If the artist of the past integrated himself into society, he became its tool, forced to pander to the ruling class. When, in Berlin in the 1950s, Brecht himself chose to reject Baal's antisocial stance and seek to serve his society, he did so in the confidence that the state sought to benefit the people as a whole, not just a ruling class. In a socialist state, an artist could write in the service of society with a clear conscience. In 'On looking through my first plays', Brecht ascribes his inability consistently to apply this line of argument against Baal to his own lack of strength. He does, however, ironically compare his Baal with the life-affirming Chinese god of happiness, whose supporters suggest the workers should take over the factories, and who cannot be killed. Baal is not susceptible to reform by a mature Brecht in the 1950s, but perhaps Baal too is the outcome of an intuitive revolutionary inspiration.

Brecht shares with Goethe a capacity to project experimentally an aspect of his own character as a writer without striving to present the whole. In *Torquato Tasso*, Goethe had focussed on the poet's problems in constraining his nature to fit it within the frame of acceptable court behaviour. In *Baal*, Brecht does not present a picture of himself as a bohemian writer but of the bohemian writer in himself. There is, of course, an elemental urge to *épater le bourgeois* in this first play by a young man who was himself in the process of rejecting a comfortable, bourgeois background. But the play does not show the scenes of sex and drinking as images of unrestrained pleasure. They are, rather, part of Baal's voracious and all-embracing appetite for experience. Conventional concepts of pleasure and pain are not relevant here. Baal can refuse no sensory experience if he is to remain true to his purpose as a poet, whether it be the (for an audience titillating) indulgence in sex with a pair of sisters, or his death in the forest, variously described as 'miserable' and 'sordid'. None of these experiences is to be preferred over the others. Baal must remain open to them all if his poetry is not to be limited in its expression and relevance. And he must reject the safety and physical comfort of Johst's indoor world, as well as the emotional comfort of stable relationships. He cannot restrict himself to caring for Sophie, nor for any one man or woman. If people want to go with him, they may, but Baal will not slow down to make allowance for them. Baal affirms the raw life force, as did the Baalim when Moses brought from the mountain to the followers of Yahweh the tablets of stone bearing the new social restrictions. In 1926, when preparing yet another 'stage version', Brecht tried to make the phenomenon of Baal more acceptable to an audience by pointing up the moral objections to his behaviour with scene titles like 'Baal misuses his power over women'. But Baal is not simply a selfish hedonist and immoralist. The point of his rejection of an easy life in favour of a life on the road is lost if he is seen to represent merely a negative role model. Baal's freedom from social conventions and his receptivity to all experience are essential to his integrity as a poet. It is, paradoxically, integrity which can be seen as Baal's central trait, and it is the search for integrity, in whatever form and for whatever conditions, which will characterise Brecht's writing throughout his life.

Baal is anything but a generalised image of the suffering, romantic artist. He suffers and dies in the play, but he accepts his death, as he has accepted all experience, as the fulfilment of a demanding contract with the natural world, freely entered into in order to realise his destiny as a poet. His desire to make love to plants is a desire, not to rid himself of personal identity, but to experience and give expression to his total integration in nature. As a character, he embodies many of the features admired by writers of the pre-romantic *Sturm und Drang* movement. He is a man of sudden and intuitive action rather than contemplation, and his poetry's vitality and truth result from the fact that he writes from direct, physical experience of the natural world.

As a study of an artist, *Baal* harks back to the portrait of the playwright Lenz in Büchner's short story, and there are further debts to Büchner, particularly to his *Woyzeck*, in the episodic 'Stationen' structure and 'filmic' style of writing, as well as in the varying depths at which the characters are realised. Where the expressionist playwrights avoid the harsh and demanding side of creativity in their portrayal of the 'poet' (as in *Der Einsame* or Sorge's *Der Bettler*), Brecht clings to that side of Büchner which influenced the German naturalists – his lack of romanticism and his ability to stare the truth of a situation in the face. In having Baal perform in a cabaret, Brecht also locates him in a very different tradition of German writing, reaching back via Wedekind to Grabbe and, again, to Büchner. This, he proposes, is where the true life of German poetry is to be found, not in the 'high culture' tradition to which Johst attempts to attach his Grabbe. If the atmosphere in Johst's play is one of tragedy, and his poet predictably melancholic, Brecht in *Baal* shows early evidence of his comic gift and of his prodigious talent as a theatre poet. Lyricism pervades the play, from Baal's haunting descriptions of nature to the songs he sings (as Brecht himself did) to his own ragged accompaniment. Baal's lyricism is vital and assertive, mirroring the individual tone of Brecht's lyric poetry during his time in Augsburg.

Baal may be Brecht's first play, but in its cool representation of sensational and offensive images on stage we can detect the beginnings of Brecht's ideas on the role of the theatre. In a diary entry for 10 February 1922, he records the hope that he has, in *Baal*, avoided a common artistic error: 'that of trying to carry people away'.[4] Already, and despite the nature of the material, Brecht has the intention of distancing the audience from the onstage action, of not violating their 'splendid isolation', and of encouraging a critical attitude in them by inhibiting over-identification with the characters in the play. While reflecting the bohemian lifestyle Brecht was himself attempting to lead at the time, *Baal* also adumbrates concerns and techniques which were to be central to Brecht's writing for the rest of his life.

DRUMS IN THE NIGHT

In *Drums in the Night*,[5] Brecht writes a play in a genre that was becoming familiar to post-war German audiences, that of the *Heimkehrerdrama*, in which returning soldiers of the defeated German army face the difficulty, or impossibility, of reintegrating into a society which rejects them as symbols of a recent past that it wishes to forget. The pre-war expressionist concept of the New Man (*Der Neue Mensch*), who was to have risen in brotherhood and love from the cleansing fire of the war, had died in the trenches. In his place, there returned either the emasculated hero of Toller's *Hinkemann* (1923–4), who, after rejection by his wife, takes a job in a cabaret biting the heads off live rats, or the socialist New Man of Toller's *Die Wandlung* (1919), who returns from the trenches disillusioned with nationalism, espouses the cause of the international brotherhood of man and becomes a revolutionary leader. (The genre retained its currency. One of the most effective *Heimkehrerdramen*, Borchert's *Draussen vor der Tür*, was written after the Second World War by a soldier recently returned from the Eastern Front.)

Both the setting and subject of the play are unusual for Brecht, as is its five-act form. In the vast majority of his writing for the stage, the contemporary issues which he is actually addressing are distanced, either historically or geographically. Brecht is at pains to place *Baal* in 1904 and *In the Jungle of the Cities* in Chicago. The problem dealt with in *Drums in the Night* is a contemporary one in a contemporary setting, and this should be pointed up by the parody of the then-current expressionist style in the play. As it would be in *Fear and Misery of the Third Reich*, Brecht's concern is not universal but immediate and localised; its transposition into his customary parable format would blunt the edge of his message.

Although recognisably a *Heimkehrerdrama*, *Drums in the Night* bears all the hallmarks of Brecht's originality in its analysis of a social situation. His returning soldier, Andreas Kragler, adopts neither of the courses which might be expected of an expressionist *Heimkehrer*: he does not despair and commit suicide nor set himself at the head of the revolutionaries. Brecht draws a startlingly refocussed picture of the events in Berlin during the Spartacist uprising, reaching unmistakably towards the conclusion that revolution is not to be brought about by essentially romantic calls to arms. Perhaps Kragler is viscerally aware of this after his contact with the 'real' world during the war. Much later, Brecht's Galileo would voice pity for a land that has need of heroes. Kragler's deafness to the Spartacists may indicate Brecht's early recognition that, to succeed, a revolution must be well enough conceived to manage without heroes. Or is he simply not interested?

Is the play the chronicle of an anti-hero unaware of his revolutionary duty? Or is it Brecht's analysis of the German non-revolution? His discomfort with *Drums in the Night* later in his life is palpable, and the suggestion that Kragler was intended to excite revulsion in the audience cannot be sustained by reference to the text.[6] On the other hand, Kragler's choice of social conformity and his rejection of revolutionary engagement might, retrospectively at least, be seen as paradoxical 'virtues' by analogy with the paradoxical 'vices' described in Brecht's later 'ballet', *The Seven Deadly Sins* (1933). Kragler chooses to accept the world as it is and to take refuge in anonymity. The irony in such an argument would not have satisfied a Communist Party which called for Kattrin to be promoted as the hero of *Mother Courage*. The wiser recognition is that *Drums in the Night* was (and is) not a call for action or inaction but, once again, an experiment. It does not present the playwright's answer but the strikingly unexpected course of action of an individual character.

The play's unconventional tone was misjudged in its première at the Munich Kammerspiele, when the director, Otto Falckenberg, took advantage of its sparse expressionist features – colour imagery, stark characterisation, red moon – to produce a standard piece of expressionist theatre. Brecht was far from happy with the result. Falckenberg had missed the point: that Brecht had employed familiar expressionist icons with ironic intent. In this production, not by any means for the last time, Brecht's sense of irony was misunderstood, as was the grotesque humour in the characterisation of Murk and the Balicke family. Brecht equates their war profiteering with their *petit bourgeois* respectability. Such people are the backbone of capitalism, profiting as they do off the backs of the working class and off the sacrifices of the soldiers in the war. Kragler's post-war anguish is mocked (ironically) when Murk and Balicke decide that, for their part, they must substitute baby carriages for the munitions production from which they have prospered in the war. The rich seam of grotesque inspiration which Brecht had first called on for his depiction of the socialites in *Baal* here once again throws into sharp contrast the cooler presentation of the 'hero'.

Despite Falckenberg's simplistic reading of the play, his production caused something of a stir, initiating, among other things, the long-running dispute between the critics Herbert Ihering (who championed Brecht) and Alfred Kerr (who did not). Ihering's awarding of the prestigious Kleist Prize to Brecht led to a number of other productions of *Drums in the Night* (although the citation stated that the award was for his first *three* plays, it was widely assumed to apply to this one in particular), which established Brecht as a playwright, and encouraged both directors and publishers to take an interest in his other plays.

IN THE JUNGLE OF THE CITIES

Throughout his life Brecht had a love–hate relationship with America. It represented for him the apotheosis of the hated system of capitalism, in which the many are callously exploited for the profit of a few. Above all in Chicago, men were consumed by the meat-packing yards in much the same way as the animals they killed. Both the horrific, dehumanised picture of the mechanised stockyards of Chicago painted by Upton Sinclair in his novel, *The Jungle*, and its message of hope through organised labour, profoundly influenced Brecht's thinking. The description of the unbearable conditions experienced by Garga and Jane Larry owes much to Sinclair, as does the later play, *Saint Joan of the Stockyards*. On the other hand, Brecht was fascinated by what he pictured as America's freedom from the restrictions of the European bourgeois tradition. It was, for him, a genuinely new world, a country where anything could happen, where rules could be broken. Buildings could be taller than anywhere else, women more beautiful and men stronger. There were cowboys and prairies in America (Brecht had read about them in Karl May's novels), but it was the culture of the giant cities which Brecht found so seductive. In this cruel but exhilarating world, the law of the jungle was exercised by gangsters to whose lives he had access by way of novels and the cinema. Their music was jazz, they drove fast cars, they smoked cigars and the sports they watched were intensely physical: boxing and six-day cycle racing. It was, after all, in imitation of American names that Brecht changed his first name from Berthold to Bertolt (or Bert). Both the positive and the negative stimuli from his mental picture of America are equally represented in his setting of the C. Maynes Lending Library in Chicago. *In the Jungle of the Cities*[7] also shows the influence of the speculative exoticism of an era before package holidays. Brecht's ethnography in his picture of Schlink, the Malayan timber-dealer, is about as genuine as Shakespeare's geography. Schlink comes to Brecht from the writing of Rimbaud, whom, according to an early note by Brecht, Garga should resemble.[8] In a free, competitive environment, Brecht can give vent to the racist fears of his generation, pitting his 'hero' against an oriental opponent in a fight free from the requirements of psychological motivation imposed by the conventions of naturalistic characterisation. The environment retains an influence, but one which can be overcome by a determined combatant.

Critics have repeatedly seen the *acte gratuit* of the opening of hostilities between Schlink and Garga, the isolation of the individuals and the impossibility of communicating through language that the play displays as elements prefiguring the Theatre of the Absurd. But absurdism is informed by existentialism; the philosophy precedes the playwriting. Brecht's story of a motiveless fight to the death results from his abandoning of the conditioning factors of European thought and its drama. In the new world, where anything is possible in a society based on the philosophy that a man is the master of his own fate, Brecht sets a new sort of drama. The struggle is not absurd. It has the logic of the boxing-ring. The audience at a boxing-match would not stop to ask why the boxers are fighting; neither should the audience at *In the Jungle*. Suffice it to say that they choose to fight, and that all the other elements of the drama, the other characters, the American environment, even the Salvation Army, are employed by the antagonists solely to that end. Brecht's thesis is that the ultimate achievement of a society based on the primacy of the individual will be the total breakdown of communication, and such complete isolation of the individual that even enmity becomes an unattainable goal. There is a commonly held view that this bleak image of the world was dispelled, for Brecht himself, by his acceptance of a Marxist analysis of human relations and the functioning of society; but this presupposes that Brecht intends *In the Jungle*'s depiction of human relations to be a bleak one. Is it not, rather, another of Brecht's experiments; this time a glorying in the one-on-one combat, a once-for-all encounter usually to be found only in the contrived single-mindedness of the world of sport? Brecht was, at this time, associating with Paul Samson-Körner, a light-heavyweight boxer whose objective (*sachlich*) fighting style he admired and whose renunciation of everything outside the ring he planned to commemorate in a (in the event uncompleted) play called *The Human Fighting Machine*.

In the presentation of its leading characters as fighting machines, *In the Jungle* prefigures Brecht's excursion into the mechanistic potential of the human being in *Man is Man*, where once again the flimsiest of motivations is proffered to justify the taking apart and reassembling of a human personality as if it were a motorcar. In both plays, a man is shown to be the sum total of his actions, not of his heredity and psychological development. In this way, the subject becomes an object and can be manipulated. Remove the consciousness of responsibility, and human beings are capable equally of the tyranny of the Chicago meatpacking bosses or the Nazis, or, indeed, of the tyranny of Stalin. But this darker side of the argument will come later. In this extraordinary and uncompromising play, after staring into the void, Garga can still acknowledge the sheer exhilaration resulting from the renunciation of personal responsibility for the sake of a naked struggle for dominance between two men. His last line is, 'That was the best time' ('Es war die beste Zeit').

Perhaps the most extraordinary feature of these first three plays by a young writer is their originality. In each case, this was recognised by supporters and opponents alike. After the first night of *Drums in the Night*, Ihering wrote in the *Berliner Börsen-Courier*: 'The twenty-four-year-old writer Bert Brecht has changed the face of German writing overnight.' For the production of *Baal*[9] at the Theater in der Josefstadt in Vienna (March 1926), the 51-year-old Austrian playwright, Hugo von Hofmannsthal, wrote an introductory playlet for the director, the actors and a dramaturg, in which Hofmannsthal declares the wish of the age to be set free from the 'individual', that monstrous child of the sixteenth century, which had been nurtured by the nineteenth century. Hofmannsthal points to the anti-individualistic tendency of contemporary dramaturgy and cites Brecht as its leading exponent. After *In the Jungle*, Kerr was moved to write in the *Berliner Tageblatt*: 'Enough of politeness: this is completely worthless rubbish. Completely worthless rubbish', whereas Ihering wrote: 'When we come to look back later at this play of Bert Brecht, we will realise how acutely the feeling of new beginning is expressed in this work.' Opposition to the plays also took more direct forms. In 1923, a gas bomb was thrown by a Nazi sympathiser during a performance of *In the Jungle*, which had to be interrupted until the air in the theatre had cleared, and Joseph Stolzing wrote in his review for the Nazi paper, the *Völkische Beobachter*, of smelling a 'Jewish stench' in the theatre. The 1929 production of *Drums in the Night* at Wiesbaden led the Nazi Party to public protest in the press and a threat of 'war in the theatre'.

While the plays show great originality and, in their use of language, a genuinely new voice on the German stage, there is no coherent line of thought to link the three. Brecht rigorously maintains an integrity of approach to his subject in each, but one is left overall with a sense of lack of direction. While Brecht never claimed to be offering solutions in his writing – and it would be naive to look for a coherent political programme even in his mature work – the political analysis in Brecht's plays does become more focussed after his reading of Marx, and after the protracted debates with his circle of politically committed friends in Berlin.

One of that circle was Helene Weigel, whom he met in 1923. Another, whom he met the following year, was Elisabeth Hauptmann. These two remarkable women must certainly have contributed to another, and perhaps equally important, change in Brecht's perception of society. Throughout his life Brecht would continue relationships with a number of women (Weigel once described him to their daughter Barbara as 'faithful to too many'), but before his encounter with Weigel, and certainly in the first three plays, the female characters offer limited opportunities to their performers. One might reasonably claim that, in *Baal*, there are aesthetic and structural reasons for the concentration on the central (male) character. The play is close in form to the 'I' dramas (*Ich-Dramen*) of the expressionists. It tells the story of the poet Baal, and the other figures are no more than functions of his character. But the same defence cannot be mounted for the unsatisfactory portrayal of women in the other two early plays. The women of *In the Jungle* are treated as mere cyphers. Brecht kept changing their names, as he did those of the minor thugs, when he reworked the text, and they remain pawns in the game between the combatants. A slightly stronger case may be argued for Anna in *Drums in the Night*. Where Frau Balicke is venal and dominated by her husband, Anna has the makings of a genuine character in her determination to prevent Kragler from joining the street-fighting in the newspaper district. Having submitted to her father in the first scene of the play, she finally shows a surprising strength of purpose to win Kragler. His embracing her as they leave together indicates his acceptance of her as an equal partner in their shop-soiled relationship. But if Anna is the first of Brecht's female characters to show any spirit, she does so in order to win her man. Later, in his long collaboration with Hauptmann and his longer relationship with Weigel, Brecht will create very different women, realising more clearly their dramatic and revolutionary potential.

The early plays have not lost their theatrical appeal, although *Drums in the Night* has barely sustained it. After initially enjoying considerable stage success, with twenty-five productions during the Weimar Republic, it fell foul of the Nazis. A brief post-war revival foundered in the GDR, where its message was seen as ideologically unsound, and both subject-matter and five-act structure have lessened its appeal for directors in the West. *Baal* and *In the Jungle*, however, continue to appear on the programme of Germany's leading theatres. In December 1987, Ekkehard Schall, by then the leading actor of the Berliner Ensemble, opened as Baal in the Alejandro Quintana production at the Theater am Bertolt Brecht Platz in Berlin, and in October 1991, Ruth Berghaus's production of *In the Jungle* opened at the Thalia Theater in Hamburg, as the second in a series of what she called 'related texts' which began in autumn 1989 with her production of Büchner's *Danton's Death*.

If the three plays, each, as we have seen, a very different kind of experiment, can be seen to form a unity, it may be only through a comparison with *The Life of Edward II of England*, which was premièred at the Munich Kammerspiele in March 1924. With its historicised setting, its large cast and broad scope of action, this is the first of Brecht's plays which can usefully be called 'epic'. It was also the first of his adaptations of classic texts and his first attempt at fully collaborative writing. In both the writing and the direction of this play, Brecht entered into a new phase of his work for the theatre. Where each of the first three plays is, to some extent, a rejection of influences, *Edward II* is an attempt to lay the foundations of a new style of theatre, the development of which in practice and the definition of which in his theoretical writing would occupy Brecht for the rest of his working life.

NOTES

1 Each of the first three plays carries a dedication: *Baal* to Brecht's schoolfriend, Georg Pfanzelt, *Drums in the Night* to his lover, Paula Banholzer, and *In the Jungle of the Cities* to his first wife, Marianne Zoff. For whatever reason, none of Brecht's subsequently published plays has a dedication.

2 This essay was first published as the Introduction to volume 1 of the German edition of his plays, 1954.

3 There are three recorded versions of the text, dated 1918, 1919 and 1926, in addition to the published versions. The third of these, reworked for performance under the fuller title of *Lebenslauf des Mannes Baal*, is the one that contains the scene titles. The edition published in 1922 provided the text for the première at the Altes Theater in Leipzig on 8 December 1923.

4 Brecht, *Diaries 1920–1922*, p. 159.

5 Written in 1919 and originally called *Spartakus*, the play was premièred at the Munich Kammerspiele on 29 September 1922.

6 Brecht claimed, in 'On looking through my first plays' (1954), that the rebels were the tragic figures and Kragler the comic one.

7 A first draft was completed in 1922 and the play was premièred at the Munich Residenz-Theater on 9 May 1923 under the shorter title *In the Jungle* (*Im Dickicht*). The version rewritten for publication in 1927 was premièred at the Hessisches Landestheater in Darmstadt in December 1927.

8 *Im Dickicht – Erstfassung und Materialien*, ed. Gisela Bahr (Suhrkamp: Frankfurt, 1968), p. 134.

9 This was the production that extended the play's title to *Lebenslauf des Mannes Baal*. See note 3 above.

4

STEPHEN McNEFF

The Threepenny Opera

The Threepenny Opera is unique. Since its first performance in Berlin, at the Theater am Schiffbauerdamm on 31 August 1928, it has enjoyed a popularity matched only by the best-known Broadway musicals or the most established operas. It has led a protean existence in commercial theatres, in subsidised regional and national theatres and in opera houses. It has spawned a film, a novel and countless recordings of its music by a bewildering range of performers.

Yet it is clearly not an opera in any conventional sense; the word opera in the title implies a parody. Formally the music is too disunited to make it, for its time, a 'proper' opera, even though operatic devices such as recitative, ensembles and choruses are used. Neither is it a musical in the sense that we now accept the term, even though the Marc Blitzstein revival in the 1950s ran in New York for more than 2,500 performances. Successful Broadway musicals tend to have socially conventional plots with plenty of spectacle and picturesque romanticism, not Marxist-inspired social criticism as their motivation.

It is worth getting to know Kurt Weill a little better before going on to the work itself in more detail. Weill is a paradoxical character; a classically trained composer who in his youth was regarded as at the leading edge of the avant-garde, but who wrote 'Mac the Knife' – one of the most ubiquitous and durable popular tunes of the century. Although his growing band of hagiographers resist the notion as a way of assessing his work, Weill's career more or less falls into two halves: the German, pre-war half of avant-gardism and the American second half up to his death in 1950 when he wrote 'American' musicals – worthy pieces most of them with lots of good detachable tunes, but nothing in the same league as *The Threepenny Opera*.

Weill was born in Dessau in 1900. His father was a cantor and his mother reportedly a good amateur pianist. He did not take up music until he was

The abbreviation *BT* refers to *Brecht on Theatre*.

fourteen, but made rapid progress and enrolled in the Berlin Hochschule für Musik in 1918. From 1921 to 1924 he studied composition with Ferruccio Busoni – the iconoclastic modernist composer who practically invented twentieth-century neoclassicism in music and whose *Fantasia Contrappunctistica*, his giant work for piano, combines the purity of Bach's contrapuntal thought with revolutionary intellectualism. Busoni died in 1924, a victim of his own habitual drinking and smoking. It is impossible that Weill, who supported himself at this time by playing the piano in beer halls, was not profoundly influenced by Busoni's intellect, his theoretical writings and his extraordinary stage works, including the unfinished *Doctor Faust*.

Weill wrote a number of 'modernist' works during the first part of the 1920s: a first symphony in 1921; *Zaubernacht*, a dance pantomime for children, in 1922. *Frauentanz*, a song cycle for soprano and wind instruments was performed in 1924 and in March 1926 *Der Protagonist*, a commission from the Dresden Opera based on Georg Kaiser's one-act play, firmly established Weill as one of the leading composers of his generation. His modernism differed significantly from the expressionism of the Second Viennese School of Schoenberg, Berg and Webern – the other great intellectual thrust in the German-speaking musical world. Weill's instincts led him much more in the direction of socially aware art-forms, and, although it was to be some time before he abandoned 'intellectual' music for good, his stirrings towards a broad-based popular approach are evident in *Der Protagonist* and the other works of the period.

As a means of supplementing his income Weill had been contributing to the publication *Der deutsche Rundfunk* since 1924. In March 1927 Berlin Radio broadcast Brecht's *Man is Man* with incidental music by Edmund Meisel which Weill reviewed favourably. It is possible that Weill had met Brecht earlier, but it was not until this date that they came into contact professionally. In *The Days Grow Short*, Ronald Sanders suggests that Brecht and Weill got together in Schlichter's restaurant in Berlin in the company of Lotte Lenya (whom Weill had married in 1926) and 'some mutual friends of the composer and the playwright who had brought them together'.[1] We can only speculate on how the meeting happened, and our popular image of these two *enfants-terribles* in the Berlin of the 1920s will be disappointed if we don't imagine a boozy, smoky, into-the-early-hours, outrageously radical, talk about how the world will be saved by art, piece of theatrical history being created! It doesn't matter; the meeting was a success. Weill's emerging theory of *Zeitoper* (opera for the times) obviously found approval with Brecht, although Brecht, whose feelings about conventional opera verged on the murderous, must have forcefully made clear his feelings about the role of the librettist. Whether Weill completely took in Brecht's objections to a conventional role is a matter of some doubt, as disagreements about the fundamental nature of this relationship were to cause particular problems a few years later and ultimately lead to the breakdown of their short collaborative life. Still, it is easy to imagine in the euphoria of a fruitful meeting that they believed that anything was possible. Composers and writers nearly always get on well at first, but one of them will often emerge as the dominant partner – whether it is the composer because he or she has the commission and therefore holds the balance of power and the key to the means of production, or the writer, whose force of personality and status enable him or her to dominate the proceedings from a literary and often unmusical perspective.

The terms *Gebrauchsmusik* and *Gemeinschaftsmusik* (most usefully translated as 'functional music' and 'communal music') are generally associated with the Donaueschingen Festival (The Festival of German Chamber Music – *Deutsche Kammermusik*) which was started by the German composer Paul Hindemith in 1921. From a modest beginning this festival became an important part of the contemporary music scene in Germany in the 1920s and was host to numerous important premières. It was the claimed spiritual home in Germany to no less a figure than Stravinsky. Whatever ideas of 'high' art Donaueschingen may have started with, the influence of the French (particularly the composer Milhaud), of jazz, and the cosmopolitan and intellectual forces of the time led to the wholehearted embracing of *Neue Sachlichkeit* (translated by Sanders as 'new objectivity'). There is no doubt that the Festival, which moved to Baden-Baden in 1927, became as important for its social influence on participants as it was for its musical interest, and it was at the 1927 Festival that Brecht and Weill's first collaboration, the *Songspiel Mahagonny*, was premièred.

Songspiel Mahagonny, or *Das Kleine Mahagonny*, is based on six poems in Brecht's *Hauspostille* and, at only 30 minutes long, was designed as 'an exercise in style' for the full-length opera, *The Rise and Fall of the City of Mahagonny*, which was already in planning. It combines six trained and untrained voices in a vernacular, popular style with 'rough' tunes (some contributed or at least suggested by Brecht) and a sour-sweet orchestration, more than hinting at jazz, from an idiosyncratic band of a dozen or so musicians and including saxophones, elements of a jazz drum set and trombone lines tending towards the flatulent. The effect of the music is of a slightly out of tune, 'I'm not sure if that's the right note' feel, which soon becomes addictive and lends a distinctive colour and tone to the proceedings. The notion that the work can be performed by untrained voices (let alone an amateur orchestra) is deceptive, for while the work loses a lot if sung operatically, the technical requirements of the vocal lines, particularly some treacherous harmonic writing, demand singers with a high degree of musicianship. This issue may seem of mere technical interest – a problem to be sorted out by conductors and music directors – but it has a significance which will become of importance when discussing performance styles in *The Threepenny Opera*.

At the start of 1928 Brecht and Weill were involved in numerous projects. Weill's new one-act opera for the Leipzig Opera, *Der Zar lässt sich photographieren (The Tsar Has His Photograph Taken)*, was about to open in February. Both Brecht and Weill had continued work on the libretto for the full-scale *Mahagonny*, which was ready by the start of the new year, and Brecht was also working on at least two other projects – a re-write of Hasek's novel, *The Adventures of the Good Soldier Schweik* for Piscator and George Grosz, and his own (in the event, unfinished) play, *Joe Fleischhacker*.

It would seem unlikely then that either man was touting for work when, in the spring of 1928, Brecht was introduced to Ernst-Josef Aufricht at Schlichter's. (Schlichter's again! – the course of theatrical and musical history and, no doubt, all other arts would be immeasurably duller if it were not for the bars and restaurants of the world.) Aufricht, a none-too-successful actor who had just come into family money, had taken a lease on the Theater am Schiffbauerdamm, and had gathered together a team of people (which included Erich Engel, who was currently directing Brecht's *Man is Man*, and who would direct *The Threepenny Opera*) to find a suitable play with which to open the theatre in the late summer. It seems that they were having some difficulty in finding a suitable work and Brecht's first suggestion, *Fleischhacker*, would not do either. Brecht then suggested an adaptation of John Gay's *The Beggar's Opera* (retitled *Gesindel – Scum*), which he had been toying with in collaboration with Elisabeth Hauptmann. As most accounts have it, Aufricht thought that the idea 'smelt of theatre', which was hardly surprising – *The Beggar's Opera* had served John Gay well, and Nigel Playfair had successfully revived the work for 1,463 performances at the Lyric Theatre, Hammersmith (London) in 1920. Brecht showed Aufricht what was already on paper and Aufricht was impressed enough to make the decision to open with the work on 31 August. Brecht now went a stage further and proposed that Weill be involved with the music. It is not clear exactly how Brecht originally conceived Weill's involvement, nor how he explained it to Aufricht and the others. Perhaps it seemed unimportant to distinguish too pedantically between arranging existing music and composing new music, and it may be that Brecht was deliberately vague on the subject. Everyone would have been aware (or quickly made themselves aware) that the original *Beggar's Opera* music was a collection of popular tunes arranged by Christoph Pepusch, and that Frederic Austin had used the same material re-orchestrated for the Hammersmith production. (All other adapters of *The Beggar's Opera* have followed the same path of re-arranging and/or re-orchestrating the original tunes, including Benjamin Britten in the 1948 production for the English Opera Group.) Whatever Aufricht's understanding of the situation, the mention of Weill's name was enough to send him scuttling off to the Charlottenburg Opera to hear *Der Zar lässt sich photographieren* and *Der Protagonist* which were playing in a double bill. Aufricht, with the characteristic conservatism for which theatrical producers are renowned, was frightened by Weill's 'atonality' (although Weill's scores from this period technically deploy no such thing), and asked Theo Mackeben, who had been engaged as musical director for *The Threepenny Opera*, to have Pepusch's original arrangements standing by. We can be certain that Weill had no intention of simply re-arranging existing music and, although there are vestigial remnants of original tunes in the final score, the music is almost entirely new.

If the exact chronology of the events leading up to the decision to go ahead with *The Threepenny Opera* is a little unclear, what is established is that contracts were signed by the end of April, and by 10 May 1928 Brecht and Weill (and their families) were ensconced in Le Lavendou in the South of France, furiously writing a work that was to be premièred in less than four months. Even for the established professionals that Brecht and Weill must have considered themselves by now, this was cutting things rather fine. The relaxed atmosphere of the South of France and the Brechts and Weills *en famille* would not appear to be the most conducive to hasty creation, but both men obviously found that it suited them up to a point. By July they were back in Germany with the work under way but still unfinished. Work was well enough advanced to start rehearsals on 1 August.

Our hindsight and historical perspective tells us that *The Threepenny Opera* is an important work. It set the tone for what was to become a series of collaborations between Brecht and Weill, and it established both men in the popular theatre in a way that they had not enjoyed before. In Weill's case particularly it must have had a fundamental impact on his whole approach and philosophy, although it is unlikely that he viewed it that way when he was writing it. Both were meticulous planners of their work, and the speed at which *The Threepenny Opera* project was taken up and completed suggests that neither Brecht nor Weill considered it to be a work of seminal importance – more a summer project worth doing because the money was always welcome, and the reopening of the Theater am Schiffbauerdamm was too good an opportunity to miss. (Professional writers and composers, whatever their principles, tend also to be opportunists, aware that Aufrichts don't come along every day, and they are often willing to make time to jam in yet one more project if they think that it will be useful.)

The writing work on *The Threepenny Opera* continued in rehearsals. The rehearsals themselves were a famous catalogue of disasters and no one seriously expected the work to be a success. Massive cuts were made, casting was changed and new music was added. The work's most famous detachable song, 'The Ballad of Mac the Knife', which, in a well-ordered world, would have been planned from the beginning as a show-stopper, was added at the last moment – no doubt just as well, because its hastily placed positioning as the first vocal utterance in the piece sets up the whole of the rest of the work. All in all (and this is with a certain degree of license) the project must have had something of the atmosphere of a musical comedy try-out, or perhaps the well-intentioned but hastily organised chaos of *ad hoc* political theatre – although that denies the frustration and anger that it must really have caused to the professionalism of the serious-minded individuals involved. It must have been agony for Weill. Like all good pieces of theatrical mythology, the result was a triumph. Aufricht's faith in Brecht was vindicated (as producers are always vindicated when the box-office does well), and the Theater am Schiffbauerdamm established as the leading left-wing theatre in Berlin.

The Threepenny Opera is not, as I have said, an opera. Neither was its source. John Gay had set out to ridicule the taste for Italian Opera, which was at its height in London in 1728. There is some dispute about the significance of the anti-Walpole satire in *The Beggar's Opera*, but there is little doubt that it was a revolutionary work, 'a play about a social group that had never had a play written about them before'.[2] For its first audience, it was a fresh and exhilarating experience, cleaning out the cobwebs in popular musical theatre of the time, and playing for sixty-two performances while making the fortunes of its creators and cast. The fact that later revivals (including the 1920 one) to some degree or other prettified the music to the point of emasculation does not seem to have deterred Brecht and more particularly Weill (there is no special evidence that Weill heard the 1920 score although no doubt he could have obtained a copy if he'd wanted to). Brecht clearly seized on the satirical and wider political possibilities of the original, and Weill was obviously in harmony with him in creating a work suited to the time. Weill would have been acutely aware of the satirical implications of a Beggar's or *Dreigroschenoper*. Even though his works were hardly conventional, his reputation had been largely established through the operatic medium and he would have understood the social and professional implications of a parody of the operatic system probably better than Brecht.

If later versions of *The Beggar's Opera* are regarded as essentially re-vamping John Gay's original, it would be wrong to think of Brecht and Weill's *Der Dreigroschenoper* simply as an adaptation. *The Threepenny Opera* is to all practical intents and purposes a new work. Perhaps one should properly say that it takes *The Beggar's Opera* as its model or inspiration. It would be dull to make a complete comparison here (even if space allowed), and a reading of both texts will soon make clear the differences in incident and location. What is more important to understand is that Brecht used *The Beggar's Opera* for his own purposes. As John Willett has mentioned, 'in Gay the target was an aristocracy whose affairs were much like those of the underworld; here (in *The Threepenny Opera*) it is a bourgeois society which allows there to be an underworld at all'.[3] Actually, the precise authorship of *The Threepenny Opera* was a matter of some dispute at the time of its première. The original playbill merely acknowledges Brecht as 'adapter' with Hauptmann as translator and notes that there are interpolated ballads by François Villon and Kipling. Weill, however, does get sole credit for the music. This situation changed after the first publication of the libretto and Brecht became author of the work, but not before Brecht had to defend himself against charges of plagiarism for 'forgetting' to acknowledge one of the translators of the interpolated material – a fact which, as Stephen Hinton reminds us,[4] led to Brecht's famous remark about 'fundamental laxity in matters of intellectual property'. Whatever the case, and there is no dispute that Brecht lifted various chunks from a variety of sources including his own work, the 'feel' of the eventual *Threepenny Opera* is of a fresh, original work even if, to use Hinton's useful term, it is a montage.

In a textual analysis it will be found that *The Threepenny Opera* follows the same basic plot as *The Beggar's Opera*. Some of the more important changes are that Brecht updates the action to around the end of the nineteenth century; Jeremiah Peachum is now the leader (Godfather?) of the London beggars rather than a fence, and various scenes and locations, notably the Soho marriage of Macheath and Polly, are entirely new. Out of sixty-nine tunes in *The Beggar's Opera* only one survived in Weill's score – Peachum's 'Morning Chorale'; the rest of the music is Kurt Weill's. Brecht claimed that he had donated music to Weill, going so far as to say that he had 'dictated ... bar by bar, by whistling and above all by performing'. Composers who have worked with strong-willed authors no doubt may have experienced something similar to Brecht's 'dictation' – although not many authors working with an established composer would be so bold as even to hint that they were responsible, even in part, for composing the music. Brecht had made similar suggestions about the *Songspiel Mahagonny* (possibly with more justification), but it is probably safe to assume that

Weill, a tolerant and affable collaborator, would, for the most part, have been prepared to listen to Brecht's musical ideas more in the spirit of absorbing the style rather than being prepared to use verbatim what Brecht was singing and whistling. Weill hardly needed Brecht's tunes, but he might well have been interested in getting to the bottom of what Brecht thought the music should be doing. Besides which, while Brecht may have candidly admitted to 'laxity in matters of intellectual property', Weill was deeply conscientious when it came to such things and had by now evolved a musical style that relied for its distinctiveness as much on its harmonies and orchestration as on individual melodies. Brecht had a high opinion of his own musical abilities, later going so far as to record his own version of 'Mac the Knife'.[5] However useful the experience might have been, perhaps in the event Weill merely listened indulgently while Brecht expounded his musical ideas, rather than force his personality too much in discussing (as opposed to actually writing) the music. Weill would have known that his own stamp would be on the final result no matter what initial sources started the flow of musical ideas.

The fact is that the music of *The Threepenny Opera* is highly distinctive and contributed immeasurably to the work's success at its première and throughout its subsequent history. The role of the music and its performance was, and is, a cornerstone of the whole style of the work. Partly, this is because of Brecht's attitude to opera and singing in the theatre, but it is also because *The Threepenny Opera* came along at a time in Weill's career when, with his attitude to *Zeitoper* becoming more firmly rooted, he was able to compose a practical demonstration of his beliefs in a way that the confines of established opera had not allowed him to do. This would ultimately contribute to a sea-change in the course of his musical development.

Brecht made no secret of his contempt for conventional opera and wrote vehemently about his attitudes to it. He regarded opera as 'culinary' – a mush of elements, and, writing a few years later in his notes to *The Rise and Fall of the City of Mahagonny*, he says,

> Our existing opera is a culinary opera. It was a means of pleasure long before it turned into merchandise. It furthers pleasure even where it requires, or promotes, a certain degree of education, for the education in question is an education of taste. To every object it adopts a hedonistic approach. It 'experiences', and it ranks as an 'experience'. (*BT*, p. 35)

At the risk of over-simplifying, Brecht's objections seem to revolve around the idea that opera, by the all-embracing nature of music and spectacle, tends to draw its audience into its emotion in an uncritical fashion – the experience of opera is purely one of pleasure without any higher judgement being required. This is as valid a criticism of conservative opera today as it was of opera in the Germany of the 1920s. As Brecht mentions in the same article, it is precisely for its backwardness that the opera-going public adores opera, and the majority of opera buffs make no real value judgements nor exhibit any active critical response when, for instance, Pinkerton, in nearly a quarter of an hour's worth of indulgently swamping moonlight music, cynically woos the eponymous heroine of Puccini's *Madam Butterfly* after his patronising mock marriage to her. There is no place in Puccini and others (and I'm sorry to pick on Puccini as there are many other aspects of his operas to be admired) for a critical response – the music leaves no room for it and the opera does not want it. Brecht felt that the music must take an attitude and strike a position and his feelings about singing in the theatre were equally unequivocal. 'Nothing is more revolting', he said, 'than when an actor pretends not to notice that he has left the level of plain speech and started to sing.' He believed that the singer must be direct: 'his aim is not so much to bring out the emotional content of the song but to show gestures' (*BT*, p. 45–6).

The casting of *The Threepenny Opera* reflects the directness of Brecht's approach to singing. *Songspiel Mahagonny* had acknowledged the need for well-trained, operatically orientated, singers for at least part of its casting. *The Threepenny Opera* makes no such requirements and the first performance cast Harald Paulsen, well known as a musical comedy star, as Macheath; Roma Bahn, a music hall actress, was eventually cast as Polly and (without working through the entire cast list) *The Threepenny Opera*'s most durable interpreter, the performer most closely identified with the work, and for over fifty years its most avid protector, Lotte Lenya, Weill's wife, was cast as Jenny. Whatever the talents of the cast, and in the case of the performers mentioned they were not inconsiderable, their main strengths did not lie in operatically produced singing, but they must obviously have rested in the ability to perform the songs in the way that Brecht and Weill required. This provides us with a clear indication of how the work should be cast today, for while it is a mistake to cast the work with opera singers, it is equally wrong to employ actors who do not have strong musical talents, and, just as importantly, the ability to strike the right kind of balance between an 'epic' and a more mellifluous delivery – something that requires an instinctive musical intelligence.

It would also be wrong to think that Brecht alone created the philosophical and practical conditions necessary for this uniquely *Threepenny Opera* blend of the intelligent singing actor. Weill's music is ideally suited to performers of the type that were cast in the first production. Less demanding technically than *Songspiel Mahagonny*, *The Threepenny Opera* score contains musically clever and highly inspired vocal writing. To take a few examples, the *Moritat* ('Mac the Knife') is a simple enough tune when sung on its own, and the popularity and speed with which it was taken up by legions of amateur and professional singers (and others) since 1928 attests to that. In *The Threepenny Opera* it is first sung with a simple type of barrel organ accompaniment, but, from the third verse, the orchestra develops more intricate rhythmic patterns which eventually lead to canonic imitation of the first phrase and increasingly complex chromatic accompaniment figures. The effect is to place the Ballad Singer in a constantly evolving musical world which retains our musical interest for nine verses while making few demands on the performer other than that he learn the tune properly and stay with the band. Similar devices are employed elsewhere and in the Third Finale the chorus is assigned a relatively simple part while the accompaniment moves around them *Allegro Vivace* in a suitably galloping six-eight time. Even the recitatives for Tiger Brown in this Finale should be easily handled by an actor who understands the main purpose of recitative – to impart information with musically interrupting comments. Areas which can give trouble (and one should not underestimate the real singing demands of all the parts) are Macheath's 'Gerettet!' which lies high for the average baritone (as the part is frequently cast, even though it seems that Weill had expected an operetta tenor) and certainly the 'Jealousy Duet' can cause Lucy some problems if she is not a singer of some experience, as Brecht and Weill discovered when Lucy's aria had to be cut from the original production because Kate Kühl could not handle it. (This aria is now published in an appendix to the Universal Edition version of the miniature score.) The orchestra itself lends a unique flavour to the sound, and the original orchestra, a collection of Berlin studio musicians playing under the banner of the 'Lewis Ruth Band', played a variety of more-or-less jazz instruments (but including a decidedly non-jazz harmonium), doubling up in unlikely combinations. The original band parts indicate seven musicians, but for modern performances this can be somewhat confusing if one sticks to the letter, as some of the doublings are rare (to say the least). The picture has become even more confused since audiences have become more familiar with recordings of Weill's arrangement of the music for wind ensemble, *Kleine Dreigroschenmusik*, which, although officially not much bigger in terms of instrumentation than the stage version, always feels more orchestral than the original.

Brecht had said of Weill, talking about the *Songspiel Mahagonny*, 'up until that time, Weill had written relatively complicated music of a mainly psychological sort, and when he agreed to set a series of more or less banal *song* texts he was making a courageous break with a prejudice which the solid bulk of serious composers stubbornly held' (*BT*, p. 86). This suggests (characteristically for Brecht) that Weill by himself might never have dreamt of the ideas of *Zeitoper* or been aware of *Gebrauchsmusik*. In fact, as we know, Weill was particularly conscious of the social functions of music even before 1929 when he wrote, '*The Threepenny Opera* takes its place in a movement which today embraces nearly all the younger musicians. The abandonment of "art for art's sake", the reaction against individualism in art, the ideas for film music, the link with the musical youth movement and, connecting with these, the simplification of musical means of expression – they are all stages down the same road'.[6] Somewhat adopting Brecht's strident tone, but still in keeping with what Weill had been, and still was, clearly moving towards, he goes on to say:

> Only opera remains stuck in its 'splendid isolation'. Its audiences continue to represent a distinct group of people seemingly outside the ordinary theatrical audience. Even today new operas incorporate a dramaturgical approach, a use of language, a choice of themes such as would be inconceivable in the modern theatre ... Opera originated as an aristocratic branch of art, and everything labelled 'operatic tradition' goes to underline its basic social character. Nowadays, however, there is no other artistic form whose attitude is so undisguisedly social, the theatre in particular having switched conclusively to a line that can be better termed socially formative. If the operatic framework cannot stand such a comparison with the theatre of the times (*Zeittheater*), then that framework had better be broken up.

With very few changes, Weill might just as well have been speaking about the current popularity of consumer opera – rehashes of the old war-horses on giant television screens, in arenas seating tens of thousands and, in an eviscerated form, at globally televised football matches! Here is opera at its most culinary, and it is a great pity that a genuine interest in opera on the part of the widening audience to whom mass media have provided access should not also be accompanied by some deeper critical approach, rather than simply providing an opportunity to market a product and merchandise spin-offs less concerned with the art form than with the antics of opera personalities.

In the light of what we know about Weill's later career (admittedly somewhat forced on him by pressure of events in Germany in the 1930s), *The Threepenny Opera* was not a chance encounter with a man like Brecht who weaned him off culinary opera and manipulated him into writing epic theatre, but a deliberate and conscious (if unplanned) effort on the part of a thinking musician to follow a new path which would lead him into unknown and hostile territory. *The Threepenny Opera* did not change Weill's attitude to opera, but rather confirmed what he already knew or suspected: that a different approach, one that we now might call music theatre, was needed. The demise of his relationship with Brecht was probably inevitable, but their achievement in *The Threepenny Opera* and subsequent works provides an inspiration to continue searching for a socially aware music theatre which takes the best from opera and theatre and transforms them into a dynamic and balanced whole, where, as in the case of *The Threepenny Opera*, the whole is decidedly greater than the sum of the parts.

NOTES

1 Ronald Sanders, *The Days Grow Short*, p. 80.
2 Mark Pappenheim, quoting John Caird in an article 'Low life and high art', in the *Independent*, 28 March 1992, p. 26.
3 John Willett, *The Theatre of Bertolt Brecht*, p. 30.
4 Stephen Hinton, ed., *Kurt Weill: The Threepenny Opera*, p. 11.
5 Top Classic-Historia H 625.
6 See *Collected Plays*, vol. II (ii), p. 98.

5

JOEL SCHECHTER

Brecht's clowns: *Man is Man* and after

Brecht was not a great comedian, but several of his friends were. Both Karl Valentin and Charlie Chaplin influenced the playwright, and led him to invent stage characters who could be described as political clowns. The first of these clowns, Galy Gay, appeared in 1926, as the humble Irish porter who becomes a 'human fighting machine' in *Man is Man*.

The play remains an important document of Brecht's political humour, as well as of his development of epic theatre and a Marxist aesthetic in the 1920s. It has also been regarded as a critique of militarism, imperialism and what Brecht later called 'the bad collective' which destroys individualism; but the comic aspects of the play deserve special attention, since they reveal Brecht's innovations in political clowning. As if to acknowledge his closeness to comedy, Brecht has characters in the play speak of scenes in Begbick's canteen as 'numbers' – that is, variety acts like those performed in music halls.

The play's innovations moved the clowning of Brecht's contemporaries from cabarets and films into German theatres which were far more solemn, and less appealing to working-class audiences, than the popular art forms in which Valentin and Chaplin performed. Early in his career Brecht called for more 'fun' in the theatre, and the fun of clowning by Chaplin and Valentin became a model for Galy Gay's adventures in *Man is Man*. 'It's a jolly business' to see a man 'surrender his precious ego', Brecht once said about Galy Gay's agreement to give up his name and identity, and accept that of Jeriah Jip (*BT*, p. 19). This 'jolly business' is advanced through music hall numbers and songs in an episodic structure. Brecht entertains the public with cabaret-like routines at the same time as his fragmented plot uncovers conditions which lead to military recruitment, war and the destruction of civilian life. Most of the civilian casualties are 'peasants, artisans and shop-keepers, most of them friendly, hardworking people' whose shelter burns at

The abbreviation *BT* refers to *Brecht on Theatre*.

the end of the play; but Gay's civilian life is also destroyed, through his grotesquely comic transformation into a soldier.

MARX THE TEACHER OF SATIRE

'Friendly, hardworking people', and the public seeking fun in cabarets and sports events, were of interest to Brecht's favourite spectator, Karl Marx. Around the time that *Man is Man* had its première in Darmstadt in September 1926, Brecht decided that Marx 'was the only spectator for my plays I'd ever come across ... A man with interests like his must of necessity be interested in my plays' (*BT*, p. 24). Marx never actually read Brecht's plays (he died in 1883); but his approach to politics and economics inspired Brecht to politicise clowning as no playwright had before. The critic Walter Benjamin once noted that Marx was 'a teacher of satire', and 'it is with Marx that Brecht has gone to school'.[1] (Although Marx's influence in the political sphere is said to have ended in 1991 with the collapse of the Soviet empire, his influence on comic playwriting continues through Brecht's influence on more recent theatre.)

Marx was less comic than Brecht; but he described social contradictions between and within classes, and diverse forms of profit, which lend themselves to humorous interpretation. Brecht translates Marx's understanding of the economic motives behind war into comic terms in *Man is Man* when one soldier asks another 'who this war's against'. The answer, from a Brecht schooled by Karl Marx and music hall comics, is: 'If they need cotton, it's Tibet; if they need wool, it's Pamir.' The troops end up in Tibet, led by Galy Gay, whose understanding of trade and economics is mocked by Widow Begbick when she asks how he can be 'such a materialist' as to buy a fish. Gay becomes a bigger materialist, and wages a war for cotton, after he attempts to sell an elephant; he enters the army as a businessman, in other words.

Galy Gay's business deal gives comic form to Marx's theories of capital and exchange. Volume I of Marx's *Capital* argues that money is 'a great leveller; it extinguishes all distinctions'.[2] In *Man is Man* the promise of financial profit leads Gay first to 'extinguish all distinctions' between his counterfeit elephant and other, more authentic war elephants which are heard offstage; and he never suspects that Billy Humph, the elephant, is merely two men under a military map, with a gasmask as their trunk. Gay assumes Billy is genuine because Widow Begbick is willing to pay for the creature. He also later agrees to 'extinguish all distinctions' between his identity and that of Jip, after a trial staged by the machine-gun unit threatens to extinguish him completely – by execution – for the elephant swindle.

The vaudeville turns through which these exchanges of money and extinctions of identity are initiated suggest that Marx was not the only one behind the scenes, however.

VALENTIN THE WHITEFACED CLOWN

Karl Valentin sometimes parodied business deals as Brecht did in the sale of the counterfeit elephant. Shopkeepers, firemen, military band players, professionals with small roles in the economy and the defence of society often fared badly in Valentin's cabaret sketches. Their ambitions and bids would exceed their abilities, or, as Brecht once said of Valentin, 'Here we are shown the inadequacy of all things, ourselves included'.[3] But Valentin himself was more than adequate as a comedian.

Brecht met the comedian in 1919, a year before he began writing *Galgei*, which he later retitled *Man is Man*. A photograph from the period shows Brecht playing clarinet at a fairground booth with Valentin on tuba and Valentin's cabaret partner, Lisl Karlstadt, ringing a cowbell. Brecht worked with this team in 1922, when they staged a midnight cabaret performance of songs and sketches, billed as 'The Red Raisin', in Munich. Valentin continued to influence the playwright's work on *Man is Man* as late as 1931, when Brecht revived his play and staged it in a style quite similar to some of Valentin's cabaret sketches.

Critic Denis Calandra has noted, 'Looking closely at Brecht's arrangements as a director in the 1931 *Mann ist Mann* ... one cannot help but recognise Valentin's stage pictures.'[4] The grotesquery of Galy Gay and the other soldiers onstage in Berlin with their padded shoulders, trouser-covered stilts and vests laden with murderous weapons, rivals that of the dwarfs, giants and cross-dressed women in Valentin's own acts. In both cases, with their physical features exaggerated and misshapen, the performers resemble sideshow eccentrics.

Galy Gay, lifting weights in front of the soldiers, looks like the clown in a traditional circus routine, where the smallest man in the ensemble tries to lift dumb-bells as strong, tall companions watch him struggle. For the most part, however, Brecht's racist soldiers regard their enemies, not themselves, as misfits and brutes, especially when the enemies are Asians who booby-trap a temple, as the bonze Wang does.

Karl Valentin's comic aggression was rarely savage; it often began with innocent verbal misunderstandings, as Galy Gay's interest in elephants does. When the soldier Polly says 'What an elephant', in a reference to Galy Gay's thick wit, the simple porter mistakes derision for the offer of an elephant, and begins a comedy of errors that leads to his trial and mock-execution.

2.   Peter Lorre as Galy Gay, second from left, in the 1931 production of *Man is Man* (design by Caspar Neher). 'The performers resemble sideshow eccentrics.'

Karl Valentin's stubborn, comic personae would frequently persist in misunderstanding their partners, as do the soldiers who make over, rather than mistake, Gay's identity.

Valentin's naive sense of humour also contributed to Brecht's concept of epic theatre. Brecht told Walter Benjamin that the cabaret clown more or less invented epic theatre while advising him on a production of *Edward II* in 1924. Brecht was in Munich adapting and directing Marlowe's tragedy, and he asked Valentin, 'one of his closest friends', for comments on the battle scene.[5] Valentin said that the soldiers are scared, they're pale; Brecht chose to show this condition by giving them chalk-white faces – faces Valentin and other clowns wore in the circus and cabaret. The unfamiliar, startling appearance given to Brecht's soldiers in *Edward II* was the start of epic theatre. These men were not 'acting' fear through internally motivated behaviour, but demonstrating it with the artifice of whiteface. In 1931 Brecht led Peter Lorre back to this 'epic' acting style when he directed Lorre in the role of Galy Gay. Lorre whitened his face with powder during the play, 'instead of allowing his acting to become more and more influenced by fear of death "from within himself"', according to Brecht (*BT*, p. 55).

CHAPLIN THE EPIC ACTOR

In the same 1931 letter (to the *Berliner-Börsen Courier*) which discusses Lorre's performance, Brecht observed that 'the actor Chaplin ... would in many ways come closer to the epic than to the dramatic theatre's requirements'. Although he did not say Chaplin would be perfect for the role of Galy Gay, he wanted an actor 'to mime the basic meaning underlying every (silent) sentence' in the role, as Lorre had. Brecht saw Chaplin perform mime in this way many times, notably in 1926 when he watched *The Gold Rush*.

Later, when Brecht defined 'social gest' as a component of his theatre, he could have been recalling any number of Chaplin's films with their multitude of pratfalls. To Brecht, 'gest' was not merely a matter of physical gesture, but a matter of 'overall attitudes' which gestures can embody. He wrote that 'one's efforts to keep one's balance on a slippery surface result in a social gest as soon as falling down would mean "losing face"; in other words, losing one's market value' (*BT*, p. 104). The playwright saw Chaplin perform such falls, and created similarly precarious moments in his 1931 production of *Man is Man*. Brecht's friend, the Soviet writer Sergei Tretyakov, reported of the 1931 Berlin production: 'Giant soldiers armed to the teeth and wearing jackets caked with lime, blood and excrement, stalk about the stage holding on to wires to keep them from falling off the stilts inside their trouser legs.'[6] To preserve their stature as battlefield giants, Brecht's actors performed a sort of low-wire circus act, leaning against the wires so as not to lose balance and lose face.

Brecht met Chaplin in Hollywood several times between 1945 and 1947, and it is possible that in this period Brecht influenced the comic film-maker. He discussed *Monsieur Verdoux* with Chaplin before the film was completed, and its indictment of profitable war preparations in Europe recalls some of Brecht's own ironic references to war as a business practice.

Both the Little Tramp and Galy Gay are meek and compliant when first seen, and both 'cannot say no', as Mrs Gay says of her husband. But each of these clowns, like Chaplin's Verdoux, triumphs over his adversaries because he endures hardships (execution in Gay's case) as if they are pratfalls, from which the clown rises, quaking but not conquered, to the dismay of his adversaries.

One of Gay's Chaplinesque recoveries occurs when he wakes on the train to Tibet, discovers the Widow Begbick lying next to him and hears that they've slept together. A sheepish, Chaplin-like grin might be seen on his face as Gay, with no recollection of the previous night, says, 'Isn't it funny? Almost indecent, isn't it? But a man's a man, you know. He isn't entirely his own master.' Here sexual prowess comically, erroneously becomes part of the new, fictive identity constructed for Galy Gay by his masters in the army.

Gay's inadvertent success in love and war points toward a form of subversive comedy which Brecht elaborated in later plays. *Mr Puntila and his Man Matti*, *Schweyk in the Second World War* and the dialogue between two refugees in *Conversations in Exile* feature characters who survive adversity by enduring it, and outliving abusive authority if they cannot control it. To do this they often speak what the German critic Hans Mayer has called 'slave language', a coded vocabulary of resistance to authority which sounds like obedience.[7] (Brecht also learned this language from the Czech novel, *The Adventures of the Good Soldier Schweik*, which he adapted for Piscator's stage in Berlin.) Complying with outrageous orders, carrying them out fully like Galy Gay 'who can't say no', agreeing a passbook equals a person, these characters undermine authority by letting it contradict and trip itself with impossible, ill-conceived plans. Indications of this comic strategy occur in *Man is Man* when Galy Gay accedes to the requests of the machine-gun unit, then begins to rule it; he follows the questionable logic that men are as interchangeable and expendable as machine parts, to the extent that he becomes a fearless, uncontrollable fighting machine himself.

In fact, Gay becomes the bloodthirsty, five-shot hero Bloody Five ceases to be mid-way through the play. Bloody Five won his infamous name after his five pistol shots executed 'five Hindus, standing with their hands behind their backs'. His savagery against helpless victims leads the soldier Jesse to say of Sergeant Fairchild (alias Bloody Five): 'From a human point of view, one might regard your conduct as indecent.' Later, when Galy Gay defeats the Fortress of Sir El-Djowar with five cannon shots, his conduct is also 'indecent' as he leaves the shelter of several thousand refugees in flames. 'But what's that to me?' asks Gay, in a repartee as cruel as his five cannon shots.

GALY GAY THE MECHANICAL BALLET DANCER

By the end of the play, Gay as Jip displays a machine-like, inelastic behaviour which the philosopher Henri Bergson defined as a source of laughter. Initially the porter is too human, too pliant and changeable to be the 'human fighting machine'. But he becomes a monstrous version of the person once described by Soviet film-maker Dziga Vertov as 'the new man, free of unwieldiness and clumsiness [who] will have the light, precise movements of machines'.[8] Like the cannon with which he destroys a Tibetan town, Galy Gay as Jeriah Jip performs technologically precise acts of war. If there is any humour here, it occurs when Gay, like Chaplin in *Modern Times*, performs a mechanical ballet with a machine – a cannon. Like Chaplin, he is new to the machinery of modern times. 'Show me how this thing works, Widow Begbick', says Gay of the deadly instrument. A brief, comic lesson in artillery techniques ends in a less comic storm of cannon-fire against peasants, artisans and shopkeepers.

When Brecht wrote *Man is Man*, he expressed great enthusiasm for technological innovations and the changes of which humanity, aided by science, was capable. He praised Galy Gay as an example of malleable human identity made possible after the revolution in Russia and other parts of Europe. The subjugation of an individual identity to that of a collective was endorsed by the affirmations of comedy, and by the decision of the co-authors of *Man is Man* (Emil Burri, Slatan Dudow, Caspar Neher, Bernhard Reich, Elisabeth Hauptmann) to call themselves 'The Brecht Collective'. In 1927 Brecht wrote, 'Galy Gay is by no means a weakling ... he becomes the strongest of all once he has ceased to be a private person ... [he] comes to no harm, he wins' (*BT*, p. 19). But after the Nazis proved themselves to be more adept than Brecht's Marxist-influenced friends at marshalling a mass movement, the author wrote in 1954 that *Man is Man* was a play about the 'bad collective (the "gang") and its powers of attraction', and Gay's 'growth into crime'.[9] In retrospect, the play contains both these perspectives within it: the comic, optimistic fable of Gay's triumph and the story of an individual's criminalisation and psychological destruction.

SMITH, THE MAN WHO LOST HIS HEAD

The destruction of an individual was portrayed quite graphically by Brecht later in a 'Clown Act', the third part of the 1929 *Baden-Baden Cantata*. This variation on Galy Gay's transformation shows a man named Smith sawn apart by two violent 'friends' who say they will alleviate his pain. When his ear, legs, arm and head hurt, they offer to cut off the appendages. Smith consents to their treatment, much as Gay agrees to change his name and attend his own funeral in *Man is Man*. Ronald Hayman comments on the 'Clown Act': 'the business of sawing off limbs one by one becomes a vaudeville variant on the theme of dismantling the individual personality'.[10] The play itself concludes that the 'moral' is: 'Man does not help man.'

The inspiration for this clowning may have come from an unnamed 'eccentric clown' Brecht saw in September 1920; his diary notes that the clown, who 'banged himself on the head, developed a large bump, sawed it off and ate it', displayed more 'wit and style' than 'the entire contemporary

3.   The sawing apart of the grotesque giant in the *Baden-Baden Cantata* is just beginning.

theatre'.[11] The 1920 head-sawing trick resurfaced in Brecht's 1929 'Clown Act', and caused spectators at the Baden-Baden Festival to riot, according to actor Theo Lingen, who first played the role of Smith.[12] Evidently the refined audience felt its sensibilities were under assault, as well as Smith's.

Before he completed *Man is Man*, Brecht collaborated with Karl Valentin on yet another violent scenario. In a film which Brecht helped write, the cabaret comedian portrayed a barber whose razor-shave severed a customer's head. The taking apart and reassembly of the body in *Mysteries of the Barber Shop* (1923) anticipates the shooting and resurrection of Galy Gay, and Bloody Five's self-castration to restore his name and lost reputation as a man sexually dependent on no one.

The violence in these scenes reflects more than Brecht's love of clown acts. He witnessed terrible acts of brutality when he was a medical orderly in the First World War, and later when German demonstrators clashed with police and Nazis began their stormtroop tactics, including disruption of his plays, in the Weimar Republic. These events, not merely cabaret acts or film slapstick, introduced the playwright to violent conflicts to which he gave new, grotesque form in his plays. Valentin and Chaplin showed Brecht how comedy could contain this violence, and criticise it, through scenes in which its victims were naive, its perpetrators, grotesque and inhuman tyrants.

Man is Man conveys some of Brecht's fiercest opposition to war and militarism, through its mordant depiction of an army that will fight any enemy at a moment's notice, and recruit almost anyone willing to stand for roll-call. The transformation of a harmless porter into a dangerous soldier in *Man is Man* recalls Brecht's youthful song, 'The Legend of the Dead Soldier': in 1922 at Trude Hesterberg's Wild Stage, Brecht shocked Junkers in Berlin with this song about a corpse which is dug up, inspected by an army doctor, judged fit for battle and sent back to the Front. Here, as in *Man is Man*, a soldier was manufactured almost like a cannon; his assembly required a medical exam, a business deal, or a mock trial instead of a metal works – and the product is cannon fodder, not a cannon. Such procedures continue in our own day, as new identities are manufactured for leaders of state, their armies and their enemies, by highly paid advisers who produce media images and slogans instead of goods or social programmes.

POST-BRECHTIAN CLOWNS

Brecht's politicisation of comedy, his Marxist-influenced explorations of comic naivety and resistance to authority through clowning have served as models for other, more recent theatre artists. The Italian political satirist Dario Fo began theatre work in the late 1940s by reading 'Gramsci, Brecht and Mayakovsky, who were to become his chief sources of inspiration', according to critic Tony Mitchell.[13] In one of Fo's best plays, *Accidental Death of An Anarchist*, naive questions from the lead character, a fool portrayed by Fo himself, undermine the state's authority by following police accounts of a death to their logical but absurd conclusions. The play, based on actual testimony concerning the 'accidental [in fact, police-produced] death' of an anarchist under arrest, went beyond Brecht's fables to offer extremely timely, topical commentary on injustices Fo and his collective uncovered in their country's legal system. As much as anything else, it is Fo's development of Brecht's *faux-naif* clowning that has made him Europe's leading, contemporary political playwright.

An American satiric theatre group, the San Francisco Mime Troupe, has adapted comedies by Brecht and Fo, and continues producing its own, original plays as well. The denouement of one Mime Troupe play, *The Mozamgola Caper*, features a speech comic only in its defiance of capitalist economic logic: an African leader who has escaped assassination attempts by buffoonish opponents declares that his nation and thirty-three other countries will not pay their international debts 'to those who were the architects of our underdevelopment'.[14] His declaration of economic independence is a non-violent slap at the play's biggest fool, a CIA agent named DeBarge who, before his defeat, sings a rap song warning the Third World: 'Run your country in your own way / But first you better clear it with the USA.'

Perhaps the final word on Brecht's political comedy belongs to the Russian director Yuri Liubimov, whose innovative productions at the Taganka Theatre in Moscow popularised Brecht and the Soviet satire of Bulgakov. Liubimov staged Brecht's *Good Person of Szechwan* in 1963, before epic theatre had a following in post-Stalinist Russia; and he adapted Bulgakov's novel *The Master and Margarita* for the stage after a struggle with the censors. In a 1990 interview, Liubimov said, 'I consider Brecht to be the founder of political theatre.' This, from a director whose country gave birth to Meyerhold and Mayakovsky, is rather startling in itself. Liubimov added that Brecht 'is not simply a playwright who introduced only political wit', an important reservation, since clowning was hardly Brecht's only contribution to modern political theatre.[15] Still, Liubimov's own staging of Brecht and Soviet satire continues a tradition of political clowning Brecht advanced through *Man is Man*.

NOTES

1 Walter Benjamin, *Understanding Brecht*, p. 84.
2 Karl Marx, *Capital*, vol. I, trans. Ben Fowkes (New York, 1977), p. 229.

3 Brecht, quoted by Klaus Völker in *Brecht Chronicle*, p. 34.

4 'Valentin and Brecht', *The Drama Review*, 18 (March 1974), p. 91.

5 Benjamin, *Understanding Brecht*, p. 115.

6 Tretyakov, quoted by John Willett in *The Theatre of Bertolt Brecht*, p. 148.

7 Mayer, 'Bertolt Brecht and the tradition', in *Steppenwolf and Everyman*, trans. Jack Zipes (New York, 1971), pp. 118–27.

8 Vertov, *Kino-Eye*, trans. Kevin O' Brien (University of California Press, Berkeley, 1984), p. 8.

9 Brecht, 'On looking through my first plays', in *Collected Plays*, vol. II (New York), p. 245; also in *Collected Plays*, vol. II(i) (London), p. 108.

10 Ronald Hayman, *Brecht: A Biography*, p. 143.

11 Brecht, *Diaries 1920–1922*, p. 32.

12 Lingen, quoted by Hayman in *Brecht: A Biography*, p. 143.

13 Tony Mitchell, *Dario Fo: People's Court Jester* (Methuen: London, 1984), p. 37.

14 San Francisco Mime Troupe, '*Mozamgola Caper*', in *Theater Magazine* (New Haven, Winter 1988), p. 71.

15 'Iurii Liubimov in dialogue', in *The Brecht Yearbook* 16, (1991), p. 122.

6

ROSWITHA MUELLER

Learning for a new society: the *Lehrstück*

The centrality of the *Lehrstück* (learning play) to Brechtian theory was only slowly understood by a wider circle of international, critical audiences. Whether it was the lack of a comprehensive theory dealing with these works, or the Cold War hangover that rendered their texts particularly unpalatable, the result was a more-or-less total misunderstanding of this group of plays written between 1926 and 1933. A prominent and influential example of misreading was Martin Esslin's interpretation of the learning plays in his book *Brecht: The Man and His Work*. It is significant that Esslin translated the term *Lehrstück* as 'didactic plays', because in his view Brecht was writing communist thesis if not propaganda plays. Not until 1972, when Reiner Steinweg published his first volume dedicated to the construction of a coherent theory of the *Lehrstück*,[1] which Brecht had provided in fragments and sketches only, was the relation of the learning plays to the rest of Brecht's work fully appreciated.

Conceived and written contemporaneously with works like *Mahagonny* and *Radiotheorie*, the learning plays belong to the nexus of Brecht's most innovative writing. In his 'Notes to Mahagonny', he drew a sharp line between renovative art, which is designed merely to stimulate audiences' appetites for cultural consumption in an effort to save the existing institutions, and genuine innovations which aim at a transformation of the entire cultural apparatus 'from places of entertainment into organs of publication'.[2] Very early in his career as a playwright, Brecht coined the term 'culinary' to refer to both a particular form of art and an attitude of reception. In 'culinary' art the understanding of how a play is put together, how it is produced and performed, yields to the mere savouring of the finished product. In his anti-opera *The Rise and Fall of the City of Mahagonny*,

This essay is based on arguments introduced in chapter 2 of Roswitha Mueller, *Bertolt Brecht and the Theory of Media* (University of Nebraska Press, 1989). It appears in its present form with the kind agreement of the University of Nebraska Press.
The abbreviation *GW* refers to *Gesammelte Werke*.

which was first performed in Leipzig in 1930, Brecht characterised opera as the epitome of 'culinary' art-forms in bourgeois culture. While passive consumption is, as Walter Benjamin had pointed out, the attitude of the exploiter, the situation in the case of the mass media, which, by the 1930s, had taken over the function of opera, is more complex and more pervasive. Exploitation rebounds upon the audience itself. Brecht coined the term 'inploitation' (*Einbeutung*)[3] for the spectators' position, ambivalently split into exploiter and exploited. He saw the audience as the cause and as the victim of a system that divides both terms – on the one hand, it marks work and productivity as devoid of pleasure, and on the other it keeps pleasure free of productivity for the sake of work.

This focus on audience reception, the insistence that the audience develop an altogether different attitude, is at the core of Brechtian theory. It also represents the connecting link that allows his theory to be read through disciplines other than the theatre: 'Changes in media production are not only aimed at a new type of supply for the apparatuses, but at the new attitude of the spectators. What is common to all of Brecht's efforts is that they consider the audience's active involvement central.'[4] An audience capable of interacting with the work of art and the producer in any field of cultural endeavour stands at the top of Brechtian alternatives for artists in his time. His most thoroughgoing and comprehensive analysis of the economic conditions of artistic production was written on the occasion of the *Threepenny Opera* trial. The trial involved a contract between Brecht and the Nero Film Company which specified his right to collaborate on the script of the planned film version of his *Threepenny Opera*, which had been a box-office success in the theatre. This right was rescinded, however, as soon as the film company found his new rendition to be substantially different from the original. The legal decision in favour of the film company came as no surprise to Brecht. He had not taken his case to court solely in the hope of winning, but for the purpose of a sociological experiment. The experiment was planned to be a theoretical exposition of the relation between bourgeois ideology and bourgeois practice, tested on the concrete example of Brecht's involvement with the film industry, the press and the judicial system.

Brecht tried to demonstrate that the pressure to create saleable goods forces the film company to contradict 'the great bourgeois ideology', which holds inviolate authors' rights to their intellectual products. Reality contradicts this: 'The author is being engulfed in the technological process which is seen as commodity production. The protection of the authors' rights is denied because the producer "is burdened with an exorbitant financial risk". Intellectual interests may be protected as long as this protection does not cost too much.'⁵ The only intellectual struggle in the arts left in our epoch, Brecht remarked, points to an interesting overestimation of all means of production. 'The businessman, in this case as everywhere, prevails over the worker, the owner of the means of production is *eo ipso* considered productive' (GW, xv, p. 136).

For Brecht, this is also the condition under which the work of art or the cultural product is turned into a commodity and the cultural worker is proletarianised. About the artists and intellectuals who believe in their independence, he wrote: 'Thinking that they are in possession of an apparatus, which in reality owns them, they defend an apparatus over which they no longer have any control.' He went on to describe the exact workings of this loss of control: 'The producers are completely dependent on the apparatus, economically and socially; it monopolises their effect, and progressively the products of writers, composers and critics take on the character of raw materials: the finished product is turned out by the apparatus' (GW, xvii, pp. 1005–6). Brecht used the term 'apparatus' as a broad category to include every aspect of the means of cultural production, from the actual technological equipment, to promotion agencies, to the institutions such as the opera, the theatre, the radio etc., as well as the class that is in possession of the means of production. Thus the terminology itself points up the connection between culture and politics. In Brecht's view, the cultural apparatus functions, among other things, to stabilise the existing social relations both politically and economically. He saw this in terms of a selection process: 'By means of the (cultural) apparatus, society absorbs what it needs in order to reproduce itself' (GW, xvii, p. 1006).

The results of Brecht's political and economic analysis of the *Threepenny Opera* trial are instrumental in forming his concept of 'refunctionalisation' (*Umfunktionierung*), which understands function as the pivot between artistic and social production. Function as Brecht understood it includes and describes both aesthetic technique and the conditions of artistic production. Yet there is an anticipatory (if not utopian) move involved in Brecht's concept of refunctionalisation on which both his radio theory and his *Lehrstück* theory are based. Benjamin explained Brecht's concept of refunctionalisation as the structural reorganisation of the relationship between the stage, the author and the audience – or in the case of radio, between the producer and the listener – in order to bring about a more democratic mode of communication. It is evident that these structural and functional changes entail political as well as formal differences. The whole notion of refunctionalisation must be seen in the context of Marxist material aesthetics (*Materialästhetik*) elaborated in the early 1930s by a small circle of artists and theoreticians (Brecht counted Eisler, Piscator, Heartfield, Grosz and

Benjamin among them). The shared goals of this group involved as a major concern the elimination of the gap between the production and the consumption of art. This notion of art for producers was inspired by the young Soviet avant-garde artists whose forward-looking ideas spread to Berlin through the work of cultural mediators like Tretyakov.[6]

The anticipatory aspect of Brecht's theory is most highly developed in the *Lehrstück*. While the theoretical and practical purpose of Brecht's epic theatre was to work with democratic ideals under the conditions of capitalist societies bringing bourgeois ideology to bear upon its own presuppositions, the historical basis for the *Lehrstück* is a society in transition to socialism. Within this context, the central concern is to find ways of learning that are adequate for the new state. Lenin's question about how and what one should learn is the impulse for the *Lehrstück*. Nevertheless, these differences in historical place and time do not imply discontinuity with epic techniques. Brecht emphasised that epic techniques are the basis for the *Lehrstück* but that many of the projected goals of the 'new drama' can be realised to their full extent only within the context of a *Lehrstück*. Brecht's own development as an artist must be considered with this precise historical specificity in mind. The degree of technical perfection of his plays, according to his own testimony, is not subject to the maturation process of the playwright, but depends on the specific social and historical moment of his creative efforts. Since technique, in Brecht's terms, is inseparable from social function, 'only that measure of epic theatre that is acceptable today'[7] can in fact be used. As a result, the playwright found himself in the curious position of judging his later, so-called great plays to be less advanced with respect to technique than plays he had written many years before. He wrote of the *Life of Galileo*, perhaps the most popular of his works in the English-speaking world: '*The Life of Galileo* is technically a great step backward ... First the *Fatzer and Brotladen* fragments should be studied. These two fragments are the highest standard technically.'[8] When social conditions were no longer appropriate for its practice, Brecht discontinued work on the *Lehrstück* and reverted to the *Schaustück*.

In the 1920s when Brecht was engaged in experiments with the *Lehrstück*, the proletariat represented a rapidly growing force in Germany. Communist workers' choirs, for example, which Brecht could draw on for his plays, had a membership of half a million people. This was the new audience Brecht had in mind when he wrote that the 'new production' was interested not in conquering the old theatre and its audience, but in making theatre available to a different audience altogether. The new production, 'which corresponds to the sociological situation, can be understood only with respect to its contents as well as its form by those who understand the situation' (*GW*, XV,

p. 129). Brecht never lost sight of the specific socio-historical conditions and their requirements. When the political situation in Germany was no longer propitious for radical socialist transformation, he temporarily suspended the *Lehrstück* project. Yet concessions to the times were made on the level of adjustments, not compromise. The epic *Schaustück* can hardly be termed illusionist. Towards the end of his life, and in the context of the German Democratic Republic, Brecht once again revived the concept of the *Lehrstück*, even if only in the form of topical ideas, such as the importance for bureaucrats of realising their own redundancy.

The most far-reaching impact of the *Lehrstück* resides, not in its themes, but in its structural innovation, which aims at a total abolition of the division between performance and audience. It is precisely this attention to the active audience that cuts across disciplines and remains a challenge for the theatre as well as for the media. One such interdisciplinary focus on the active participation of the audience was proposed by Brecht in his learning play *The Flight over the Ocean* (originally called *Der Flug der Lindberghs*), which was performed at the Baden-Baden Music Festival in 1929. The play is an exercise in the use of radio as an apparatus for communication rather than for distribution. As such it is a model for a theory of the media. It has model character both in its form as *Lehrstück*, which radically alters the performance/audience (and by implication the sender/receiver) structure of the play, and in its content, which discusses the attitudes requisite for a future audience.

The stage set of the 1929 performance of *The Flight over the Ocean* demonstrated the apparatus/listener split. On the left side of the stage was the radio orchestra, its singers and the technical apparatus; on the right side was the listener, who read and sang the part of the pilot. The rear wall of the stage served as background for the written explanation of the theory underlying the play. *The Flight over the Ocean* is a celebration not only of the technological feat of the first airplane crossing of the Atlantic, but also of the new technological media and their communicative potential. Beyond the glorification of this technological feat, which ends with a dedication to future exploits, 'das noch nicht erreichte' ('that which has not yet been achieved'), Brecht writes the central concern of the *Lehrstück* into the text itself – namely, the education of individuals to enable them to become members of a collective. Upon arrival, the pilot announces:

> My name is so and so. Please carry me
> to a dark shelter, so that
> no one may see my
> natural weakness.
> But report to my comrades of

the Ryan Company in San Diego
that their work was good.
Our motor has persisted.
Their work was without flaw.

The pilot, representing the individual yields to the community of workers who have produced the technological apparatus: 'The apparatus represents the community, the state and the wealth of the whole, to which the individual does not stand in opposition but becomes part of through the speaking exercises.'[9]

> The community asks you: Repeat
> The first flight across the ocean
> By jointly
> Singing the notes
> And by reading the text.

A year after the Baden-Baden performance, Brecht suggested that the following experiment be conducted to point out how important and decisive the staging is for the text of *The Flight over the Ocean*. In this experiment, the part of the pilot was to be acted by a popular hero who, by causing the audience to identify with him, would have separated them from the masses. The play was to be performed before an audience in a traditional concert situation, split between performance and audience. Brecht concluded from this example that in the event of a *Lehrstück* performance in this traditional setting, which is a possible but nevertheless wrong kind of performance, the part of the pilot must be sung by a choir in order not to offset the purpose of the whole play.

The second play of this kind, *The Baden-Baden Cantata of Acquiescence*, was an immediate critical success at the Baden-Baden Music Festival of 1929, where it was performed together with *The Flight over the Ocean*. Brecht was amazed and at the same time alarmed by this success. He feared that he had provided the tools for the 'individual dogmatism and opinionatedness of the literati', since the formal aspects of the *Lehrstück* were accepted immediately. Without teaching (*Lehre*), Brecht insisted, this form is 'not especially exciting' (GW, XVII, p. 1026). He also disagreed with Paul Hindemith, who had composed the music for this *Lehrstück*. In his instructions for the piano excerpt for the *Lehrstück*, Hindemith had written that, since the purpose of the learning plays was simply to let everyone present participate and not primarily to create specific acts, the form of the piano music should be adjusted to whatever purpose was at hand. Brecht explained the misunderstanding as a consequence of the purely experimental purpose of the Baden-Baden performance, and he added that this performance was meant to be a one-time 'self-understanding'.[10] Invoking the usual scenario of experimental drama, Brecht wrote, 'The value of learning in this kind of musical exercise, when coupled with a contemplative text stimulating to the imagination of the student, would be negligible.' And he continued: 'Such an artificial and shallow harmony could never, even for a minute, be a counterbalance to the formation of collectives on the broadest and most vital basis which tear the people of our times apart with quite different forces' (*GW*, XVII, p. 1028).

The *Baden-Baden Cantata* of 1929 is a grotesque clown scene in which a person's limbs are amputated under the guise of helpfulness. The play explores cruelty, violence and death and broaches the subject of complicity between the helper and the forces of power and violence. The agreement or acknowledgement (*Einverständnis*) of these negative forces cannot be equated with senseless submission, but is part of the playwright's insistence on facing the negative as part of life. What has to be learned (the *Lehre*) is thus truly an aspect of the formal dialectics of the *Lehrstück*. Any attempt to emphasise only one or the other does not do the entire project justice.

Nevertheless, there are recorded remarks by Brecht apparently minimising the importance of *Lehre*. The most notable of such remarks was recorded by Pierre Abraham following an interview with Brecht in 1956. In this interview, Brecht explained that the *Lehrstück* should not be scrutinised for 'proposition or counterproposition, arguments for or against certain opinions, pleadings or indictments that represent a personal point of view, but only physical exercises meant for the kind of athletes of the mind that good dialecticians should be. Well- or ill-founded judgements are a wholly different affair that bring into play elements that I have not introduced into these debates.'[11]

While Esslin dismissed this remark by Brecht as simply tongue-in-cheek, it is the cornerstone of Reiner Steinweg's comprehensive compilation of statements by Brecht relating to a theory of the *Lehrstück*. Steinweg's analysis of the extant texts leads him to the conclusion that the *Lehre* is to be understood not as 'recipes for political action', but as the teaching of dialectics as a method of thinking. Steinweg goes on to characterise the *Lehrstück* as an attempt to furnish a model for the 'dialectical simultaneity, the mutual dependence, and the reciprocal positing and counterpositing of theory and practice of theoretical thought and practical behaviour' (Steinweg, *Das Lehrstück*, p. 118).

While this is undeniably correct, it does not distinguish the *Lehrstück* sufficiently from the epic *Schaustück*. Epic theory aims at the unity of theory and practice in an attempt to change the spectators' attitude from a passive to a productive one. The critical ability of the audience is sharpened to recognise the contradictions in bourgeois society and to hold their own experience up to comparison with the way these contradictions are presented. Thus norms of behaviour and action and the resulting social relations are no longer taken for granted but are understood in their historicity. The *Lehrstück*, however, goes beyond the epic *Schaustück* in significant ways. Thematically as well as structurally, the *Lehrstück* is based on premises that are radically different from those of epic plays. Apart from *The Exception and the Rule*, which was originally planned as a *Schaustück*, none of the learning plays deals explicitly with the contradiction in bourgeois society. There is no Puntila, no Shen Te/Shui Ta to be found in a *Lehrstück*, just as there is no fixed text or actor/audience separation. And, most importantly, the central contradiction – that between producers and means of production – is completely erased. 'The great pedagogy changes the role of acting completely; it annuls the system actor/audience; it recognizes only actors who are at the same time students' (*ibid.*, pp. 23–4). The audience is either completely dissolved as onlookers or is given an active role. Other learning plays demand preparation and exercise from the public before the performance. When there is a homogeneous group of people – for example, a school class or a workers' choir instead of an amorphous group that happens to congregate for a particular performance – it is advisable to drop the term audience altogether. In this instance, the audience is the producer. The performance/audience gap is entirely dissolved – one is identical with the other. Thus, structurally as well as thematically, the *Lehrstück* has left bourgeois society behind. The *Lehre* itself, learned in practical exercises, is concerned with the acquisition of a number of attitudes – not specific political decisions – that are necessary for a strategy in the political struggle towards a socialist society. Learning how to think dialectically is central and applies to the content (the specific *Lehre*) just as much as it does to the formal arrangement.

One of the influences on Brecht during the time in which he formulated the *Lehrstück* experiment was the Latvian actress Asja Lacis, who had organised and directed children's theatre in Russia immediately after the Revolution. Brecht met Asja Lacis in 1923 in Munich, where she subsequently worked with him as assistant director of his play *The Life of Edward II of England*. She gave Brecht exact information about the new Russian theatre and about children's theatre in particular. Walter Benjamin, whom Lacis introduced to Brecht in 1929, had written a theory of children's theatre based on her practical experiments in Soviet Russia. The similarity of this document to Brecht's conception of the *Lehrstück* is unmistakable. It also illuminates the dramatic practice of the learning plays.

In his 'Program for a proletarian children's theatre', Walter Benjamin designated the stage as the place where all life can appear in its unlimited fullness and at the same time be framed and defined. Both aspects are necessary for a proletarian children's theatre: 'The education of a child requires that his total life be affected. Proletarian education requires that the child be educated in a circumscribed area.'[12] The enormous importance of theatre in the education of children is based on the insight that the stage provides a space that fuses reality and play or, as Brecht put it, a place where learning and entertainment are not separated. Further, the notion of *Lehrstück* is contained in Benjamin's description of proletarian children's theatre, particularly with respect to the stress on the process of learning, while considering the performance itself an incidental event: 'Here performances are incidental; one could say that they come about as an oversight, almost as a practical joke of the children who one day interrupt their studies in this way, studies which in principle are never complete.'[13]

The performance, Benjamin argued, 'stands opposed to the educational build-up of activity in the sections, as release does to tension'.[14] He therefore divided the programme into two parts, 'the pattern of tension' and 'the pattern of release'. The educational training that falls under the pattern of tension is structurally a fairly self-directed process in which the children's experience becomes the sole arbiter of their learning selection. There is no direct moral influence on the part of the director, only the mediated influence through the material, the lesson, the performance. The children themselves take collective responsibility for changes and corrections in the lessons. Asja Lacis emphasised this point in her memoirs: 'We demonstrated that it was correct for adult leaders to keep themselves entirely in the background. The children believed that they had done everything themselves – and they did it in play. Ideology was not forced upon them, nor was it drilled into them. They appropriated all that corresponded to their experience.'[15]

Finally, the 'Program' does mention the director's place in this learning situation. Observation is preferable to admonition; in fact, it is the cornerstone of education: 'To the observer, however (and this is where education first begins), every action and gesture of the child becomes a signal. These are not so much, as psychologists like to think, signals of the unconscious, of latent powers, repressions, or censors; instead, they proceed out of a world in which the child lives and gives commands.'[16]

Thus, the child's every gesture is considered a creative impulse, and the final performance is a synthesis of the gestures. Improvisation is a fundamental condition for performance, for signalling gestures can arise only if there is complete lack of restraint. This latter point is peculiar to the children's theatre; it is only mildly echoed in Brecht's *Lehrstück* theory in his encouragement of 'personal invention'. By contrast, the main emphasis in the *Lehrstück* rests on straining to reach the highest possible awareness of the text and the corresponding critical ability to change it. Another difference between children's theatre and the *Lehrstück* is their respective positions on the need for discipline: 'The discipline which the bourgeoisie demands from its children is its stigma. The proletariat disciplines only the maturing proletarians; its ideological class education begins with puberty. Proletarian education proves its superiority by guaranteeing to children the fulfilment of their childhood.'[17]

Perhaps it would not be too speculative to propose that the admitted necessity for theoretical training and discipline after childhood is taken up by the *Lehrstück*. In connection with *The Flight over the Ocean* and its proper performance, Brecht wrote: 'This exercise serves discipline, which is the basis for freedom ... such exercises will be useful to the individual only insofar as they are useful to the state, and they are useful only to a state that intends to serve everybody in equal measure. *The Flight over the Ocean* therefore has neither aesthetic nor revolutionary value independent of its application' (*GW*, XVIII, p. 126).

The *Lehrstück* can thus be seen as the correlative for adults of a pedagogy in the theatre, which Benjamin had spelled out in collaboration with Lacis in the 'Program'. The notable difference between the children's theatre and the *Lehrstück*, the notion of discipline, at the same time raises questions about the *Lehrstück* as a possible instrument of indoctrination. It is possible, for example, to see structural similarities between *Lehrstück* performances, in which the text is read by an announcer onstage and repeated by the audience-performers, and Lenin's notion of a vanguard Party leading the masses. Similar observations could be made about the structural division of the *Lehrstück* into document and commentary (which roughly corresponds to a division into dramatic and reflective passages in the play, possibly also related to the 'pattern of tension' and 'pattern of release' described by Benjamin). According to Steinweg, the function of the commentary may be identical with that of the 'ideological secretary' Brecht mentions in the draft of a play closely resembling a *Lehrstück*. The commentary can be read by a narrator or by characters in the document.

In the *Baden-Baden Cantata*, for example, the 'reading of the commentary text' is performed by one of the members of the choir, simply called 'the speaker'. Steinweg establishes the relation between this teacher-narrator figure of the commentary and the Keuner figure in Brecht's Keuner stories. The commentary introduces the elements of reflection into the document and at the same time is a model for a new teacher–student relationship. In a note to his unfinished play, *The Fall of the Egoist Johann Fatzer*, Brecht

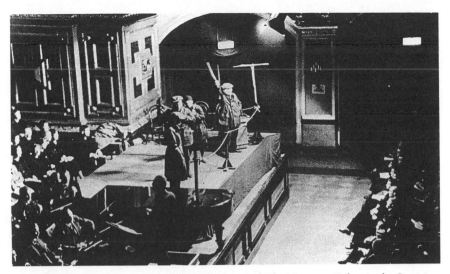

4.   Teo Otto's design for the 1930 performance of *The Measures Taken* at the Grosses Schauspielhaus, Berlin, reinforces Tretyakov's description of the *Lehrstück* as 'a political seminar of a special kind'.

responds to the question about the content of the commentary as follows: 'Opinions (theories) which are necessary for the collectivist state and the road to it: the revolution.' In the same context, Brecht also wrote: 'The pupils should memorise those parts of the commentary the teachers consider difficult before they understand them' (Steinweg, *Das Lehrstück*, pp. 20–1). The question is whether this leader/pupil distinction within the *Lehrstück* implies authoritarian rule and the simple transmission of a number of revolutionary slogans.

Steinweg proposes a different way of formulating the question. He understands the 'opinions' and 'theories' to be a dialectical disposition that is appropriate in evaluating specific theories, that is, the ability to test specific teachings in material reality. This, however, seems to be only part of the picture. Steinweg bases his conclusion on a reference Brecht made to the songs of the control chorus in *The Measures Taken* as 'theories'. Because Steinweg disregards the actual teaching content in the passages referred to, he once again proposes a purely abstract meaning of the concept of 'theory'. However, Brecht's notion of theory is closely related to Lenin's usage of this term and has to do with general statements about concrete political action and strategy. This view is corroborated by Hanns Eisler's remark (recorded by Tretyakov) describing the *Lehrstück* as 'a political seminar of a special kind concerning questions of strategy and tactics of the party'.[18] There is a great number of strategic points made in the text of the control chorus of

The Measures Taken. In the song 'Praise of the USSR', the chorus establishes the role of the Soviet Union as the teacher and leader of the 'fate of the world' (*GW*, II, p. 636); the song 'Praise of Illegal Work' represents an exhortation to engage in the class struggle specifically as an underground effort. To the workers of a paper-mill, the chorus suggests going out on strike; it praises the subordination of every virtue to the virtue of fighting for communism; it further extols the Party as the vanguard of the masses. In short, the chorus incorporates the theoretical tenets of official Marxism–Leninism, which at that historical point represented the main revolutionary force for informing and assisting the struggle of the Chinese peasants.

Nonetheless, it should be stressed that the *Lehrstück* cannot be contained as a kind of dogmatic Marxist–Leninist thesis play. It remains a genuinely utopian project. As far as the general goals of the *Lehrstück* are concerned, these theoretical tenets are not meant to dominate the play as eternal truths. While Brecht departed from and made use of current political theories, he approached them undogmatically. Aware of their faulty and time-bound character, he opened them up for discussion. Brecht expressly pointed out that the commentary may be changed at any time: 'It is full of mistakes with respect to our time and its virtues, and it is unusable for other times' (Steinweg, *Das Lehrstück*, p. 21). In that sense, the 'opinions' or 'theories' are a pre-text, a provisional statement summarising the state of the arts and theory as a starting-point for further development. The structure of the *Lehrstück* is rigorous, as Brecht called it, but only so as to make insertions and changes easier, facilitating the addition or deletion of passages. As mentioned above, one of the ways Brecht incorporated a traditional audience into the context of a *Lehrstück* was to hand out questionnaires after the performance so people could write their opinions. One of the questions asked after the performance of *The Measures Taken* reads: 'Which of the pedagogical tendencies in *The Measures Taken* do you object to for political reasons?' These opinions, according to Brecht, were used in rewriting the play.[19]

The process of such rewriting is best documented in Brecht's two versions of the Japanese Noh play *Taniko* (based on Elisabeth Hauptmann's translation from Arthur Waley's *The No-Plays of Japan*). His original play *He Who Said Yes*, which follows *Taniko* very closely, met with strong criticism on the part of the actors/audience, a school class in this case. The central 'attitude' to be learned in this play is quite similar to the final 'lesson' in *The Measures Taken*: the subordination of the individual to the good of the community or the revolutionary cause. Just as the young comrade was 'eliminated' in *The Measures Taken* to avoid jeopardising the revolution, the young boy who miscalculated his strength and enlisted in a difficult expedition to fetch medicine for his village was abandoned by his comrades and left to die. This decision was made in the interest of the efficient execution of the mission. The schoolchildren's reaction to this ending was negative enough for Brecht to rewrite the entire play with a new title, *He Who Said No*. A comparison of the two texts shows that the new version is radically different. Brecht abandoned altogether the theme of individual subordination to the general cause; instead, he turned it into a discussion of the need to change 'great old traditions'. First, Brecht eliminated the purely private emotional reason for the boy's departure, the sickness of his mother. Whereas in the first version the mother is in dire need of the medicine, in *He Who Said No* she is feeling better. Thus the intrusion of individual emotion into the affairs of the community, so fatal for the young comrade in *The Measures Taken*, is eliminated in *He Who Said No* by a simple change of circumstances. That Brecht felt the need to change the boy's motive is an interesting illumination of his insistence on *Lehre*. The teaching of the subordination of the individual to the common good is not simply revoked, but rather supplemented, expanded and complicated with another *Lehre*, the necessity to revise old customs.

The boy's final refusal to submit to the traditional self-sacrifice is set up in a number of ways. While in the first version there is no explicit reference to the need for the boy's total agreement with anything that might occur during the journey, in *He Who Said No* he is asked: 'But would you be in agreement with everything that might happen to you on the journey?' The answer is 'Yes'. This is the prelude to the theme of 'following the great tradition'. In the face of this rather brutal custom, the boy's refusal becomes an instance of refreshing dialectical practice: 'Your learning can wait, by all means. If there is anything to be learned over there, which I hope there is, it could only be that in our situation one must turn back. And as far as the great custom is concerned, I cannot see any sense in it. I need a great new custom that we should introduce immediately, the custom of thinking anew in every situation.'

Brecht, then, was unwilling to scrap the attitude of self-sacrifice in its original context; instead, he shifted the emphasis in the whole play just enough to prepare for the notion that individual sacrifice can also be meaningless, that unreflected acquiescence is the opposite of the desired dialectical attitude. It also represents the complementary side to the whole debate of the individual versus the state. For this reason Brecht preferred to have both plays performed together whenever possible, to illustrate perhaps the most important of his thoughts on the practice of the *Lehrstück* and its function in preparing the road to a new society: 'To be in agreement also means: *not* to be in agreement.'[20] The dialectics of this thought are as simple as its social ramifications are intricate.

While Brecht dismissed the bourgeois construction of 'the individual' because it is by definition pitted against the masses (a judgement based not only on Marxist theory but, as he tried to demonstrate in the *Threepenny Opera* trial, on the process of disintegrating the individual inherent in capitalist production), he nevertheless resurrects the importance of the human subject in another context: 'The split personality that the old philosophers anticipated is realising itself: thinking and being is splitting in the person in the form of an enormous sickness. The person goes to pieces, is out of breath, metamorphoses, becomes nameless, no longer hears any reproach, flees from its expansion into its smallest denominator, from its expendability into nothingness – but in its smallest denominator it recognises, relieved about the transition, its new and basic indispensability within the whole.'[21] And as Brecht had pointed out in the case of *The Flight over the Ocean*, the collective whole, the state, is acceptable only in as far as it serves everyone in equal measure. Given its feudal context, the instant critical success of *He Who Said Yes* angered Brecht and provided another reason to pair it with *He Who Said No*.

From this vantage point it is again possible to pose the question of authoritarianism. Does the exercise that recommends the repetition of a text necessarily mean submission to authoritarian rule? In another passage of the *Fatzer* fragment, Brecht describes the relation between technique and attitude, which in turn sheds light on the connection and distinction between imitation, copying and criticism. He argues that the 'style of writing determines the choice of thoughts, the attitudes of the writer, and the purpose of writing'. (Steinweg, *Das Lehrstück*, p. 16). By imitating and copying the commentary or by taking on its attitudes, the student will recognise 'the shortcomings of the commentary in its greatness and smallness, in its arrangement and its taste' (*ibid.*, p. 16).

Brecht has been accused of behaviourism because of his treatment of style, gesture and attitude as prior or equal to thought. Probably the clearest statement of Brecht's views can be found in the text to the *Threepenny Opera* trial. He observed: 'Behaviourism is a psychology that was created by the need for commodity production to arrive at methods that could influence the buyer, that is, an active psychology, progressive and revolutionary (cathected). It has its limits in consonance with its capitalist function (the reflexes are biological, only in some Chaplin films are they already social).' And he continued, 'The great American comics present humans as objects; they could have an audience of reflexologists' (*Brecht on Theatre*, p. 50). This positive evaluation of the treatment of humans as objects stands in seeming contrast to Brecht's preoccupation with consciousness within the structure of performance and reception. The problem is complex. Brecht's emphasis on the social dimension in the formation of the subject, coupled with his insistence on gesture, attitude and action, brings him into closer affiliation with the Russian school of reflexology (whose leading figure, Vladimir Bechterev, was the teacher of Asja Lacis). 'The defeat of reflexology', Brecht noted with apparent regret, 'was caused by its mechanistic application', and thus paved the way for 'the victories of phenomenology'.[22]

In his book *General Principles of Human Reflexology*, Bechterev defined the aim of reflexology as the 'strictly objective study, in their entirety, of the correlations of the human being with the environment through the mediation of man's facial expressions, his gestures, the content and form of his speech, his behaviour, and, in general, everything by which he manifests himself in the environment'.[23] Bechterev bases his theory on the physical law of identity of matter and energy. He consequently assumes that consciousness and the nervous system coincide and that there is no fundamental difference between mental, psychic and physiological processes. Similarly, Brecht saw reciprocal influences between emotional, intellectual and physical states: 'Just as moods and thoughts can lead to attitudes and gestures, attitudes and gestures can also lead to moods and thoughts.'[24]

As biosocial entities, humans are capable of development through social interaction, Bechterev argued, and he insisted that imitation was the basis of social life. What sustains the development of imitation in the biological scale of animal life is that imitation is the result of selection: 'Imitation cannot be "blind" without any correctives on the part of the individual, who, through imitation, notes certain phenomena which are new to him.'[25] Imitation is thus understood as the most basic element of learning that includes the possibility of alternative choice. Similarly, Brecht's *Lehrstück* experiments are centrally concerned with the relation between imitation and learning as well as with the element of choice. The participants are called upon to copy the text and the style of acting until criticism has changed it. This point represents the juncture of Brecht's preoccupation with the subject in his dramatic theory and his emphasis on behaviour: 'The *Lehrstück* rests on the expectation that the actors may be socially influenced by executing certain attitudes and repeating certain speech patterns' (*GW*, XVII, p. 1024).

At the same time it is important to point out that this juncture between subjective consciousness and external behaviour, which Bechterev grounded in scientific laws, also corresponds to Brecht's understanding of dialectics and as such undergirds all of his work. Most of Brecht's reflections on dialectics follow the insights of his Marxist mentor Karl Korsch, who had proclaimed the coincidence of reality and consciousness in his heretical *Marxism and Philosophy* (1923). This book tried to restore historical materialism, from its perceived reifications by the Second International into a set of economic principles, to the status of a theory of social relations, not restricted to a partial aspect of society. Korsch branded as metaphysical all dualistic approaches to consciousness that would consider it as secondary or as a reflection of concrete material processes. Brecht's comprehension of the coincidence and reciprocal influence of subjective and objective levels explains much of the ambivalence and contradictoriness in his work. But it also provides the foundation upon which his notion of the unity of theory and practice rests, a notion which is crucial not only to his *Lehrstück* conception but to his entire epic theatre. This coincidence rescues the concept of production from its association with an exclusively economic determination and aligns it with intellectual production, that is, criticism, from which flow the dissolutions of a number of familiar opposites, such as pleasure and learning, work and creativity or thought and feeling.

The *Lehrstück* has followed these unities down to the more tenacious level of patterns of behaviour, attitudes and gestures. Realising that content can change but that it can also be corrupted by old forms, Brecht knew that nothing was really to be gained until new contents had taken shape in everyday attitudes. To this end, Brecht sought to reconstruct the formation of behaviour, gestures and attitudes in the learning process through imitation. By beginning at the point at which certain persistent patterns were formed, Brecht thought it was possible to unravel the patterns originally learned and replace them with new ones, this time consciously chosen. Historically, this utopian project is closely linked to the expectations for a new society which existed in Germany before the rise of fascism. The challenge of the *Lehrstück*, however, has not diminished, and remains as vital today as it was in Brecht's time.

NOTES

1 Reiner Steinweg, *Das Lehrstück. Brechts Theorie einer ästhetischen Erziehung*. This was followed by two more volumes on the *Lehrstück*, edited by Steinweg: *Brechts Modell der Lehrstücke, Zeugnisse, Diskussionen, Erfahrungen* (Suhrkamp: Frankfurt, 1976), and *Auf Anregung Bertolt Brechts: Lehrstücke mit Schulern, Arbeitern, Theaterleuten* (Suhrkamp: Frankfurt, 1978).

2 Brecht, *Gesammelte Werke*, vol. XVII, p. 1016. This and all subsequent translations from original German texts are my own unless otherwise stated.

3 Siegfried Unseld, ed., *Bertolt Brechts Dreigroschenbuch* (Suhrkamp: Frankfurt, 1960), p. 98.

4 Dieter Wohrle, *Bertolt Brechts medienästhetische Versuche* (Prometh Verlag: Cologne, 1988), p. 59.

5 Unseld, *Bertolt Brechts Dreigroschenbuch*, p. 112.

6 Werner Mittenzwei gives a comprehensive account of *Materialästhetik* in 'Die Spur der Brechtschen Lehrstücktheorie', in Steinweg, *Brechts Modell*, pp. 225–54.

7 Brecht, *Arbeitsjournal*, vols. I and II: II, p. 912.

8 *Ibid.*, vol. I, p. 41.

9 Rainer Nagele, 'Brechts Theater der Grausamkeit: Lehrstücke und Stückwerke', in *Brechts Dramen*, ed. Walter Hinderer (Reclam: Stuttgart, 1984), p. 308.

10 Steinweg suggests a parallel usage in Marx and Engels, *The German Ideology*.

11 Steinweg, *Das Lehrstück*, p. 61.

12 Walter Benjamin, 'Program for a proletarian children's theater', trans. Susan Buck-Morss, *Performance* 5 (1973), p. 29.

13 *Ibid.*

14 *Ibid.*, p. 31.

15 Asja Lacis, 'A memoir', trans. Jack Zipes, *Performance* 5 (1973), p. 29.

16 Benjamin, 'Program', p. 30.

17 Lacis, 'A memoir', p. 27.

18 Steinweg, *Brechts Modell*, p. 120.

19 Brecht, *Die Massnahme: Kritische Ausgabe mit einer Spielanleitung von Reiner Steinweg* (Suhrkamp: Frankfurt, 1972), p. 238.

20 Steinweg, *Brechts Modell*, p. 62.

21 *Ibid.*, pp. 96–7.

22 *Ibid.*, p. 125.

23 Vladimir Bechterev, *General Principles of Human Reflexology* (Jarrolds: London, 1933), p. 81.

24 Steinweg, *Brechts Modell*, p. 125.

25 *Ibid.*, p. 235.

7

CHRISTOPHER McCULLOUGH

Saint Joan of the Stockyards

In writing an essay on the play *Saint Joan of the Stockyards* to be included in a collection of essays under the title *The Cambridge Companion to Brecht*, I am acutely aware of the consequence of making an entry into a canon. The writing of the essay cannot be taken in isolation; it will take its place alongside others, some on individual plays, some on aspects of Brecht's stagecraft and dramaturgy. Each essay may be read individually, but they will equally be 'read' as part of the *Companion* and potentially as part of the construction of a canon of work. In one sense all the contributors to this volume are engaged in the making of an historical narrative. By selecting the essay titles, by deciding the order of those titles, we are party to the construction of a narrative that may be seen as the 'making' of one Brecht. Or even the deconstruction of another Brecht. That we are all working independently may of course produce a very interesting narrative; one which may well challenge the assumptions created by the idea of a *Cambridge Companion*. In the way that our experience of a television programme cannot be entirely divorced from the pattern of the overall programming of the evening, I want to approach *Saint Joan of the Stockyards* as much from the perspective of its *Cambridge Companion* narrative as from any notional 'historical' narrative. Perhaps inevitably the two narrative discourses are inextricably interwoven. Brecht argued, as has been pointed out by Elizabeth Wright in *Postmodern Brecht*,[1] that the author is not the creator of an original work, but someone who produces art from the materials of history. As contributors to this volume we are working from a number of simultaneous histories: the Germany of Brecht's lifetime, perceptions of Brecht's personal life and the historical narrative suggested by this book. In this sense I cannot separate *Saint Joan of the Stockyards* from the *Lehrstücke* of Roswitha Mueller and the 'Zelda syndrome' of John Fuegi. Perhaps the question to be tackled by this essay is not how does *Saint Joan* fit into this great narrative, but what potentiality does it possess to be the vehicle by which the reader's attention may be drawn to the narrative?

The possibility of such an intervention is aided by the fact that the play has, by and large, been neglected over the years by both critics and theatre practitioners. *Saint Joan of the Stockyards* has attracted comparatively little attention since it was written some time between 1929 and 1931. Its first production was as a radio play directed by Alfred Braun on Berlin Radio and broadcast on 11 April 1932. It was not until 1959 that it received its first stage performance, in Hamburg. The period of Brecht's work from which this play emerges is possibly the most interesting or the most frustrating, depending on how you intend to construct the writer and his work. The reasons for this seeming neglect of the play are complex, but we may assume that in part the critical evaluation of *Saint Joan,* and of the other early plays, is connected with the priority accorded to later plays such as *Mother Courage, Galileo* and *The Caucasian Chalk Circle.* In the view of many critics and theatre practitioners the answer is straightforward: the later plays are better written and offer greater scope for an engaging theatrical experience. This may of course be true, but equally it may depend ultimately on what narrative is constructed between object/event and reader/audience. One thing that is clear is the evidence that the later plays, because they seem to approximate more closely to bourgeois values concerning the matter of great humanistic art, are more easily appropriated (and naturalised) into what Brecht himself would have identified as 'dramatic' theatre.[2] The crude antagonisms of early responses to Brecht's work (certainly in England) tend to be supplanted by the more subtle ideological appropriations away from Brecht's Marxist aesthetic, into a remaking according to humanistic sensibility; something that amounts to a naturalising of Brecht into the scheme of a bourgeois hegemony.[3] By recognising the 'tragedy' in his later plays, that evidently Brecht did not, Esslin, Bentley and others aim to rescue 'art' from 'politics'.

Eric Bentley's argument in his introduction to his collection of essays, *The Brecht Commentaries,* elucidates this cultural process quite clearly.[4] Bentley's critique of Brecht is based on the perception that 'Brecht wished his work to be read as a revelation of the world, not of its author . . . The world is not always revealed in his works: sometimes it is veiled, sometimes distorted. But *he.* . . . is always revealed.' For Bentley the work is inseparable from the artist. The work of the artist is the product of a unique vision. To know the work is to know the artist and the experience for the reader/audience is offered as one that transcends historical and ideological contextualisation. 'I don't, in any case, require that a reader take an interest in me; only that he take an interest in Bertolt Brecht; or rather his work; or rather, as I was saying, his work and him: his work *as* him and him *as* his work.'

The salient question regarding *Saint Joan* must focus on its ideological context: the narrative that may be perceived between it as a playtext and other of Brecht's texts of the late 1920s and early 1930s, rather than that between it and the later plays produced in America and the post-war German Democratic Republic.

John Willett in *Brecht in Context*[5] locates the play not only in the period of the *Lehrstücke*, but also ideologically with Brecht's reading of Marxist theory and the further research that went into the *Lehrstücke*. Willett records the occasion when Brecht watched a banned parade from the window of Fritz Sternberg's flat on 1 May 1929. Brecht was attending Sternberg's lectures on Marxism, but it was the experience of seeing demonstrators gunned down by the police that gave him his practical impetus towards ideological commitment. Willett argues that this point in Brecht's work marked the end of his first experiments with a 'scientific' theatre in the form of the *Lehrstücke*; the point where he cannibalised Elisabeth Hauptmann's *Happy End* (songs by Brecht) to make *Saint Joan of the Stockyards*. The question that I wish to raise in this essay, emanating from the earlier comments relating to the narratives by which we appropriate a play's signification, relates to the potential ideological location of *Saint Joan*. Is it possible to argue that the play is best read as part of the *Lehrstück* experiment, a planned transition to socialist art? The radical potentiality of *Saint Joan* lies in its links with the idea of the *Lehrstück*, its problems in the idea that it is an early experiment in preparation for later plays. It is a question of deciding which are the most significant narratives by which culturally to locate the play. If judged by the values of the later plays, even taking into account how far those texts depart from the values ascribed to Aristotle or Diderot, then *Saint Joan* appears stilted and even prosaic in spite of the author's employment of, in addition to prose, blank verse, unrhymed verse, Salvation Army hymns and what Eric Bentley calls Brecht's menagerie of Chicago. But if there is the potential to see the play as part of the *Lehrstück* experiment, then a very different signification is possible. That the play represents itself more as a 'play to be performed in the theatre' than as an open-ended experiment in theatricalised political debate, isn't much of a help in determining its worth; indeed its structural patterning and its stagecraft conspire to reveal its weaknesses on both counts. It lacks the radical purposes and stagecraft of the *Lehrstücke*.

The Measures Taken is the *Lehrstück* that shares with *Saint Joan* many similar themes. Interwoven with *Saint Joan*'s central theme of the interdependence of capitalism and religion is the image of the young person with altruistic humanistic desires which, paradoxically, prove antagonistic and destructive towards the aim of the revolution, since altruism finally serves to restore the status quo. The remaining commonality between the two plays may be observed in the fact that both were products of collaboration rather than the efforts of a single author: *The Measures Taken* – B. Brecht, S. Dudow, H. Eisler; *Saint Joan* – B. Brecht, E. Hauptmann, H. Borchardt, E. Burri. However, the argument that may prove of value to a contemporary eye seeking evidence of radical theatre in this period may well have to support the *Lehrstück* against a 'play' which, though obviously linked to the experiment, strays in a rather ponderous manner, weighed down by the scholarship of its parodic intertextuality, towards more conventional concepts of dramaturgy and theatrical practice. By 'conventional' I mean, in this instance, a play that is contained within the concept of being performed on stage, by professional actors, with formalised scenery and having a specific point in time that is denoted as the end. Although Brecht's ideal audience for *Saint Joan* was radically different from the audience anticipated by naturalist or expressionist writers, its role was still passive in contrast to the potentiality of the audience (if there was actually such a social grouping) engaged with the *Lehrstücke*.

Brecht offers clues as to the potentiality of the *Lehrstück* in his essay, 'The German drama: pre-Hitler'.[6] There is not the space in this short essay to investigate with any degree of thoroughness the nature of the *Lehrstück*, nor of course is it the responsibility of this essay to do so. However, in the spirit of foregrounding possible narratives within *The Companion*, it may be worthwhile to refer briefly to some of the aims of these theatre experiments. The import of Brecht's essay is best summarised by selective quotation, as follows:

> the conflict of classes, war, the fight against disease, and so on... formed nothing but effective background for a sort of sentimental 'magazine story' that could have taken place at any other time ... The learning play is essentially dynamic; its task is to show the world as it changes (and how it may be changed)... philosophers discussed these learning-plays, and plain people saw them and enjoyed them, and also discussed them... I tried to work outside the theatre, which having for so long been forced to 'sell' an evening's entertainment, had retreated into too inflexible limits for such experiments... These experiments were theatrical performances meant not so much for the spectator as for those who were engaged in the performance. It was, so to speak, art for the producer, not art for the consumer.

In its content, perhaps more than in its dramatic and social structure, *Saint Joan* has a potentiality for radical political thought. It is directly materialist and anti-metaphysical, almost laying the foundation for *The Mother* which was written in the same period, but in which the central female figure is allowed the opportunity for a more overt espousal of revolutionary thought and action. While Joan Dark could well be seen as a precursor to the figure of Pelagea Vlassova, the focus in *Saint Joan of the Stockyards* is clearly on the dialectic between the interdependent claims of capitalism and religion and revolutionary action. Joan Dark's personal epiphany draws on the same irony as does the dilemma of the Young Comrade in *The Measures Taken*. Joan, like the Young Comrade, is susceptible to a liberal humanistic response to human misery. However, their respective conclusions as to why that misery exists and what to do about it are very different. The authors of the two plays are dealing, in both cases, with the dialectic between an altruistic humanistic response to the *misery* of human beings in the moment, and the broader more distant goal of the revolution – to eradicate the *cause* of human misery. The difference is that, whereas *The Measures Taken* is dealing with an intrinsically open-ended debate around the issues, *Saint Joan of the Stockyards* engulfs us in the narrative of Joan's epiphany.

Joan's narrative is by no means a simple affair of woman loses old belief; woman finds new belief. Closely associated with this narrative are the important elements (important to the sense of irony that I would argue is at the heart of all of Brecht's attempts at objectifying our perception of human experience) that make up the complex interrelationships between the rich and the poor, religion and capitalism and Joan and the other members of the Black Straw Hats Mission. Our first encounter with Joan Dark is as the Black Straw Hats leave their Mission House: the first of Joan's descents into the depths. Her first speech in Scene 2 is misleading and the audience may be forgiven for thinking that she is about to embark on a critique of the economic status quo of this mythical Chicago:

> In gloomy times of confusion
> Disorder by order
> Planned caprice
> Dehumanised humanity
> When there is no end to unrest in our cities...

It is made clear very quickly that the problem as perceived by Joan centres on the lack of God in people's lives; particularly in the lives of the poor. Many times during the play they are seen, by the Black Straw Hats and by Pierpont Mauler and his like, as being brutish and wicked. For Joan in this early speech, it is necessary:

> To prevent the brute strength of the short-sighted people
> From shattering its own tools and
> Trampling its own bread-basket to pieces –
> We wish to reintroduce
> God.

It is clear later on in this scene that Joan, though starting from this specific ideological position, wants to know the causes of poverty. The pattern for the rest of the play traces this quest for causality, interweaving it with the various positions, and eventual collusion, between the 'bosses' and the Black Straw Hats. Scene 4 delineates Joan's second descent into the depths (of poverty). As well as being a crucial moment, this scene expresses (or exposes) the central didactic argument of the play. Slift, a speculator, has, at Mauler's request, taken Joan into the district of the stockyards in order that she see for herself the wickedness of the poor. The experiences that Joan witnesses in this scene show her, not only the effects of poverty in the lives of people who have been brutalised by their poverty, but also the cause of the poverty. Our focus is not on a contemporary rendering of a tragic status quo wherein pain and suffering are our only reference points. We, through Joan, are allowed to see that the behaviour of human beings is not something inbred into a class, or even a race, of people, but that historical conditions cause events and dictate the actions of people. Slift asks Joan, after showing her the 'wickedness' of various working people, if she has not seen, 'that their wickedness is beyond measure?'. Her reply is in the form of a long speech that ends the scene and functions as an argument around which the tensions of the play are to gather. For Joan it is the first insight into the causes of poverty; an insight that will eventually culminate in her perceiving how the actions of her religious group help preserve the balance of power in favour of the rich. And this is before Snyder, the leader of the Black Straw Hats, sells out to Mauler and his cohorts in return for the rent to keep open the Mission. What Joan has been shown by Slift is not 'the wickedness of the poor', but 'the poverty of the poor'. Her speech ends with the couplet,

> O thoughtless rumour, that the poor are base:
> You shall be silenced by their stricken face!

The first step for Joan's emancipation from religion has begun. She now begins to see the causes of actions, but she still clings to the belief that hearts will melt at the sight of misery. But what is it that Joan is moving towards? I have used the term epiphany with a heavy sense of irony; for any other employment of the term would serve only to reinforce the image of Joan as a special individual; a tragic heroine with religious overtones. The effect would be to marginalise the workers' chorus even more than it already is and to place the economic turmoil of Chicago into a background against which Joan's personal tragedy is enacted. Eric Bentley in his comments on *Saint Joan* in *The Brecht Commentaries* offers a curious reading of the play.[7] His stance is determinedly anti-Marxist and, by implication rather than through a direct critique, he attacks the ideological movement of

Joan's progress in the play. Bentley's approach focusses on Brecht's intention to avoid having Joan besieged by epigrams, as he sees Shaw's *Major Barbara* so caught. But while he admits to Brecht's intention to see Joan Dark 'entangled in circumstances', he seeks to distance her from those circumstances by arguing that it is to opinions that she is won over; the 'opinions' (in Bentley's view) of atheism and quite possibly communism. For Bentley, *Saint Joan* 'belongs to Brecht's agitprop phase'. In one sense Bentley is justified in the view that Joan is won over to opinions. Indeed it is the very focus on the individual plight of Joan that almost robs the play of any effective dialectical alternative to the efforts of The Black Straw Hats to alleviate misery:

> JOAN: But those who are down below are kept below
> So that the ones above may stay up there
> And the lowness of those above is measureless
> And even if they improve that would be
> No help, because the system they have made
> Is unique...
> THE BLACK STRAW HATS, *to Joan*: Be a good girl! Hold your tongue!

In claiming that the ideological positions of atheism and communism are 'opinions' rather than ideas, Bentley is, by implication, claiming authority for his own 'ideas'. He makes no secret of his opposition to Brecht's ideological view of the world in the essay 'About this book'. The consequence of this opposition is a claim to the authoritative high ground of interpretation by emphasising the personal symbiosis created through a relationship that was part professional and part personal. Bentley cannot see 'any Brecht poem or play except as an extension of the man I knew'. It is, of course, difficult (but not impossible) to challenge this mode of personalising art and relationships. Certainly the critical debate over the intentional relationship of author to text is an aid. Perhaps the pertinent debate in the case of Brecht emerges from the questions now being raised about the authorship of the earlier plays. Does it matter who wrote the plays (except perhaps in the determining of royalties)? Eric Bentley and Martin Esslin both employ a subtle and beguiling line of argument on Brecht in their scheme to disengage the artist from his political ideology. It is worth giving serious attention to the point that their need to see Brecht as the lone authorial genius as a yardstick by which to assess the artistic merits of the plays paradoxically challenges Bentley's own opinion on 'opinions'. The possibility that the earlier plays, such as *Saint Joan of the Stockyards*, were the products of collaboration would seem entirely appropriate to the argument that the ideological alternatives to Joan's religious faith are substantially more than 'opinions'.

NOTES

1 Wright, *Postmodern Brecht*, p. 1.
2 For further discussion of this point, see Christopher McCullough, 'Brecht and brechtian: estrangement and appropriation', in *Political Theatre*, ed. Graham Holderness (Macmillan: London, 1992), pp. 120–33.
3 See, for example, T. C. Worsley's review of *The Caucasian Chalk Circle* in the *New Statesman*, 14 July 1956.
4 Bentley, 'About this book', in *The Brecht Commentaries*. The quotations that follow are from pp. 15–17.
5 Willett, 'Changing role in politics', in *Brecht in Context*.
6 First published in English in *Left Review* (London, 1936). Also in *Brecht on Theatre*, pp. 77–81.
7 See Bentley, *The Brecht Commentaries*, pp. 81–3.

8

JOHN FUEGI

The Zelda syndrome: Brecht and Elisabeth Hauptmann

In a famous Brecht poem, the question is asked: 'Every ten years a great man. Who paid the bill?' (*Poems*, pp. 252–3). Curiously, the question is one that has never seriously been put in the case of Brecht himself. In the essay that follows, I will set forth some preliminary findings on a question that has received remarkably little attention in more than half a century of Brecht studies: who wrote what and what was the cost of that writing to others? Though a few scholars have identified various individual works as written by someone other than Brecht, no scholar has stepped back to ask, if many of the trees were planted by someone else, what of the Brecht forest remains? The question is a vast and inordinately complex one. I will limit my detailed observations to the contributions made by Elisabeth Hauptmann (1897–1973), and will only generally note the strikingly similar cases of Margarete Steffin (1908–41) and Ruth Berlau (1906–74).

Reading the diaries of the late teenager and young adult Bertolt Brecht, one sees that he was uncomfortable working alone on anything except short poems, and regularly took things from published sources as well as taking things from friends in his closest circle, most particularly Caspar Neher, Ludwig Prestel and Georg Pfanzelt. As an 18-year-old he compares himself to two successful German playwrights, boasting: 'I can write, I can write plays, better than Hebbel and wilder than Wedekind.' But he also notes: 'I am lazy. I'm unable to become famous'.[1] A little later, a notebook of the then 20-year-old Brecht reflects the fact that his writing was reliant on others when he labels a group of then still unpublished poems: 'Songs for the Guitar by Bert Brecht and His Friends'. However, once the songs find their way into print a few years later, they become songs by Bertolt Brecht, with no acknowledgement of the work of others and no royalties to his friends. Such was the magnetism (sexual and otherwise) of Brecht that though Pfanzelt complained privately about his work being taken, Brecht was not challenged in public about what he had done.

It was not that the magnetic young Brecht could not write (the evidence of various early and late poems gives abundant proof of his poetic talent), but it was that he would often prefer taking the work of others rather than going to the trouble of writing things himself. A diary entry for 4 October 1921 says: 'I've been wallowing in the Rimbaud volume, borrowing a passage here and there.' He did indeed wallow and borrow, and the first recognition of this was a hostile review in the autumn of 1924 pointing out that the play *In the Jungle of the Cities* 'spoke entire passages from the work of the French poet'.[2] Furthermore, the 1923/4 work on *Edward II* incorporated about one line in six from Walter Heymel's copyrighted German translation of the English original.

What is clear with both the poetry and the plays is that taking over the work of others was a habit long before Brecht moved to Berlin in the autumn of 1924 and his meeting there with the richly gifted writer-translator, Elisabeth Hauptmann, with her near-native fluency in English and her excellent school French. She would begin, I believe, to provide a stream of texts later to be published under the expensive 'Brecht' label. She, with her almost British understatement, would sometimes admit what she had done. On one occasion in the 1950s, driven to desperation by statements from Brecht that she knew to be wrong 'from the ground up', she would note: 'Up until thirty-three I either wrote or wrote down most of the poems. There was hardly anyone else there who wrote. Hardly anyone to provide material, no one else from January 1925 on.'[3]

The evidence now available validates her claim. In 1925, she turned out a series of beautiful renderings of some of Kipling's most difficult dialect verse. This would not have been possible for Brecht to do as his knowledge of English was, as his close friend Hans Otto Münsterer pointed out, 'next to nothing'. James Lyon, an authority on Brecht's poetry, has noted of Hauptmann's renditions of Kipling: 'Brecht liked her translations.' 'In fact', as Lyon notes, '[Brecht] made relatively few changes in her texts of "The Ladies", "Cholera Camp" or "Mary, Pity Women", the only ones where her preliminary translations are available for comparisons.' But, although Hauptmann must be credited with fully 80 to 90 per cent of these texts, 'The Ladies' came out in the magazine *Die Dame* in 1927 as Brecht's. List Verlag did the same with 'Cholera Camp' and 'Mary, Pity Women'. When Professor Lyon asked Hauptmann about this, she said 'she intentionally omitted her name because Brecht's alone carried more weight'.[4]

The story of how Hauptmann, in the mid-1920s, very much in love with Brecht and hoping to marry him, began to contribute 80 to 90 per cent to works that the world was told were by Brecht might seem at first an aberration in literary history. But it may not really be as exceptional as it first appears. There is a striking parallel from the same period in American

5.   Brecht and Elisabeth Hauptmann in Brecht's studio, 1927. This is the Brecht of Schlichter's portrait.

literature. It is now known that one of F. Scott Fitzgerald's most typical short stories, a piece called 'The Millionaire's Girl', was actually written in 1929 by Zelda Fitzgerald. Even though the literary agent, Harold Ober, knew the story was by Zelda,[5] he recommended publishing it as an F. Scott piece in *The Saturday Evening Post*. The *Post*, he said, would pay $4,000 (a fortune in the wreck of the economy after the Wall Street collapse) for one F. Scott story. If the same piece appeared in *College Humor* (where Ober had been selling Zelda's work – as sometimes retouched by F. Scott – under the byline 'By F. Scott and Zelda Fitzgerald'), the going price was $800. F. Scott needed both the money and to be seen by his public as a productive writer. He was drinking heavily and having difficulty completing things. Zelda was persuaded to go along with the deception.

Within months of agreeing to the *Post* scam (the most egregious of what was a whole series of deceptions), Zelda Fitzgerald began to exhibit the signs of mental distress that would lead to her incarceration and eventual death in an institution. Zelda Fitzgerald's willingness, however reluctantly, to allow her own creative efforts to be published under the name of her more famous husband parallels, I believe, what Hauptmann repeatedly allowed to happen. Brecht, like F. Scott, was having trouble finishing things. And Hauptmann, like Zelda Fitzgerald, knew that the fees paid would be higher if her work was published under the more famous name.

In both these cases, as well as those of Steffin and Berlau (all of which I subsume under the general heading of 'The Zelda syndrome'), there is evidence that the literary establishment knew something was radically amiss, yet turned a blind eye to the deception. If someone was willing to create a 'Brecht' or an 'F. Scott Fitzgerald' and then allow these works to be published as though they were the genuine article, the practice would be accepted with equal readiness in New York, Paris, Berlin and Moscow.[6]

For Hauptmann, as for Zelda Fitzgerald, this process began modestly and grew largely unchecked throughout the second half of the 1920s. John Willett notes matter-of-factly: 'Elisabeth Hauptmann . . . wrote him the two English-language "Mahagonny Songs" which have ever since figured among his poems'.[7] In an interview with James Lyon, Hauptmann said it was 'self-evident' she had written the 'Alabama Song'.[8] The surviving archival copies of the two *Mahagonny* songs are marked in Hauptmann's hand, 'English by Hauptmann' on one and 'By Hauptmann. Brecht's handwriting' on the other.[9]

From late 1924 on, after Hauptmann met Brecht, 'it is often difficult to know who', writes Willett, 'wrote exactly what'.[10] At the most basic level, radical change had come about. In his analysis of the original manuscripts of 'Brecht' short stories, for instance, John Willett conservatively and laconically notes, 'the major responsibility was quite likely to be Hauptmann's'.[11] What brings Willett to this conclusion is that the manuscripts often show few or 'no marks of Brecht's hand'. Based on the manuscript evidence, Willett concludes that at least seven of the eleven short stories that comprise 'Brecht's Berlin Stories' are probably by Hauptmann. Only three, in Willett's view, are by Brecht.

In the second half of the 1920s there begin to emerge works significantly different from the originally exclusively *macho* Brecht texts of the Augsburg and Munich days. As John Willett succinctly puts it, the works produced after Hauptmann arrived on the 'Brecht' scene were ones 'clearly voicing for the first time a woman's point of view'. Not only do women's roles become richer, more three-dimensional after Hauptmann's arrival, but there is a sovereign, wholly assured series of adaptations of English-language originals, and to a somewhat lesser extent French also, that reveal the hand of someone who really knows the original language and can brilliantly create a nuanced German adaptation.

The shape and focus of plays begins to alter as the strong central figure of Widow Begbick is introduced in *Man is Man* and then will later be recycled in *Mahagonny* and *Mother Courage*. And the poems that Hauptmann works on, largely on her own, sympathetically reflect the condition of women, while those that Brecht works on on his own continue to reflect a virtually 'Mac the Knife' point of view where women are casually raped and murdered. In the realm of theory and dramaturgical practice, it is Hauptmann's discovery (through the English translations of Arthur Waley) of Japanese and Chinese sources that forms the basis of a revolution in modern staging that persists to the present day.

In the winter of 1927/8, friends in England sent Hauptmann a copy of John Gay's *The Beggar's Opera*, the 1728 parody of corrupt London society and of that society's favourite composer, Handel. She was immediately fascinated by the work of Gay with its sympathy for London's exploited poor, its savage satire on British society and, in *The Beggar's Opera* and its, in some ways, even more radical successor, *Polly*, with its strong female roles.

Brecht showed little interest in Hauptmann's 'Beggar's Opera' project.[12] But one day in the second half of April, Brecht was sitting at his usual place at Schlichter's restaurant with cigar and newspaper when the Berlin impresario, Ernst-Josef Aufricht, came in. Aufricht was looking for a play to reopen the Schiffbauerdamm Theater which he had just leased. Brecht eagerly began to talk about a play called *Fleischhacker*. He did not mention that if it were ever to get finished (which it never did), it was already promised to Piscator. Aufricht did not like the sound of *Fleischhacker* anyway and called for the bill. As he got up to leave, Brecht said, 'Then I've got something on the side. You could look at six or seven scenes from it tomorrow. It's an adaptation of John Gay's *Beggar's Opera*.'[13]

The very next day, Aufricht was taken with the 'insolence and dry wit' of the text. He was convinced he was reading authentic Brecht. The mistake was understandable, for of course he was reading a text just as authentic as a number of other texts by Hauptmann that had been appearing over Brecht's signature.[14]

A contract was drafted at Brecht's direction and arrangements made to sign it at the offices of the firm of Felix Bloch Erben on 26 April.[15] Brecht invited Weill to go along to the signing but did not include Hauptmann. This was despite the fact that the text delivered to FBE was clearly hers. Fortunately, FBE's original hectographically reproduced version of this text has survived. It is currently part of the holdings of the old East Berlin Academy of Arts where it is still treated as though it were a Brecht text. But when the American scholar, Ronald Shull, working in tandem with the former East German scholar, Joachim Lucchesi, took a look at the type-

script, they saw it 'relied heavily on Gay's original piece including the reten-
tion of a number of song texts of Gay in Hauptmann's translation'.[16] Given
the existence of this text, plus the fact that Hauptmann was the only person
in the workshop who had the skills to render such complex English into
German, there is little doubt that most of the fabric of the work that FBE
would market globally was hers. Nevertheless, she would earn 12.5 per cent
from the German market while Brecht took 62.5 per cent of the world
market.

Rehearsals for *The Threepenny Opera* began at the Schiffbauerdamm
Theater on 1 August 1928, using of necessity the tentative version that
Hauptmann and Weill had produced. Some of Hauptmann's renderings of
Kipling ballads, including the Kiplingesque 'Cannon Song' that had been
used earlier in 1928 in the Berlin production of *Man is Man*, had been inser-
ted. The surviving manuscripts indicate that the songs that Hauptmann
herself was responsible for are the ones telling a story from a woman's
point of view. One of these, 'The Song of Pirate Jenny', reveals Hauptmann's knowledge of *Polly*, where Gay presents his heroine doing battle
with pirates. Another Hauptmann song appears to be the now very famous
'Barbara Song'. Finally, the 'Jealousy Duet' is an almost verbatim translation by Hauptmann of Gay's original words. In the light of all this, it is
difficult to argue with what Klaus Völker, one of the most knowledgeable
people in the world when it comes to the Brecht circle, has told me in a
number of interviews: 'Elisabeth Hauptmann was responsible for as much
as 80 or even 90 per cent of the published text of *The Threepenny Opera*.'[17]

When Brecht finally reached Berlin on 20 August, he made some additions
to the play. The most significant of these were the four Villon ballads that
he had taken over virtually verbatim from an early twentieth-century
volume of translations by K. L. Ammer;[18] a volume which included versions
of what would become some of the most prominent 'Brechtian' songs in the
play. The 'Ballad of a Pleasant Life' contains one of the most famous lines in
'Brecht': 'Nur wer im Wohlstand lebt, lebt angenehm' ('Only he who lives
well, lives pleasantly'). The 'Ballad of the Pimp' is also straight Villon/
Ammer, as is the 'Ballad of the Famous' that was used here and then taken
over later in *Mother Courage*. When Brecht presented 'his' work to the
team working on the final stages of *The Threepenny Opera* in August 1928,
the others saw these pieces as typical Brecht songs. They were. He had
stolen from Ammer's translations from the time of his first plays onward.

Although Brecht managed to keep Hauptmann very much behind the
scenes with *The Threepenny Opera* and sold her work as his, this happened
to a somewhat lesser extent with *Happy End*, the work written as a successor to *The Threepenny Opera*. As John Willett notes, the latter work 'was

put together in the summer of 1929 much as its predecessor had been a year earlier. That is to say *there would be a basic script written by Hauptmann for which Brecht would write songs to be set by Weill'* [my emphasis].[19] Without the remark being italicised, one could almost miss Willett's matter-of-fact observation that Hauptmann was as responsible for *The Threepenny Opera* as she was for *Happy End*.

With the help of the archives of the Felix Bloch Erben company in Berlin, and the Kurt Weill Foundation in New York and New Haven, and the memoirs of Aufricht, we can reconstruct the unhappy course of *Happy End* and the Brecht scam behind it. From Aufricht and from Kurt Weill we know Brecht represented himself originally as the author of *Happy End*. He said he had worked with Hauptmann on the text and claimed (to preserve the parallel with *The Threepenny Opera*) that the new play was based on the work of an American author called Dorothy Lane. But what happened next is that Brecht unexpectedly married Helene Weigel on 10 April 1929. Shortly after this came Hauptmann's suicide attempt, and, after her recovery, Hauptmann directly challenged Brecht's position as supposed co-author. From the FBE files we learn that on 26 April 1929, Hauptmann gave Brecht the following memo:

> I have written a play that will appear under the pseudonym Dorothy Lane and that has already been accepted for production at the Theater am Schiff-bauerdamm in Berlin. The work is appearing through the stage publisher Felix Bloch Erben. You have obligated yourself to me to write the lyrics for the songs for this piece. I have informed Felix Bloch Erben of this and you have acknowledged the existence of my contract with Felix Bloch Erben. I, on my side, have informed Felix Bloch Erben that you reserve the right to use the texts of your songs in separate book publication and in cabaret appearances.[20]

Brecht responded: 'I have declared myself ready to write the songs. I may use these songs, following the terms of my contract with Felix Bloch Erben, for cabaret etc. etc.'

Hauptmann was now, as FBE knew, the contractor, able to force Brecht to acknowledge that his role was *only* that of sub-contractor, the supplier of lyrics to be slotted into Hauptmann's text. Her contract with the firm of Felix Bloch Erben was drawn up on the standard printed form that presupposed that all playwrights were male. The contract reads: 'Herr [*sic*] Fraulein Hauptmann of Berlin W.50, Spichernstrasse 16' would market her 'intellectual property', a work called 'Happy End' and written under 'the pseudonym of Dorothy Lane' with FBE. Hauptmann left the office that day with her very own cheque for 5,000 marks in hand. Later, to her horror, Brecht would sabotage both the production and Hauptmann's effort at independence by inserting an irrelevant text at the end of the play on opening night, thus contributing to the premature closing of the production.

At this same time, the critic Alfred Kerr declared in the *Berliner Tageblatt* that Brecht had plagiarised from a German translation of Villon in *The Threepenny Opera*. The great satirist, Kurt Tucholsky, noting also thefts from Rudyard Kipling, began in his comedy routines to refer to a certain 'Rudyard Brecht'.[21] The controversy spread to the streets of Berlin as a Tucholsky joke began to circulate. One person asks of another, 'Who is the play by?' The other person replies, 'Brecht'. At which the first says, 'Then who's the play by?[22]

On 6 May in Ihering's hospitable *Berliner Börsen-Courier*, Brecht replied to Kerr's allegation. It was true, he wrote, that he had forgotten to include the name of the Villon translator, but that was because he had 'a fundamental laxity in questions of literary property'. He also denied that the work included any Kipling. He may even have believed this claim and been unaware of how much Kipling Hauptmann had kept in. Brecht's riposte about his own contempt for intellectual property, particularly when published in Berlin's equivalent of *The Wall Street Journal*, cleverly made Kerr look old-fashioned in worrying about such things. Brecht opined further in the *Film-Kurier*, 'Literary property is an item that should be classed with allotment gardens and such things.'[23]

The myth Brecht was promoting here of his own progressiveness with regard to questions of property has been, until the present day, widely believed. It would persist even though Piscator pointed out in 1929 in his *The Political Theatre* that Brecht had repeatedly shouted at the Piscator Collective, 'My name is a brand name, and whoever uses this brand name has to pay for it.'[24] When Hauptmann's friend and fellow playwright (and fellow-lover of Brecht's) Marieluise Fleisser, tried in her play *Tiefseefisch* (Deep Sea Fish) to have her exposé of Brecht's exploitative practices staged in Berlin in 1930/1, Brecht threatened reprisals and forced its withdrawal.[25]

While Brecht was publicly deriding intellectual property, privately, on 17 May 1929, he signed a new 'General Contract' with Felix Bloch Erben. The head of the firm, Fritz Wreede, committed FBE to pay Brecht 1,000 gold marks a month for seven years. Significantly, the deal was to include plays 'written in cooperation with one or more other authors'. Having signed a contract only days before with Hauptmann, Wreede now knew of Hauptmann's contribution to work marketed under the Brecht label. In signing the new agreement Brecht was, of course, counting on Fritz Wreede's discretion not to reveal that the same Brecht, who was declaring in print that he had a fundamental laxity in questions of intellectual property, was selling the products of the Brecht factory at the highest possible price. Brecht's basic laxity was with the property of others, but he would allow no such laxity by others in using the work sold under his brand name.

The work that Hauptmann and Brecht did in the winter of 1928/29 marked an unusually sharp shift in the workshop's orientation. When I did my first interview with Elisabeth Hauptmann in 1966, she told me in her quiet, understated way how she remembered this change in direction coming about. In the autumn of 1928, one of Hauptmann's closest English friends, Margaret Mynatt, had visited her in Berlin and brought her a copy of Arthur Waley's English versions of *The No-Plays of Japan*. 'I was,' Hauptmann told me, 'overwhelmed by Waley'. Attracted to the austere beauty of these late fourteenth- and early fifteenth-century plays, she began to translate several of them into German. The project was, as she told a later interviewer,[26] strictly her own and she very explicitly did not show the work to Brecht. Aware that Waley had taken liberties with the original, Hauptmann enlisted native speakers of Japanese to help improve the accuracy of the texts. As she indicated to an East German interviewer in 1966, this was strictly her own work, done for her own pleasure.[27] However, Kurt Weill happened to see her translation of the play *Taniko* and showed her work to Brecht. Immediately, as the surviving texts show, Brecht took over most of her work word for word.[28] In one interview with me she quietly acknowledged that she was responsible for 80 per cent of the play *He Who Said Yes* and that she had suggested the direct audience address method that is essential to *The Mother*. She also told me in the same interview that she wrote much of *The Measures Taken*.[29]

From a whole list of texts she contributed to in the *Lehrstück* mode, Hauptmann then turned in the early 1930s to the Salvation Army and American materials that she had used in *Happy End* and in short stories, published under her own name, to create with Brecht and another associate, Emil Burri, the play *Saint Joan of the Stockyards*. Jan Knopf, author of a widely used handbook on Brecht and theatre, notes of *Saint Joan*: 'From the work materials one can determine that no small part – including the text – of the preparatory work was provided by Emil Burri and Elisabeth Hauptmann who were also responsible for the plot; *Brecht's work consisted primarily of checking up on suggestions, editing and expanding the text*' (my emphasis).[30]

It is now becoming clear, after scholars have spent decades finding ways to work past artificial barriers in East German archives, that without Hauptmann we would have no *Threepenny Opera*. Just as surprising perhaps is that it is her adaptations/translations of Arthur Waley's English versions of Japanese plays and the theoretical writings of Seami that undergird the whole genre of the *Lehrstück* as developed in the 'Brecht' workshop. John Willett says as much when he points out that the two key originators of the *Lehrstück* form are Paul Hindemith and Elisabeth Hauptmann, rather than, as is so often erroneously assumed, Bertolt Brecht. 'There is', says Willett of the *Lehrstück* form, 'no good evidence that it ever was, as so often assumed, [Brecht's] particular invention.'[31] Similarly, we now know that 'Brecht's' Chinese poems would not exist without Hauptmann.[32] There is also a doubt, at we have seen, that most of the Berlin short stories, including the prize-winning 'Die Bestie', would exist without her. And, after the Second World War, it is clear that without Hauptmann much of the new play repertoire of the Berliner Ensemble would not exist.[33] Nevertheless, despite her almost endless list of contributions to the 'Brecht' *œuvre* from 1925 to about 1932, and again from 1945 to Brecht's death in 1956, her name remains largely unknown. So far, despite the fact that her work was vital to reshaping the modern stage, there is no entry under her own name in the main reference works on the German or on world drama. She, like Zelda Fitzgerald, remains largely a non-person.

In the space available here it is impossible, except in outline, to note the importance, similar to that of Hauptmann, of Margarete Steffin. The research of the Danish scholar Rudy Hassing[34] and the Berlin critic Inge Gellert[35] has begun to show that Steffin's contribution to 'Brecht', from about 1932 to 1941, is similar in scope and importance to that of Hauptmann. There is also evidence, and again we must be grateful to Rudy Hassing for his efforts, together with those of Hans Bunge, of the contributions made to 'Brecht' by Ruth Berlau.[36] Similar efforts, I am convinced, need to be made in the case of Hella Wuolijoki (his collaborator on *Puntila*, still begging at the time of her death for money due to her from Brecht), Ernst Ottwalt (murdered in the gulag), Emil Burri, and Martin Pohl (arrested on a trumped-up charge by the Stasi).

Returning to the question asked at the beginning of this essay, we can finally sketch out an answer to who helped create the 'great man', Bertolt Brecht, and at what cost. In Hauptmann's case we know of at least two suicide attempts during Brecht's lifetime. The story of Berlau's life is even sadder. And in the case of Steffin, her several abortions, together with the almost constant neglect of the tuberculosis she had contracted before meeting Brecht, led directly to her death. Aware that Brecht completed little unless she was there, she neglected her illness in favour of turning out thousands of pages of translations that were then marketed as by 'Brecht and Steffin',[37] and on working on the great plays of the exile period, plays such as *Galileo, Mother Courage, Señora Carrar's Rifles, Fear and Misery of the Third Reich, The Good Person of Szechwan, Arturo Ui, The Horatii and the Curiatii, The Trial of Lucullus, The Days of the Commune*, and *The Caucasian Chalk Circle*.

As the life and work of various, sad, too-long neglected women and men who worked with Brecht at various times begin to come into scholarly focus, we can better understand what Brecht meant by 'collective' work. It can now be shown that before the collapse of Weimar and after the creation of the GDR, the landed estate-owner Brecht, all his protestations about 'Poor Bert Brecht' to the contrary, was an extremely wealthy man, selling what was often the fruit of the labours of his closest associates while steadfastly refusing to provide Elisabeth Hauptmann, Ruth Berlau, Hella Wuolijoki, Martin Pohl and Steffin's heirs with money legally and/or morally due to them. It was a 'collective' where Brecht overwhelmingly collected and where others contributed to his fame and financial welfare.

What I have provided here is only a beginning.[38] With the collapse of the GDR, we need to re-examine the entire 'Brecht' canon to provide, wherever possible, answers to the question: who really wrote what? Perhaps with a fresh (what Martin Esslin has called for for years), 'non-hagiographic' approach to the 'great man', we can begin to recognise the voices of the various people who worked in the Brecht factory to create poems that have earned their place as some of the greatest work ever written in German, and who helped write plays that now regularly compete on world stages with Shakespeare, Molière, Chekhov and the best of the classic drama of Greece. Finally, we can listen both to and for the voices of the various people who were responsible for the creation of what, despite evidence to the contrary, are still being globally marketed as the 'Collected Works of Bertolt Brecht'.

NOTES

1 Fragment was published in *Sinn und Form*, 1988/9.
2 See Dieter Schmidt's excellent *'Baal' und der junge Brecht* (Metzler: Stuttgart, 1966), p. 50.
3 Elisabeth Hauptmann, *Julia ohne Romeo* (Aufbau: Berlin, 1977), p. 230. This small collection of Hauptmann's work was published in GDR in 1977.
4 See James K. Lyon, *Bertolt Brecht and Rudyard Kipling*, pp. 5, 55, 56, 58. Lyon does not believe Brecht usually went directly to English sources to get his Kipling. He writes, 'The overwhelming evidence speaks for translations.'
5 See James R. Mellow, *Invented Lives* (Houghton Mifflin: Boston, 1984), pp. 340ff.
6 Brecht regularly published both Steffin's and Hauptmann's work in Moscow under his own name in the 1930s, although his own lack of foreign-language skills made his role as 'translator' wildly implausible.
7 p. viii in Willett's notes to the English language-version of *The Rise and Fall of the City of Mahagonny*.

8 Reported to me in a conversation with James K. Lyon on 1 March 1992 at the Delaware Brecht Conference.

9 See Willett, 'Bacon ohne Shakespeare? The problem of Mitarbeit', in *Brecht, Women, Politics*, ed. J. Fuegi, G. Bahr, J. Willett (Wayne State University Press: Detroit, 1983), p. 123.

10 Willett in *Bertolt Brecht in Britain*, ed. N. Jacobs and P. Ohlsen, p. 14.

11 This, and the two following quotations are from *Brecht, Women, Politics*, ed. Fuegi *et al.*, pp. 128 and 125.

12 In a letter dated 9 May 1928, Brecht still refers to the text as something that Erich Engel plans to do under the title 'The Beggar's Opera'.

13 Ernst-Josef Aufricht, *Erzähle, damit du dein Recht erweist* (Propyläen: Berlin, 1966), p. 64.

14 For a good discussion of the layers of the text and the importance of Hauptmann's work in the process, see Lucchesi and Shull, *Musik bei Brecht*, pp. 388–407.

15 The date stamps on the contract are fuzzy but the time frame can be reconstructed from internal evidence. The FBE contract specifies that it will go into force as soon as final agreement and a finished text are delivered to the Schiffbauerdamm Theater. Obviously, therefore, the FBE signing had followed the original meeting with Brecht at Schlichter's.

16 Lucchesi and Shull, *Musik bei Brecht*, p. 390.

17 Fuegi interview with Völker, 28 September 1990, Berlin.

18 See Lucchesi and Shull, *Musik bei Brecht*, p. 390.

19 Brecht, *Letters 1913–1956*, p. 582.

20 This is the first publication of these documents from Hauptmann's private papers.

21 Cited in Willett, *The Theatre of Bertolt Brecht*, p. 94.

22 'Im Theater ... Von wem ist dieses Stück? Dieses Stück ist von Brecht. Von wem *ist* also dieses Stück?'. Kurt Tucholsky, *Lerne lachen ohne zu weinen* (Berlin, 1931), p. 346.

23 Cited in Völker, *Brecht: A Biography, pp. 132–3*.

24 Piscator, *The Political Theatre*, ed. and trans. Hugh Rorrison (Eyre Methuen: London, 1980), p. 196.

25 It is now available in Fleisser's three-volume *Gesammelte Werke* (Suhrkamp: Frankfurt, 1972).

26 See notes on O. Schirmer's 1966 interview in Steinweg, *Das Lehrstück*, pp. 65–6.

27 The interview is in *Julia ohne Romeo*, pp. 175–7.

28 This was seen as early as 1959 by Willett (*The Theatre of Bertolt Brecht*, pp. 96–7) and in 1961 by R. Grimm. See his *Brecht und die Weltliteratur* (Nuremburg, 1961), p. 19. What was not begun at this time, however, was a systematic assessment of just how much Hauptmann was responsible for.

29 Interview in Berlin, 9 November 1970.

30 Jan Knopf, *Brecht-Handbuch* (Metzler: Stuttgart, 1980), p. 107.

31 Willett in *Brecht, Women, Politics*, p. 125.

32 I am grateful to Ms Paula Hanssen for this information. Her forthcoming dissertation at the University of Illinois traces various Hauptmann contributions to 'Brecht'.

33 See my essay, 'Whodunit: Brecht's adaptation of Molière's *Don Juan*', in *Comparative Literature Studies*, II, no. 2 (June 1974), pp. 159–72.

34 Rudy Hassing is preparing a biography of Steffin and has kindly shared his research notes with me.

35 See particularly the 1991 Rowohlt/Berlin volume of Steffin's writings, *Konfutse versteht nichts von Frauen.*

36 Some of these are dealt with in the 1992 film, *Red Ruth: That Deadly Longing.*

37 These works, published in Moscow, were from the languages Brecht did not know. Earnings from deliberately misattributed work seem to have constituted the main support of the Brecht group in the late 1930s.

38 For vastly more complete documentation, see my forthcoming *Brecht & Co.: An Archaeology of Voices* (1993).

9

ELIZABETH WRIGHT

The Good Person of Szechwan: discourse of a masquerade

Brecht is known for his radical rethinking of the theatre in the light of Marxist thought. He has succeeded in providing a methodology for a materialist critique by deliberately making ideology appear in the theatrical discourse.[1] Political society is to recognise itself as a production rather than as a mimetic representation, but the question is who controls the production? According to Marxism it is the capitalist machine, but according to feminism it is the patriarchal one that is responsible for oppressing at least half of society, namely women. Brecht's presentation of women has not won him much acclaim from feminists.[2] In his work the social positions of both men and women are seen as externally determined – often the exploiting male and the exploited female – while internalised ideals or anti-ideals of femininity and masculinity are reproduced without any distancing devices. There are, on the one hand, a variety of 'good', politically correct, mother-figures (Grusha, 'the Mother', Shen Te), and, on the other, a selection of asocial rebels (Baal, Azdak, Yang Sun) who, in order to maintain their place at the margins of society, conduct themselves aggressively in relation to women.

Brecht's 'good person' (*der gute Mensch*) is masculine in German, *Mensch* being the generic term for mankind, but nevertheless it can and here does represent a woman. The woman, Shen Te, masquerades as a man at critical moments in the plot: unable to fulfil the Imaginary mandate of being 'the good person' in the Symbolic, Shen Te produces a 'male' half, Shui Ta, to perform the phallic function of exercising reason and control. 'Imaginary', 'Symbolic' and 'Real' are Jacques Lacan's 'orders' (replacing Freud's 'agencies'), modes of positioning the individual in relation to language and the material.[3] For Lacan, however, the term 'individual', in popular parlance synonymous with 'ego', is a precarious concept, since the ego is an Imaginary narcissistic, albeit necessary, construction. The crucial feature of the Lacanian subject is that it is alienated by virtue of its very entrance into language, a system which both joins and divides. As soon as the subject is caught in the defining network of the signifier it is divided between fixed identifications and actual being. Access into the Symbolic inevitably produces a split in the subject between the *moi*, the mis-recognising consciousness, and the *Je*, which only symptomatically appears in the gaps of consciousness. For Lacan, alienation is a structural condition of subjectivity *per se*. The splitting of subjectivity produces the sexual division and bestows symbolic gender.

In a celebrated article Joan Riviere sets out that womanliness is a cover-up to conform with social constructions of femininity, a masquerade, whereby *the* woman as a category does not exist except by miming and parodying that which is expected of her.[4] Joan Riviere's patient used womanliness as a mask to hide the possession of masculinity. In Freudo-Lacanian theory both sexes repudiate femininity, both have a masculine relation to the mother, seeking to be the phallus that she wants/lacks. Womanliness is a 'feint' or 'cover-up': 'there is no absolute femininity beneath the veil, only a set of ontologically tenuous codes that normatively induct the feminine subject into the social practice of "being" woman through mimesis and parroting'.[5] As a woman, then, Shen Te is already implicated in a masquerade: she is the 'good woman' wanting to live up to being 'an Angel to the slums' (p. 106),[6] thereby placating her suitors and the father-gods, who respectively derive economic and moral advantage therefrom. The appearance of her male half, Shui Ta, is a defence against the failure of this masquerade, thus reversing the strategy of Riviere's patient, whose 'feminine' impersonation (coquetry) came to the rescue of her 'masculine' one (success and achievement).

Shen Te is split into the good exploited female and bad exploiting male. In her first masquerade, as Shen Te, she is attractive for her very helplessness and innocence, while as Shui Ta, her second masquerade, she is attractive for her power. Divided by her masquerades, she occupies the hysterical position in that she performs (both in the sense of functioning in and acting out) the historically specified form of symbolic identification. On the whole Brecht's female characters are shown as admirable to the extent to which they develop their 'womanliness' into a form of political strength – there is a long list of motherly figures, apart from 'the Mother', which includes Kattrin, Grusha, Frau Sarti (in *Galileo*). But Shen Te starts her masquerade with a handicap: as a prostitute she masquerades as a fantasy object. Although for Brecht her profession 'demonstrates' economic necessity ('Let me admit: I sell myself in order to live', p. 10), for the gods, to whom she makes this admission and who cautiously pay her for their overnight lodging, she is a lure and forbidden source of (obscene) enjoyment: 'But please let nobody know that we paid. It might be misinterpreted' (p. 11).

These considerations are necessary in dealing with Brecht's presentation of a person, who would be (essentially) good, were it not for the prevailing economic conditions: 'I should certainly like to be, but how am I to pay my rent?' (p. 10). Her doubts rest on the fact that she is a prostitute, albeit with the traditional topos of having a heart of gold. For Brecht her ego is thus not alienated by its very constitution, since a self is presumed outside or before an alienation has taken place. This alienation is produced because 'something is wrong with this world of yours': 'To be good while yet surviving / Split me like lightning into two people' (p. 105). The question posed by the play is, however, not what is good or what is bad, but whether it is possible to *be* good in the world as it is at present. To this end the playwright stages an 'experiment' which probes the prevailing state of the world and investigates the complaints of its inhabitants that it is impossible to be 'good'. In this essay I would like to conduct my own experiment: to what extent is Brecht too speaking as a split subject, so that he is doubled in his discourse, speaking from an Imaginary position in the Symbolic Order while being spoken by it, believing that he is launching his attack from a stable position, while himself not being immune to the Symbolic's alienating effects?

The plot of the play runs as follows:[7] three gods arrive in the capital of Szechwan, a province in China, looking for lodging, having descended from the clouds in legendary fashion. They have heard rumours that it is impossible to be good in the world as it is and have therefore come to see whether there are any good people left; if this is the case, the world can stay as it is. The waterseller Wang, anxious to propitiate them, engages on a thankless search for a willing host. In triumph and relief he produces Shen Te, the local prostitute, who is willing to accommodate them, though she has to forgo a client and will lose the means to pay her rent. On leaving her lodgings the gods, after some misgivings regarding their status, bestow a generous sum of money on her. As a good person Shen Te opens a tobacconist's shop with the money thus acquired, doling out free bowls of rice and cigarettes to all who appear. By the end of the day her business is already near ruin: a homeless family of eight is using her premises as a free lodging house, while at the same time cynically suggesting that she invent a tough cousin as the true owner of the shop. Shui Ta, the cousin, duly turns up next morning and, with the help of the local police, briefly gives the family their marching orders. Shen Te/Shui Ta now function as split off from each other: whenever Shen Te runs into financial trouble through a generous impulse, Shui Ta turns up with a tough solution. This is particularly the case when Shen Te falls in love with the unemployed pilot Yang Sun: she borrows money to help him to a job as a pilot in Peking, only to find that when there is not enough money for two, he plans to leave her behind. The agreed marriage ceremony does not take place, but he retains a portion of

6. 'Three cheers, and one cheer more / For the good person of Szechwan.' Karl von Appen's design for the 1957 production by the Berliner Ensemble.

the money and goes off. Meanwhile Shen Te, hopelessly in debt and now with child, is determined to survive, even though this means accepting a cheque from Shun Fu, the barber, as rich as he is infatuated. To everyone's surprise and alarm, Shen Te disappears and Shui Ta returns and starts a business. Soon the owner of a thriving tobacco factory, he employs the now penniless Yang Sun, who rapidly works himself up by a series of ruthless ploys. He becomes increasingly puzzled by Shen Te's absence. It is through his accusations that Shui Ta is brought to trial, charged with the murder of the missing Shen Te. During the trial Shen Te is praised for her goodness and Shui Ta arraigned for his misdeeds. When Shen Te/Shui Ta sees that the judges are the three gods she takes off her mask and accounts for the necessity of her masquerade and split. Her appeal to the gods for help is in vain: barely conceding the occasional use of the masquerade, the triad ascends with 'three cheers, and one cheer more / For the good person of Szechwan' (p. 108). In the epilogue an actor transfers Shen Te's appeal for help to the audience: something has to change, but who or what should it be?

The experiment begins with the gods searching for a good person. The usual attempt to establish an ethical system is thus reversed: instead of a subject in search of an ego-ideal (a father, a god, the rational, the good), the gods are looking for ideal ego – a self-confirming mirror-image – in order to

justify their existence. Far from representing the Law, the gods show themselves to be dependent on Imaginary ideals. The institution of the Law, the
police, is in fact corrupt and morally bankrupt, unlike the ineffectual gods
who are at least conscious of their roles as ego-ideal, in that they are
anxious not to claim their rights of enjoyment as paid-up lodgers of the
prostitute. The police by contrast accept the cigars offered by Shui Ta as a
bribe; enjoyment is here shown as attendant upon power. The transaction is
the same as the boy taking the cakes, since the cigars are not paid for, but
the boy is hauled off as a thief. Because Shui Ta and the police control the
sources of enjoyment, the same economic rule can be broken, rendering the
Law duplicitous and obscene.

Brecht is clear in his exposure of the bourgeois capitalist order and its
gods who go along with it.[8] As a prostitute Shen Te is on the lowest rung of
the ladder in that she herself is the commodity. With the financial backing
from the gods she attains petit-bourgeois status as a shop-owner, a rung
above the workers, while the previous shop-owners, alienated from their
own class, sink to the *Lumpenproletariat*, the refuse of all classes. Through
Shen Te, Brecht demonstrates that a successful business in the capitalist
world depends on taking rather than giving. To balance the giving of the
'good' person, a 'bad' person is needed to take it back, just as in *Puntila* the
'drunk' generous side of the landowner is a trade-off for the 'sober' mean
side.

What is missing from this analysis is an examination of the material conditions of gender behaviour outside its relation to class. The prostitute Shen
Te is forced to sell her body for money: an early version of the play was
called *Die Ware Liebe*, 'commodity love', to resonate with the notion of
'Die wahre Liebe', 'true love'.[9] To get the newly impoverished Shen Te out
of this double-bind, the police officer advises Shui Ta to find a rich suitor,
the barber Shu Fu – in other words, to sanctify the sale of herself by entering
into a marriage contract with a single willing buyer: 'you can't earn your
living by love, or it becomes immoral earnings ... respectability means, not
with the man who can pay, but with the man one loves ... all you need do is
to find a husband for her' (p. 30). So far, so good. Brecht has made the same
point in *The Threepenny Opera*: bourgeois marriage is a form of legalised
prostitution. What is omitted from this critique is the relation of class
oppression to sexual repression. Albeit by dint of omission, the play also
'demonstrates' that the advantages accruing to men from the subordination
of women are not merely confined to class: neither 'cousin' Shui Ta (were he
a 'full' presence), nor lover Yang Sun, nor protector Shu Fu, not to speak of
the gods, are likely to offer any support for Shen Te's child. Producing children is a form of unpaid production for which Brecht has supplied no

estrangement effect, unless it be supplied by the audience's response in the theatre to (1) Shen Te's anticipatory maternal enjoyment and (2) her Imaginary staging of the male hero's arrival:

> The world awaits him in secret. In the cities they have heard the rumour: someone is coming now with whom we must reckon. *She presents her small son to the audience*:
>
> An airman! Salute a new conqueror
> Of unknown mountains, inaccessible countries! One
> Carrying letters from man to man
> Across the wastes where no man yet has trod!
>
> *She begins to walk up and down, leading her small son by the hand.* Come my son, inspect your world. (p. 70)

For Brecht, Shen Te's great moment is not as the odd couple – soft philanthropist/hard entrepreneur – rent apart, but as 'The Mother' of future combatants, the proletarian woman who can produce the vanguard of the revolution and whose motherhood will extend to protecting him like 'a tiger, a savage beast' (p. 77). Her male child is to be the romantic traveller and Imaginary coloniser of the earth's waste places, the possible utopian inheritor of a future undivided existence, carrying always the insignia of the Symbolic – the Letter destined to arrive, unsubvertible communication from 'man to man'. Here the text displays a set of values and interests in common with traditional bourgeois modes of thought, in particular a general representation of humanity that is blatantly masculine. To historicise Shen Te's discourse of the maternal will surely be a challenge for a future producer of this piece, a politico-theatrical response to 'what sort of measures you would recommend' (p. 109).

It is hardly surprising, then, that feminists feel that Marxism regards itself as a form of Master-knowledge, one that 'takes the position of the subject, the knower, and its radical "partner", such as feminism, is assigned the role of object of knowledge'.[10] Being locked in 'dichotomous thinking', Marxism tends to prioritise the first term on the basis of the logical paradigm A/not-A, where A affirms and not-A negates.[11] With the Shen Te/Shui Ta dichotomy Brecht has merely reversed this in making Shen Te represent the affirmative – 'she can't refuse' (p. 7), or 'say no' (p. 14) (the negative pole of power), whereas Shui Ta specialises in the negative (the positive pole). This opposition is soon sublated into a new greater dichotomy of active male professional conquerer-son and passive female proletarian mother, 'demonstrating' the assumption that while the division of classes is a fact of history, the division of sexes is a fact of nature: women just *are* mothers, while men are (high) flyers.

Shen Te is placed in a subordinate position by a number of different systems and not just by a single mechanism – that of a woman with property within capitalism and its market economy. Her oppression is economic as a prostitute, psychic as a romantic beloved, social as a pregnant mother. There is here an ensemble of social practices that mutually reinforce one another. Moreover, the various reactions to her in each of these positions ally with each other to disempower her in specifically concrete ways. Where in her 'masculine' masquerade Shen Te is immediately accepted as a shop/factory-owner, in her 'feminine' masquerade she is repeatedly called to account. Shui Ta as a man inspires confidence without further credentials for being 'sharp as a knife' (p. 16) and for his 'decisive action' (p. 29), while Shen Te as 'Angel of the slums' is used and exploited both by her fellow citizens and her lover. The gods, the Other, desire her to 'freely follow the impulses of her gentle heart' (p. 22) and Shen Te's desire accords with this, declaring that 'to love, honour and cherish a husband would be very pleasant' (p. 10). As rejected lover she weeps, but as mother she vows to be 'a tiger, a savage beast / To all others if need be. And / It need be' (p. 77), which means further 'masculine' masquerade. It is not that Brecht is unaware of the sexist behaviour of Shen Te's lover (YANG SUN: 'You want to appeal to her reason! She hasn't any reason!', p. 53), but that he sees this sexist behaviour primarily as economically determined, rather than discursively constructed, an effect of capitalist rather than gender oppression.

In developing the concept of hegemony beyond that of rule or master-principle, Antonio Gramsci defined it as a complex contingent interrelationship of various groups and institutions within civil society, an ensemble of social practices in collusion, mutually reinforcing one another by making compromise alliances with a range of social forces in order to form a bloc. This bloc, in institutions, cultural relations and ideas, establishes a basis of consent for the existing order, a fabric difficult to tear, since its parts are mutually supportive in practical and ideological ways. At its simplest it is the strategic organisation of consent, *either* for the status quo *or* for progressive change.[12] Where Brecht mainly sees a single mechanism oppressing the worker, Gramsci's model of society can take account of the interrelationship between a number of systems, such as gender and class. The post-Marxist Ernesto Laclau reads Gramsci's Marxism as a break with the dichotomous thinking of eighteenth-century rationalism: 'Hegemony exists when that which would have been a rational succession of stages is interrupted by a contingency that cannot be subsumed under the logical categories of Marxist theory.'[13] This *contingency* shows itself both in inescapable antagonisms that cannot be foreseen and in the resistance of the social to a transparent analysis,[14] effects that Brecht's texts are not immune to. In the present case, there is the example of the gratuitous assault by the wealthy barber Shu Fu on the poor water-seller Wang, laming his hand with the curling tongs (p. 41) – a moment of pure antagonism, an excess, which Brecht turns into a crude economic dilemma (the more serious the injury, the greater the chance of compensation for the water-seller – in thus trying to collude with the system Wang becomes a card-carrying member of the *Lumpenproletariat*).

According to Laclau, the true nature of the hegemonic relationship cannot be conceived consciously: the task and the agent move together but without a fully rational understanding presiding over them. Negativity and opaqueness are parts of the social that cannot be overcome by a final *Aufhebung*, a dialectical resolution, into a supposed positivity and transparency, and this, Laclau considers, is comparable with the Lacanian notion of a constitutive *lack*.[15] One cannot accede to an identity without a division being imposed, making two: for Lacan, Real (material) lack, the unsymbolisable remains of the living body and its experiences, is the inevitable consequence of the loss of the primal object – the mother – and an inescapable part of the constitution of the subject. Both the Imaginary (from the viewpoint of the subject) and the Symbolic (from the viewpoint of society) operate as if there were no lack, the Imaginary by a fantasy of plenitude (e.g. Shen Te's romantic love and maternal joy), the Symbolic by appearing to promise fulfilment (the gods as perceived by Wang and Shen Te). But at least two songs in the play admit the bankruptcy in the Symbolic: in 'The Song of the Smoke', lack (*Mangel*, translated as 'hunger') features as lack of hope (pp. 19–20), while 'The Song of Green Cheese' ('Das Lied vom Sankt Nimmerleinstag' – 'Never-Never-Day') declares through five stanzas that only 'when the moon is green cheese' will the earth become a paradise (pp. 68–9). In these songs the lack in the Other is of course figured as an anti-myth, as a challenge to bourgeois inertia and complacency. The message comes across loud and clear in the case of the water-seller Wang, trying to sell water in the rain:

> I sell water. Who would taste it?
> – Who would want it in this weather?
> All my labour has been wasted.   (p. 90)

Wang is at the mercy of nature, because the division of labour within the capitalist system has specified a role that can become futile at a moment's notice, a kind of built-in redundancy. These specifically economic contradictions leave the more radical elements of social antagonism unacknowledged, but the barber's unprovoked attack could be taken as an unconscious recognition that the Symbolic itself is structured around lack, where the water-seller is the symptom of lack in both the subject (his own poverty) and the Other (the Symbolic's empty (dry) space). Brecht, however, prefers to perceive lack as principally in the capitalist system, rather than in the Real of the subject, that portion of being that falls outside the Imaginary and Symbolic, 'the traumatic kernel the symbolization of which always fails'.[16] Shen Te cannot find a signifier which is her own, she cannot say it 'all' (p. 108), she cannot represent herself in the Symbolic as either 'good' or 'bad', her sobbing a testimony to the failure of either Shen Te or Shui Ta to fill the lack with words (p. 92).

But the Other cannot fully symbolise itself either. The gods themselves 'know' this:

> No matter: one pays one's debts. One cannot afford even the appearance of irregularity. The letter of the law has first to be fulfilled; then its spirit.
>
> (p. 39)

Hence their looking for an ideal ego to refurbish their tarnished dream of plenitude.[17] They decide 'to settle on Shen Te' (p. 98), who 'is strong, healthy and well built, and can endure much' (p. 106), and who can reconfirm their own status as ego-ideal, as being in the place from which she wants to be observed, for as gods they can only function by virtue of those who perform their adoration of them.

But Shen Te breaks apart through trying to carry out the mandate of the gods: she can neither be the 'good person' producing Imaginary plenitude, nor can she stop trying to fill out the void in the Symbolic, the lack in the Other. When her second masquerade fails, her hysterical position comes to the fore, for she resists the specified Symbolic identification of 'good person': 'But do you not understand that I am the wicked person whose many crimes you heard described?' (p. 106). She perceives that in order to survive she must sustain a dual masquerade, spoken by the Symbolic when called upon to help, speaking from the Imaginary when in love: 'goodness to others / And to myself could not both be achieved. / To serve both self and others I found too hard' (p. 105). Shen Te is a hysterical subject by the end of the play, asking – Why me? Why do I have this mandate? What does the Other want of me?

So what of Brecht's experiment? Brecht exposes elements which he sees as holding a system in place, showing up their ideological function at a given moment in history. The gods, for instance, are presumed into existence by the disempowered, such as Wang and Shen Te, while the barber Shu Fu and the airman Yang Sun attempt to beat the system on its own terms. Brecht's project in 'historicising' the events is to show how the actions of the individuals derive their meaning from their social and political relations at a specific moment in history. The apparently exotic context sharpens the incongruity of the persistence of these outmoded forms: the estrangement effect of the masks, far from pointing up universal elements of human nature, foregrounds the artificiality of the attitudes adopted. In one performance of this play the masks were dispensed with, the actors slyly pulling at the sides of their eyes, saying 'Look, we're Chinese.' The characters are made to enact their roles in order to disrupt their identification with the capitalist Other, showing in their speech and bodily movements (Wang prostrating himself before the gods, the policeman smugly accepting the cigars) the automatism of these performances. By this gestic means Brecht believes he has been able to historicise the discourse of the body.

Speaking as he is from an Imaginary position in the Symbolic, yet believing himself to be a stable subject, Brecht has failed to acknowledge the constitutive nature of lack. The historicised discourse thus turns into a hystericised one, in that the antagonisms show within the characters as well as between them: the short-lived romance between Shen Te and Yang Sun (depending on her idealisation of the phallic, bourgeois hero and his response to her 'womanly' masquerade) testifies to the impossibility of the sexual relation (Lacan).[18] The hystericised discourse shows that Brecht is not immune to being spoken by the Symbolic, at a level of ambiguity beyond that of the duplicity of capitalism.

NOTES

1 See Terry Eagleton, 'Brecht and rhetoric', *New Literary History* 16 (1984–5), pp. 633–8.

2 See Sara Lennox, 'Women in Brecht's work', *New German Critique* 14 (1978), pp. 83–96; see also Ann Hermann, 'Travesty and transgression: transvestism in Shakespeare, Brecht and Churchill', in *Performing Feminisms: Feminist Critical Theory and Theatre*, ed. Sue-Ellen Case (Johns Hopkins University Press: Baltimore and London, 1990), pp. 294–315 (pp. 302–8).

3 For definitions and explications of the three orders, see the 'Translator's note' in Jacques Lacan, *The Four Fundamental Concepts of Psycho-Analysis*, trans. Alan Sheridan (The Hogarth Press: London, 1977), pp. 279–80, and Malcolm Bowie, *Lacan* (Fontana/Collins: London, 1991), chapter 4.

4 See Joan Riviere, 'Womanliness as masquerade', in *Formations of Fantasy*, ed. Victor Burgin, James Donald and Cora Kaplan (Methuen: London and New York, 1986), pp. 35–44; first published in *International Journal of Psychoanalysis* 10 (1929). For the relation between Riviere's notion of 'masquerade' and Lacan's theory of sexual difference, see Stephen Heath, 'Joan Riviere and the Masquerade' in Burgin *et al.* above, and Ellie Ragland-Sullivan, 'The sexual masquerade: a Lacanian theory of sexual difference', in *Lacan and the Subject of Language*, ed. Ellie Ragland-Sullivan and Mark Bracher (Routledge: New York and London, 1991), pp. 49–80.

5 Emily Apter, 'Masquerade', in *Feminisms and Psychoanalysis: a Critical Diction-ary*, ed. Elizabeth Wright (Basil Blackwell: Oxford, 1992), p. 243.

6 Subsequent quotations from the play refer to page numbers in the *Collected Plays*.

7 For Brecht the plot is exceeded by what he calls the *Fabel*, a term not easily translated, since it designates not only what is narrated but how; see Elizabeth Wright, *Postmodern Brecht*, p. 28.

8 For what immediately follows I am indebted to Jan Knopf, *Brecht-Handbuch* (Metzler: Stuttgart, 1980), pp. 204–8. For a useful source-book of commentaries, documents and reviews of the play, see *Brechts 'Guter Mensch von Sezuan'*, ed. Jan Knopf (Suhrkamp: Frankfurt, 1982).

9 Knopf, *Brecht-Handbuch*, p. 201.

10 Mia Campioni and Elizabeth Gross, 'Love's labour's lost: Marxism and femin-ism', in *A Reader in Feminist Knowledge*, ed. Sneja Gunew (Routledge: London and New York, 1991), pp. 336–97 (p. 371).

11 *Ibid.*, pp. 372–3.

12 See 'Hegemony', in *A Dictionary of Marxist Thought*, ed. Tom Bottomore (Basil Blackwell: Oxford, 1985), pp. 201–3; see also Ernesto Laclau, *Hegemony and Socialist Strategy: Towards a Radical Democratic Politics* (Verso: London and New York, 1985), pp. 93 148 (pp. 134–45).

13 Laclau, 'Psychoanalysis and Marxism', in *New Reflections on the Revolution of Our Time* (Verso: London and New York, 1990), pp. 93–6 (p. 95).

14 See Slavoj Žižek, 'Beyond discourse-analysis', Appendix in Laclau, *New Reflections*.

15 Laclau, *New Reflections*, p. 5.

16 See Slavoj Žižek, *For They Know Not What They Do: Enjoyment as a Political Factor* (Verso: London and New York, 1991), pp. 197–209.

17 There is a distinction to be made between 'ideal ego', the (unconscious) narciss-istic formation, originating in the mirror phase, tied to the Imaginary, and 'ego-ideal', the coalescing of narcissism and collective ideals. It is the difference of how one sees oneself and how one wants to be seen. The gods would like Shen Te, as 'ideal ego' (good person), to re-establish them as 'ego-ideal' (worth looking up to). For a more detailed elucidation of these concepts, see J. Laplanche and J.-B. Pontalis, *The Language of Psychoanalysis* (The Hogarth Press: London, 1973), pp. 144–5 and pp. 201–2.

18 See Lacan, *Encore*, Le Seminaire XX, 1972–3 (Seuil: Paris, 1975); for a translation of the two central chapters, 'God and the jouissance of The woman' and 'A love letter', see *Feminine Sexuality: Jacques Lacan and the 'école freudienne'*, ed. Juliet Mitchell and Jacqueline Rose, trans. Jacqueline Rose (Macmillan: London, 1982), pp. 137–61.

10

ROBERT LEACH

Mother Courage and Her Children

Mother Courage and Her Children was written in 1938 and 1939 at a particularly difficult time for 'progressive' or 'radical' writers, especially those with affinities with the *avant-garde* of previous decades. Politically, in the face of rampant Nazism and fascism, Stalin had decreed that Communists must work for a 'popular front' of anti-fascist forces, which seemed to require artists to seek new forms of 'popular culture'. But in Soviet Russia, there was no such 'popular front', and the slightest deviation from the increasingly tortuous 'Party line' was being viciously stamped on. The Great Terror and the Show Trials silenced all dissent at home and left foreign well-wishers baffled.

Meanwhile, the Party's artistic line caused fearsome debate to rage about the nature of progressive, especially Communist, literature, and Brecht found his own ideas frequently denigrated and his work dismissed in circles where he ought to have felt welcome. The debate centred on notions of 'reality', and the writers' relationship to it. The period of mass industrialisation, as Marx had pointed out in *The Communist Manifesto*, was characterised by 'constant revolutionising of production, uninterrupted disturbance of all social conditions, everlasting uncertainty and agitation . . . '[1] If contemporary life was fragmented and chaotic – and modernist writers and artists agreed that Marx was correct about this – how should they deal with this phenomenon? Various methods were tried: many of the 'isms' of twentieth-century art, futurism, imagism, cubism, constructivism and others, began as fresh attempts to penetrate the fragmentation. The groups usually comprised like-minded artists who wished to work in parallel through the same or similar new techniques, such as montage, interior monologue, factography and so on, and many of the individual artists professed Communist, or at least radical and left-wing, allegiances.

In the 1920s, some of Marx's previously unknown works were published for the first time, edited by Hungarian activist, Georg Lukács, who thus acquired prominence in progressive and Communist literary circles. In 1932, in the pages of the German Communist Party's literary journal *Linkskurve*, Lukács launched a furious attack on the documentary style of the proletarian novelist and Brecht collaborator, Ernst Ottwalt, from a position extremely close to the one that was to be adopted at the Soviet Writers Congress under the influence of Zhdanov in August 1934. The correctness of Zhdanov's position, especially as mediated by Lukács, was perhaps most fiercely debated by those writers and intellectuals who were refugees from Nazism in the mid-1930s, as they questioned their own measure of responsibility for what had happened in Germany. Thus, Alfred Kurella declared in 1937 that 'Expressionism leads to Fascism',[2] while Lukács continued to pillory an ever-increasing number of modernist writers as 'formalists', exempting only a tiny few, such as the extreme futurist Mayakovsky, who had for some perverse reason been accepted into the Stalinist pantheon. Zhdanovian orthodoxy had become pervasive by the end of the 1930s, and Lukács detected signs of repentance among writers such as Feuchtwanger, Döblin and even Brecht who, he announced, 'were making strenuous efforts to overcome ... subjectivist tendencies'.[3]

Brecht replied first in a series of notes and short essays, which were not published at the time. In these he was concerned to point out the anti-Marxist nature of Lukács's criterion of 'timelessness', his reliance on novels to prove his case as against poetry or drama, and his *apparatchik* mentality, which preferred judgement to dialogue. Lukács's cautious welcome of the publication of *The Informer*, a scene from *Fear and Misery of the Third Reich*, made Brecht feel 'as if I were a sinner returning to the bosom of the Salvation Army. At last something taken from life itself!'. As Brecht noted, however, Lukács had 'overlooked' the fact that the play was a 'montage of 27 scenes and ... that it is really no more than a catalogue of gestures'.[4] If Lukács had known the whole work, Brecht implied, he would have dismissed it as 'subjectivist', for to him a montage technique was incapable of revealing the objective relations between the surface appearance of life and the reality of hidden social currents beneath.

Lukács saw the dialectic of appearance and essence as the crucial field for realism, suggesting that the great works of literature created a true-to-life surface but were simultaneously able to reveal the underlying social forces which were not apparent in day-to-day existence. The appearance and the essence reacted together to create true realism; they were the form and the content which made up the work, the thesis and the antithesis of traditional dialectics which found their synthesis in the masterpiece, at least in the cases of his most admired writers, Balzac and Tolstoy. The idea of Balzac and Tolstoy as exemplars for twentieth-century dramatists may seem faintly absurd to us now, but it was dangerously real in the late 1930s. Brecht's second, and more lasting riposte, to Lukács's line of argument was to create the play *Mother Courage and Her Children*, which may be seen as a further and clinching contribution to the argument.

Brecht's 'dialectics' in *Mother Courage* are quite different from Lukács's. Instead of the synthesising of form and content into the whole and rounded work, Brecht presents a spikier, looser number of components which interact dialectically but never synthesise. Brecht believed that Marx's analysis denied the sort of graspable, perhaps static, reality implicit in Lukács's conception. For Lukács, reality was governed by underlying forces which were beyond human control, indeed almost beyond human understanding, but for Brecht this was mystification which vanished when a work's *function*, which Lukács's analysis never contemplated, was considered. Brecht wanted his theatre to intervene in the process of shaping society, so that Lukács's duality of form and content was replaced (to over-schematise briefly) by a triad of *content* (better described in Brecht's case by the formalist term 'material'), *form* (again the formalist term 'technique' is more useful here) and *function*. In Brecht's dramatic form, these three constantly clash but never properly coalesce to compose a rounded whole. (This can be illustrated by the way Brecht's plays tend not to have conventionally acceptable endings: Mother Courage's problems are by no means resolved at the end of this play.)

Thus Brecht's concept of the work's function radically affects his dramaturgy. He is not content to accept, as Tolstoy was, for example, the author's unquestionable omniscience with regard to the reality presented. (Tolstoy's attitude to the Napoleonic Wars may be compared instructively with Brecht's attitude to the Thirty Years War.) Brecht is interested in the author's own relationship to that reality. He sees certain events, and certain attitudes displayed, and uses them as the starting-point. Incomplete, perhaps, they provide gestures ('material') with which to begin. As Walter Benjamin explains,

> The gesture has two advantages over the highly deceptive statements and assertions normally made by people and their many-layered and opaque actions. First, the gesture is falsifiable only up to a point; in fact, the more inconspicuous and habitual it is, the more difficult it is to falsify. Second, unlike people's actions and endeavours, it has a definable beginning and a definable end. Indeed, this strict, frame-like, enclosed nature of each moment of an attitude which, after all, is as a whole in a state of living flux, is one of the basic dialectical characteristics of the gesture. This leads to an important conclusion: the more frequently we interrupt someone engaged in an action, the more gestures we obtain. Hence, the interrupting of action is one of the principal concerns of epic theatre.[5]

The 'interrupting of action' we may describe as the 'technique'. It is specifically the interrupting which Eisenstein called 'montage' and Brecht called
'epic theatre': 'it is the retarding quality of these interruptions and the episodic quality of this framing of action which allows gestural theatre to become
epic theatre', Benjamin concludes.

The technique of interrupting is active and interventionist. For the actor,
it is the justification for the Brechtian rehearsal exercise 'Not this ... but this
...', and for the audience, it is the means by which the world is seen as
changeable, the rise of Arturo Ui as resistible. Imperceptibly, these remarks
about technique have led to a consideration of the function of Brecht's
theatre, which is to 'learn how to see and not to gape, To act instead of
talking all day long'.[6] The interruption therefore is thoroughly 'indiscreet' (a
favourite term of Brecht's: the music in *The Threepenny Opera*, he said,
was to be a sort of 'copper's nark'), serving as a means not only of pointing
up something which a socialist realist play would flow over, but pointing it
up in such a way as to energise the spectator, to stimulate her or him into an
awareness of the possibility for change. Thus, if fragmentary events or attitudes culled from real life form the starting-point for Brecht's play, becoming involved in it, taking part in it, is its end.

Mother Courage is an almost programmatic illustration of this alternative
kind of dialectical theatre, because its power derives precisely from the
relationship between the material, the technique and the function, the
'gesture', the 'interruption' and the 'stimulation'. When Mother Courage
sings 'The Song of the Great Capitulation', for instance, the *material* is the
way we complain to our superiors. From this perspective, the subject of the
complaint is of little consequence, the point is that Mother Courage is complaining – 'They cut everything in my wagon to ribbons with their sabres
and then claimed a fine of five thalers for nothing and less than nothing' –
and the Young Soldier is also complaining – 'Saved the colonel's horse and
didn't get the reward'.[7] The gesture is the gesture of complaining, caught in
two almost random attitudes.

The *technique* of interruption is then strenuously applied. The stage
presents a vivid comparison between the two characters, Mother Courage
stoical and determined, sitting and waiting, and the Young Soldier furious
and energetic, marching up and down, shouting. The scene proceeds crab-
wise, through an unpredictable series of interruptions, which provide a
number of 'frame-like' moments, each highly 'indiscreet'. First Mother Courage's patient determination is interrupted by the entry of the furious Young
Soldier. Then his frenzied stamping up and down is interrupted by the
Scrivener – 'Be seated!' (*The young soldier sits.*) 'And he *is* seated', remarks
Mother Courage wryly. His gesture, in other words, is uncompleted. The

song interrupts the action, and it is worth noticing that the song itself is interrupted several times by the singer's asides:

> Long, long ago, a green beginner
> I thought myself a special case.
> (None of your ordinary run of the mill girls, with my looks and my talent and my love of the higher things!)
> I picked a hair out of my dinner
> And put the waiter in his place.
> (All or nothing. Anyway, never the second best. I am the master of my fate. I'll take no orders from no-one.)

Because the gestures are constantly interrupted, often by means as 'artificial' as a song, we begin to see the material, in this case complaining, in a fresh light. Perhaps complaining to the high-ups is futile? Perhaps it is necessary? The scene has been indiscreet about complaining, and we need to rethink our attitude to it. The indiscretion leads to an understanding of the *function* of the scene, though there is no conclusion in the usual sense of the word. Because both complainers in the scene decide against carrying their complaints through, we should not imagine that Brecht is saying, 'Don't bother to complain, don't rock the boat.' What he is saying is, 'Be aware of what complaining involves' and 'How can complaining change things?'. He is interested in directing our attention towards ways of complaining which will be effective. Brecht does not pass judgement on his characters, he uses their gestures, copied from life and then interrupted, to stimulate us into at least reflecting on the problems which we often express through gestures. This is what is meant by an interventionist theatre, and is precisely opposite to what Lukács required. It is worth noting, however, that the next scene demonstrates that Mother Courage herself has not capitulated in the battle to make a living:

> *Two soldiers are being served at a counter by Kattrin and Mother Courage.*
> MOTHER COURAGE: What, you can't pay? No money, no brandy!

Once we are able to analyse the play in these terms, we understand Brecht's praxis more deeply. He presents us with a series of gestures, warlike gestures, for instance, when Eilif describes his victory over the peasants to his commanding officer in Scene 2, or when the soldiers descend on Halle in Scene 11. Each gesture is pregnant with meaning in itself. Thus, Eilif's gesture of triumph takes the form of 'The Song of the Fishwife and the Soldier', which he sings while 'at the same time [he] does a war dance with his sabre':

7. Helene Weigel as Mother Courage. 'Each gesture is pregnant with meaning in itself.'

To a soldier lad comes an old fishwife
And this old fishwife, says she:
A gun will shoot, a knife will knife
You will drown if you fall in the sea.
Keep away from the ice if you want my advice
Says the old fishwife, says she.
But the soldier lad laughed and he loaded his gun

And he reached for his knife and he started to run:
It's a hero's life for me!
From the north to the south I shall march through the land
With a knife at my side and a gun in my hand!
Says the soldier lad, says he.

The song, sung directly to the audience, is exhilarating (though perhaps Eilif's frenzy may carry a hint that he understands some of the song's irony). He performs before the Commander, who is relaxed and, if not dismissive of Eilif, is merely amused by him, his story providing an excuse for cracking a bottle of Falernian. But our response is further modified by the presence of Eilif's mother, herself a sort of 'fishwife' with some of the same sort of homespun philosophies which Eilif, like the soldier in the song, has ignored. We may nod sagely, and admit the wisdom of the fishwife's advice. But even as we watch Eilif perform, we simultaneously see his mother swindle the cook out of a gilder, forcing him to pay this exorbitant sum for a scrawny old boiling fowl. Moreover, Brecht takes some care to inform us of the social status of each of the characters – Eilif, the private, is trying desperately to impress his phlegmatic Commander, who in turn bawls bossily at his cook. The 'warlike gesture' turns out to contain a multitude of ramifications: the scene is a 'social gest' in Brecht's terms, 'a pregnant moment' in Roland Barthes'.[8]

The meaningfulness of this 'gesture', however, is greatly enhanced when it is recollected, even half-recollected, by the spectator as he or she watches Scene 11, for here is another 'warlike' gesture, but one which presents something quite different from Eilif's vigorous song-and-dance. Brecht presents the attack on Halle obliquely, a fragmentary glimpse of a tiny episode, certainly not the sort of comprehensive overview which Tolstoy, for example, presents of the battle of Austerlitz in War and Peace. Brecht chooses to silhouette a few muddled and rather frightened soldiers creeping about in the night, their furtive plot disrupted by a disabled girl banging on a drum, attempting to wake the town to what is happening. That is all. When Kattrin climbs to the roof to do her drumming, the soldiers are completely nonplussed and the image of their bafflement is unforgettable. It is especially powerful, of course, as a contrast to the pretend bravery of the young man, Eilif, and his boasts earlier. The peasants pray, the soldiers fumble frantically to find a way to get her down and Kattrin goes on drumming.

In the end, they manage to stop her by setting up and firing a musket, a shattering noise which effectively interrupts the drum as the drumming interrupted the soldiers' stealthy advance. Thus does Brecht draw attention to the action itself, the reality of war, and stimulate us to reconsider that, rather than the anecdote of the brave dumb girl. And throughout the play,

Brecht focusses our attention by way of gesture and interruption: peace is interrupted by war; direct address is interrupted by conversation; song by speech, and the method of singing, *Sprechstimme*,[9] is a method of interrupting singing with speaking and vice versa; Mother Courage's failure is interrupted by her success as a businesswoman, her mother's pride by her grief; even the melodrama of the shooting of Kattrin as she drums to awaken Halle is interrupted by comedy:

> 1st SOLDIER: ... Show us which your mother is and we'll see she ain't harmed.
> *Kattrin goes on drumming.*
> THE ENSIGN: *pushes him roughly aside*: She doesn't trust you; with a mug like yours it's not surprising.[10]

In the first scene the would-be recruitment of the sons is interrupted by the sale of the belt, the sale of the belt by the loss of Mother Courage's eldest son; the sale of the capon in the next scene is interrupted by his return, a hero. The bargaining over the capon is echoed by the bargaining Eilif reports he carried on with the peasants, and this series of gestures of bargaining reaches its climax with the bargaining Mother Courage indulges in (for quite understandable reasons) as Swiss Cheese faces the firing squad. The reverberations are almost endless, and they are set up by concentrating on 'pregnant moments' rather than on the more conventional means of unfolding the story.

This method profoundly affects other aspects of the drama, in clear contradistinction to Lukács's precepts. The creation of character was for Lukács one touchstone of a true realist: 'The realist must seek out the lasting features in people, in their relations with each other and in the situations in which they have to act; he must focus on those elements which endure over long periods and which constitute the objective human tendencies of society and indeed of mankind as a whole.'[11] Some years later, looking back at Brecht's mature work, especially *Mother Courage*, Lukács decided that his former opponent had come into the fold: 'Where Brecht's characters had once been spokesmen for political points of view, they are now multi-dimensional. They are living human beings, wrestling with conscience and the world around them. Allegory has acquired flesh and blood; it has been transformed into a true dramatic typology. Alienation-effect ceases to be the instrument of an artificial, abstract didacticism; it makes possible literary achievement of the highest order. All great drama, after all, must find means to transcend the limited awareness of the characters presented on the stage.'[12]

Apart from the magisterial tone, this criticism simply fails to address the problems Brecht is concerned with. For him, 'character need not be completely defined': character is only of interest in so far as it illuminates the fleeting event which provides the writer, or the actor, with a usable gesture. '"This way of joining up", "this way of selling an elephant", "this way of conducting the case", do not altogether add up to a single unchangeable character but to one which changes all the time and becomes more and more clearly defined in the course of "this way of changing".' This does not mean, of course, that 'this way of changing' proceeds smoothly from one kind of human being to another, that the character grows or develops in the usual sense. Indeed, Brecht goes so far as to assert: 'The coherence of the character is in fact shown by the way in which its individual qualities contradict one another.'[13] Thus we are presented in *Mother Courage* with a central character who is basically selfish and uncaring but whose attitude occasionally, especially towards her daughter, is hopelessly sentimental. She is kind – she gives a cloak to the Chaplain, she allows Kattrin to have the red boots – but also unkind – she refuses to give shirts for bandages, and heartlessly she proclaims: 'War is a business proposition: Not with cream cheese but steel and lead.' She is courageous when denying Swiss Cheese, cowardly in her scene of the Great Capitulation. Courage itself is an ambivalent quality: 'The poor need courage. They're lost, that's why. That they even get up in the morning is something – in *their* plight. Or that they plough a field – in war time. Even their bringing children into the world shows they have courage, for they have no prospects.' Mother Courage acquired her name because she 'drove through Riga like a madwoman, with fifty loaves of bread in my cart. They were going mouldy, I couldn't please myself.'

Mother Courage is thus a paradox – clever when selling a capon, stupid when taking the Chaplain's advice to stock up – because Brecht is simply not interested in the kind of character creation Lukács admires. Brecht is concerned to jolt the audience into some kind of reaction, and making fully rounded characters is unlikely to further this purpose. Mother Courage's pigheadedness, which to some critics makes her seem tragic, should be seen as a particular social gest, which Brecht uses at a particular moment. Her 'character' appears so strong because he chooses his frame-like gests carefully and presents them with economy and great vividness. Because each 'pregnant moment' is recognisable and amazing, a spectator is apt to imagine that the character in them is 'convincing' because that is what is usually the case. '"This way of changing" ... hardly strikes the spectator who is used to something else.'[14]

Something of the same is true of Brecht's uses of his source material. For instance, in *Mother Courage* Brecht draws on Grimmelshausen's seventeenth-century novels, *The Adventures of Simplicius Simplicissimus* and

Mother Courage. For Lukács, this is 'the popular, realistic literature of the past'. Referring to Brecht's composer, Hanns Eisler, he comments: 'It may be left to the Eislers of this world to take the book to pieces and estimate their montage value; for the living tradition of German literature it will continue to survive intact in all its greatness ... Only when the masterpieces of realism past and present are appreciated as *wholes*, will their topical, cultural and political value fully emerge.'[15] For Brecht, such a view of Grimmelshausen's picaresque method is not so much inadequate as irrelevant.

Simplicissimus (which, by the way, gave its name to an expressionist journal which Brecht also abhorred) and *Courage* are both chronicles of the Thirty Years War, and both take their protagonists through a series of adventures by means of unrelated but vivid individual scenes. Brecht does not dramatise any of Grimmelshausen's scenes; what he does is to take the tone and the method to create his own parallel story. This can best be seen by comparing scene titles. Grimmelshausen's chapter 27 is headed: 'Courage's husband is killed in battle. She herself escapes on her mule, meets a troop of gipsies and is taken by their Lieutenant for his wife. She foretells the future to a young lady in love, robbing her of her jewels the while. But her success is short-lived. She is soundly beaten and made to give them back.'[16] Compare this with the heading for one of Brecht's scenes: 'Before the city of Ingolstadt in Bavaria Mother Courage is present at the funeral of the fallen commander, Tilly. Conversations take place about war heroes and the duration of the war. The Chaplain complains that his talents are lying fallow and Kattrin gets the red boots. The year is 1632.'

The implicit fragmentariness of these headings suggests that Grimmelshausen, like Brecht, is seeking something other than to be 'appreciated' as a *whole*. It is more profitable to link these two writers with the typical 'popular' style which both might be seen to be working towards, and which is certainly not the same as that of the 'masterpieces of realism'. How far Brecht understood popular tradition in an intellectual sense may be open to question[17] but he was never guilty of writing about the 'sturdy realism of folk art' composed by 'true sons of ancient Homer',[18] as Lukács does. The true popular tradition is characterised by such features as non-psychological characterisation, as in melodrama and the Italian *commedia dell'arte*, and by montage techniques, as in music hall or circus. The actual true sons of Homer are those singers of tales described by Albert Lord, and their fundamental techniques are precisely these.[19]

These sung tales, or ballads, generally depend for their meaning on their montage, which is how *Mother Courage* also impinges on the spectator. Montage is a rhythmic device which exposes reality or truth in a specific manner. In *Mother Courage*, Brecht is particularly concerned with the relationship between the 'little person' and the major forces of history, as Lukács argued the great realists were. But by breaking up the flow of the drama, by fragmenting the totality and using montage, interruptions, non-psychological characters and gestures, Brecht confronts the spectator not with reality itself, but with attitudes towards reality. Bourgeois society, like Lukács himself, tends to present institutions and transactions as beyond our powers of control ('The pound rose on the foreign exchange markets as a result of share price movements'). Brecht's theatre aims to undermine this response precisely through techniques described by Lukács and Zhdanov as 'formalist'.

NOTES

1 Marx and Engels, *Manifesto of the Communist Party* (Foreign Languages Publishing House: Moscow, n.d.), p. 51.
2 Ernst Bloch, *et al.*, 'Discussing expressionism', in *Aesthetics and Politics* (NLB: London, 1977), p. 16.
3 See Georg Lukács, 'Realism in the balance', in *Aesthetics and Politics*, pp. 58–9.
4 *Ibid.*, p. 58.
5 Benjamin, *Understanding Brecht*, p. 3.
6 *The Resistible Rise of Arturo Ui*, p. 96.
7 This and following quotations (except where noted) from *Mother Courage and Her Children*, trans. Eric Bentley (Methuen: London, 1962).
8 Roland Barthes, *Image-Music-Text* (Fontana: London, 1977), p. 73.
9 'As for the melody, he (the singer) must not follow it blindly: there is a kind of speaking-against-the-music which can have strong effects, the results of a stubborn, incorruptible sobriety which is independent of music and rhythm. If he drops into the melody it must be an event; the actor can emphasize it by plainly showing the pleasure which the melody gives him.' *Brecht on Theatre*, p. 45.
10 The quotation here is from *Collected Plays*, where the translation is more pointed than Bentley's.
11 Lukács, 'Realism in the balance', p. 47.
12 Lukács, *The Meaning of Contemporary Realism* (Merlin Press: London, 1963), p. 88.
13 *Brecht on Theatre*, pp. 124, 56, 196.
14 *Ibid.*, p. 56.
15 Lukács, 'Realism in the balance', pp. 55–6.
16 Hans von Grimmelshausen, *Mother Courage* (The Folio Society: London, 1965), p. 8.
17 See his dubious, and politically motivated, definitions in 'Popularity and realism', in *Aesthetics and Politics*, p. 81.
18 See Lukács, 'Realism in the balance', p. 55; also Völker, *Brecht: A Biography*, p. 257.
19 See Albert B. Lord, *The Singer of Tales* (Harvard University Press: Cambridge, Mass., 1960).

11

DARKO SUVIN

Heavenly food denied: *Life of Galileo*

A REACTIONARY MASTERPIECE?

Brecht's *Life of Galileo* is probably his most popular single work, both on stage and in print: in German, it outsells all other works by Brecht (2.4 million copies up to 1990). Yet it is also by far the most heavily rewritten of all his plays, with at least one turnabout in the ultimate horizon and intended message; Brecht was never quite comfortable with it; and he died in the middle of directing its rehearsals, not having (as I shall argue) fully resolved the play's horizon. The harsh vocabulary in his note of 25 February 1939, three months after writing the first version, can be taken as valid for all the extant versions:

> LG is technically a great step backward ... too opportunistic. One would have to rewrite the play totally if one wanted to have this 'breeze that comes from the new shores', this rosy dawn of science. All more direct, without the interiors, the 'atmosphere', the empathy. And all directed toward planetary demonstration. The composition could stay the same, the character of Galileo too. (*AJ*, 1, p. 32)

Though Brecht all along believed with good reason that the final self-condemnatory speech of Galileo's could – 'with a strictly epic performance' – subsume the empathy into this great figure under the necessary estrangement (*AJ*, 1, p. 27), he was aware that centrally significant ambiguities remained. A sketch of the three main versions, usually called the 'Danish', 'American' and 'Berlin' versions, may be useful here.

The first version, written with the help of Margarete Steffin in Denmark

In addition to the abbreviations *GW* (*Gesammelte Werke*) and *BT* (*Brecht on Theatre*) this essay uses *AJ* (for *Arbeitsjournal*) and *LG* for the play in all its three versions. Quotations from the text are, with occasional modifications, from the Sauerlander and Manheim translation (*Collected Plays*, vol. v, pp. 3–98). All other translations are my own.

(1938/9) and performed in Zurich (1943), was fed by various sources, notably by Georgi Dimitroff's final plea in the 'Reichstag fire' trial staged by the Nazis in 1933, where he compared them to the Inquisitors vainly trying to suppress Galileo's truth. The play's horizon is one of skilful tactics against the rulers, as discussed in Brecht's seminal essay 'Five difficulties in writing the truth' (GW, XVIII, pp. 222–39). But already here Galileo is a rich and somewhat contradictory figure who has both betrayed science and smuggled out the *Discorsi* via Andrea. A rewriting begun in 1944 in California was completed in intimate collaboration with Charles Laughton, who financed the play and played Galileo in Los Angeles and New York (1947). From the outset (see AJ, II, p. 411) Brecht decided to strip Galileo of any valid excuse for his treason, now seen as one against the people rather than simply against the scientific profession; this was brought into sharpest focus by the A-bomb explosions over Japan. The 'American version' is thus diametrically opposed to Brecht's first ideas to write a 'learning play' (*Lehrstück*) about a sly anti-fascist saboteur biding his time, still strongly present in the Danish version. Enriched by many splendid particulars, the American is also a stripped-down 'stage version' (AJ, II, p. 446), published only in English and cannibalised after 1947 into the third 'Berlin version', which restores many cuts and adds further details and focussing gained through three months of rehearsals. Clearly, the rewriting was unfinished, yet firmly orientated toward the overall horizons of the 'American version'. Thus LG exists with two main horizons: the 1930s 'LG 1', where Galileo is a sinner against Reason who is not only more sinned against than sinning, but also finally redeemed by the *Discorsi*; and the 1944–56 'LG 2', where this overwhelming central figure is not merely an extrapolation from – or to – Oppenheimer but primarily the Epicurean intellectual destroyed as person and as politically liberating potential by class society outside and inside him. LG 1 can be called a finally optimistic People's Front version, LG 2 an integral if 'awful warning' -type socialist version with undigested remnants of LG 1.[1] This will be further argued below, where I am throughout referring to the final, 'Berlin' version.

The textual history may provide a clue why Brecht did not fully come to terms with the story: for example, in the world of the play there is no evidence that Galileo was at the time of his trial strong enough to withstand the state apparatus, so that I do not see how this story could illuminate a fall from supremely useful to alienated and co-opted science. Brecht himself noted that the play has two themes: first, 'that in this societal formation the thirst for knowledge grows perilous to life, since it is developed and punished by society', and second, 'the decisive difference' between 'pure' and socially revolutionary science (AJ, II, p. 465). Though the latter theme was preferred by him at the time of actual and potential A-bomb use (as well as of abuse of the 'science' of Marxism), the text strikes a deep chord in all spectators concerned with intellect versus power, with people caught between the institutionalisations of power and of knowledge. Therefore, I shall explore the relative weight of the first theme. This will be done, first, by means of a brief survey of the play's agential system and of its plot. Second, I shall interpret Brecht's insistence on the story (*Fabel*) by not limiting it to the linear sequence of events but stressing its metaphoric system(s).[2]

AGENTIAL SYSTEM AND PLOT OF *LG*: THE KNOWERS AND AUTHORITY

I propose that the thematic domain of *LG* is the pursuit of knowledge in class society: science should be knowledge making life for (the) people easier, but it is alienated by ruthless pressures of authority into 'pure' or specialised knowledge disregarding people's pursuit of happiness and the very existence of humanity. The play's strong polarisation between the life-furthering and death-dealing camps starts from an updated Leninist model of society, yet the contradictory Galileo, protagonist and indeed emblematic representation of the positive potentials, partakes of both poles and finally moves from the positive to the negative one; so does Andrea, his shadow and one-sided successor. The goal of 'productive' or 'critical' science for the people is not attained, the corruption of the (potential) best has resulted in the worst. Beyond individualism and in spite of the surface 'illusionism' or realism, Brecht's constellation of dramaturgic agents returns – as usual – to a stance akin to folk-tale, baroque or medieval narration. Here, it is a quest story (such as the Grail one); but the quest fails. The two camps are opposed as Knowledge and Authority, as central institution of power with a basis in the ruling classes (here the Catholic Church and landowners) against a budding counter-establishment around Galileo which never allies itself with its potential political basis (here the popular classes). Galileo's troop or 'brotherhood' best reveals the parabolical nucleus of Brecht's agential system, a neo-Marxist version of morality play. Of the three disciples, Federzoni the artisan is popular practice, the peasants' son Little Monk popular ethics, while Andrea's impressionable, subaltern curiosity contributes the element of 'pure' knowledge, easily channelled into élitist specialisation when sundered from the first two. Integral science should fuse these three facets, but Galileo privileges the third over the second.

This is why his debate with the Little Monk (Scene 8) is compositionally and ethico-politically the central scene of the play.[3] Scenes 1–7 and 9–13 can be called Galileo's 'two campaigns', with epic repetition and foreshortening

– the first a protracted offensive resulting in failure at Scenes 7–8, the second (after an eight-year interval) a briefer one culminating in the carnival Scene 10 and resulting in final protracted failure (11–13); after a nine-year interval, Scenes 14–15 provide the epilogue and summation. Further, the Knower's offensives and defeats modulate between an euphoric and dynamic atmosphere where Cognition dominates (roughly, Scenes 1–3, 6 and 8–10) and a dysphoric and enclosed one where Authority dominates, as well as between public and private spaces: Galileo is at home in the space of scientific experiment, cut off after Scene 9; he may even infiltrate the authoritarian space (e.g. in Scenes 2 and 6), just as the unruly Carnival people briefly takes over the streets, but the two never fuse in plebeian politics, so that he ends confined in a closed space of total surveillance by authority, prefigured by the space of the plague, but now wilfully repressive. Finally, the underlying tensions are built up by a rich texture of echoes between and variations on figures, objects, events, gestures and locutions, most significantly in the metaphoric systems of seeing and nourishment (see *Short Organum*, p. 63, *BT*, pp. 198–200).

A mature Marxian allegory differs from a Christian one in the dialectic of contradiction which runs not merely between the camps but also inside each camp and indeed some key figures. Pope Barberini himself is shown, in the magnificent robing scene, as devolving from goodwill toward science to reification by the power apparatus; in the Knowledge camp, the Little Monk is won over from static casuistry to dynamic understanding of ebb and flow, while Andrea's orientation and exile perpetuates Galileo's corruption and fall into political isolation. All such dramaturgic agents partake of the characteristic Brechtian bipolarity, which is of a piece with the dominance of concrete and changing situations rather than of an individualist, static Self.

SEEING AND EATING: THE ENCOMPASSING METAPHOR OF HEAVENLY FOOD

LG is dominated by discussions about proper looking. Its central objectification, the telescope, visually dominates the two periods of Galileo's scientific 'offensive', while the imaginative referral to looking through it is almost ubiquitous. In all significant cases, this semantic field concerns – in the very first words we hear from the state – 'the light of knowledge' (*GW*, III, p. 1231): it is a metaphor for understanding and cognition. Though it encompasses also the old, Ptolemaic or passive seeing according to which Man is seen by God and the world is a stage, Galileo's stance, building upon the telescope's making visible the invisible, is that people must decide how to see the world. I shall treat these references first as a series of drawn-out metaphors and as a 'metaphoric theme' leading to a complex seeing in and of *LG*. Second, I believe they fuse with the metaphoric theme of nourishment into a common tenor, the duality of food for the stomach and food for the mind. In a traditional vocabulary I shall call this possibly central cognitive organon of *LG earthly and heavenly food*.

RIGHT SEEING AND WRONG SEEING: THE TELESCOPE, THE BATTLE OF THE BOOKS, THE LIGHT THAT FAILED

An opposition between right seeing and wrong seeing is established from the opening instructions of Galileo to Andrea; *glotzen* (to gape) – Brecht's favourite swearword at stupidity since his early plays – is connected with passive acceptance of surface impressions such as the sun's daily movement. However, the opposition is not simply one of surface versus inner truth. Right or good seeing depends on the pertinence of the object chosen for investigation, on the kind of interest at stake: in Scene 2 (the telescope demonstration) the senators look at women, an appetising lunch and fortifications, while Galileo notifies Sagredo that the moon has no light of its own and may prove Copernicus' hypothesis, and that the Milky Way is composed of uncountable stars. But right seeing is not simply a matter of seeing 'facts', as Galileo implies in his more ingenuous or demagogic moments. Barberini notes, praising Galileo's sly metaphor of apparent shore movement from ship, that 'What we see ... need not be correct ... But what is correct, to wit, that the Earth turns, cannot be observed! Clever' (p. 49). Correct seeing is slyly indirect, like the sun's flaming image thrown onto the screen in Scene 9 and subjected to sceptical questioning. It depends also on the model or hypothetical framework used: the chair carried round the washbasin and the apple with embedded splinter in Scene 1 are as correct as the Copernican wood-model, but the Ptolemaic astrolabe breaks in Scene 4. Obversely, even a very plausible hypothesis is not enough unless it is in feedback with proof through observation: *seeing* the rough edge of the moon becomes meaningful only after this is *explained* as gigantic mountains; only then can 'heaven be abolished' (p. 19). Even more impressive is the black-out in the middle of this scene, signifying the verification of Jupiter's moons by a computation using astronomic tables. Denoting the passage of some hours by scenic convention, the interruption also connotes, in an exemplary estrangement (*Verfremdung*), the waning of the crystal spheres and of the whole medieval image of the world. The antonym to gaping is thus a union of theoretical knowledge (the calculation) and of correct, heretofore unheeded observation. It is an active process of checking the abstract by the concrete, and vice versa – a Baconian induction/deduction which is well defined, by contraries, when Aristotle fails such a verification, since the needle floats (Scene 9). All of this is meant when Andrea in the play's last speech exhorts the boy (the *posteri*, those who come later – including us) to 'learn to open your eyes'.

Galileo's insistence on the importance of things seen for the first time is systematised by him into a general epistemological and political principle in the dispute with the Court Schoolmen:

> The moons of Jupiter don't lower the price of milk. But they have never been seen before, and yet they exist. The man in the street will conclude that a good many things may exist if he only opens his eyes! . . . doctrines believed to be unshakable are beginning to totter, and we all know that there are far too many of them. (pp. 35–6)

Right seeing is correlative to an alliance with the people or assumption of the view from below, to the sceptical draught from the new coasts 'that lifts even the gold-braided coats of princes and prelates', revealing empty heavens (p. 5). The people is deeply interested in change, in news that 'somebody's seen a pear growing on an apple tree' (p. 68). It also understands power relationships in society (as witness Mrs Sarti's exemplum of her bringing the dinner to Galileo, p. 25), and its Singer takes the authority of Galileo's telescope as a look into an at least semi-serious future upside-down world of plebeian self-government. This metaphoric theme culminates in one of the greatest moments in a play that abounds in great moments, Scene 8, in which the Ptolemaic and the Copernican seeing are brought to earth and grounded in the daily lives of the great popular mass. The Little Monk sees the peasants' terrible daily grind as assuaged by the belief that the eye of God upon them makes sense of it (cf. the upper-class variations on that eye in Scene 7). Galileo dismisses that as the psychology of exhaustion caused by the upper classes' wars and economic exploitation, even while 'the greatest machinery before our eyes', the heavens, could provide the model for machines making their toil unnecessary and the earth fertile – provided one could 'see [not only] the divine patience of your people' but also 'their divine wrath' (pp. 57–8).

The telescope leads the spectator into this domain, but it remains occasionally ambiguous and finally neutralisable. Andrea's first look through it confirms the church's monuments, 'the copper letters: GRACIA DEI [on the campanile]' (p. 15). The telescope alternates between crassest exchange-value and use-value. In Scene 3, Galileo crosses the divide into alienating his daughter by refusing her a look through it; in the same élitist vein, Andrea in the next scene lets go the chance of having the boy-duke look through it. Perhaps only the heroic high points of the work on the phases of Venus during the plague and on the sunspots, and the Carnival scene where – the

only time in the play – it is shown how the people 'directed the telescope at
... princes, landlords, priests' (p. 93), are free of such ambiguities. The telescope is also caught in a network of rich oppositions to other stage objects
and visual metaphors: the wooden models of world-systems, the household
objects used for heliocentric demonstrations, the water-bucket, the much
discussed (and in 1947 back-projected) instruments of torture, the globe. But
its most significant relationships may be those to two other kinds of 'seeing
machines' or heuristic organons – the right and wrong *books*.

From the scene where Galileo repeatedly begs the court pseudo-scientists
to look through the telescope, while they will trust their eyes only when
reading Aristotle (p. 31–6, prefigured on pp. 12–13), an impression may arise
that correct observing through optical instruments is in this play opposed to
a wrong world-view arrived at through books. This is not so, for Brecht had
a clear understanding of the theory–practice feedback loop. Like the telescope, writings are organons whose use depends on the pragmatic context
of user-subject, focus-object and interests served. *LG* is a play polarised,
among other things, between two founding texts, the old Aristotle and the
new *Discorsi*. Aristotle is bad because irreconcilable with observation and
used by the ruling class as a substitute for, and indeed bar to, a proper
'seeing for oneself' (p. 5; see also the pompous use of the world-as-a-book
metaphor by the Procurator, p. 16). Furthermore, Aristotle is confined to
Greek or Latin and thus esoteric – for the rulers and their ideologists only. It
was the fate Brecht most feared for Marxism,[4] and this political aspect
dominates the seeing and writing tropes of *LG*. Even the *Discorsi* grows
negative, a sign of treason to the people and to science, when Galileo dis-
sociates it from the popular 'pamphlets against the Bible': 'I've written a
book on the mechanism of the universe, that's all. What people make or
don't make of it is no concern of mine' (pp. 75–6).

On the contrary, books that can help the glance through the telescope to
understand reality are precious: they are spiritual food always compatible
with material food. The play opens with Galileo's request to Andrea: 'Put
the milk [and bread, DS] on the table but don't shut any books', while the
Florentine Court party refuses equally the telescope and Mrs Sarti's pastry.
Galileo's own book is flanked on the positive side by texts he cites from
Horace, tending to prove the aesthetic necessity and quasi-erotic pleasure
(Priapus!) of self-governing scientific enquiry. The Bible is ambiguous:
popular pamphleteers as well as the Carnival crowd take Galileo to be a
'Bible-buster', while he sincerely says that the Bible is (with Homer, and one
presumes Horace and the mathematical tables) his 'favourite reading'
(p. 75). Galileo can quote scripture for his own purposes at least as well as
the cardinals, as exemplified by the battle of proverbs in the ballroom scene;

a respectful Christian critic can therefore exclaim that Brecht seems to have studied biblical hermeneutics. The telescope can be used as commodity, toy and military instrument; equally, Galileo's *Discorsi* becomes in his final interview with Andrea a 'curse'. It occasions one of the most important formulations and condemnations in the whole play (and one of the most Brechtian, though of Benjaminian origin):

> Oh, irresistible sight of the book, that hallowed commodity! The mouth waters and the curses are drowned. The Great Whore of Babylon, the murderous Beast, opens her thighs, and everything is different! Hallowed be our haggling, white-washing, death-fearing community! (p. 93)

Such a play-length complexity issues in the final question of whether the supremely important manuscript with which Andrea crosses the border is a good or bad vector to the future.

A final cluster within the theme of seeing is that of *blindness* (or *myopia*) *versus light*. Weak sight is physical: physics stands here for cognition and ethics, a traditional use from Oedipus and Tiresias on, but this cluster also allows for temporal development. Galileo is at the beginning a Sun Hero, the knight of 'the clear light of science', and he formulates its remarkable credo:

> Sometimes I think: I'd let myself be locked up ten fathoms below ground, in a dungeon to which no light filters through, if in return I could find out, What is light? And the worst of it: What I know, I must tell others. Like a lover, a drunkard, a traitor. It's an unalloyed vice, I know, and leads to ruin. (p. 59)

This orientation is counteracted not only by outside repression but also by general human frailty ('Face to the stars we are like worms with dim eyes that see very little', p. 14) and by Galileo's particular failing, which compounds a sharp focus on immediate material advantages with political blindness (see Sagredo's cautions, pp. 23 and 27, and Mrs Sarti's on p. 67). Such hints grow into an avalanche after Galileo's political fall. Waiting for his arrival from the Inquisition dungeon (which is, like his final internment, an ironic inversion of the one he almost wished for so that he might understand light), his disciples at first vainly trust that 'no force can make unseen what has been seen' but later refuse to see him (pp. 83–4). And in our final glimpse of Galileo we find out that his eyes are quite dim and that his recantation has led Descartes to 'stuff his treatise on the nature of light into his desk drawer' (another dungeon). Brecht the director commented: 'Galileo is sitting in his jail, and he has not found out what light is.'[5] In this scene Galileo gives forth his final Bible citation: 'If thine eye offend thee, pluck it out.' At its end, the daughter to whom he had told, when he refused to let her look through the telescope, that the night was clear or bright, repeats that to him, now at her mercy. Myopia and blindness mean a self-caused imprisonment in isolation from the people; knowledge about (insight into) nature will become a curse unless accompanied by knowledge about society.

FOOD OF THE STOMACH AND OF THE MIND

The references to food and eating are less numerous in *LG* than those to seeing, and they are as a rule found either directly or not too indirectly linked to seeing. It seems useful to take a cue from Galileo's indignant declaration, 'I despise people whose brains are incapable of filling their stomachs' (p. 26), and divide these references into food for the stomach and for the mind. The former are supposedly literal and the latter certainly metaphoric. This means that occasionally the same tenor can have a literal and a metaphoric vehicle, as is the case with the two apples from the Tree of Knowledge, one conveyed by Andrea's stage object in Scene 1 (which he doesn't eat in order to repeat the demonstration for his mother) but the other conveyed by the Little Monk's 'gobbling down' the manuscript of Galilean physics in Scene 8. Here this alimentary parallel to gaping – the Brechtian *fressen* famous from *The Threepenny Opera* but as important in some other plays[6] – is judged positively: gobbling is the reverse of goggling. The encompassing metaphor of the play, that of heavenly food, is arrived at by fusing the references and metaphoric series of food and of seeing as cognition. In that sense, even the literal references to food belong here at least by semantic contagion.

The common denominator or analogical ground between eating and seeing-cum-thinking is that both are sensual pursuits as well as pleasures centred in the brain.[7] It is often shown and expressly stated in the play that Galileo likes to eat. He also likes to think, for 'Thinking is one of the greatest enjoyments (*Vergnügungen*) of the human race' (p. 24), and 'his thinking comes out of sensuality' so that 'he can never say no to an old wine or a new idea' (p. 80). As if to prefigure this judgement by the new Pope, almost the whole Scene 9 is a counterpoint of Galileo's delight in Sicilian wine and in the possibility of sunspot investigation opened up by the dying of the old Pope; in places, this delight both issues in an approximation to a poem in prose centred on the drawn-out metaphor of pleasurable degustation and mimics that degustation verbally. Heavenly and earthly food are here in a feedback loop: each helps the other. Galileo thinks better when he has breakfasted (and his back is being rubbed by Andrea after a body ablution which also ushers in the great 'aria' on the new times): 'Galileo ... *works* in a sensual way' (GW, XVII, p. 1127). Conversely, the Jupiter moons had a chance to foster the correct stance of scepticism and innovation and thus indirectly affect the price of milk; the people wanted to use the tele-scope for expropriating the expropriators of 'the fruits of science'. Yet at the end Galileo must note that the scientists had failed in transferring proper seeing from heavens to earth, so that 'credulity still dooms the struggle of the Roman housewife for milk' (p. 94).

The melding of gustatory and intellectual appetite is Galileo's dominant 'gestic stance' (*Gestus*). If anything is clear in *LG*, it is that the proper stance of the ideal spectator is to admire this horizon of a consistent Epicurean praxis. As in the plague scene, Galileo needs both the mathematical tables (food for the mind) and the bread and milk (food and drink for the body). The play, however, teaches how and why, in class society, those pursuing knowledge cannot, in direct proportion to their significance for the system, have both. In theological language appropriate to this upside-down, Feuer-bachian creed: Galileo cannot save both body and soul, he is being forced to choose. Barberini told him so, rightly if cynically, in the ballroom ante-chamber scene, which is introduced by the chorus as wining and dining him, although all we see is food for the brain being perverted. It is the parable of the Roman she-wolf's children:

> Two little boys, the story goes, received milk and shelter from a she-wolf. Ever since then all the she-wolf's children have had to pay for their milk. In return, the she-wolf provides all manner of pleasures, heavenly and earthly; from conversations from my learned friend Bellarmine to three or four ladies of international repute, may I show them to you? (pp. 49–50)

Opposed to this upper-class parable is Galileo's desire to enjoy the fleshpots *and* the science (p. 26). In class society, this constitutes an insoluble antagonism within both the world's body and the protagonist's representa-tive body.[8]

A further irony is that (as Brecht put it *à propos* Mother Courage) he who sups with the devil needs a long spoon. Galileo's weak eyes are both literal or bodily and metaphorical or cognitive: giving up the soul did not quite save even the body. At the end he not only writes the *Discourses* at the expense of his eyesight and bodily comfort, but both his brain and his stomach are strictly controlled: the brain has to deliver to the archbishop recurrent commentaries on the church's ideological saws, the stomach is delivered only poor food vetted by the church (except for the mysterious geese – but even those he cannot have properly, with apple and thyme). The two are expressly linked by Virginia's demanding the comments in exchange for the vegetables and cheese as well as by Galileo's snide praise of the church's charity soup instead of higher pay for the workers; both are finally debased by the manner in which the erstwhile heavenly food is consumed.

THE KNOWER, THE PEOPLE, AND UTOPIAN
DE-ALIENATION FOR US

If *LG* works mainly by analogy, as a parable, its overriding tenor or meaning is the *defeat of a pursuer of knowledge in class society*. Galileo's central trait (like that of Joan Dark and arguably of Brecht) is, 'I've got to know it'; but the pursuer does not become a purveyor of life-furthering knowledge. What is the reason and the meaning of this defeat? Has Galileo come 'objectively' too soon, or has he merely missed (or even, as emblem of a *trahison des clercs*, upset) the boat of a realistically possible plebeian revolution? Is he (and are we) living at a time of the societal revolution's difficult but exhilarating rise – splendidly shown from the great 'aria' of Scene 1 to the joyous experimentation of Scene 9 – or of its difficult and depressing decline – as in the gloomy second part of *LG*, where blindness prevails over (in)sight. In the latter case, Galileo could not have done more than he did, and his work is (for all secondary vacillations) heroic; in the former case, he could and should have done significantly more, and he is (for all secondary declarations) a traitor. In the latter case the spectators can learn from Galileo by heroic extrapolation, as from an 'optimistic tragedy'; in the former, by contraries foregrounded in his speech of self-condemnation, as in a black comedic chiasmus. Brecht's '*LG* 1' was written against the heroic horizon, though characteristically it was a 'heroic cowardice'.[9] In '*LG* 2', under the enormous impact of the atom bomb (but also of Stalinism), he decided for the horizon of betrayal. Yet this horizon has never been fully established, despite all the rewritings. The consequences of such an inconsistency are partly good, adding to the richness of Galileo's contradictory characterisation – and making the play palatable to bourgeois audiences, from liberals to post-modernists – but largely bad, adding up to a confusing oscillation between praise and condemnation, extrapolation and analogy, Aristotelian and Brechtian dramaturgy.[10]

Galileo's downfall, we are told, stems from not having openly allied himself with the rising classes. This makes him a very interesting anti-hero: one who gave up the fierce wholeness of desire by giving in to, and internalising, the terrible pressures of the environment. In this case it is the noble desire to enjoy both earthly and heavenly food, the militant, future-oriented knowledge for the people *and* the triumphant, instant gluttonous satisfaction for oneself. His dilemma is a variant of Shen Te's: how is one to be good to others and oneself too? In Brecht's stern version of poetic justice, he will end up having neither: a punishment for the new hubris of having refused the salvific alliance with the people. However, just who and where are the rising lower classes? The answer is, I fear, that a power nexus sufficient for a cognitive decision about the representative knower's historical chances of success is *not shown* in *LG*. The play does not dynamically, gestually connect the scientific troop and the lower classes. Brecht's brief touches impressively characterise the dramaturgic agents who represent the people. But there is no people as an – even repressed – coherent array (and not simply a suffering and sometimes dangerous mass) in *LG*. The stupendous dialogue with the Little Monk about the Campagna peasants does not quite compensate for this lack of gestual and notional connection. The wonderful and very gestual Carnival scene comes and goes without much relation to what precedes and follows. The only evolution in lower- or middle-class characters can be seen in Andrea and Virginia who – like Galileo himself – grow away from the people as a political subject. This is in stark divergence to the presentation not only of Galileo and his troop but also of the ruling classes, who are sketched in economically but at times dynamically, showing how they interconnect and form a coherent political subject – say, the church's and the landowners' interests; the link between the Cardinal Inquisitor and Virginia through her confessor.

The double alienating split within the revolutionary body politic (intellectuals versus physical workers) as well as within the representative protagonist's sensuality (thinking versus eating), is irreparable in the world of *LG*. No tinkering short of a rewrite, not even Brecht's late addition of Vanni, can change this. The play functions as an awful warning demonstrating a twofold alienation – that of the sensual microcosm and political macrocosm. On the macrocosmic side, 'the question is not the planets, but the Campagna peasants' (p. 57) and the Roman housewives: will intellectuals spur them to become their own lords and masters? Within science this would mean reintegrating into it the Little Monk's question about the effects of ethics on science. On the microcosmic side, the question is how to unite the outgoing pleasure of seeing and the ingesting pleasure of eating. Taking these two as reverse sides of the same utopian coin, the question may be phrased as: *how can an ethico-politically alert, formalised but practical science help the working people to see and understand, thus to become self-managing subjects who can unite earthly food and scientific seeing in the pleasures of the mindful body* – as prefigured by the initial Galileo. Everyone to realise his or her own Galilean potentials: nothing less than this is Brecht's immodest, revolutionary utopian horizon.

Finally, the play's two themes of the endangered knower and the corrupted science fuse in Galileo's being a physicist (cf. *AJ*, I, p. 177). In this roundabout way, the Brechtian insistence on science as a modern form of destiny can be recuperated for interpretation. The play's upshot is to raise in us the overarching question; what is knowledge – science, or any systematic cognition such as perhaps gourmandise (love of good fare) – for? Is it a life-furthering science for the people or a death-dealing science for the ruling classes? Establisher of (individual and collective) integral pleasure or total destruction? Heavenly food or demonic possession?

The other major example of unresolved oscillation in *LG* is the powerful final scene. I have argued at length[11] that Scene 15 itself opposes a victorious Sun Hero to the Dark Age – stupid authority looking for forbidden books and superstitiously cruel children; and that this is appropriate to '*LG* 1', where it stems from, but not to '*LG* 2', where Andrea is the emblem of science devolving into a 'race of inventive dwarfs' (*GW*, III, p. 1345) and witches are seen instead of heavenly bodies. Does the decisive manuscript Andrea is smuggling prefigure Marx or Teller? Should the spectator say yes or no to it (today without Brecht's restriction to 'bourgeois')?

> In *Galileo* the moral is of course in no way absolute. Had the bourgeois societal movement which uses him been shown as a descending one, he could have safely abjured and accomplished by this something quite reasonable. (See *Yea-Sayer* and *Nay-Sayer*!) (*AJ* II:500).

I believe Brecht had finally not made up his mind. In 1948 he treated science (Galilean and Marxist) as critique and learning, 'the most important pleasure of our age' (*AJ*, II, p. 518); in 1954 he had concluded that 'the term [scientific age], as commonly used, is too polluted' (*GW*, XVI, p. 701).

Thus, the vehicle of Brecht's parable shows at the end how the frustrated knower of Scene 14 and the frustrated people of Scene 15 are already in a kind of zombie, death-in-life state. But the utopian tenor, for us, not only remains unscathed but even gains in force by horrifying contrast to 'What if this goes on?' In that sense, Brecht's fable is necessarily unfinished:

> How long
> Do works endure? As long
> As they are not completed
> . . .
> Useful works
> *Require people . . .* (*Poems*, p. 913)

NOTES

I wish to thank the SSHRC of Canada for a research grant and a Leave Fellowship in 1986–7 when the spadework for this essay was done. Much of the essay reproduces in abbreviated form material from my article originally published in *The Brecht Yearbook* 15, pp. 187–214. Permission to use it is hereby gratefully acknowledged.

1 For some of the best comments on the play, see Hans Bunge (and Hanns Eisler),

Fragen Sie mehr über Brecht (Rogner and Bernhard: Munich, 1970), here particularly p. 252.

2 For the argument that metaphoricity underlies all narrativity, see Suvin, 'On metaphoricity and narrativity in fiction', in *SubStance*, no. 48 (1986), pp. 51–67. For a more detailed analysis of sight and food metaphors in *LG*, see Suvin, 'Brecht's parable of heavenly food', in *The Brecht Yearbook* 15 (1990), pp. 187–214.

3 Compare Rainer Nägele in *Der Deutschunterricht* 23, no. 1 (1971), pp. 86–99, who however seeks to establish rather too strict analogies between pairs of scenes on either side of the axis of Scene 8.

4 See Brecht's 'Driven out with good reason' (*Poems*, pp. 316–17), and Pierre Deghaye, *Galilée et le mysticisme astral* (différence: Paris, 1977), chapter 6. Deghaye (pp. 42–4) is the Christian critic cited in the next paragraph.

5 Käthe Rülicke, in Werner Hecht, ed., *Brechts 'Leben des Galilei'* (Suhrkamp: Frankfurt, 1981), p. 141. Rülicke's observations on Brecht's directing of *LG* (pp. 91–152) are valuable.

6 See Suvin, *To Brecht and Beyond*, chapter 5.

7 Brecht here inverts the alimentary metaphorics of the Christian tradition – forbidden fruit, last supper, hunger and thirst after righteousness, earthly food (milk, meat, bread, wine) and food of eternal life etc. – at the same time as he latches on to a materialist tradition, beginning with the classical 'salt' as food and acute reason, that was at its strongest in France (Feuerbach was the torchbearer in Germany).

8 Galileo's refusal to be introduced to the courtesans seems to me part of a deliberate system of Brecht's. In *LG*, food or thinking is a 'seduction' (*GW*, III, p. 1256), and 'the urge to research' is a 'violent desire for pleasure' parallel to 'the urge to reproduce' (*GW*, XVII, p. 1109). Yet, except for a single stanza from the Singer's wife in the carnival scene, sex – the major sensual rival to food – is absent from *LG*. If one were to treat the play naturalistically, this would invite concern about the historical Galileo (a man with many paramours and children) or about the dramatic character's relationship with Mrs Sarti, neither of which makes any sense. Still, the absence of erotics from practically all of Brecht's major plays deserves attention.

9 See Reinhold Grimm, 'Ideologische Tragödie und Tragödie der Ideologie', in Siegfried Melchinger *et al*, eds., *Das Aergernis Brecht* (Basilius P: Basel, 1961), p. 112.

10 See Hans Mayer, 'Galilei, Brecht und die Folgen', in *Festschrift für E. W. Herd* (University of Otago Press: Dunedin, NZ, 1980), pp. 167–79.

11 See Suvin, 'Brecht's *Life of Galileo*: scientist extrapolation or analogy of the Knower?', in *Forum Modernes Theater*, 5, no. 2 (1990), pp. 119–38.

12

MARIA SHEVTSOVA

The Caucasian Chalk Circle: the view from Europe

Written between 1941 and 1944 during Brecht's exile in the United States, *The Caucasian Chalk Circle* is made up of two stories, Grusha's, which starts in Scene 2, and Azdak's, which does not begin until Scene 5, the penultimate scene of the play. These two stories converge in Scene 6 where the problems that had been posed at the outset and highlighted throughout the sequences involving Grusha are resolved, thus bringing the whole action to a more or less 'happy' end. Since happy endings are not characteristic of Brecht's drama, this particular example of harmonious conclusion to anything but harmonious events (and to anything but a transparent argument) has prompted a number of commentators to draw special attention to the 'liberating, life-enhancing quality' of the play or its 'unified understanding'.[1] The scholars who emphasise the joyful, morally affirmative and/or politically optimistic outlook provided by the play's dénouement are usually also the ones who believe its two stories are organically linked. Their opinion runs counter to the authoritative view of John Willett and Ralph Manheim for whom the work is an 'awkward combination of two largely unrelated stories', despite which it is nevertheless 'a truly epic work embodying many of Brecht's special ideas, tastes, and talents'.[2]

Disagreement over the play's structure and its implications for the meaning of the whole is an inevitable consequence of Azdak's arriving so late in the piece. By this time Grusha's story has almost run its course. The revolt led by the fat prince against Georgi Abashvili, Governor of Grusinia, has taken place, as a result of which the Governor is executed. Meanwhile his wife has fled without all the dresses and shoes she had hoped to salvage, accidentally leaving behind their child Michael. Grusha has gone through a night vigil watching the sleeping child who was abandoned by his nurse, this second abandonment duplicating the egotistical and fear-ridden behaviour of Michael's biological mother. After a tableau intended to suggest her conflict over whether or not to take Michael, Grusha decides to take him, and heads for the northern mountains in order to save Michael and herself from the soldiers who support the Palace revolt. Before this decisive moment occurs, however, Grusha has a short and oblique exchange with Simon, from which it transpires that they are in love and will wait for each other till the end of the war. To all intents and purposes the war has been raging for some time and, although treated with indifference by the governing élite, as indicated early in Scene 2, has indiscriminately swallowed up the common people represented emblematically by Simon, several anonymous soldiers and one or two voices among the beggars and petitioners who illustrate the Singer's opening account of the desultory life and times of Georgi Abashvili. The picture of war, Princes' revolt and Palace Guard mutiny is complicated by the carpet-weavers' uprising and the riots that have broken out in the outer town – these latest events implying that a revolutionary situation has flared up in counterpoint to the *coup d'état*. All this, where Grusha's story is interwoven with Grusinia's history, is sketched in with rapid, bold strokes by the Singer's song-commentaries, the succinct segments of dialogue between different speakers and the stage directions which, together with the songs and dialogue, are fundamental not only to the play's narrative but to its dramatic action as well. In other words, telling, contextualising, showing and doing are not separate occurrences but coincide in the same play-section or frame.

The sociopolitical circumstances in which Grusha takes flight are foregrounded in Scene 3. Here she buys milk for Michael, her reactions to the peasant selling it indicating that his price is exorbitant. She deceives the aristocratic women, whom she meets by chance, so as to get Michael onto a carriage that only wealthy fugitives can afford. (The women are somewhat euphemistically described in a stage direction as 'elegant ladies'.) When this attempt to offload him for his as well as her own good fails, she leaves him on a peasant woman's doorstep. The latter, when face to face with the Ironshirts in pursuit of Grusha, betrays the very child she had coveted as long as neither loss nor danger was to be incurred in having him. Each incident builds up the narrative and allows the reader or spectator to grasp the point that Grusha, for all her pragmatism and common sense, is also motivated by care and concern for those needing them, even though she manifests this kindness in an elementary rather than intellectually developed or emotionally refined way. Hence Brecht's idea of her as a 'sucker'.[3] When she is confronted, in turn, by the Ironshirts whose bullying corporal is about to seize Michael, Grusha hits the offending corporal over the head, seizes the child and escapes once again. Grusha's own song, together with those of the Singer and the musicians, explain how she has bonded with Michael through their shared hardships and has at last consciously and deliberately decided to keep him, this act of knowledge and awareness contrasting greatly with the deterministic way in which events imposed a 'decision' on

Grusha in Scene 2. Furthermore, it is by now clear that *keeping* Michael is a qualitatively different phenomenon from *taking* him.

From the point of view of plot, then, the process of learning undergone by Grusha is indispensable for what follows. Grusha goes toward the ravine, crosses the rotten bridge against all odds, and leaves the pursuing Ironshirts and stranded merchants behind her. Scene 4 shows her putting up with abuse from her brother's wife, marrying an apparently dying peasant in order to have a roof over Michael's and her head, meeting Simon some years later who thinks the child is Grusha's son and, as the scene ends, running after the Ironshirts who have finally caught up with Michael and are carrying him off to Natella Abashvili. Grusha, who has become Michael's mother by deed, confirms to the Ironshirt berating her that he is her child. She had just denied this to Simon, thereby telling Simon a truth which he mistook for a lie. Grusha's story is suspended on this latest in a whole host of paradoxes which, besides being necessary for the plot, demonstrate the interconnection between individual actions and the social situations that give them sense and meaning – even in a world that seems to have lost all sense and meaning.

What the plot sets up, in fact, is a social dynamic between the numerous figures that appear and drop out of sight. Consequently, instead of simply displaying relationships between individuals, each group of figures is animated by the interaction between social classes that constitutes social relations as such. In other words, as is typical of Brecht's corpus, encounters between individuals are informed by the interests, habits, assumptions and aspirations pertinent to the class, or social group within a given class, to which the individuals interacting with each other belong. In this way, Brecht shows that what may be thought to be a purely individual action is social through and through.[4] The social relations presented in *The Caucasian Chalk Circle* are not considered to be generically 'human' and, therefore, true for all time. They are embedded in the specific conditions of war, and so on, outlined above. The peasant who cheats Grusha, a servant from his own class, does so on the grounds that war engenders economic hardship. To his mind, this justifies profiteering and exploitation irrespective of who is being exploited, fellow peasant or gentry. Moreover, the peasant's lack of compassion for Grusha shows that there is no 'natural', self-evident or intrinsic class solidarity between them, any more than there is anything 'naturally' greedy about him or 'naturally' maternal about her. A similar line of reasoning is evident in the scenes with the innkeeper. The innkeeper can get richer quicker from the opportunities provided by the war. While doing so he also acquires the power of contempt over his superiors, whether they be morally superior (Grusha) or superior by pedigree (the 'ladies'). The traits distinguishing him socially from the aristocratic women whom he fleeces, on the one hand, and Grusha, to whom he shows as little mercy, on the other, are exacerbated by the conditions in Grusinia. Put differently, this means that the rules of commerce which shape his world view in times of peace now work more efficiently for his benefit. The satirical sketch of capital accumulation drawn here is repeated with relevant variations in Scene 4, where the merchants hide their merchandise. Their gesture is a class sign: they have goods to run away with while Grusha has none. Although the movement is done quickly (and the image arising from it held briefly), its meaning in terms of the social interplay evident up to this moment is quite clear. By the same token, the aristocratic women's recoil from Grusha's cracked servant's hands is an extremely eloquent social sign-gesture.

The social dynamic of Grusha's story does not rely on inward-looking, psychologically detailed explanations for this or that motive or this or that outcome. Everything is communicated outwardly, through what happens when it happens rather than through states of mind and soul. And this is precisely why Brecht, when mounting *The Caucasian Chalk Circle* with the Berliner Ensemble in 1954, used his theatre's turntable stage to such great advantage by having all changes of setting during Grusha's journey through the mountains come towards her.[5] The changing landscape highlighted the main events of the narrative; and, of course, events in any story involve the actions of protagonists. The motion of space in time (the passage of time being suggested on stage, as in the text, through narrative sequence) allowed the spectators' gaze to fix on the external conditions that gave rise to, and accounted for, not only Grusha's but everybody else's actions, all of them demonstrating something about each other.

How external manifestations or surface appearances have to be taken at face value is brought out admirably in the vignettes dealing with Grusha's marriage to Yussup the peasant, surely among the funniest scenes in twentieth-century theatre. Grusha's brother has to get rid of her because 'people are already talking about a child with an unmarried mother' (p. 47). Her future mother-in-law needs her to work on the farm because Yussup is supposedly dying. Grusha, who has told Michael that 'being poor and cold as well puts people off' (p. 46), has no alternative but to accept the arranged marriage which might as well be a funeral. In the words of the roguish monk who, like the guests, is more interested in food and guzzling than sentiments, either a 'hushed Wedding March or gay Funeral Dance' (p. 52) would be suitable for a situation in which one thing and its opposite are both true. When Yussup, in a fantastic *coup de théâtre*, suddenly sits up because he hears that the war is over, the extraordinary activities reach a mock climax. The audacity of this scene is entirely consistent with the energetic 'grotesque realism', as Mikhail Bakhtin describes Rabelaisian laughter, of the stream of vignettes creating the whole.[6] The war may be over, 'but the soldiers on both sides are the losers', and 'only one side's bigwigs can win' (p. 53). At the end of Scene 4 this transparent critique of war is repeated by the Singer, whose song of battle and of soldiers dying is a third-person account of Simon's experiences. The statements made by the song in a matter-of-fact way about things as they are (that is, at face value) replace once again the first-person accounts and personalised viewpoints of characters to be found in psychological theatre or in what Brecht termed 'dramatic theatre' (sometimes 'bourgeois theatre'), Ibsen being, more often than not, the example he loved to hate. Similarly, Grusha does not give direct expression to her thoughts. The Singer narrates what, in 'dramatic theatre', would have been a reply to Simon. He also tells about Grusha's feelings ('unhappy girl', p. 60), her departure for the city in search of Michael, and the impending trial initiated by the 'real' mother.

Enter Azdak. Although Azdak's entrance is abrupt, it has been anticipated in three ways: through the Singer's narrative ('On the Judgement Seat sat Azdak', p. 60); through the tone of the wedding–funeral (whose comic and vibrant 'grotesque realism' is intensified in Scenes 5 and 6 which are dominated by Azdak); in the figures of Yussup and the monk whose ingenuity, resourcefulness and cunning make them reduced versions of Azdak, minus Azdak's passion for justice. Besides which, Azdak is essential for the resolution of a tale that hinges on a decision about Michael. It would be impossible, for all these reasons, to separate Azdak's story from the rest. In addition, the guests at the wake–celebrations tell of how the Grand Duke, who had been deposed earlier on, was now being restored to power with the help of the Shah of Persia. Persia was the enemy with whom Grusinia had been at war. Azdak, the Singer says at the beginning of Scene 5, hid an unknown fugitive in his hut when the Princes' revolt first broke out. The stranger then turns out to be the Grand Duke, foe of the people of Grusinia but friend of their enemy the Shah. Thus an event that occurs in the past, at the time Grusha's story begins, unobtrusively links Azdak's story to hers.

Furthermore, the theme of war is quite pronounced throughout, acting as a linking device between the relatively wide range of events taking place. How, in war, an alliance between rulers takes precedence over the welfare of the ruled is a recurring motif in Scene 5. Nowhere is this particular motif more explicit than in the zany mock trial announced as the 'People of Grusinia versus Grand Duke' (p. 70). Azdak, who plays the role of the Duke, almost immediately adopts the role of his accusers. By playing two roles in one he is able to satirise the rulers all the more sharply. As the Duke he admits that he had the war conducted by his Princes. As the Duke's accusers he affirms that 'if people realize Princes talk same language as Grand Dukes, may even hang Grand Dukes and Princes' (p. 71). The focus, in both cases, is the allied interests of rulers. Azdak continues his burlesque, which doubles as an indictment, with 'Princes have won *their* war'. The war, from the point of view of the people, was lost: 'War lost only for Grusinia, which is not present in this court.' Azdak's biting joke reinforces his judgement against the Grand Duke. The same judgement is extended to the fat prince whose increasing hysteria, albeit having a comic purpose, is to be interpreted as a confession of guilt. Azdak's judgement (the term meaning both 'analysis' and 'condemnation') also reiterates the judgement of the guests at Grusha's wedding (representatives of the 'people') concerning the alliance between lords against them. Whether the lords are from Grusinia or Persia is immaterial. Their alliance is a *class* alliance. When the chips are down, the ruling classes will bury their differences and hold firmly together. The term 'people' not only evokes the idea of a mass or crowd, but also implies the existence of a collective subject who, instead of being a leading protagonist in the fate of Grusinia, has been sold out by whoever was in control. Azdak suggests nothing less in the fake trial where real (and serious) judgements are made.

The war trial concludes with yet another contradiction when Azdak the rascal is made a judge. The rest of Scene 5 presents selected moments in Azdak's career which demonstrate, always with enormous humour, how he deals with trickery, blackmail, greed and mendacity in order to bring justice to the poor. The case of the old woman who receives, as if by magic, a gift of a stolen cow and ham from the robber Irakli is a deliciously outrageous example of how Azdak turns so-called normal juridical procedures upside down: he rewards the needy and oppressed and those who, like Irakli, break the law to help them, and punishes those who think only of protecting their property and money, which are commodities protected by the law. In the words of the Singer and his musicians, 'To feed the starving people / He broke the laws like bread ... Two summers and two winters / A poor man judged the poor' (p. 80). The segment with the old woman is also of paramount importance because it firmly links the theme of justice, which emerges from Scene 5 as a matter of *social* justice rather than of legality or of the letter of the law, to the theme of war introduced at the very beginning of the play. The connection between the two themes is clinched when Azdak, in unusually lyrical mode, likens the woman to 'Mother Grusinia, the woebegone ... whose sons are at war' (p. 79).

The poignancy of this moment is short-lived. Azdak swiftly reverts to his boisterous, unseemly, hard-drinking self, his persona recalling pell-mell the mock-kings, wise fools, ribald monks, mountebanks, jugglers and so on, filling the topsy-turvy world of carnival as Bakhtin identifies it for the Middle Ages and the Renaissance. Bakhtin's concept of carnival, besides referring to a whole range of activities that, in his view, define popular culture, entails the idea that carnival is the means by which the popular classes criticise and subvert the established social order. Parody and inversion are the forms most commonly used to deride the status quo. Carnival, then, is a time of freedom for the people when it seems possible to abolish hierarchies, eliminate inequalities, thwart monolithic powers – in short, construct an enlightened world. The network of issues involved in Bakhtin's 'carnival' is useful for understanding what commentators on Brecht generally concede to be an extraordinary, though sometimes puzzling, scene. Azdak, when perceived as a carnivalesque folk hero, helps us to understand Brecht's vision of a society where the 'have-nots', as his hero calls them, can at least begin to have and also change institutional structures, as Azdak does.

Scene 5 concentrates on Azdak's reign. It begins at the same time as Scene 2, when war, popular insurrection (the carpet-weavers' revolt) and civil war force Grusha to escape with Michael to the mountains. It ends as Azdak's story dovetails with Grusha's story. Scene 5 could be described as a flashback that, although not a flashback on Grusha from within her tale, nevertheless cuts into it, as if from the outside looking in. This interruption does not occur simply because Brecht disliked linear narratives. It happens so that the connecting links between the two tales can suddenly jump into view. Two years have passed when Scene 5 ends. Scene 6 focusses on the present, that is, at the point of time when Grusha and Azdak meet and when, consequently, their stories fully converge. The linchpin holding their stories tightly together is the test of the chalk circle by which either Grusha or Natella who, in the meantime, has been demanding the return of Michael, will be proclaimed by none other than Azdak the true mother of the child.[7]

It is not long before Natella's hidden motives are revealed. She needs Michael to unblock the revenues of her estates, capital and greed going hand in glove, as they have throughout the play. Grusha, for her part, loves Michael. Azdak, who has understood the situation perfectly well, generates a good deal of suspense by his tricks and pretences which finally goad Grusha into a tirade against him. Grusha mistakenly assumes that he is in collusion with Natella and her lawyers and therefore with the ruling classes they represent ('But you've let yourself become their servant. So that their houses are not taken away, because they've stolen them', p. 92). Grusha also takes Azdak to be the watchdog of a legal system devised by rulers for their own ends ('But you're on the look-out, otherwise they couldn't drag our

8. Ernst Busch as Azdak and Angelika Hurwicz as Grusha in the Berliner Ensemble's 1954 production of *The Caucasian Chalk Circle*, designed by Karl von Appen.

men into their wars'). Once again the themes of war and justice are brought together.

From here on, Grusha and Azdak's combined story rapidly comes to a close. The chalk test is carried out twice. Grusha refuses both times to pull Michael out of the circle because she cannot bear to hurt the child that she has raised. She proves by her action that the true mother is the caring mother, and so gets the child. Azdak divorces her from the peasant she has married. She is now free to marry Simon. Natella loses her estates. The city gains a garden for children. Justice is done for the just. The unjust are undone. Even so, the play does not close on an unqualified happy ending. The feudal order of the Grand Duke is restored. Grusha and Simon have to leave town. Azdak, the harbinger of social change, disappears, never to be heard of again except in legends and folk-tales – or in Brecht's theatre.

What, then, is to be made of the epilogue/moral of the story that confirms Azdak's judgement? The moral is: 'That what there is shall belong to those who are good for it, thus / The children to the maternal, that they may thrive; / The carriages to good drivers, that they are driven well; / And the valley to the waterers, that it shall bear fruit.' The reference here to the waterers of the valley recalls Scene 1 which is like a prologue to *The Caucasian Chalk Circle*. The scene tells of a dispute between two collective farms in Georgia shortly after the Second World War. One group of peasants wishes to resettle the valley where they had previously produced excellent goat's cheese. They had moved their goat-herds, albeit on advice from the authorities, at the approach of Hitler's armies. By doing so they effectively abandoned the land to the enemy. The other group wishes to irrigate the valley for orchards and vineyards. Its members are partisans who defended the valley against the Nazi invasion. The problem is amicably solved, the valley going to those who had fought and suffered for it and would nurture the land and, literally, make it grow. It is, of course, significant that life-giving water will be brought to the land. The performance prepared for the occasion is 'The Chalk Circle', a Chinese legend revised to fit a chapter of Georgia's medieval history and which, the guests are told, bears on the problem at hand.

Now, such a legend actually exists. Brecht uses it in conjunction with folk-tale elements from the European tradition (quests, journeys, obstacles that must be surmounted, chance events that prove to have been there by design, 'magical' solutions, and other folk-tale qualities permeating the play). And he uses the legend to give the prologue, the core of the work (which is the play within the play connecting Grusha and Azdak's stories) and the very short epilogue summing up the proceedings, the aura as well as the authority of folk-wisdom. The prologue is a framing device. But its tale of the valley is analogous with Grusha's tale which, as we have seen, fits into Azdak's. The structure is that of Chinese boxes (or Russian dolls?). The epilogue/moral draws its full sense and meaning from this interlocking structure.

Furthermore, although Brecht adapted the Chinese legend to suit his purposes (in the legend, for example, the biological mother is the nurturing mother), he appears to have kept the general drift of its moral and philosophical argument.[8] Just the same, he gave it a new dimension by transposing the argument to a war context. This meant that the argument now had quite a different resonance, its reach going well beyond the area covered in the original. The war context at issue is not confined to old Grusinia, Brecht's fantasy name for Georgia. It incorporates modern Europe. Scene 1 underlines this fundamental point by detailing the time and circumstances in which the play within the play, and the lessons to be drawn from it, take place. The context is a Europe that has only just begun to emerge, in ruins, from the Nazi onslaught. Since the whole of *The Caucasian Chalk Circle* is an interlocking structure, what is relevant to one part of it is relevant to another. Thus Scenes 2 to 6, which are in a completely different time-frame, lock into Scene 1, thereby superimposing their setting of international war, civil war, upper-class strife and popular uprising on Scene 1. The reverse also holds, Scene 1 superimposing its pattern on the design of the scenes behind it. This composition may well illustrate the collage and montage techniques discussed by Brecht in his writings on the theatre and which he claimed were the essential components of his work. What is certain is that the process of capturing heterogeneous elements in one Gestalt-like image has the effect of bringing past and present together, each throwing into relief and illuminating the other. It is worth recalling, in the framework of this argument, that Brecht, when discussing with Eric Bentley a projected volume in English translation including the *Chalk Circle* and *Galileo*, thought it useful to point out to his American disciple that the plays 'were written in times of revolution and world war'.[9] Brecht's remark suggests that the 'times' bear on the meaning of *Chalk Circle* irrespective of the distance created twice over by its appeal to a fourteenth-century Chinese model, on the one hand, and a fictitious medieval Georgia, on the other.

Given the preceding observations, it would be reasonable to argue that, whatever else it may be, the *Chalk Circle* is an allegory not from a Chinese or Caucasian perspective, but from a European viewpoint, of Europe in revolution and war; further, that Brecht uses the legend of the chalk circle to make some indirect, discrete comments on the post-war settlement and division of Europe planned for after the defeat of Germany. Talk of a post-war settlement started between Churchill and Roosevelt as early as 1941 when the Atlantic Charter was drawn up outlining the principles 'on which a post-war settlement might be based'.[10] Discussions about the dismemberment of Germany were under way by 1943, agreement on the subject, according to most historians' accounts, being reached relatively easily by Churchill, Roosevelt and Stalin at Teheran (which is in the Caucasian region) in November of that year. Similarly, discussions about zones of occupation took place before decisions were finally approved at the Yalta conference (again in the Caucasus) in February 1945. Meanwhile de Gaulle, who had been excluded from these deliberations, was anxious to have France participate in the divisions and settlements of Europe, especially because the future of Germany would affect the future place of France on the continent.

In the light of Brecht's acute awareness of events and debates in Europe while he still lived there, whether in Germany, or later in exile in Denmark, Sweden and Finland, it would be perfectly appropriate to assume that he kept his ear to the ground (and to the radio) for information on Europe during his exile in the United States. News was all the more likely to have crossed the Atlantic because of America's forestalled, but nevertheless anticipated, entry into the war. Apart from such factors beyond Brecht's control, there was the control he exercised in respect of his own political choices. Politics was the driving force behind Brecht's exile in America. And exile is bound to have sharpened his perception of Europe. But, although extenuating circumstances made their impact, Brecht had taken his position against Nazism for communism. This is why insisting upon his anti-militarism as if it were an abstract phenomenon and not rooted in a specific time and place with specific reasons for explaining it is inadequate. Reluctance to concede that Brecht's anti-militarism is steeped in anti-nazism and anti-capitalism which, in *The Caucasian Chalk Circle*, at least, looks like a populist, even utopian-populist version of communism, marked the reception of his plays in general, in Western Europe as well as the United States, straight after the war. It also marked the reception of the Berliner Ensemble's production of the *Chalk Circle* in Paris in 1955. This response has kept on reappearing in studies of Brecht since then, and will doubtless keep on reappearing now that the fall of communism in Europe and the advent of an integrated capitalist Europe post-1992 appear to be giving licence to all forms of dismissal, Brecht's particular variant of utopian communism included.

Whatever the future of Europe may be, the countries of Europe in the scenario provided by *The Caucasian Chalk Circle* are like Michael and Grusha – or the valley and its fruit-growers – in one. The 'Golden Age' of Grusinia (p. 96) at the time of Azdak is quite different from the age envisaged in Scene 1. This second age had not yet come about at the time Brecht was writing his play. He believed, though, that it should come about and that, with effort and care, alias proper nurturing, it might even come about, if only for a short time, and will continue to inspire others to aspire for it.

NOTES

1 Jan Needle and Peter Thomson, *Brecht*, p. 205, and Darko Suvin, *To Brecht and Beyond*, p. 181.
2 Introduction to the play in *Collected Plays*, p. xiii.
3 Brecht, 'Notes on *The Caucasian Chalk Circle*', *Tulane Drama Review*, 12, no. 1 (1967), p. 95.
4 The indelibly social character of all human action – gestures, words, activities, attitudes and so on – is integral to Brecht's much discussed, often maligned and sometimes confused notion of *Gestus*. For an interesting use of this notion see Elin Diamond, 'Brechtian theory/feminist theory: towards a gestic feminist

criticism', *The Drama Review*, 32, no. 1 (1988), pp. 82–94. There can be no doubt that, if Brecht is useful for feminist criticism, he is indispensable for the sociology of the theatre. For related observations, see my essays on 'The sociology of the theatre' in *New Theatre Quarterly*, 5, nos. 17 and 18 (1989).

5 See John Fuegi, *Bertolt Brecht: Chaos, According to Plan*, p. 148.

6 Bakhtin, *Rabelais and His World* (Indiana University Press: Bloomington, 1984). Subsequent references to Bakhtin are also to this book. Bakhtin's notion of space-in-time, or the 'chronotope', would be extremely helpful in understanding the narrative structure of *The Caucasian Chalk Circle* and the reliance of this structure upon the organisation of space, always with precise reference to time, in the play. See Bakhtin, *The Dialogic Imagination* (University of Texas Press: Austin, 1981), pp. 84–258.

7 Fuegi, *Bertolt Brecht*, p. 134 noted that Brecht, in his 1954 staging, had Ernst Busch play the Singer as well as Azdak, which had the effect of linking the various parts of the play together. As I suggest in my essay, what appear to be disconnections are a clever illusion, a 'brechtism' designed to throw mud in our eyes so that, when cleaned, we can use them all the better for seeing with.

8 For a detailed examination of Brecht's debt to Chinese legend and, it seems, the play by Li Hsing-tao based on it, see Antony Tatlow, *The Mask of Evil*, pp. 291–302.

9 See Brecht, *Letters 1913–1956*, p. 412.

10 James Joll, *Europe Since 1870: An International History* (Penguin: Harmondsworth, 1976), p. 425.

3
THEORIES AND PRACTICES

13

CARL WEBER

Brecht and the Berliner Ensemble – the making of a model

In October 1946 Brecht wrote from American exile to his oldest friend and collaborator, the designer Caspar Neher: 'It would be nice if the Theater am Schiffbauerdamm in Berlin, for instance, were available to us again.' The war and Hitler's reign over, Brecht had set his mind on getting a theatre of his own and finally achieving what must have been an ultimate goal that never before had seemed attainable. In a letter to Neher of December the same year, he stated: 'I'm convinced that we'll build up a theatre again.'

It took Brecht little more than two years to realise his ambition. In April 1949 the East Berlin authorities, that is, the Politburo of the Socialist Unity Party, agreed to provide the financial support for his project: a company under Brecht's artistic guidance that was to be managed by his wife Helene Weigel as 'Intendant'. She would also be the company's leading actress. His plan to take over the Theater am Schiffbauerdamm, however, had to wait until the company in residence would move into the Volksbühne theatre, still to be rebuilt from its ruins at Luxemburg Square. The Intendant of the Deutsches Theater, Wolfgang Langhoff, offered Brecht his two houses, the Deutsches and the Kammerspiele, as a provisional home where the company could perform two to three times a week.

At the Deutsches Theater there was already a Brecht play on the boards since 11 January 1949: *Mother Courage and Her Children*, in a production co-directed by Brecht and his old friend Erich Engel (who had staged the legendary *Threepenny Opera* of 1928 at the Schiffbauerdamm), with Helene Weigel in the title role. The triumphant reception of the opening, by the audience as well as critics from all four occupied zones of Germany, had probably been the decisive event for the authorities' consideration of Brecht's Berliner Ensemble project.

During the protracted and often difficult negotiations, Brecht had complained in his journal about 'the foul breath of provincialism' he encountered in a meeting with the party's establishment. Nevertheless, the socialist government granted him the wherewithal to explore – with collaborators of his choice – the concept of 'a theatre for the children of the scientific age', as he had called his paradigm for a new theatre. Before he finally took up residence in Berlin in May 1949, Brecht had tested the waters for his project at the Zurich Schauspielhaus as well as the revived Salzburg Festival but, due to political and/or economic reasons, neither place could offer a situation even remotely comparable to the one in East Berlin. It was partly because of such options that Langhoff made the generous offer to share his theatres with the new Ensemble. He, like the leading critic and old promotor of Brecht, Herbert Ihering, and other friends, was worried Brecht might turn elsewhere with his project. The chance to participate in the building of a first socialist state on German soil must have been irresistible to the Marxist playwright, even while he recognised many of the mistakes made in this effort to create what he held to be the only desirable society of the future. Still, in a journal entry of 7 May 1949, Brecht concluded a little poem describing his new residence in East Berlin with the line: 'On top of the cupboard containing my manuscripts / My suitcase lies' (*Poems*, p. 416). He continued his efforts to obtain an Austrian passport, which he received in 1951, and when he heard in June 1949 that the production of *Mother Courage* was being considered for a National Prize Second Class, he let the government know that he would refuse it. Two years later he received the First Class Prize.

In the spring and summer of 1949 Brecht and Weigel put together their company, using members of the *Mother Courage* cast as a nucleus while adding actors known to Brecht from the years before his exile, such as Gerhard Bienert, Erwin Geschonneck, Therese Giehse (who had been the Mother Courage of the Zurich première in 1941), Leonard Steckel (the Zurich Puntila of 1948), Friedrich Gnass, and later Ernst Busch. There were others he had met after the war in Switzerland, like Regine Lutz (also of the *Puntila* cast), and Hans Gaugler (who had played Kreon in Brecht and Neher's 1948 staging of his *Antigone* adaptation in the Swiss city of Chur), as well as a number of actors Brecht discovered at various Berlin theatres. Eventually the company was an eclectic mix of older actors from leftist theatres of the Weimar Republic, others who were products of the Nazi theatre, young performers, many of them trained in East German conservatories where Stanislavsky's method was the guideline, and also several actors from amateur groups. Brecht made insistent efforts to attract a number of famous exiles to his new company, among them Erwin Piscator, Peter Lorre, Fritz Kortner, and Elisabeth Bergner, but regrettably only the director Berthold Viertel and the actor Curt Bois accepted their old friend's invitation. Brecht succeeded, however, in assembling a collective of artists with whom he had worked during different periods in his life, among them the director Erich Engel, the designer Caspar Neher, the composers Paul Dessau and Hanns Eisler, the Danish writer and director Ruth Berlau (who had developed the concept of model books for Brecht's productions) and Elisabeth Hauptmann, his closest dramaturgical collaborator before they both had to leave Germany in 1933.

Brecht had scant confidence in theatre schools; he firmly believed in learning-by-doing and began to gather a group of young directing assistants and dramaturgs. Benno Besson and Egon Monk joined the Ensemble in 1949 and soon became directors with the company, as did Manfred Wekwerth, who arrived in 1951 and eventually was to be the Ensemble's artistic director, from 1977 to 1991. Peter Palitzsch was hired from the Dresden Volksbühne in 1949 as the company's principal dramaturg; he designed the famous Berliner Ensemble logo which, as a neon sign, can still be seen slowly turning at night on the roof of the Theater am Schiffbauerdamm. There were also Lothar Bellag, Hans Bunge, Klaus Küchenmeister, Käthe Rülicke, Peter Voigt, Carl Weber and others, who came as assistants and eventually became directors and/or dramaturgs with the Ensemble. Though Brecht hardly intended to create a school, the substantial number of young theatre artists who worked under his guidance as directing, dramaturgy and design assistants, plus the many apprentice actors hired by him or Weigel, were all later to exert a pervasive influence on the German theatre during the second half of the century.

To avoid foreseeable scheduling conflicts with Langhoff's company at the Deutsches Theater, the nearby ruins of a former army barracks were partly rebuilt as a rehearsal hall, containing a stage that duplicated the measurements of the Deutsches, a small auditorium, some office space and a property shop. Here, in Max Reinhardt Strasse, Brecht had his office and conducted rehearsals, while the Ensemble's official address was Luisen Strasse 18, around the corner, where Weigel's office, the administration and the dramaturgy were housed.

Company and staff assembled, the Ensemble started its first season in September 1949 with rehearsals of the opening production. On 12 November 1949, the curtain with Picasso's dove of peace (the emblem Brecht had chosen for his new company) rose for the Berlin première of *Mr Puntila and his Man Matti*, directed by Brecht and Erich Engel, with set and costumes by Caspar Neher and music by Paul Dessau; as in the Zurich première, Puntila was played by Leonard Steckel. The performance was received 'with much laughter and many curtain calls' as Brecht noted in his journal. He added, however, 'It is only as much epic theatre as can be accepted (and offered) today . . . But when will there be the true, radical epic theatre?'. Five years later he was to speak of a 'dialectic theatre' which had subsumed the features of the 'epic'; Brecht regarded the earlier term as too limiting fully to define his envisioned new theatre.

During his first visit to Germany since 1933, in August 1948, Brecht saw a performance at the Constance theatre and grimly stated to his friend Max Frisch: 'One has to start from point zero again!'. The Berliner Ensemble was intended to be such a new start, the model for a rebuilding of German theatre culture from its ruins. It was a task that, according to Brecht, was not so much a matter of mortar and bricks as of aesthetics and philosophy. Brecht had designed a master-plan for his company, and the three productions following the successful *Puntila* were to demonstrate his programme.

There were three specific traditions he wanted to pursue:

Drama that presented the agenda and history of social revolution.
Plays from the classic and modern repertory which critically probed class society, to be staged in new radical readings.
Comedies from the German and international theatre to establish a tradition which, in comparison to other cultures, the German theatre was lacking, as Brecht was not alone in feeling.

Brecht had intended to open the company's first season with a play from the revolutionary tradition, the adaptation of Nordahl Grieg's drama about the Paris Commune uprising of 1871, *The Defeat*, or *The Days of the Commune*, as was the title of the text that Brecht and Ruth Berlau had prepared in Zurich. Copyright problems, however, and the predictable ideological reservations of the party made Brecht opt for *Puntila*, which also seemed to be a likelier crowd-pleaser. Comedy as a satirical treatment of the class struggle, rather than revolutionary drama, was thus the first public presentation of the new Ensemble and eventually would dominate its repertoire. The second production, which opened only six weeks later, presented an example of modernist critical realism, Maxim Gorky's *Vassa Zheleznova* with Therese Giehse in the lead. This was also a gesture towards the Russian military administration where Brecht had ardent supporters in the cultural officers A. Dymschitz and I. Fradkin. The director Berthold Viertel conducted rehearsal in a manner greatly different from Brecht's; he insisted, for instance, on full identification of the actors with their parts. Brecht was not at all averse to having such work done with his young company and made energetic efforts to persuade Viertel to join the Ensemble as a resident director; unfortunately the increasingly hostile Cold War climate led to Viertel's decision to settle in Vienna.

The third project was Lenz's *The Tutor*, a tragicomedy from the *Sturm und Drang* movement of the late eighteenth century, practically forgotten by the German theatre when Brecht decided to adapt it. The performance text was created with a team of collaborators: Berlau, Besson, Monk and Neher. This was the collective working method developed by Brecht in the years before he had to leave Germany, a procedure which became a hallmark of the Berliner Ensemble in subsequent years, and for a long time after Brecht's death. Brecht and Neher staged the production which Neher also designed; the Swiss actor Hans Gaugler gave an unforgettable performance as the protagonist Läuffer. Before the opening on 15 April 1950, Brecht told the company: 'Tonight the audience may flop, don't let that disturb you.' Well, the audience didn't flop, and the performance became perhaps Brecht's and Neher's greatest collaborative triumph. The production provided a model for the fresh critical reading of a classical text, presenting a metaphor that revealed the intellectual's precarious position in society; in Läuffer's case it leads to self-castration as the only way to appease – and survive in – the existing social order. In a prologue, the tutor Läuffer proclaims: 'I'll tell you what I'm teaching: The ABC of German misery!'. Brecht said he intended the production as, among other things, a contribution to the current debates about the reform of the GDR's school system. It was open, of course, to many other readings and elicited critical responses which branded adaptation and production as 'negative'. Brecht countered: 'The positive in *The Tutor* is the bitter fury aimed at a situation of undeserved privileges and slanted ways of thinking, a situation unworthy of humanity.' The attacks and Brecht's defence were early indications of a quandary the Ensemble had to live with for some time.

It took nine months to prepare and stage Brecht's next project, the first work to represent the tradition of revolutionary drama he intended to establish. *The Mother* had been written in 1931 and staged by Brecht in January 1932; the very free adaptation of Maxim Gorky's novel used *Lehrstück* techniques to facilitate the interaction of the performance with the contemporaneous struggle of the German left during the Great Depression and Hitler's electoral advances. In his staging that opened exactly nineteen years later on 13 January 1951, Brecht celebrated the revolution triumphant, as shown especially in the final scene with its chorus 'In Praise of Dialectics', accompanied by a brief montage of documentary film clips from the Russian and Chinese revolutions. The hardships and mistakes the party had to contend with in its struggle, however, were not hidden. The production process was an early instance of the research and development efforts for which the Ensemble was soon to become famous. Extensive dramaturgical and design exploration, and more than seventy rehearsals preceded the preview performances, previews being another innovation Brecht introduced to the German theatre – a result of his production experiences in the

United States, no doubt. Caspar Neher designed sets and costumes. Helene Weigel played, as in 1932, Pelagea Vlassova, a role which even more than Mother Courage became her hallmark; she played it again under Brecht's direction in Vienna in 1953, and at the Berliner Ensemble for twenty years until her death in 1971. Ernst Busch joined the company with the production. Brecht created the role of the party organizer Lapkin to enable the older Busch to perform the songs, in Eisler's settings, that he had sung as Vlassova's son Pavel in 1932.

Of all the productions Brecht directed for the Ensemble, *The Mother* was in many respects the most faithful rendering of the epic theatre concept as he had defined it before and during his exile years. The set was 'quoting' an environment rather than representing it; there was extensive use of projections and scene titles; the small chorus, in its songs to the audience, commented on the fable and/or the actions shown on stage; there was an enchanting ease and, yes, elegance with which even the most serious scenes were performed. All this added up to a grand demonstration of Brecht's epic paradigm, the most striking example probably being the scene when Vlassova receives the news of her son's execution. While the chorus addressed the audience with the powerful 'But when he went to the wall to be shot . . . ', Weigel sat hunched on Vlassova's cot at the other side of the stage, staring blindly at a small piece of paper she held with both her hands. This simple image combined with Eisler's very lyrical setting of the song created a theatrical moment of absolute lucidity and at the same time immense emotional impact. (Yes, emotional beyond all expectation; there was hardly a performance without an audience gasping and openly in tears during the scene.) This, and the by-now famous drum scene of *Mother Courage*, gave irrefutable evidence how mistaken the claims were that Brecht's epic theatre had to be cold, severe and dryly didactic. Nevertheless, in spite of the production's great popular success, there were massive ideological attacks which accused it of formalism; on the occasion of a Central Committee conference, one high-ranking party functionary called it 'a hybrid of Meyerhold and Proletkult' – a reproach not to be taken lightly in the East Berlin of 1951 when Stalinism was at its peak.

The Ensemble was only in its second season when Brecht entrusted a production – and a rather ambitious project, at that – to one of the young assistants he had invited into the company in 1949. Egon Monk directed, under Brecht's guidance, *Beavercoat and Red Cock*, a text which Brecht and a collective of young collaborators had constructed from two comedies by Gerhart Hauptmann, *The Beavercoat* and *The Red Cock*; these plays of Hauptmann's naturalist period shared the pivotal character of Mother Wolffen, a shrewd survivor from the impoverished *Lumpenproletariat* of

provincial Prussia. The inimitable Therese Giehse gave an imposing performance of Wolffen in a production which sharpened and concretised
Hauptmann's satiric attack on the misguided values and virtues of social
climbers during the early years of the Hohenzollern Empire. Though the
opening in March 1951 was well received, the play had to close after only
fourteen performances, since the Hauptmann heirs disapproved of the
dramaturgical surgery Brecht's team had performed on the text.

The Ensemble started its third season in the fall of 1951 with a revival of
the by-now legendary *Mother Courage* of 1949. Several new actors were in
the cast which was, of course, still headed by Helene Weigel and Angelika
Hurwicz as her deaf-mute daughter Kattrin. Ernst Busch now played the
Cook, Erwin Geschonneck (the Matti of *Puntila* and von Wehrhahn of the
Hauptmann plays) was the Chaplain, and the young Regine Lutz appeared
as Yvette. In this slightly modified restaging by Brecht, *Mother Courage*
became the flagship of the Ensemble's repertoire and soon was to be recognised as a turning-point of twentieth-century theatre, quite like Stanislavsky's Chekhov stagings fifty years earlier. The impact of the original
performance in January 1949, however, could hardly be repeated: the audience approached the Deutsches Theater through streets lined with ruins and
rubble, without streetlights under the cold winter sky; they were the survivors of the most devastating war to hit Germany since the Thirty Years War
with which they were confronted on Brecht's stage, challenging them to
observe human attitudes so utterly and shamefully familiar to them.

Brecht decided it was time to evaluate and put on record what had so far
been achieved by his Ensemble, one reason being that the work was increasingly under attack for formalist and other deviations from the official guidelines of socialist realism. Together with his young collaborators he compiled
the volume *Theaterarbeit*, a detailed documentation of the six productions
the Ensemble had presented. Dramaturgy, directing, acting, design and
other aspects of the work were explained and discussed in a most comprehensive manner; an abundance of photographs and sketches documented
the visual features of each project. It is probably the most thorough investigation of a company's working practice ever published; it also amounted to
what is a manual of theatre crafts that has not yet been surpassed.

The Ensemble's next productions were both directed by leading actors of
the company, proof of Brecht's inclination to break down the barriers
between the specialised theatrical professions, and also evidence of his great
respect for actors and their artistic sensibilities. In January 1952, Therese
Giehse's staging of Kleist's *The Broken Pitcher*, one of the few classic
German comedies, continued Brecht's effort to establish a tradition of
comedy performance. Giehse also played one of the leading parts in the

production which was closely supervised by Brecht, as we can observe in many photographs taken during rehearsal. It may have been a shrewd tactical move to have Giehse direct the Kleist play which, after all, was the first work from the classic German canon to be presented by the Ensemble; as she was not only a nationally famous actress but also a Swiss resident, Giehse was a less probable target for those GDR critics who were just waiting to attack Brecht for disrespect towards the German classics – as they soon would do with a vengeance on the occasion of his *Urfaust* version.

Two months later, a production directed by the actor Ernst Busch opened. N. F. Pogodin's drama *Kremlin Chimes* was a Soviet play of 1942, part of a trilogy with Lenin as the central character. The project is rarely mentioned when the Ensemble's repertoire is discussed, though it was the company's only bow to the official dogma of socialist realism with which Pogodin's play was in accordance. Even so, the author's famous earlier work *Aristocrats* had come close to meeting Brecht's epic prescriptions, and *Kremlin Chimes* still employed some such techniques in its dramaturgy. There was reason to assume that the project might pacify some of Brecht's adversaries in the party and the critical establishment. It is also interesting that Brecht offered Busch the direction at a time when the actor had considerable difficulties with the Party; entrusting the set design to John Heartfield demonstrated Brecht's support of another artist who was out of favour with the cultural *apparatchiks*. The production was competent and well acted but not much different in style from stagings of similar plays by Langhoff and other better East Berlin directors.

When several of the younger actors and his assistant Egon Monk approached Brecht with the idea of a workshop production of Goethe's *Urfaust*, Brecht immediately accepted their plan to explore a work from the German classic tradition, in further pursuit of ideas previously tried with *The Tutor*. Soon Brecht was actively involved in the project, restructuring Goethe's fragment and eventually even adding rhymed 'bridge-texts' to be recited between scenes. *Urfaust* opened first at the provincial theatre of Potsdam, in April 1952, and a year later in Berlin with a partly new cast. Brecht regarded it as an experiment in testing a contemporary, critical reading of works from the canon which the official terminology referred to as the 'Great Classic Heritage'. The establishment's response was devastating. The Party paper's review accused the production of 'formalism' and 'cosmopolitanism'. Claiming that Brecht's position was 'alien to the people and anti-national', the critic warned him: '[he] should be aware of the situation the German people is faced with, of the challenges it has to confront'. The Party boss Walter Ulbricht threatened during a congress of artists and intellectuals: 'we won't permit that one of the most important works of our great German poet Goethe is formalistically disfigured'. Brecht had already provoked the Party's anger with his and Paul Dessau's opera *The Trial of Lucullus* in 1951, and also by offering a somewhat less than enthusiastic statement on the occasion of a Stanislavsky Conference in 1953, convened to establish once and for all that the Russian director's system was the only appropriate practice for the GDR theatre. The barrage in response to *Urfaust* amounted to what Brecht had called in his play *Galileo* a 'showing of the instruments'. The sudden illness of the actor playing Faust (Paul Albert Krumm) offered a welcome pretext to discontinue the show after only six performances at the Deutsches Theater.

In Brecht's lifetime, the Ensemble did not again produce a work from the German classic canon, and though Brecht had considered the rehearsals of *Tutor* and *Urfaust* as a preparation of his actors for the work on Shakespeare, he did not stage either *Hamlet* or *Coriolanus*, both projects he had been very keen on. (One must add here that Brecht did not feel any actor in the company was ready to play Hamlet and had thought of Peter Lorre, who had turned down an invitation from the Ensemble. Brecht had also not been able to persuade Ernst Busch, the only actor he believed right for the role, to play Coriolanus.)

Meantime the 1952–3 season's first productions had been Brecht's *Señora Carrar's Rifles* and *The Trial of Jeanne d'Arc at Rouen 1431*, adapted by Brecht and Benno Besson from Anna Seghers's radio play which had used the actual transcripts of the trial. The productions were directed by Monk and Besson, respectively, under the artistic supervision of Brecht, a further step in his strategy to develop young directors. Helene Weigel played Senora Carrar, and Ekkehard Schall was seen as her son, his first role with the Ensemble of which he was later to become the leading actor. Käthe Reichel played Jeanne, her second leading part after Gretchen in *Urfaust*. Both productions were kindly received but did not create quite the stir, positively or negatively, of earlier openings.

In *The Trial of Jeanne d'Arc*, Brecht and Besson experimented with new ways of shaping crowd scenes. A fairly small number of important company actors represented both the people of Rouen and the English soldiery; they did this by working out minutely detailed responses of the individual crowd members who were commenting on the trial and, finally, watching Joan die at the stake.

During the early 1950s Brecht had worked intensively on plans for a play about the contemporary GDR, based on the achievement of a then famous model worker, Hans Garbe. Brecht thought it appropriate for the project, and also timely, to employ techniques which he had developed during his *Lehrstück* period twenty years earlier; even the title *Büsching*, the protagonist's name, was taken from a character in the *Lehrstück* fragment *The Fall of the Egoist Johann Fatzer*. The obvious problems any radical treatment of such a topic had to encounter in the political climate of the GDR eventually brought the project to a halt. *Katzgraben* by Erwin Strittmatter, then, would remain the only play concerned with contemporary East German issues Brecht produced at the Ensemble. Brecht had come upon the text when he was a member of a jury for a playscript competition. Strittmatter's comedy did not win, yet Brecht invited the author to develop it further for the company. Brecht and a group of collaborators used the summer of 1952 to create with Strittmatter a greatly revised script; besides other changes, the complete text was put into free-form blank verse. In February 1953 the play went into rehearsal. Brecht regarded it as a project of the greatest political importance and devoted to it much energy and invention; the number of comments he wrote during the rehearsal process exceeded those of any other Ensemble production. The comedy depicted the social shifts in the East German countryside after the Second World War when former farmhands who had been given land from expropriated big estates were struggling with the established village hierarchies; it was Strittmatter's comedic treatment of the rural class struggle which had attracted Brecht to the text. Most of the company's leading actors were in the cast; Weigel, for one, played magnificently the small role of a rich farmer's wife in a sharply etched, cartoon-like fashion. Eisler had written some songs for the piece and Karl von Appen designed the set.

Von Appen had been invited from the Dresden State Theatre on Palitzsch's recommendation, and Brecht was sufficiently impressed by his work on *Katzgraben* to appoint him head of design at the Ensemble. Since Neher had ceased working with the company, von Appen soon became Brecht's preferred designer and also an important directorial collaborator. Von Appen's sets and costumes showed the dour drabness so prevalent in much of what used to be provincial Prussia, a fitting environment for the bitter and funny class warfare in which Strittmatter's village people were entangled. In the final scene the play tried to present a glorious outlook towards a collective future, but this optimistic and upbeat ending could not be made to work, hard as Brecht tried and to his considerable chagrin. The opening in late May 1953 did not receive the deserved acclaim, the artfully detailed production was not recognised for its frugal beauty. A few weeks later the violent events of 17 June – with the government's clumsy handling of the wage situation and the resulting uprising of large parts of the East German population which was quickly crushed by Soviet tanks – eclipsed whatever impact this unique Brecht staging of a GDR play might have achieved.

This is not the place to elaborate on Brecht's attitude during the fateful events of June; as is well known, he refused to distance himself from the Party and its government though he clearly stated his critical views about their policies, a statement the Party successfully managed to suppress. Of great concern to him was certainly the continued existence of the Ensemble that depended, after all, on the goodwill of the party leaders.

During the following months, Brecht completed the first draft of a new play, *Turandot, or the Whitewashers' Congress*, which he planned for the Ensemble. He also participated in many discussions regarding a necessary change of the GDR's cultural policies. In October 1953 he staged, with his assistant Manfred Wekwerth, *The Mother* at Vienna's Scala Theater, while in Berlin Besson was rehearsing a production of Molière's *Don Juan* in an adaptation by himself, Brecht and Hauptmann. At the same time, several of the young assistants were at work on shorter projects, according to Brecht's proposal of small-scale, highly mobile productions which could be performed in any given space, an effort to revive agitprop traditions of the 1920s and early 1930s. One result of these experiments was Wekwerth's successful and, in the context of Brecht's goal to create politically invasive theatre forms, important staging of Hauptmann's and Wekwerth's adaptation of a Chinese agitprop farce, *Millet for the Eighth Army*, originally written and performed in the Chinese countryside to rally support for Mao's Red Army during the anti-Japanese war of the 1940s.

In November 1953 Brecht began rehearsals for *The Caucasian Chalk Circle*. He intended to open the play at the Theater am Schiffbauerdamm, the new home the company was to occupy, at last, in the spring of 1954. The musical score was composed by Paul Dessau who had invented a new instrument for the occasion, a 'gongspiel' to serve his settings which were strongly influenced by Middle Eastern and Asian music. Von Appen was designing, Angelika Hurwicz and Ernst Busch were playing the leading roles of Grusha and Azdak. Due to Brecht's insatiable drive for perfection and his never-tiring fertile imagination, rehearsals eventually extended over nearly eleven months, and the show was not ready to open until October 1954.

The Ensemble inaugurated its new house, on 19 March 1954, with Besson's *Don Juan* which had already been playing since November at the Deutsches Theater. The adaptation stressed the comic, or rather satiric, aspects of the piece; the protagonist was neither a tragic nor a demonic hero but a callous, arrogant, quite ridiculous libertine who hunted women like deer in the forest, as mere trophies. The set by Hainer Hill presented a park of Versailles vista, framing the games of the feudal hunter (played by the not so young and somewhat portly Geschonneck) and his shrewd but hapless servant Sganarelle (Norbert Christian, with the company since 1952).

The Caucasian Chalk Circle was by far the most lavish and multi-layered production Brecht ever directed, definitely a departure from the frugal aesthetics of his earlier stagings for the Ensemble. Von Appen's sets and costumes were rich, colourful and full of delightful visual surprises. Brecht explored new possibilities of epic presentation and used to this end numerous details which he seemed to have discovered in Broadway musicals and Hollywood movies during his American exile. The acting spanned the whole gamut from the broadest farce to the most tender and lyrical moment, and the term 'culinary', which Brecht once used so disparagingly for a kind of theatre he despised, would be quite appropriate when we talk of his *Chalk Circle* production. It was to become one of the most popular performances of the company, but the opening in October 1954 was treated by the Party paper as a non-event; no review appeared. A sharply negative critique in the magazine *Theater der Zeit* warned: 'Watch out, dead end!'. On the other hand, the president of the GDR, Wilhelm Pieck, demonstratively attended a performance to show his support of Brecht.

What strengthened Brecht's position even more effectively was the Ensemble's triumphant appearance at the first Festival International d'Art Dramatique in Paris in July 1954, where *Mother Courage* won first prize. Brecht's company created a sensation, and the visit brought him immediate recognition as a leading figure of the contemporary theatre. The house at Schiffbauerdamm soon became the Mecca for numerous theatre professionals from Europe and the Americas. This could not fail to impress on the GDR authorities what a valuable asset the Republic had in Brecht's Berliner Ensemble. International success and political changes in the Soviet Union – what used to be called 'the thaw' – combined to improve the company's status, and when the Stalin Peace Prize was awarded to Brecht on 21 December 1954, his and his theatre's position in the GDR was irrevocably secured. In June 1955, *The Caucasian Chalk Circle* was shown at the second Paris Festival, where Brecht received the standing ovation of an international audience.

Brecht had committed the Ensemble to stage *Winterschlacht* by Johannes R. Becher, expressionist poet, old friend, and the newly appointed Minister of Culture. The eminent Czech director Burian was invited to direct the play, but his concept and working methods quickly caused problems with the company and dramaturgical staff. When Burian resigned, Brecht had to take over and mounted the production in collaboration with Wekwerth. With Eisler's symphonic score, von Appen's designs and Ekkehard Schall in his first leading role, the play opened in January 1955. Schall's portrayal of a young German soldier during the battle for Moscow, formerly a convinced Hitler youth who turns against the atrocities of the Nazi system, was severely censured in the reviews for his unheroic *Gestus*, and so was the production as a whole for its failure to comply with the accepted clichés of an emotionally stirring performance. Brecht felt the need to write several lengthy comments on the production's reception, but none of them was published before his death; he avoided involving himself in arguments about formalism in the theatre, which were so prevalent during those years, and tried rather to make his points with the work on his stage.

Winterschlacht was to be the last production completed by Brecht. After long deliberations, Ernst Busch had finally been chosen for the role of Galileo and Brecht started rehearsing the play *Life of Galileo* in December 1955. In late March 1956 Brecht had to stop working, due to a viral infection he had brought back from his visit to Milan for the opening of *The Three-penny Opera* in Giorgio Strehler's production, which Brecht immensely admired. Erich Engel, his old friend and collaborator, was eventually to finish the *Galileo* production after Brecht's death: it opened on 15 January 1957.

The Ensemble presented, however, four other productions during its last season under Brecht's guidance. These were all comedies, in tune with his intention of setting a standard for comedy performance in the German theatre. Two came from the English-language repertoire, one from Russia and one from the classic Chinese theatre. It is quite obvious that after the *Urfaust* controversy Brecht preferred to introduce works from the classic international repertoire which had been rarely, if ever, performed in the German theatre, and were unfamiliar to its critical watchdogs in the GDR. All these productions were directed by former assistants, dramaturgs or actors; as if with foresight, Brecht thus established a strong presence of young directors who might soon be ready to shoulder the company's responsibilities. The plays were, in order of opening: *Trumpets and Drums*, Brecht's, Besson's and Hauptmann's adaptation of Farquhar's *The Recruiting Officer*, directed by Besson; *The Ward* or *Good Deeds Hurt* by Alexander Ostrovsky, directed by Angelika Hurwicz; *The Day of the Great Scholar Wu*, adapted from excerpts of classic Chinese comedies and directed by Peter Palitzsch and Carl Weber; *The Playboy of the Western World* by John M. Synge, adapted by Brecht, Palitzsch and Wekwerth, and directed by Palitzsch and Wekwerth. Of these, *Trumpets and Drums* was the most important project. It was designed by von Appen, the music composed by Rudolf Wagner-Regeny, and Regine Lutz played young Victoria who joins the army to capture her man. The production was as farcical as it was elegant and swift in its pacing; it displayed a self-referentiality as 'performance' which was surprising and new at the time. Von Appen's sets were derived from etchings of the period, achieving a lightness for which the

9. The Berliner Ensemble's production of *Trumpets and Drums* (1956), designed by Karl von Appen, with (from left to right) Regine Lutz, Gerd Biewer, Sabine Thalbach, Annelies Reppel and Norbert Christian, 'achieving a lightness for which the Ensemble had not been particularly known in the past'.

Ensemble had not been particularly known in the past. The adaptation had reconstructed the text and moved the story from the original's War of the Spanish Succession to the American War of Independence, introducing aspects of class struggle and political progress which the original did not contain. The production was one of the Ensemble's unqualified successes, and consequently Brecht selected it to join *Mother Courage* and *The Caucasian Chalk Circle* for the London invitation season in September 1956.

It was the brush-up rehearsals for this London season which became Brecht's last working days in his theatre. Though not feeling well, he had come to town from his country house to work on the productions scheduled for London. He was too weak to call out his directions to the stage from the centre of the auditorium, as was his habit, and a microphone had to be installed to amplify his voice. Angelika Hurwicz, who was waiting for an entrance backstage, was hardly aware of what she implied when she remarked: 'My God, that sounds like a voice from the grave.' The next day, Brecht could not attend rehearsal. Two days later he died, on 14 August 1956. When the coffin was moved from his apartment in Chaussee Strasse to the cemetery next door for the brief and very private burial, his assistants and dramaturgs walked with it, and throughout the day actors and other members of the company stood guard at the graveside. A few weeks later, the Ensemble opened its first London season with *Mother Courage*, an event which marked the beginning of the playwright's fame as one of the great innovators of world theatre.

It was Brecht's work at the Ensemble which brought him to the attention of the international theatre community and eventually resulted in his status as the most performed German playwright of the international repertoire. It was also this work which put Brecht's indelible stamp on much of the theatre of the second half of the twentieth century. What made his practice so unique and impressive that it became such an admired and often emulated model? After all, he had only seven years and seven productions of his own with the company before he died so prematurely. Perhaps the most compelling aspect of his productions was the clarity with which the story was told. In Brecht's view, every single detail of a production had to serve the telling of the *Fabel*, to use his own term. What he called *Fabel* was the plot of the play told as a sequence of interactions, describing each event in the dialectic fashion developed by Hegel, Marx and, in Brecht's last years, also by Mao. This may sound quite theoretical, but in Brecht's practice the *Fabel* was something utterly concrete and practical. Acting, music, the visual elements of the staging, in short, everything an audience perceived, had to contribute to the storytelling and make it lucid, convincing, entertaining and 'elegant' – as Brecht liked to put it. One result was that the Ensemble's productions were quite well understood by international audiences who could not follow the German text. Brecht insisted that the configuration and movement of actors and objects on stage should clearly 'tell the *Fabel*'. If they were to watch a play through a glass wall blocking all sound, the audience should still be able to follow the essential story. He also insisted that each of the performance elements: acting, design, music and so forth, should remain a recognisable separate entity while it contributed to the *Fabel*'s presentation.

Brecht liked to speak of a 'storytelling arrangement', which meant the specific blocking of actors and all props employed in a scene. He regarded this arrangement as the most important means to achieve a clear presentation of the *Fabel*, and the term 'scenic writing' may best convey what he was aiming for. In actual rehearsal, Brecht proceeded very slowly with the blocking, sometimes spending from two to four months in the process, and often testing up to twenty different versions of a scene's grouping before deciding on a final option – which then again was scrutinised several times and changed if he was not satisfied. During this slow and fastidious process, the actors developed also many other aspects of their performance, working towards the appropriate *Gestus* of their stage character.

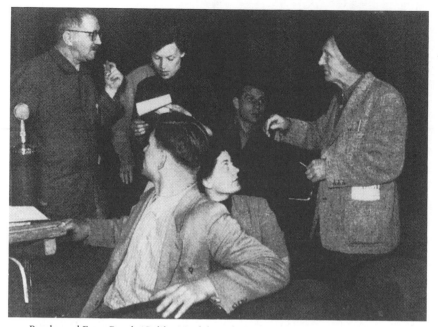

10. Brecht and Ernst Busch (Galileo) in debate during a 1956 rehearsal. Isot Kilian refers to notes, Manfred Wekwerth observes from behind, whilst Hans Bunge turns to look at Brecht and Käthe Rülicke to look at Busch.

Gestus was the other essential ingredient in Brecht's work as playwright and director. The term defines the total persona the actor creates on stage by way of his physical demeanour, facial expression, vocal utterances, costume and so forth. The *Gestus* was to be mainly determined by the social position and history of a character, and Brecht instructed his actors to develop it by careful attention to all the contradictions to be discovered in the actions and verbal text of the role. Again, this may sound quite abstract, but was achieved during rehearsal in a most practical, even playful manner.

Brecht constantly encouraged his actors to try out every feasible choice of a particular detail, often spending hours on about two minutes worth of printed text. Yet there were never extended discussions on any aspect of the work during rehearsal; when actors began to explain their ideas, Brecht replied: 'Let's have a look', and the intended action or line reading was performed on stage. If Brecht liked the offer, he immediately incorporated it into the scene; if not, he suggested further changes or another possibility. His ability to elicit the actors' sense of play and their inventive imagination was uncanny. Outside of rehearsal, Brecht had sometimes a baffling patience with an actor's lengthy ruminations, but never during the work on stage. He truly loved actors, and they returned this love in kind. It was only when an actor or technician showed a deliberate lack of commitment that Brecht would become angry and might explode into one of his notorious verbal outbursts. He firmly held that talent showed itself most of all in what he called 'the interest', meaning curiosity and commitment to the project at hand. He expected it from everyone in the company during rehearsal, in response to his own intense commitment. Nevertheless, the mode of most rehearsals was playful and at ease; sometimes observers would compare it to the attitude of children at play in a sandbox.

Brecht's deft and seemingly effortless guidance of his actors made it possible to forge within a few years the coherent ensemble of quite idiosyncratic individuals with which the critic Kenneth Tynan, for one, was so impressed: 'They neither bludgeon us with personality nor woo us with charms, they look shockingly like people – real potato-faced people' (*Tynan on Theatre*, pp. 240–1). As mentioned earlier, this company was put together from actors of the most disparate backgrounds, and it was Brecht's practice, not studied theoretical or ideological indoctrination, that taught and moulded them into the unique Berliner Ensemble.

Little as the theory of epic theatre or dialectics were mentioned during rehearsals, they were much discussed and applied during the long period of gestation which each project went through before rehearsal began. The thorough and extremely detailed preparation included countless discussions in which a text was dissected to determine which *Fabel* it might yield. Brecht encouraged his designers to draw numerous sketches exploring options of the scenes' groupings. This often resulted in a kind of storyboard to be used as a point of departure by Brecht when he began to block a production, without restricting in any way his or the actors' liberty to arrive at very different solutions.

There were many other innovative practices Brecht developed with his team of collaborators: for instance, the way the Ensemble's playbills were put together, or the work with audiences in pre- and post-performance meetings; the volume *Theaterarbeit* provides illuminating examples. Much of what became standard procedure in the Ensemble's pre-production process was eventually adopted by many German directors and dramaturgs, the most prominent of them perhaps the creative team which guided the famous Schaubühne of Berlin.

There were two proverbial sayings which Brecht loved to repeat: 'The proof of the pudding is in the eating' and 'The devil is in the detail' – and they, indeed, encapsulate much of what his work at the Ensemble was about. His care for the minutest detail, his attention to the do-able, his insistence on the importance of the *Fabel*, that is, the narrative aspect of theatre, his conviction that visual perception is at the core of the theatrical experience, and, of course, his conviction that the theatre has a mission to further the progress of human society by showing it as changing and changeable, and to do this in an entertaining manner – these were the elements which shaped his work with the Ensemble.

They will remain as his legacy, and they have informed as well as changed the practice and theory of theatre during the second half of this century. The direct or indirect influence of Brecht's achievement with the Berliner Ensemble has been evident in the work of such diverse theatres as the Schaubühne, the Théâtre du Soleil, or the Royal Shakespeare Company, in the productions of Peter Brook, Yuri Liubimov, Roger Planchon, Peter Stein, Giorgio Strehler and other leading contemporary directors, and in the texts of playwrights as different as Arthur Adamov, Edward Bond, Tony Kushner and Heiner Müller, to name only a few.

In early 1953, Brecht bitterly noted in his journal: 'Our performances in Berlin have hardly any echo at all ... Our efforts might be completely meaningless unless our mode of playing can be resurrected later, that is if their value as teaching material is eventually realised.' History has shown that Brecht's pessimism was premature, and that the meaning of his work with the Ensemble has been gloriously confirmed.

14

PETER BROOKER

Key words in Brecht's theory and practice of theatre

INTRODUCTION: DIALECTICS

The most damaging yet most common error in discussions of Brecht's theory has been to see it as fixed and unchanging, and to view it therefore as either dogmatic, communist-inspired abstraction or revered holy writ. Behind these views lie different perceptions of Marxism and the rights and wrongs of political art. Brecht began to think through the ideas with which he is most commonly associated in the late 1920s and early 1930s. His emphasis and terminology changed in these years, as well as subsequently, and many see in his later remarks and essays (especially *A Short Organum for the Theatre*, 1948) a belated acceptance of the conventions of realism and the realities of emotional experience suppressed by the supposed sterile intellectualism of his earlier years. In this way Brecht has often come to be admired as a great writer, particularly in the West, *in spite* of his theory: as at once reconciled with his own youthful hedonism and with the forms and verities of an art above theory and politics. In fact, this is simply to read Brecht in terms of one favoured aesthetic ideology rather than another, and to compromise his art and ideas as much, though in another direction, as a protective state socialism ever did. If we are to approach his ideas more constructively, we need to understand how they emerged and changed in particular artistic and social circumstances, and see them, moreover, as belonging with clusters of related terms and concepts in what was a developing self-critical aesthetic and theatre practice. Some of these terms (the idea of a 'pedagogic' or 'scientific' theatre, even of an 'epic' theatre) receded or were rejected, while others (an emphasis on 'pleasure', on 'productive attitudes', on 'naivety' or the description of his theatre as a 'philosophical people's theatre') emerged in the late 1940s and the last years of Brecht's life.[1] The three key terms introduced below should not therefore be

The abbreviation *BT* refers to *Brecht on Theatre*.

regarded as the *only* important terms, nor as evenly weighted, either in Brecht's career or for subsequent readers, critics and artists.

We therefore need first to appreciate that Brecht's artistic categories over-lapped and changed, not because of any lack of rigour or principle on his part, but because these ideas were intimately connected to a changing prac-tice – in poetry, fiction and film – as well as theatre. Secondly, we need to accept that this body of work, itself conditioned by and responsive to his-torical conditions, was expressly political. As Brecht put it, 'For art to be "unpolitical" means only to ally itself with the "ruling" group' (*BT*, p. 196).

Brecht was fond of quoting Marx's eleventh thesis on Feuerbach, 'The philosophers have only *interpreted* the world in various ways; the point, however, is to *change* it.' His object, he said, was to apply this to the theatre (*BT*, p. 248). The most consistent theoretical source for Brecht's political/artistic project was accordingly Marxism, as is well known. Significantly, however, this meant more precisely for Brecht the classic tradition, in texts by Marx, Lenin and Mao Tse-tung, of dialectical materialism. 'Dialectics' appears consequently as a further key term in his writings, from the early 'The dialectical drama' (1931) to the later essays grouped as 'Dialectics in the theatre' (1948–55). The ideas of *Verfremdung* and *Gestus* discussed below were also spoken of, directly and indirectly, as operating in dialectical terms.[2] Brecht's Marxism was in conception, therefore, neither mechanical nor deterministic; and nor was his art. In another important term, it was an 'interventionist' art (the concept of *eingreifendes Denken* – 'interventionist thinking' – Brecht derived in particular from Lenin), and as such distinct from socially concerned naturalism, reportage, official socialist realism, propaganda, or agitprop. Brecht sought to use the resources of art, in ways consistent with the tenets of dialectical materialism, to historicise and negate the commonplace and taken-for-granted, to prise open social and ideological contradictions, and so both demonstrate and provoke an awareness of the individual's place in a concrete social narrative. The artis-tic devices which we know by key words in Brecht's theoretical vocabulary were means to this end: their desired effect, one might say, being to trigger change in the material world by changing 'interpretations' ('human feelings, opinions, attitudes', as Brecht otherwise put it) in the analogous, experimen-tal world of the theatre.

Theory and practice and art and politics were therefore combined in Brecht's commitment to dialectics and to material change (which he con-ceived on a very broad front: speaking, for example, of 'the full unfettering of everybody's productivity' whether the products were 'bread, lamps, hats, pieces of music, chess moves, irrigation, complexion, character, plays etc.').[3] This should guide our assessment of his own work and the later productions of his plays, but extend also to those who wish to learn in less direct ways from Brecht's example and precepts. In his notes on the production of *Antigone* which was to initiate the composition of the Model Books for his plays, Brecht writes how 'The act of creation has become a collective creative process, a continuum of a dialectical sort in which the original invention, taken on its own, has lost much of its importance' (*BT*, p. 212). The ideas and first productions of plays were therefore springboards and blueprints; provisional texts available for fresh inscription in a changed set of circumstances. As this suggests, subsequent work which looks to Brecht will be 'Brechtian' to the degree that it revises and reorientates an 'original' Brecht; understood – to adapt the view of Manfred Wekwerth, Brecht's successor at the Berliner Ensemble – less as a full stop than a colon.[4]

Much that has occurred in radical theatre, film-making and criticism has proceeded in just this way, setting Brecht in a dialogue with new theory and new priorities.[5] In recent years, however, and particularly under the influence of theories of postmodernism, any 'continuum of a dialectical sort' seems to have run aground. For now, the ideas and principles of rationality, progress and critical distance, derived from the Enlightenment heritage, are said to be discredited or impossible. As a 'grand narrative' of human liberation in this tradition, Marxism has consequently come under fresh suspicion. At the same time, the originally subversive or critical artistic devices of the radical avant-garde or left modernism with which Brecht was associated are said to have been neutralised in an all-absorbent mass consumer culture.[6] These new developments in theory, art and culture raise large and unresolved issues. If there is a sense in which postmodernism does indeed take us beyond Brecht, however, this 'Brecht' will have to be understood in the terms indicated above: not as a dogmatic ideologue whom it is easy to dismiss, but, less conveniently, as already profoundly open to change.

EPIC THEATRE

'Epic' is the description most commonly applied to Brecht's theatre. We should realise that the term was in use in German debates before Brecht adapted it, however, and that for Brecht too it had several sources: the political theatre of Erwin Piscator and German agitprop; the cabaret of Frank Wedekind and the work of the music hall comedian Karl Valentin; Charlie Chaplin and American silent film; Asian and revolutionary Soviet theatre; as well as Shakespeare and Elizabethan chronicle plays.

Brecht's principal early statement on epic theatre was his notes on *The Rise and Fall of the City of Mahagonny*, published in 1930, though he had used the term from 1926. In this essay, 'The modern theatre is the epic theatre', he presented a table of contrary features showing 'certain changes of emphasis as between the dramatic and epic theatre' (*BT*, p. 37). In Brecht's view, drama, and contemporary German drama especially, invited its spectators to empathise with the emotional destiny of its central individual characters. Audiences were encouraged to surrender to the suspense and consolations of the well-made play, faithful to the unities of time and place and their naturalistic depiction. Brecht associated these conventions with the categories of 'mimesis', or imitation, and 'catharsis', the purging of the emotions of pity and fear, first outlined by Aristotle in the *Poetics*. Aristotle had connected these functions specifically with tragedy, and there is a sense in which Brecht's arguments made fresh claims, by contrast, for the tradition and techniques of comedy.[7] In describing his own theatre as 'non-Aristotelian', however, he was also questioning a traditional formal distinction (drawn by Aristotle and notably by Goethe and Schiller in the German tradition) between the genres of epic and drama rather than simply between dramatic modes. In addition he was clearly also questioning drama's supposed ideological effects. Brecht saw drama as illusionistic and individualistic, a reactionary prop to petty-bourgeois morality, at a time when both artistic conventions and ideology had been superannuated by unprecedented social and economic change. Scientific and technological advance and corporate capitalism had decentred and subordinated the individual. A new 'epic' theatre was therefore required which would be adequate to the new subject-matter ('the great themes of our times ... the building-up of a mammoth industry, the conflict of classes, war, the fight against disease', *BT*, p. 77). 'Epic' would present individuals as socially constructed and malleable ('The continuity of the ego is a myth' Brecht had declared as early as 1926, *BT*, p. 15) and above all introduce a new narrative accent and range.

At times Brecht also hailed this as the 'theatre for a scientific age'. In the event this was a confusing description since 'science' in his early writings could mean new technologies and industries, or the natural sciences, or a sociological perspective, or Marxism. Later it was anyway rejected as being too narrow and because the expression 'scientific age' fell out of favour (*BT*, p. 276). It is also sometimes thought that Brecht intended 'a scientific theatre', rather than a theatre 'for a scientific age', by this description, and that this implies a clinical, dispassionate mode of analysis. Hence the (unfounded) charge that Brecht outlawed feelings and amusement when in fact he wished to prevent empathy (one type of feeling) and encourage instead the broad pleasures, whether high or low, of a productive life – including the pleasures of learning and the passions of a committed, critical attitude. 'Reason and emotion can't be divided', wrote Brecht; the object of epic theatre was to 'examine' not 'just to stimulate' emotions (*BT*, p. 162).

In so far as epic theatre was, or became, a more consistently Marxist theatre (and might by that token be thought of as 'scientific'), it sought to produce a knowledge of the 'causal laws of development', to divide rather than unify its audience, to intervene in and so transform ideas and attitudes. Its domain was crucially therefore the domain of consciousness and ideology. As such, it could aim to counter the soporific ideological effects of drama (epic theatre 'turns the spectator into an observer, but / arouses his capacity for action / forces him to take decisions', *BT*, p. 37) but could not of itself destroy capitalism or prevent Nazism. In theatre, as Brecht put it, 'the puzzles of the world are not solved but shown'.[8] Accordingly, to realise its aims as a fully dialectical materialist theatre, it required that the contradictions it revealed be taken up beyond itself, in the material world outside the walls of the theatre.

Brecht had summarised the new features of epic theatre in the mid-1930s as follows:

> The stage began to tell a story. The narrator was no longer missing ... Not only did the background adopt an attitude to the events on stage ... the actors too refrained from going over wholly into their role ...
> The stage began to be instructive.
> Oil, inflation, war, social struggles, the family, religion, wheat, the meat market, all became subjects for theatrical representation. Choruses enlightened the spectator ... Films showed a montage of events from all over the world. Projections added statistical material. And as the 'background' came to the front of the stage so people's activity was subjected to criticism ... The theatre became an affair for philosophers, but only for such philosophers as wished not just to explain but also to change the world.
>
> (*BT*, pp. 71–2)

Following the examples of Meyerhold and Piscator, Brecht employed stage machinery, films, placards, music, chorus, as well as mimesis for this new narrative theatre. The result was a 'separation of the elements' rather than the traditional, organically fused work of art. The narrator or narrative function was made explicit and narrative proceeded, not in a continuous linear direction, but in a montage of 'curves and jumps' (*BT*, p. 37) – dialectically, in other words. Episodes were joined in such a way that 'the knots are easily noticed' (*BT*, p. 201). Each scene was to stand 'for itself': text, music and setting working in counterpoint, adopting attitudes, said Brecht, to the play's social content (*BT*, p. 39). 'Epic' was the general term therefore for all those technical features of a Brecht production – the use of a spare stage, white lighting, half curtain, masks, emblematic props, selectively authentic costume, tableaux, and acting style – which contributed to its analytic narrative perspective. If it were to succeed in its political function a performance would gain assent to this perspective, 'alienating' its audience from conventional forms of identification and clichéd modes of perception and understanding.

Brecht's association of 'epic' with new social themes ('oil, inflation, social struggles, the family, religion, wheat, the meat market', *BT*, p. 71) suggests that epic narratives were to be topical. Although this was sometimes roughly the case (in *Saint Joan of the Stockyards, Mahagonny, Fear and Misery of the Third Reich, Arturo Ui*), Brecht's stories were more often parables (*Round Heads and Pointed Heads, The Caucasian Chalk Circle, The Good Person of Szechwan*) or worked as historically distant parallels to contemporary issues and events (*Galileo, Mother Courage, The Days of the Commune*). In later years Brecht came in fact to prefer the term 'parable' for his work. It offered, Ernst Schumacher reports, 'simplicity and easy assimilation'; it was 'indirect', 'cunning' and 'concrete in abstraction'.[9] Even a play such as *The Mother* was 'historically alienated' whereas the direct treatment of contemporary events was fraught with problems. It was at this time too that Brecht returned to an explicit use of the term 'dialectics' to describe his theatre. 'Epic' he came to think of as too limited and as open to distortion. The concept was 'too slight and too vague for the kind of theatre intended' he wrote in the 'Appendices to the Short Organum' (*BT*, p. 276). And in two late notes he declared:

> An effort is now being made to move from the epic theatre to the dialectical theatre ... 'epic theatre' is too formal a term for the kind of theatre aimed at (and to some extent practised). Epic theatre is a prerequisite for these contributions, but it does not of itself imply that productivity and mutability of society from which they derive their main element of pleasure.
>
> (*BT*, pp. 281,2)

Brecht's remarks imply that a theatre which employed the techniques of 'epic' without its objectives would be an idealist and aestheticised version of his own intentions. From the beginning, in fact, he had talked of the difficulties of successfully staging epic theatre, largely because of the radical transformation in theatre audiences and society it not only promoted but required. Even a major play such as *Galileo*, conceived and staged in exile without this necessary foundation, was as a result compromised and less than 'epic' in Brecht's opinion. The play *Mr Puntila and his Man Matti*, first performed in East Berlin in 1949, was along these same lines 'only epic as this can be accepted (and offered) today'.[10] These reservations significantly allude to the conditions rather than the techniques or internal effects of epic theatre. They lie, one feels, behind Brecht's inclination to drop the term in favour of 'dialectics' which emphasised an incomplete and continuing artistic and historical process, or more casually, in reported later remarks, the description 'philosophical folk-theatre', a plainer term than dialectics, but one which again combines the ideas of artistic and political function.[11]

It is unnerving, perhaps, but characteristic that Brecht should feel moved to qualify and challenge a well-established vocabulary. If there is a general tendency in these late remarks, it is towards simplicity and a return to beginnings. One hears the same challenge in Brecht's hint that the early 'learning plays' designed for collective performance in schools and work-places, and the controversial *The Measures Taken* especially, represented the theatre of the future.[12] The ideas of a 'dialectical' or 'philosophical folk-theatre similarly look back and forwards, to a changed theatre and society.

VERFREMDUNG

'The exposition of the story and its communication by suitable means of alienation', Brecht wrote in *A Short Organum*, 'constitute the main business of the theatre': a statement which usefully summarises the relation of *Verfremdungseffekte* and 'epic'. The new narrative content signalled by the term 'epic' was to be communicated in a dialectical, non-illusionist and non-linear manner, declaring its own artifice as it hoped also to reveal the workings of ideology. 'Alienating an event or character', wrote Brecht, 'means first of all stripping the event of its self-evident, familiar, obvious quality and creating a sense of astonishment and curiosity about them.'[13] The direct and indirect use of a narrator, the conspicuous use of songs, masks, placards and images set in a montaged narrative sequence would help maintain this level of wonder and alert self-criticism. Beyond this, however, the repertoire of estranging effects would aim to produce a double perspective on events and actions so as at once to show their present contradictory nature and their historical cause or social motivation. In a frequent image, this would be like following the course of a river and staying above it, remaining both inside and above the stream (*BT*, pp. 44, 146, 191).

Only the *Verfremdungseffekt*, said Brecht, made it possible 'to underline the historical aspect of a specific social situation ... It was principally designed to historicise the incidents portrayed' (*BT*, pp. 98, 96). As he had summarised this logic of effects in 'Theatre for pleasure or theatre for instruction', 'What is "natural" must have the force of what is startling. This is the only way to expose the laws of cause and effect. People's activity must simultaneously be so and be capable of being different' (*BT*, p. 71). *Verfremdung* would therefore produce a jolt of surprise and illumination, as the familiar and predictable were not only historicised and seen afresh but 'seen through'; judged with the eyes of a suspicious, quizzically naive spectator. The dialectical movement of events would therefore be temporarily suspended, held at a standstill as Walter Benjamin remarked, until, as a particular attitude, action or event was revolved to expose the shadow of its alternative, the taken-for-granted would be negated under the impetus of a new understanding and grasp of social alternatives. In Brecht's words, describing this full dialectical movement, 'What is obvious is in a certain sense made incomprehensible, but this is only in order that it may then be made all the easier to comprehend' (*BT*, pp. 143–4).

Brecht derived the concept of *Verfremdung*, as so much else, from a variety of sources, no one of them final. Amongst these was the acting style of Mei Lan-fang whom Brecht saw perform in Moscow in 1935. Brecht's essay 'Alienation effects in Chinese acting' which followed this visit is said to mark the first appearance of the term *Verfremdung*. He had used the term *Entfremdung* (more strictly translated as 'alienation') previously, however, and to judge from the commentary of a friend and contemporary such as Walter Benjamin, had formulated the theory of epic theatre before his trip to Moscow.[14]

It is notable that Brecht also distinguished between 'the social aims of these old devices', including the acting style of Asian theatre, and their more politicised use in German theatre (*BT*, pp. 96, 192). This distinction is relevant, in turn, to the differences between Brecht's *Verfremdung* and the Russian formalist device of 'making strange' (*ostranenie*) coined by Viktor Shklovsky, which John Willett in particular has cited as Brecht's main source (*BT*, p. 99).[15] The connections between Brecht and the Soviet avant-garde, especially Sergei Tretyakov, are an essential part of any proper assessment of his work and thinking – as are his differences from the later official Soviet doctrine of 'socialist realism'. The idea that Brecht was directly indebted to Shklovsky, or to Tretyakov, is, however, unconvincing. Bernhard Reich, for example, whose account of Brecht's and Tretyakov's shared used of the term *Verfremdung* and its connection with Shklovsky Willett accepts as proof of its derivation, also points out how Brecht's concept differs 'quite fundamentally' from this supposed source. Compared with the 'extremely formal juxtaposition' of Shklovsky and others, Brecht's 'making aware', says Reich, 'helps one to see better the content of things'.[16] Brecht's conception and use of *Verfremdung*, as this and much else suggests, entailed a degree of political insight which thoroughly radicalised the formalist device of 'making strange'. Whereas, therefore, in a telling contrast, Shklovsky spoke of art's 'laying bare of the device' as the sign of its defining self-reflexivity, Brecht spoke of art's 'laying bare society's causal network' (*BT*, p. 109).

One further possible theoretical source requires some comment. Brecht's

Verfremdungseffekt is usually translated as 'alienation device', and this suggests a debt to Marxism. Yet in Marx 'alienation' describes the condition of dehumanised labour and social relations under capitalism which Brecht wished precisely to transcend. There is an echo but no direct derivation therefore from Marx. With his closest 'Marxist teacher', Karl Korsch, Brecht viewed Marxism as an historically specific, critical philosophy of revolution which would assist social transformation through ideological struggle. As the central concept of 'epic theatre' *Verfremdung* was a weapon in this struggle, a description of the way in which art 'by its *own* means' could 'further the great social task of mastering life' (*BT*, p. 96). It would do this not by reinforcing alienation, in Marx's sense, but by uncovering and revealing it, thereby encouraging a knowledge of the conditions of alienation as historically produced and open to transformation in the real world. Brecht's debt to Marx therefore was less to the concept of alienation than, once again, to the methods of dialectical materialism. As an entry in Brecht's *Arbeitsjournal* confirmed, 'klar, dass das theater der verfremdung ein theater der dialektik ist' ('it is clear that a theatre of *Verfremdung* is a dialectical theatre').[17]

What this further suggests is that the term 'alienation' is an inadequate and even misleading translation of Brecht's *Verfremdung*. The terms 'defamiliarisation' or 'estrangement', when understood as more than purely formal devices, give a more accurate sense of Brecht's intentions. A better term still would be 'de-alienation'. But in fact that is no reason for avoiding Brecht's own term. Attention might turn then from matters of nomenclature to the relation of theory and the practical forms and effects of *Verfremdung*, including the question of their continued application – or neutralisation – beyond Brecht.

Brecht's writings do often directly discuss the use and rationale of specific devices in his plays. One example occurs in the notes to the production of *The Mother*, where the sparse stage set, the use of a canvas for the projection of texts, and Helene Weigel's acting, amongst other features, are described as explicitly designed to prevent empathy and to show events as alterable. It might be thought nevertheless that devices and effects such as these depended uniquely upon Brecht's personal direction and are therefore unrepeatable. A comparison between two productions of *The Mother* in the 1930s, under the direction respectively of Brecht in Berlin and the Theatre Union in New York, would seem initially to bear this out. For while Brecht's notes present his own production as exemplary, the second was, in his view, disastrous. (See the extracts in *BT*, pp. 57–62, 81–4.) The question of Brecht's personal control is not, however, in the end a major factor, since what he complained of most of all in the New York production were departures from the text – the conversion of a direct address by the Mother and the Chorus in Scene 1, for example, into a dialogue between the Mother and her son. This change, in the name of greater realism, ignored the distance between the figures as well as the generalising, narrative function of the Chorus and the Mother's introduction of herself 'as if . . . in the third person' (*BT*, p. 58).[18] The Theatre Union production therefore distorted the play's *explicit* estranging effects and so jeopardised the broken course and political point of the story in which Vlassova and her son's roles are reversed, and she becomes a 'revolutionary Mother'. Much depended on a way of playing and staging, evidently, but it is clear too that certain basic V-effects (of setting, delivery, posture, the montage of voices and scenes) are structurally established and 'directed' by the text, and do not depend on a particular company or on Brecht's personal supervision.

'Brechtian' effects could therefore be employed without, and indeed after, Brecht. A second objection, relating to theories of postmodern society, is not that V-effects require Brecht's unique control, but that, on the contrary, they have become so ubiquitous in modern advertising, feature films and television sit-coms as to lose all artistic and political effect.[19] Brecht had in fact anticipated this outcome in a late conversation with Ernst Schumacher. He imagines a world in which his theatre would be as normal as bourgeois theatre, and comments:

> You know, human nature knows how to adapt itself just as well as the rest of organic matter. Man is even capable of regarding atomic war as something normal, so why should he not be capable of dealing with an affair as small as the alienation effect so that he does not need to open his eyes. I can imagine that one day they will only be able to feel their old pleasure when the alienation effect is offered.[20]

The prospect Brecht sees is of a purely aestheticised V-effect, separated from its social reference and purpose. He reflects at the same time, however, that a new consciousness of this kind will also 'be enforced by external circumstances'. In the end, predictably, as this suggests, the question of the V-effect's full purchase and survival involves broadly cultural and political matters and not exclusively artistic ones. The task of the V-effect, as we have seen, is to reveal a suppressed or unconsidered alternative; to show the possibilities for change implicit in difference and contradiction. Those who suggest that V-effects are redundant are suggesting, however reluctantly, that there are no meaningful differences, or alternatives, still less any viable utopian perspective in contemporary, postmodern societies. In a world rapidly accepting the uniformities of Western-style market economies, where major historical narratives are said to be at an end, where contrasts and alternatives of a kind significant to Brecht – between, say, war and peace, East and West, or versions of consumer capitalism and socialism – have been foreclosed, this can indeed seem a realistic diagnosis. If, however, we continue to think, with Brecht, that the world remains in need of change, if we see it as more in the grip of widespread complacency than universal goodness or inescapable banality, then it is apparent that the V-effect has more work than ever to do.

GESTUS

Brecht concentrated the range of V-effects particularly upon the actor and acting style, an emphasis which distinguished his epic theatre from that of a contemporary such as Erwin Piscator. The terms *Gestus* and *gestisch* were not unique to Brecht (Willett refers to a use by Lessing in 1767 and to an article by Kurt Weill on the gestic character of music in 1929), and first appeared in his writings in the 'Notes to Mahagonny' ('The modern theatre is the epic theatre') and then in a fuller, slightly later essay 'On gestic music' (*BT*, pp. 36, 104–6). Like other key terms these too have proved difficult to translate. Willett defines *Gestus* as carrying the combined sense of 'gist and gesture; an attitude or a single aspect of an attitude, expressible in words and actions'. He chooses the obsolete English word ' "gest", meaning "bearing, carriage, mien" ' to translate *Gestus* and along with the adjectival form 'gestic' this has become established usage (*BT*, p. 42).

What needs to be added to Willett's account is Brecht's attention to the basic *social* content of a scene or action. This comes out clearly in the discussion of gestic music, though Brecht had underlined the 'moral' perspective of gests in a footnote to the 'Mahagonny' essay. 'Not all gests are social gests', he says in 'On gestic music'. Thus a look of pain 'as long as it is kept so abstract and generalised that it does not rise above a purely animal category, is not yet a social one'. The common tendency of art has been to empty the social content from any gest. 'The "look of a hunted animal" can become a social gest if it is shown that particular manoeuvres by men can degrade the individual man to the level of a beast; the social gest is the gest relevant to society, the gest that allows conclusions to be drawn about the social circumstances' (*BT*, pp. 104–5). This is thoroughly in keeping with Brecht's conception of the narrative drive of epic theatre: the realm of gest was 'The realm of attitudes adopted by the characters towards one another ... Everything hangs on the "story" ' which is 'what happens *between* people'. Thus, 'The story is the theatre's great operation, the complete fitting together of all the gestic incidents' (*BT*, pp. 198, 200).

Social gests were therefore the nuclei of epic theatre's discontinuous, dialectical narrative, and consequently the material a company would first isolate and work upon in rehearsals. The process of 'blocking' a play would mean boiling it down to its main tableaux, reducing these to their smallest significant units, and building from this foundation (see the account 'Phases of a production', *BT*, pp. 240–2). As if to emphasise this analytic approach, as well as to answer criticism, Brecht on one occasion made a silent film of the production of *Man is Man* which showed how the actor Peter Lorre successfully mimed 'the basic meaning underlying every (silent) sentence' (*BT*, p. 55). Lorre and Brecht were concerned to produce an 'external', socially situated performance rather than to penetrate a character's 'inner life'. Similarly, working with Charles Laughton in America with no common language but Brecht's poor English, both men were forced to use the language of theatre 'to translate gests':

> psychological discussions were almost entirely avoided. Even the most funda-mental gests, such as Galileo's way of observing, or his showmanship, or his craze for pleasure, were established in three dimensions by actual perform-ance. Our first concern throughout was for the smallest fragments, for sen-tences, even for exclamations – each treated separately.   (*BT*, p. 165)

As common practice, Brecht's actors were encouraged to rehearse parts in their own accents rather than 'in character', to read in the third person, to change register, to convert the present tense into the past, to include stage directions along with dialogue, to switch roles, even to use empathy (still to be avoided in a performance) (see *BT*, pp. 136–7, 195). Brecht recruited actors to the Berliner Ensemble 'with talent' but without standard theatrical or Hollywood features, de-schooling trained actors so that they would lose common habits such as 'Gravitating to the centre of the stage / Detaching oneself from groups in order to stand alone . . . Getting louder when increas-ing speed / Playing one thing out of another instead of one thing after another' (*BT*, p. 245). Like other aspects of Brecht's theatre, gestic acting was opposed technically and ideologically to the conventions of drama, and then in the post-war period to the orthodoxies of Soviet-styled socialist realism and of Hollywood, associated respectively with Stanislavsky and the Lee Strasberg school of 'method acting'. Rather than bringing a fixed char-acter into view, or losing themselves in a role, an epic actor showed his/her character in the process of change and growth, as open to comment and alteration, knotting together separated gests to produce 'his character's coherence despite, or rather by means of, interruptions and jumps'. Brecht's object remained consistently 'the most objective possible exposition of a contradictory internal process' (*BT*, pp. 55, 54 and 196 section 53).

One would like, obviously, to be able to examine the written accounts of

Gestus in relation to its live performance under Brecht's direction. Short of historical evidence of this kind the most useful illustrations remain the Model Books prepared from the performances of the Berliner Ensemble (which were *not* intended, Brecht plainly said, to fix a standard performance) and the essay 'The street scene'.[21] In this example, a witness tells the story of an accident, re-enacting it for the spectators and bystanders, changing parts (now acting the driver, now the victim), shifting from the first to the third person; his purpose being to show how the accident occurred and how it might have been avoided. The bystanders are put in a position to corroborate or criticise the account, to learn from it, and to form their own judgement.

Whereas, as mentioned earlier, it might be objected that Brecht's theory and practice were esoteric and unique, 'The street scene' shows how gestic technique consciously redeployed everyday behaviour. (One might think of a mugging as the scene of a particularly contemporary street gest.) Epic actors would treat their roles similarly, 'acting them out', as observers or reporters, rather than surrendering to the role or inviting empathy; they would play their character as a stranger, or as if from memory. They would therefore demonstrate the social gest implicit in an action or event in such a way that its contradictory emotions and motives were situated or 'historicised'. Often, as Brecht said, this involved 'quoting' words and actions (a device unfamiliar to drama perhaps, but common to narrative). As Brecht summarised these features:

> To achieve the V-effect the actor must give up his *complete conversion* into a stage character. He *shows* the character, he *quotes* his lines, he *repeats* a real-life incident.[22]

Above all epic acting is marked by its double, dialecticising function. Thus actors show their characters while themselves being shown, situating action and events as moments of decision, defined by a penumbra of possible but unadopted alternatives ('to build into the character that element of "Not-But"', *BT*, p. 197). The object being, as ever, to alert audiences to the contradictory, alterable course of history.

It is often thought that Brecht retreated from theory to practice in later years (Willett, *BT*, p. 243). But it would be more accurate to recognise the fully materialist, that is to say, practical accent of his theory, and its necessarily physical expression on stage. The theory of gestic acting was a theory of performance, of course, and in that sense the most literal embodiment of Brecht's dialectical materialism. In itself this was no guarantee of its successful realisation, however. Some of the features of gestic acting, as suggested of V-effects above, were inscribed in the very language and text of a play.

Yet they depended also (and depend still) on the skill and talent of actors, on their training and experience, and on their professional and political commitment.

What is more, Brecht had always recognised that epic or dialectical theatre depended on enabling artistic and social conditions. The fact that this remained true in the mixed circumstances of post-war East Berlin brought Brecht to question and qualify earlier key terms, as we have seen. His later writings suggest both a renewed theoretical resolve (the return to 'dialectics') and an accompanying stress on dialogue and collective practice in the Berliner Ensemble. Brecht sought in this context particularly, so it seems, to combine theory and practice in a shared and undemonstrative working philosophy. A concept which summarises these newer aims, though it was not new in Brecht's vocabulary, is *Haltung*. This term runs emphatically through Brecht's writings and, as Darko Suvin has argued, carries a range of meanings ('bearing, stance, attitude, posture, behaviour and also poise and self-control').[23] The English term 'attitude' perhaps best conveys this range of physical, professional and intellectual connotations. It applies therefore to the bodily presence and bearing of actors (one remembers the importance of the lanky music hall artist Karl Valentin and of Charlie Chaplin for Brecht), to a play's V-effects (text, sets, music are said 'to adopt attitudes' to its content) and to the 'critical attitude' Brecht wished actors to adopt and encourage. These senses of the term *Haltung* or 'attitude' appear also in Willett's gloss on *Gestus* and *gestisch* (the expression of 'an attitude or a single aspect of an attitude'; 'bearing, carriage, mien') and consistently in statements on gest's features and effects. Thus, 'gest' is a matter 'of overall attitudes. A language is gestic when it is grounded in a gest and conveys particular attitudes adopted by the speaker towards other men' (*BT*, p. 104). Revealing 'the social gest of Fascism ... means that the artist has to adopt a definite attitude towards the fact of pomp' (*BT*, p. 105). The particular attitudes or bearings Brecht then recommended were by turns those of learning, critique, pleasure or productivity, and in his very last years in an additional keyword which combines these, 'naivety'.

According to Manfred Wekwerth, Brecht discovered the concept of 'naivety' in the process of considering why his theory had been misunderstood; it was because 'he had omitted one half, assuming that this was obvious in the theatre – the role of the naive'.[24] The company, says Wekwerth, had been used to Brecht's use of the term in relation to acting, but now he extended and generalised it. Thus Brueghel was naive, Lenin's use of parable was naive, and the playing of *The Days of the Commune*, then in rehearsal, should also be naive.[25] As a new concept the 'naive' united acting and theatre, performance and theory. Thus the actor must 'take up the attitude of a man who just wonders' (*BT*, p. 197), but Brecht's theatre too was 'in a naive sense a philosophical one ...', his whole theory 'much naiver than people think' (*BT*, p. 248). The 'naive' therefore fittingly joined together contraries; it was a look, a posture, an attitude of mind; it implied an intelligent simplicity, innocence and shrewdness, joining the conceptual and concrete, the popular and philosophical. A naive attitude would estrange the familiar, and problematise the self-evident, signalling a dialectical movement from the ordinary and everyday to the original and innovatory. It was thus, in short, a summary gest of Brecht's transformative, utopian perspective upon art and life.

NOTES

1 See Darko Suvin, 'Brecht: bearing, pedagogy, productivity', *Gestos* 10 (November 1990), pp. 11–28; also essays by Manfred Wekwerth and Joachim Tenschert in *Re-interpreting Brecht*, ed. P. Kleber and C. Visser.

2 This emphasis is the subject of my *Bertolt Brecht: Dialectics, Poetry, Politics*, on which some of the present discussion draws.

3 Quoted in Suvin, 'Brecht', p. 20.

4 See *Brecht As They Knew Him*, ed. Hubert Witt, p. 146.

5 See essays in *Re-interpreting Brecht*.

6 See the critical surveys in Steven Connor, *Postmodern Culture* (Basil Blackwell: Oxford, 1989) and *Modernism/Postmodernism*, ed. Brooker (Longman: London, 1992). Also Wright, *Postmodern Brecht*.

7 See Frederic Ewen, *Bertolt Brecht*, pp. 144–65, for a fuller discussion.

8 Brecht, *Arbeitsjournal*, vol. I, p. 216. (The full entry, dated 20 December 1940, is quoted in Brooker, *Bertolt Brecht*, pp. 82–3.)

9 Witt, *Brecht As They Knew Him*, pp. 223–5.

10 Quoted in Völker, *Brecht: A Biography*, p. 336, and see pp. 226, 243.

11 *Re-interpreting Brecht*, pp. 20, 47–9.

12 Völker, *Brecht: A Biography*, p. 253.

13 Brecht, *Gesammelte Werke*, xv, p. 301. The translation is Keith Dickson's in *Towards Utopia*, p. 241.

14 This is taken up in a fuller discussion of the term's derivation and provenance in Brooker, *Bertolt Brecht*, chapter 4.

15 See Willett, *Brecht in Context*, p. 219.

16 Bernhard Reich, *Im Wettlauf mit der Zeit* (Henschel: Berlin, 1970), p. 371; quoted in Brooker, *Bertolt Brecht*, p. 70.

17 *Arbeitsjournal*, vol. I, p. 216; quoted in Brooker, *Bertolt Brecht*, p. 83.

18 See *GW*, xvii, p. 1042 for the rewritten scene. Brecht's text appears in translation in *The Mother* (Eyre Methuen: London, 1978).

19 See Tony Pinkney, 'Introduction' to *Raymond Williams: the Politics of Modernism* (Verso: London, 1989), pp. 19–23; also the discussion in Wright, *Postmodern Brecht*.

20 Witt, *Brecht As They Knew Him*, pp. 227–8.

21 *Brecht on Theatre* includes an extract 'From the *Mother Courage* Model'

pp. 215–22; see also sections iv and v of notes to *The Mother*, pp. 58–9, and sections 47–67 of 'Short organum', pp. 193–201, for the most sustained account in Brecht's later writings. As well as 'The street scene' in *Brecht on Theatre*, pp. 121–9, see *Poems 1913–1956*, for 'On everyday theatre' and 'Speech to the Danish working class actors', pp. 176–9; 233–8. I consider the relevance of Brecht's theoretical concepts to his poetry in Brooker, *Bertolt Brecht*, pp. 93–147.

22 *The Messingkauf Dialogues*, p. 104.
23 Suvin, *To Brecht and Beyond*, p. 12.
24 Witt, *Brecht As They Knew Him*, p. 148.
25 *Ibid.*, pp. 148, 149.

15

PHILIP THOMSON

Brecht's poetry

INTRODUCTION

Brecht's poetry is remarkable for two things. In a writer who is best known for his plays and his theatre theory, the sheer volume of his output as a poet is surprising. There are some one thousand pages of poetry in volume IV of the *Gesammelte Werke* (Collected Works), most of which has been translated in Manheim and Willett's *Poems 1913–1956*. To this one must add the many poems that have come to light since the publication of the Collected Works in 1967 and have appeared in a supplementary volume and in *Gedichte über die Liebe* (Poems About Love). Second, though Brecht maintained that his poetry was a second string to his bow, the quality and range of his verse rank him among the handful of great German poets of the twentieth century. From the beginning, he was an extraordinarily diverse writer, and his poetry reflects this. He began early: if we set aside the juvenilia, Brecht started writing poetry of the highest quality around 1918, when he was only twenty years old. Poetry accompanied all phases of his life and career, right up to his death.

The man who changed people's attitudes to so many aspects of the theatre could have made the same claim about poetry. Though there are clear points of contact between his lyrical work and various movements in twentieth-century German literature such as expressionism and the 'new objectivity' (*neue Sachlichkeit*) of the 1920s, Brecht's best poetry consistently shows us a personal style and a range of techniques that are original, indeed often unique: so much so that in the history of German poetry he occupies the position of a virtual maverick. His work falls outside the mainstream of modern German poetry as represented by Rilke and Hofmannsthal, say, or (closer to his own generation) Trakl and Benn. The conventional view of twentieth-century German literature which identifies these poets as central has difficulty 'placing' Brecht. Not that the conventional view is wrong. The development of German poetry since the eighteenth century had been overwhelmingly determined by the influence of Goethe and the romantics. In this scheme of things Brecht's poetry falls outside the norm. His verse is characterised by an extraordinary mixture of everyday language and rhetorical phrasing, of concrete detail and suggestive rhythms. There are some similarities between Brecht and Heine, but these are above all ideological. In his own time Brecht simply resists pigeon-holing. By the time he appeared on the literary scene in the 1920s expressionism was a spent force, and in any case Brecht was antipathetic to it from the beginning. The spare and unemotional style of the 'new objectivity' that followed was more suited to his temperament, but Brecht remained his own man. He was never associated with a literary group or movement and even after his embracing of Marxism in the late 1920s remained remarkably independent as a writer.

As might be expected, it is his poetry that seems to reveal to us Brecht the private individual. Though he was of course, from the late 1920s on, first and foremost a political writer, his poetry remained substantially a vehicle for self-expression. But a note of caution needs to be sounded. Brecht's poetry is not introspective in the traditional lyrical mode. His personal utterances tend to have the function of self-projection, even of self-staging. He presents himself to an audience, his readers. In this sense we might say that, on closer inspection, Brecht's poetry presents not so much the private person as the public personage. Conventional lyrical soul-gazing was unacceptable to him both temperamentally and ideologically. In all but a handful of his poems one feels Brecht's desire to communicate with his readers directly, engage with them in an immediate way.

THE EARLY POETRY (AUGSBURG)

Brecht's first volume of poetry, the *Hauspostille* of 1927, clearly demonstrates his wish to break with conventional notions of the lyric as the merely personal expression of life experience, in language of a more or less 'poetic' character. The very title of this early collection, which brought together most of Brecht's poetry up to 1922, is typically provocative. Devotions or breviaries (*Postillen*) were collections of religious pieces – sermons, guidelines for a proper and moral life, etc. – commonly found on the bookshelf in good bourgeois homes. Brecht's 'devotions' are anything but proper, and many of them are distinctly irreligious or offensive according to then current norms of taste and modesty. These poems were also not recognisably 'lyrical' in any conventional sense. Though there is a wide range of forms and styles, the 'ballad' is the most common, and even here Brecht's use of the term could be unusual. There are powerful evocations of a wild anarchic lifestyle as in the 'Ballad of the Pirates':

> Frantic with brandy from their plunder
> Drenched in thc blackness of the gale
> Splintered by frost and stunned by thunder
> Hemmed in the crows-nest, ghostly pale
> Scorched by the sun through tattered shirt
> (The winter sun kept them alive)
> Amid starvation, sickness, dirt
> So sang the remnant that survived:
>> Oh heavenly sky of streaming blue!
>> Enormous wind, the sails blow free!
>> Let wind and heavens go hang! But oh
>> Sweet Mary, let us keep the sea!   (*Poems*, p. 18)

On the other hand there are poems of social accusation, also in a balladesque style, such as 'Of the Infanticide Marie Farrar', which tells the story of a young servant girl who secretly bears a child and kills it out of fear of discovery:

> Marie Farrar: month of birth, April
> An orphaned minor; rickets; birthmarks, none; previously
> Of good character, admits that she did kill
> Her child as follows here in summary.
> She visited a woman in a basement
> During her second month, so she reported
> And there was given two injections
> Which, though they hurt, did not abort it.
>> But you I beg, make not your anger manifest
>> For all that lives needs help from all the rest.

> ...

> Marie Farrar: month of birth, April
> Died in the Meissen penitentiary
> An unwed mother, judged by the law, she will
> Show you how all that lives, lives frailly.
> You who bear your sons in laundered linen sheets
> And call your pregnancies a 'blessed' state
> Should never damn the outcast and the weak:
> Her sin was heavy, but her suffering great.
>> Therefore, I beg, make not your anger manifest
>> For all that lives needs help from all the rest.
>>   (*Poems*, pp. 90–2)

In this poem, written when Brecht was only twenty-three, some key aspects of his approach as a writer are already apparent. Marie Farrar's pathetic story is told, in indirect speech, in much the sort of language such a girl would use: simple, lacking fluency, but unmistakably real. The effect of this low-key presentation, devoid of all dramatic highlighting, is paradoxically all the more powerful. It was an insight Brecht was to use in his later work for the theatre. The style of the police report in which the girl's story is recounted functions precisely in the way that Brecht was to define in his description of the *Verfremdungseffekt*.[1] Finally, the refrain introduces another style much favoured by Brecht, the folksy religious tone of the *Moritaten* or broadsheet-ballads, those moralising verse tales of murder and mayhem that were still to be heard in the fairgrounds of Brecht's youth.

Brecht's early poetry about his experiences with women also shows his disinclination to follow conventional lyrical patterns. There is little tenderness and no passion. The woman is always an object, a mere means of sexual satisfaction. This stance is part of the young Brecht's self-projection as a tough, sardonic and even nihilistic type. In one poem, however, Brecht drops this role and indulges in a rare lyrical evocation of a past romance.

'Remembering Marie A.'

It was a day in that blue month September
Silent beneath a plum tree's slender shade
I held her there, my love so pale and silent
As if she were a dream that must not fade.
Above us in the shining summer heaven
There was a cloud my eyes dwelt long upon
It was quite white and very high above us
Then I looked up, and found that it had gone.

. . .

As for the kiss, I'd long ago forgot it
But for the cloud that floated in the sky
I know that still, and shall for ever know it
It was quite white and moved in very high.
It may be that the plum trees still are blooming
That woman's seventh child may now be there
And yet that cloud had only bloomed for minutes
When I looked up, it vanished on the air.   (*Poems*, pp. 35–6)

Of course, one may ask whether this is really a love poem or a send-up. It would not be the only example of parody in the *Hauspostille*. The off-hand reference to the woman's 'seventh child' and the conventional romantic language of the third and fourth lines of the first stanza are suspicious. But the poem has a simple and delicate beauty, and the fact that it is inspired not by the 'love', about whom the poet can remember practically nothing, but by the recollection of the delicate cloud above, should not trouble the reflective

reader. It is not the only example of a poet's fascination with the eva-
nescence of the poignant moment rather than with the beloved.

Like the pious and uplifting books on which it is parodistically modelled,
Brecht's *Hauspostille* is divided into sections called Lessons. There is a
Lesson entitled 'Spiritual Exercises', another has the heading 'The Little
Hours of the Departed'. Brecht even includes a set of 'Directions for Use' in
which the reader is advised at the outset, with typically sardonic rudeness:

> This book of devotions is intended for the reader's practical use. It is not
> meant to be unreflectingly swallowed without thought.
> The first lesson (Rogations) is directly aimed at the reader's emotions. It will
> be best to read it in small doses.

Of the fifty poems in this first remarkable collection, the one that created
the most scandal was the 'Legend of the Dead Soldier'. Written in 1918 and,
like several other 'Devotions', set to music by the author, it was sung by
Brecht to the accompaniment of his guitar in a Berlin cabaret in 1921,
causing the prompt cancellation of future appearances. When Brecht
included the 'Legend' in his compilation for the *Hauspostille*, the Kiepen-
hauer Verlag refused to publish it. The poem finally did appear in the Propyläen (Ullstein) edition when it was published in 1927. One can see why the
'Legend of the Dead Soldier' caused such a reaction. It was not only blas-
phemous but in the climate of a recently lost war was regarded as an insult
to the German soldier and a desecration of patriotic values.

> And when the war was four Springs old
> And of peace there was not a breath
> The soldier took the logical step
> And died a hero's death.
>
> The war however was not yet done
> So the Kaiser was displeased to be sure
> That his soldier had given up like that
> To him it seemed premature.

The dead soldier is dug up, pronounced fit for active duty and, supported by
army medics and a chaplain, marches off to the front. On his grotesque
journey, his shroud now painted in the colours of the German flag, he is
gradually surrounded by a cheering crowd:

> So many were dancing around him now
> That the soldier could hardly be seen
> You could only see him from the sky above
> And there only stars can gleam.

. . .

> The stars are not forever there.
> Daylight gives new breath.
> But the soldier does as he has learned
> And dies a hero's death.[2]

As a collection, the *Hauspostille* is essentially the product of Brecht's adolescence and early manhood in Augsburg. Despite its delayed publication the volume was essentially complete by 1922. If one takes out the five 'Mahagonny' songs added later, virtually all of the other forty-five poems were written by that date, in other words by the time Brecht was twenty-four years old. The 'Devotions' thus present a youthful Brecht, in poetry that is audaciously new, provocatively different and often brilliant. The young man from the southern provinces liked to present himself as an anarchistic egotist and precocious citizen of the world, and certainly some of this was true. But the 'Devotions' also contain poems that reflect the relaxed and carefree lifestyle enjoyed by the young Augsburger in the company of the small band of boyhood friends who admired his talent and were captivated, as many people of both sexes were, by his personality. The Augsburg lifestyle is captured in poems like 'Of Swimming in Lakes and Rivers', where Brecht's new lyricism is powerfully displayed:

> In the pale summer when the winds above
> Only in great trees' leaves a murmur make
> You ought to lie in rivers or in ponds
> As do the waterweeds which harbour pike.
> The body grows light in the water. When your arm
> Falls easily from water into sky
> The little wind rocks it absentmindedly
> Taking it likely for a brownish bough.　　　　(*Poems*, p. 29)

By the early 1920s, however, Brecht had turned towards new horizons. The very last poem of this first collection announces the next stage of his life, the move to the big city. The imminent transition from the boyhood world of Augsburg to the realities of the great metropolis Berlin is expressed in typical Brechtian fashion in the famous poem 'Of Poor B.B.', in which the poet already sees himself as a denizen of the 'asphalt jungle'.

> I, Bertolt Brecht, came out of the black forests.
> My mother moved me into the cities as I lay
> Inside her body. And the coldness of the forests
> Will be inside me till my dying day.
>
> In the asphalt city I'm at home. From the very start
> Provided with every last sacrament:

With newspapers. And tobacco. And brandy
To the end mistrustful, lazy and content.

· · ·

Before noon on my empty rocking chairs
I'll sit a woman or two, and with an untroubled eye
Look at them steadily and say to them:
Here you have someone on whom you can't rely.

· · ·

In the earthquakes to come, I very much hope
I shall keep my cigar alight, embittered or no
I, Bertolt Brecht, carried off to the asphalt cities
From the black forests inside my mother long ago.

(*Poems*, pp. 107–8)

BERLIN: 1924–1933

Brecht's celebration of his successful transfer to the booming, bustling metropolis Berlin was somewhat premature. 'Of Poor B.B.' was written, according to Brecht's manuscript, in the night train coming back to the security of Augsburg after an unsuccessful and painful first attempt to gain a foothold in Berlin, the cultural and theatrical centre of Germany. That winter of 1921–2 spent in the capital took the gloss off the young Brecht's somewhat romantic notions of life in the city. He found Berlin too big (the Munich he was comfortably familiar with was only one-sixth as large). The lifestyle was alien, the people unfriendly. He had no money and few contacts, and was often cold and hungry. Like many a young hopeful before him, he found that nobody wanted to know him in Berlin. This experience of the city emerges in the next collection of poems Brecht published, the *Reader for Those who Live in Cities*, put together in 1926–7 though not published until 1930. Paradoxically, by the time he wrote these city poems in the mid-1920s Brecht *had* made it in Berlin. He was acknowledged as an up-and-coming dramatist and had a high profile in literary circles. The unpleasant confrontation with the German metropolis that the *Reader for Those who Live in Cities* gives expression to, went back to 1921–2.

1   Part from your friends at the station
     Enter the city in the morning with your coat buttoned up
     Look for a room, and when your friend knocks:
     Do not, o do not, open the door
     But
     Cover your tracks.

If you meet your parents in Hamburg or elsewhere
Pass them like strangers, turn the corner, don't recognise them
Pull the hat they gave you over your face, and
Do not, o do not, show your face
But
Cover your tracks.   (*Poems*, p. 131)

The almost paranoid tone of this is a vivid reminder that Brecht's metaphor for the big city, 'the jungle', was more than a poetic whim. The unfriendliness of city people and the lack of human warmth which the young man from Augsburg encountered in Berlin is the central theme in Brecht's work from this period, which includes of course the key play *In the Jungle of the Cities*.

No doubt the harsh experiences recorded in Brecht's work in the mid- and late 1920s were an important factor in his conversion to Marxism late in that decade. Marxism seemed to offer a rational, systematic and theoretically sophisticated answer to the questions that assailed the observer of life in a modern urban society. The last vestiges of the characteristic tone of the early Brecht, in turn exuberant and nonchalantly sardonic, give way to a kind of clinical urgency as the writings of Marxist-Leninism are systematically absorbed. In works such as *The Threepenny Opera* one can see the two attitudes, cynical humour and savage social criticism, side by side. But by 1929, the year the stockmarkets crashed, Brecht was writing overtly Marxist–Leninist poems ('The Carpet-Weavers of Kuyan-Bulak Honour Lenin', *Poems*, pp. 174–5) and by 1931, as the Nazis surged towards power and the economic crisis continued, he had placed his work in the service of the communist cause.

'A Bed for the Night'

I hear that in New York
At the corner of 26th Street and Broadway
A man stands every evening during the winter months
And gets beds for the homeless there
By appealing to passers-by.

Such charity, Brecht argues, does nothing to change the social conditions that produce the need for it. Nevertheless, a few lucky ones are temporarily helped.

A few people have a bed for the night
For a night the wind is kept from them
The snow meant for them falls on the roadway
But it won't change the world
It won't improve relations among men
It will not shorten the age of exploitation.   (*Poems*, p. 181)

This is a typical example of Brecht's poetry in general: it is economically written, its language is simple and it is formally sophisticated. As far as its content is concerned, it is characteristic of Brecht's overtly communist poetry, whose function is the illustration of a point of Marxist–Leninist doctrine. Here it is the argument that individual acts of kindness, though they may be admirable, do nothing to alter the system of 'exploitation' (Brecht's favourite word in connection with capitalism). It is an argument that is pushed to controversial extremes in the play *The Measures Taken*.

In other political poems such as 'Song of the S. A. Man', written in 1931, Brecht uses his theatre background to create dramatic monologues, simple but effective.

> My hunger made me fall asleep
> With a belly ache.
> Then I heard voices crying
> Hey, Germany awake!
>
> Then I saw crowds of men marching:
> To the Third Reich, I heard them say.
> I thought as I'd nothing to live for
> I might as well march their way.
>
> And as I marched, there marched beside me
> The fattest of that crew
> And when I shouted 'We want bread and work'
> The fat man shouted too ...   (*Poems*, p. 191)

Many of these poems, including the above, were set to music by Hanns Eisler, like Brecht a communist. At their best, these joint efforts are impressive examples of political poetry understood as poetry designed to persuade or convert, and they reflect directly their context, the battle for supremacy in the 1920s and 1930s of the two extreme ideologies, communism and fascism.

EXILE: 1933–1948

When Brecht went into exile the day after the Reichstag fire in February 1933, his overtly propagandistic work continued. Along with most of the other German emigré writers, he was driven by an urgent need to contribute to the battle against Nazism. Brecht was able to harness his considerable satirical powers to this purpose, and alongside anti-fascist plays and prose pieces he produced a stream of clever and effective poems denouncing and exposing Nazism. Brecht defended this kind of poetry, and the openly didactic verse exemplified by 'A Bed for the Night', in one of his most famous poems, 'Solely Because of the Increasing Disorder', written in 1934.

> Solely because of the increasing disorder
> In our cities of class struggle
> Some of us have now decided
> To speak no more of cities by the sea, snow on roofs, women
> The smell of ripe apples in cellars, the senses of the flesh, all
> That makes a man round and human

The traditional subject-matter of poetry is to be replaced, in these desperate times, by political and economic discussion, couched in the 'dry, indecorous vocabulary' appropriate to such discussion:

> So that this awful cramped coexistence
> Of snowfalls (they're not merely cold, we know)
> Exploitation, the lured flesh, class justice, should not engender
> Approval of a world so many-sided; delight in
> The contradictions of so bloodstained a life
> You understand. (*Poems*, p. 225)

But there is more to this programmatic statement about literary priorities than meets the eye. On the face of it Brecht is defending the overtly political literature necessary in times of 'disorder' (his peculiarly clinical term for the evils of late capitalism). The purely personal and aesthetic pleasures of literature ('the smell of ripe apples in cellars, the senses of the flesh') are forsworn. But Brecht, even the pre-Marxist Brecht, never did write the kind of traditional verse thus characterised. Second, it is a paradox worthy of this very devious writer that Brecht makes his statement of aesthetic 'self-denial' in a poem – a poem moreover which, although certainly not 'lyrical' in any conventional sense, is a small masterpiece of poetic economy of diction, formal structure and rhetorical sophistication.

The reader's conclusion that there is, for all the seriousness of the situation, an element of tongue-in-cheek in such statements would be strengthened by other poems from this period in which apparent regret for having to be 'one-sided and dry' thinly masks the political writer's proud conviction that only when it is political is literature worthwhile. This sentiment, which flies in the face of traditional German attitudes, is expressed in the well-known poem 'Bad Time for Poetry' (1939), where Brecht regretfully concedes that 'only the happy man is liked': people do not want to read of misery and ugliness. Nevertheless, though 'The girls' breasts / Are as warm as ever', that is not what makes him want to write:

> Inside me contend
> Delight in the apple tree in blossom

And horror at the house-painter's speeches.[3]
But only the second
Drives mc to my desk.   (*Poems*, p. 331)

The sub-text here is of course that anyone who prefers to write (or read) about apple-trees in blossom or girls' breasts is irresponsible and immoral. Of course, this rejection of the traditional subject-matter of poetry must be read at least in part as a rhetorical statement. Even in these 'dark times' of exile, as he moved from one country to another with a wary eye on the rampaging triumphs of Nazism, Brecht did in fact write poetry about love and sex and the beauties of nature: about girls' breasts and apple blossom, to use his own shorthand. But the exile's sense of impermanence and of imminent danger was never stilled for long.

Above the Sound hang rainclouds, but the garden is
Gilded still by the sun. The pear trees
Have green leaves and no blossom yet, the cherries
Blossom and no leaves yet.

The pleasant and peaceful scene evoked in this poem ('Spring 1938') does not last:

The starlings' twittering
Is broken by the distant thunder
Of naval gunfire from the war games
Of the Third Reich.   (*Poems*, p. 303)

What is most significant about the very considerable amount of verse that Brecht wrote in his fourteen years of exile is the number of poems that deal with his own position and status as a writer. Brecht had always been fond of self-portrayal and self-stylisation. (What else is 'Of Poor B.B.'?) This reminds us that, for all his conviction that writing, including poetry, must serve a social and political purpose, Brecht was at the same time an intensely self-aware writer, ever conscious of his image. It is above all in the poetry that he projects images of himself and puts himself in the spotlight. This does not mean, however, that this poetry is straightforwardly auto-biographical. Rather, his poetic self-stylisations are precisely that: they present a *version* of Brecht the writer. 'Bad Time for Poetry' and 'Solely Because of the Increasing Disorder' give us the earnest anti-fascist whom desperate times have driven away from contemplation of life's beauties to the serious job of fighting Hitler. In 'Why Should My Name Be Mentioned?', written in 1936, there is an apparent humility that only thinly hides the pride that is justly felt by the great writer. Once, the poet begins, he had thought that his name would be remembered for his contributions to humanity.

But today
I accept that it will be forgotten.
Why
Should the baker be asked for if there is enough bread?
Why
Should the snow be praised that has melted
If new snowfalls are impending?
Why
Should there be a past if
There is a future?

Why
Should my name be mentioned?   (*Poems*, pp. 264–5)

Brecht uses here a characteristic rhetorical strategy, pretending a humble acceptance of the obscurity brought about by the passing of time while actually inviting the reader to demur. The reader of Brecht, after all, can readily think of half-a-dozen answers to the title question. It is exactly the same strategy as Brecht employs in what is arguably the most famous poem from the exile period, 'To Those Born Later' (1938):

I   Truly, I live in dark times!
     The guileless word is folly. A smooth forehead
     Suggests insensitivity. The man who laughs
     Has simply not yet had
     The terrible news.

     What kind of times are they, when
     A talk about trees is almost a crime
     Because it implies silence about so many horrors?

This beginning echoes the sentiments expressed in 'Bad Time for Poetry'. But at the end of this long, three-part poem Brecht appeals to his future readers ('those born later') for understanding:

III   You who will emerge from the flood
      In which we have gone under
      Remember
      When you speak of our failings
      The dark time too
      Which you have escaped.
      For we went, changing countries oftener than our shoes
      Through the wars of the classes, despairing
      When there was injustice only, and no rebellion.

                    . . .

> But you, when the time comes at last
> And man is a helper to man
> Think of us
> With forbearance.   (*Poems*, pp. 318–20)

Here again, the humble plea for 'forbearance' is partly a rhetorical gambit, calculated to elicit from his readers (future or present) not just grudging toleration, but copious praise and admiration. As one of the greatest living German writers, and probably the greatest of any nationality on the left, Brecht can afford, in this mock farewell poem, to pretend modesty.

The farewell, in which the poet sends a final address to his readers, is a genre that was especially suited to Brecht's staging instinct, which prompted him again and again to present to his audience of readers images and versions of the man and the writer. Valedictory poems begin very early in Brecht's career. 'Of Poor B.B.' has something of the farewell about it. And the little poem 'I Need No Gravestone', though published among the late verse, was written as early as 1933.

> I need no gravestone, but
> If you need one for me
> I would like it to bear these words:
> He made suggestions. We
> Carried them out.
> Such an inscription would
> Honour us all.   (*Poems*, p. 218)

The fact that Brecht could write this in his mid-thirties (and there exists an even earlier version) draws our attention again to his intense self-awareness, his preoccupation with his image as a writer and a man. In mid-career he is already turning his attention to what he would like on his gravestone. Far from being morbid, this is evidence of Brecht's robust self-assurance, just as the gravestone text itself is. The poetry thus gives us insights into Brecht the man and the writer that we look for in vain in other areas of his work.

Brecht's productivity during these difficult and unsettling, if not actually desperate, years of exile was remarkable. Throwing himself into his work was as much as anything a way of surviving. The poetry gives us poignant and often dramatic evidence of the emotions and experiences accompanying the many forced relocations of the Brecht household. In the main Brecht was fortunate in his choice of refuge, finding helpful and influential admirers to provide him with the material necessities for the continuation of his work. The last stage of the exile's wanderings, however, was not so happy. America was a culture shock for Brecht. This experience too is recorded in his poetry. His reaction to the heartland of capitalism is not long coming:

soon after his arrival in California he writes a poem entitled 'On Thinking About Hell'.

> On thinking about Hell, I gather
> My brother Shelley found it was a place
> Much like the city of London. I
> Who live in Los Angeles and not in London
> Find, on thinking about Hell, that it must be
> Still more like Los Angeles.   (*Poems*, p. 367)

It is arguable that what repelled Brecht as much as the unremittingly materialistic and money-centred lifestyle of the United States was the patronage system in the arts, whereby to get anywhere at all as a writer one had to kowtow to rich philistines. The sarcastically named 'Hollywood Elegies' of 1942 express Brecht's bitterness and contempt:

> III   The city is named after the angels
> And you meet angels on every hand.
> They smell of oil and wear golden pessaries
> And, with blue rings round their eyes
> Feed the writers in their swimming pools every morning.
>   (*Poems*, p. 380)

BERLIN: 1949–1956

When Brecht finally returned to Germany in 1949, it was to a completely new situation as a writer. The Brecht of the 1920s had been a kind of *enfant terrible* and rising talent. The writer who went into exile in 1933 was a Marxist, pushed into a role of external opposition. Throughout, he had been his own man, and had as often as not deliberately chosen the maverick's path. Now, in the German Democratic Republic, he was not only a celebrity but in an important sense a representative figure, held up by the German communist state as *their* writer. It is clear that Brecht did not enjoy this new role. Though the recognition of his work and especially the acquisition of his own theatre and company were a great satisfaction to him, some of the impetus for his writing was gone.

It is above all in his poetry, and in the *Arbeitsjournal* he kept, that one can see Brecht's discomfort in his new role as *Staatsdichter* (state poet). The man who had written some of the greatest poetry of the twentieth century, from a position of dissent, suddenly found the greatest difficulty in writing *positive* verse supporting and encouraging his fellow citizens in the new Marxist–Leninist republic. Too often this kind of writing turned out awkward, wooden and stilted.

'To My Countrymen'

You who survive in cities that have died
Now show some mercy to yourselves at last.
Don't march, poor things, to war as in the past
As if past wars left you unsatisfied.
I beg you – mercy for yourselves at last.   (*Poems*, p. 417)

It was as if Brecht's temperament and talents as a writer were better suited to an against-the-grain approach. This was now, if not impossible, very difficult for him in his new position as the key figure in the East German cultural establishment. Any criticisms of the state he did make were usually cautious and almost always followed by compensatory violent attacks on the West. 'The travails of the mountains lie behind us. / Before us lie the travails of the plains' (*Poems*, p. 416), Brecht had written on his return to the GDR. The latter proved more difficult for him than the former.

Brecht was, however, a staunch defender of communism and of the German communist state. This remained the case even during the convulsions caused by the workers' uprising in 1953, brutally repressed by the authorities with the help of Russian tanks. Though Brecht's reactions were mixed and ambivalent, ultimately he came out in support of the regime. The conflicts and anguish created by this emerge in the group of poems he wrote that summer, titled the *Buckow Elegies* after the little town outside Berlin where Brecht had a summer house on the lake. A key poem is 'Nasty Morning'. It begins with a series of images conveying the poet's depression: the Buckow landscape, usually a source of pleasure for him, has lost its appeal.

Why?
Last night in a dream I saw fingers pointing at me
As at a leper. They were worn with toil and
They were broken.
You don't know! I shrieked
Conscience-stricken.   (*Poems*, p. 440)

Brecht's torment at being seen by ordinary people as a traitor who sided with the Stalinist authorities is clearly expressed here. But so, less directly, is his unwillingness to confront the real problems raised by the revolt. The *Buckow Elegies* contain some criticisms of the regime – such as the famous suggestion in 'The Solution' that, since according to the Party, 'the people / Had forfeited the confidence of the government', the best thing might be for the government 'to dissolve the people / And elect another' (*Poems*, p. 440). But none of these critical poems was published at the time, and Brecht seems increasingly to have sought refuge from the turmoil surrounding his public role in simple verse of a purely personal and non-controversial nature, such as 'The Flower Garden'. The garden by the lake in Buckow is so planted that there are flowers from March until October:

> Here, in the morning, not too frequently, I sit
> And wish I too might always
> In all weathers, good or bad
> Show one pleasant aspect or another.   (*Poems*, p. 439)

This uncharacteristic escape into the private domain indicates as clearly as anything the resignation and tiredness which overtook Brecht in the last years of his life. However satisfying these little poems are with their evocation of quiet beauty and peacefulness, they nevertheless represent, in the turbulent context of 1953, a kind of withdrawal, almost an abdication, from the active involvement in the social and political sphere that had been part of Brecht's *raison d'être*.

The *Buckow Elegies* are the last unified group of poems written by Brecht. It is arguable that, apart from the exhaustion that becomes visible in his last years, the major factor in the reduction in his output at this time was precisely the disappointment and disillusionment that the GDR, and his own public role in it, engendered. It is typical of Brecht that he is able to give expression to these feelings, and the essential ambivalence of his position, in a deceptively simple poem, also included in the *Buckow Elegies*:

> 'Changing the Wheel'
>
> I sit by the roadside
> The driver changes the wheel.
> I do not like the place I have come from.
> I do not like the place I am going to.
> Why with impatience do I
> Watch him changing the wheel?   (*Poems*, p. 439)

The possible readings of this are manifold, but the poem refers, like all the others from Brecht's last collection, to the crisis of 1953. Brecht sits 'by the roadside' during the uprising, unable to influence events. It is not he who is driving, or changing the wheel. Neither the events in the GDR up to this point nor the direction taken by the uprising and its aftermath are to his liking. He waits impatiently, but with little faith in the outcome.

No doubt because of the unavailability, until relatively recently, of Brecht's poems in English translation, his reputation as a poet has been totally overshadowed in the English-speaking world by his standing as a dramatist and as a dramatic theorist. Even in Germany it is above all as a man of the theatre that he is renowned. It has been maintained, among others by the editors of Brecht's works in English, that this is a misperception and that 'Brecht was a greater poet than dramatist'. Certainly it is true that his reputation as a poet has grown immensely in recent years. It is also true that Brecht's plays provide ample evidence that 'his language was that of a poet', as Manheim and Willett remark in their Introduction to *Poems 1913–1956*. We need not enter a pointless discussion about whether his poetic or his dramatic gifts were primary. The two areas of his work interpenetrate from the beginning. His plays depend heavily on the poet's superb and original use of the German language, and the poet continually borrows from his insights into the nature of theatre. The dramatist knows that dramatic effects are ultimately created through language, the poet applies the theatre man's knowledge about subtleties of presentation. In this way Brecht's marvellously diverse work contains perhaps unexpected unities and continuities.

NOTES

Unless otherwise stated, quotations are from Bertolt Brecht, *Poems 1913–1956*, ed. John Willett and Ralph Manheim, to whom acknowledgement is here made.

1 For a detailed discussion of the *Verfremdungseffekt*, see the essay by Peter Brooker in this volume.

2 The translation here is mine.

3 Particularly in his poetry, Brecht habitually referred to Hitler as 'the house-painter', a trade Hitler had once followed, and one to which Brecht considered him better suited.

16

KIM H. KOWALKE

Brecht and music: theory and practice

Brecht asserted in a 1935 essay that it was music which 'made possible something which we had long since ceased to take for granted, namely the "poetic theatre"' (*BT*, pp. 84–90). Music provided him with a powerful mechanism to reclaim and refunction in 'epic drama' the presentational mode of address, long a standard convention in most forms of music-theatre but discarded by modern drama after the 'fourth wall' had been dismantled by naturalism and realism. Brecht's relationship to music, therefore, was as essential as it was complex. Although little interested in musical repertoire or issues extraneous to his efforts in the theatre, ironically Brecht first gained wide public recognition through the musical settings of his works: opera librettos, plays with music, a ballet, dramatic cantatas, an oratorio, musical films, even commercial jingles. By 1931, music critic Hans Mersmann could even proclaim: 'New Music in Germany has found its poet. This poet is Bertolt Brecht.'[1] Although Brecht thereafter showed little interest in serving the modernist agenda of 'New Music', only one of his nearly fifty completed dramatic works lacks music. Over 600 of his more than 1,500 poems refer to musical genres in title or structure; intended as songs, most were set as such during his lifetime. Subsequently, despite copyright disincentives, there have been well over a thousand additional settings, including many by major composers.

Music serves as a pillar so central to many of his theoretical constructs and as a parameter so determinant for the shape, diction and delivery of his texts that Brecht's legacy cannot be fully understood or properly assessed without reference to music. Confidence in his own musicality allowed him to influence settings of his texts, to criticise compositions by the less independent of his collaborators, and even offer them his own melodies, of which almost a hundred have survived. The remarkably small number of multiple settings of Brecht's poems during his lifetime attests to the authority commanded by those composed in direct collaboration with him.

The abbreviation *BT* refers to *Brecht on Theatre*.

Today these songs are not infrequently still miscredited to Brecht rather than to the composers, with the attendant assumption that musicians who worked closely with him were transmitting Brecht's own readings of his poems.

Brecht's poetic impulses had first manifested themselves in 'songs to the guitar, [as he] sketched out verses at the same time as the music'[2] and primitively notated them with his own ecphonetic symbols. Like Wedekind's models, many of these early poems were intended to be sung either in private to a small group of friends or in informal public settings. Eyewitnesses to Brecht's mesmerising live performances – whether in theatre, cabaret or brothel – concur in their accounts of his magnetism (not to mention his entourage) of a magnitude that we now expect only of rock stars. The songs did not really exist as independent texts, *per se*, because the author's, composer's, performer's and protagonist's personae all coalesced into a single voice – Brecht's. Carl Zuckmayer described that voice as 'raw and trenchant, sometimes crude as a ballad singer's, with an unmistakable Augsburg accent, sometimes almost beautiful, soaring without any vibrato, each syllable, each semitone being quite clear and distinct'.[3] That description certainly fits the only commercially released shellac recordings of Brecht singing: the two ballads from *The Threepenny Opera* within his vocal capability, the 'Ballad of Mac the Knife' and its motivic retrograde, 'Das Lied von der Unzulänglichkeit menschlichen Strebens'. Definitely not beautiful, yet charismatic and unforgettable in effect, Brecht's razor-sharp performance from 1929 (re-released on compact disc, Mastersound DFCDI-110) slices the text's syntax to reveal new strata of sense, while the rattler-rolled r's roil the otherwise almost stoic surface of his nasal, coarse tone.

Prior to 1925 Brecht handled the music for all productions of his plays himself; each included several songs. Some were *contrafacta*, wherein one or more pre-existent melodies were stripped of their original lyrics to allow a new text to engage in provocative dialogue with the images associated with the too-familiar music, 'putting quotation marks, as it were, around a lot that was cheap, exaggerated, unreal'.[4] More numerous were strophic ballads with neutral accompaniments and primitive, recitative-like original melodies that insured textual pre-eminence. At their most successful they reified Brecht's goal: 'they must be cold, plastic, unflinching, and, like tough nutshells when they get caught in his dentures, knock out a few of the listener's teeth'.[5] Brecht's earliest critical champion Herbert Ihering wrote of *Drums in the Night* that one really felt 'the whip-driven rhythms of his sentences' only when Brecht sang and accompanied himself on the guitar. In response, audiences 'whistled, yelled, howled, and applauded'; they were anything but cool, rational, or 'distanced'.[6] Yet Brecht admitted that in these first plays 'music functioned in a fairly conventional way. There was usually some naturalistic pretext for each musical piece' (BT, p. 84).

After Brecht realised that what Hanns Eisler would later call his 'colossal musicality without technique' would be inadequate to address music's role in the non-Aristotelian, 'dialectic' drama he was beginning to envision, he regularly recruited or was recruited by professional composers, to whom he tried to harness his own musical intuitions and aspirations.[7] Unqualified to write both libretto and score (as the antipodal Richard Wagner had done), Brecht found himself in a double bind: on the one hand, music's importance within the epic model required collaboration with composers of stature; on the other, he was unwilling to serve merely as the librettist most of them were continually seeking. He feared they would insist on 'music having its own meaning' and resist his control over its composition and performance. Suspicious of all 'autonomous' music, particularly those attributes associated with the nineteenth-century tradition of *espressivo*, Brecht rejected the opulence of operatically trained voices and the narcotic sensuality of string-dominated orchestration:

> A single glance at the audiences who attend concerts is enough to show how impossible it is to make any political or philosophical use of music that produces such effects. We see entire rows of human beings transported into a peculiar state of intoxication, wholly passive, self-absorbed, and according to all appearances, doped. Their gapes and stares signal that these people are irresolutely, helplessly, at the mercy of unchecked emotional urges ... Such music has nothing but purely culinary ambitions left.   (BT, p. 89)

Brecht distrusted musicians in general, he said, because they tended to view texts as 'series of words which are there to give them the opportunity to enjoy themselves'.[8] Because music tends to stimulate the listener so seductively and potently – as though without mediation, he feared that his poems would become mere material for music and be embraced without critical reflection. Consequently his own voice, no longer present as the performer's, would be appropriated by the composer's. He intuited that 'in most encounters between poetry and music, poetry can become the more powerful of the two only by the intentional acquiescence or the unintentional incompetence of the composer'.[9] To counteract this, Brecht eventually tried to posit a new paradigm, one which challenged what he feared was fundamental to the very nature of music. If it were to escape both its formalism and emotional entanglements, music would have to be turned inside out and become '*Misuk*', the term he invented in the 1950s for the radical refunctioning of both composition and performance that he required. Not even Hanns Eisler, who shared so many of Brecht's other values, however, could endorse so restricted a definition.

> Brecht's rejection of certain sorts of music was so extreme that he invented another variety of music-making, which he called 'Misuk' ... For a musician it is difficult to describe Misuk. Above all it is not decadent and formalist, but extremely close to the people. It recalls, perhaps, the singing of working women in a back courtyard on Sunday afternoons.[10]

Ultimately the irreconcilable contradiction between Brecht's need for and suspicion of 'cultivated' music would limit its role within his post-1936 theatrical works and his wider impact on music theory and practice.

Although his younger brother Walter and, later, Elisabeth Hauptmann had already transcribed some of his early melodies, the first of Brecht's professional musical collaborators, Franz S. Bruinier (1905–28), not only re-notated, arranged and orchestrated a handful of Brecht's melodies (including 'Pirate Jenny' and the 'Barbara-Song') but also composed his own settings of several poems (including 'Surabaya Johnny'). Dead from tuberculosis at twenty-three, Bruinier was followed briefly by Erwin Piscator's house composer, Edmund Meisel (1894–1930), who arranged the 'Man is Man Song' for the poet himself to sing in the Berlin Radio 1927 production that brought him to Kurt Weill's critical attention. When Weill (1900–50) and Brecht met shortly thereafter, they immediately explored the possibility of writing a full-scale opera, then collaborated on a half-dozen other large-scale projects during the four years of the rise and fall of plans and prospects for Mahagonny. They experimented with various recipes for hybrid genres of music-theatre in which the domination of music was not a given: the Songspiel Mahagonny (Baden-Baden, 1927), the plays-with-music The Threepenny Opera (Berlin, 1928) and Happy End (Berlin, 1929), the radio cantata Der Lindbergflug (Baden-Baden, 1929; first version jointly with Hindemith), the 'school opera' He Who Said Yes (Berlin, 1930), incidental music for the Berlin production of Man is Man (1931). Independently, Weill also set assorted pre-existent poems as the cantatas Vom Tod im Wald (1927) and Das Berliner Requiem (1928). Despite unexpected public and critical success, their always non-exclusive collaboration dissolved in 1931 – when common aesthetic and sociological tenets proved insufficient to overcome the centripetal force of their divergent views of the function of music in the theatre. They managed to collaborate only once in exile, for the symphonic ballet with songs, The Seven Deadly Sins (Paris, 1933) – Weill's orchestral masterpiece, which Brecht dismissed after its première under Balanchine as 'not very significant'.

Brecht's concurrent but brief association with Paul Hindemith (1895–63),

the foremost German composer of the post-war generation, was more ran-
corous and less productive. Although Hindemith failed to complete all of
the movements assigned to him for the joint version (with Weill) of *Der
Lindbergflug*, he did finish the score for its sequel, the first of Brecht's learning plays with music. Commissioned for and premièred at the modern music
festival which Hindemith co-directed, and scored for amateur soloists,
chorus, orchestra and offstage brass band, this *Lehrstück* created a scandal
in Baden-Baden. But it was not performed again for three decades; Brecht
withdrew his text and retitled its literary revision, *The Baden-Baden
Cantata of Acquiescence* to clarify its didactic content, which had, in his
opinion, been all but buried by Hindemith's emphasis on the joys of communal music-making for its own sake. Their confrontation over the rejection of *The Measures Taken* for the 1930 New Music Festival precluded the
possibility of further collaboration.

Only in 1930, after completing his Marxist studies and setting himself the
task of extracting an economically determined aesthetic system from the conditions of the class struggle, did Brecht find his ideal musical colleague and
friend in Hanns Eisler (1898–1962), who more than matched Brecht's new
commitment to art for ideology's sake. Although Eisler had independently set
several of Brecht's poems earlier, their full-scale partnership commenced with
The Measures Taken (Berlin, 1930); it would span nearly three decades.
During this period Brecht would formulate and reformulate his theories on
the proper nature and function of music within the epic model in a series of
prescriptions to which Eisler's music (for their collaborative dramatic works)
conforms more closely than that of any other composer. Highly effective but
strictly subordinate to the text, Eisler's incidental but substantial scores for
The Mother (Berlin, 1932), and *Round Heads and Pointed Heads* (Copenhagen, 1936) served as paradigms of the delicate dialectical relationship
between text and music required 'to fulfill the demands of an epic theatre' (*BT*,
p. 89). Ironically, with the exception of the score for *Schweyk in the Second
World War* (Warsaw, 1957; rev. 1959) which he completed after Brecht's
death, none of Eisler's other incidental music for plays by Brecht – *Fear and
Misery of the Third Reich* (1945), *Life of Galileo* (1947), *The Days of the
Commune* (1950) – reached that standard of excellence. Perhaps recognising
that the design of Brecht's mature plays constricted music's role, Eisler concentrated on film scores – including *Kuhle Wampe* (1931) and *Hangmen Also
Die* (1942) – and free-standing songs, song cycles and cantatas based on
Brecht's texts. In so doing, he extended the tradition of the German *Lied* in
new directions – with an individual idiom that recaptured the technical
advances he had perfected during his years of study with Arnold Schoenberg –
to create a body of politically engaged songs of the highest standard.

During the fifteen years of exile when Brecht produced most of his finest plays, he rarely collaborated with composers to create musico-dramatic entities, as he had in the previous decade. Rather, music played a less formative role, as the dramatist maintained full control by calling in musicians only for certain numbers – after the script had been completed. Among these lesser figures were the Finnish composer/conductor Simon Parmet (1897–1969), Franz Lehar's musical executor Paul Burkhard (1911–77), and the Swiss composer Huldreich Georg Früh (1903–45). Post-war collaborations with Carl Orff (1895–1982) and Gottfried von Einem (b. 1918) aborted prematurely, while that with Rudolf Wagner-Regeny (1903–69) yielded only two scores.

In the last decade of his life, however, Brecht's principal composer was Paul Dessau (1894–1979). Although Dessau had heard *Songspiel Mahagonny* in Baden-Baden in 1927 and had already composed songs for the Paris première of *Fear and Misery* (1938), he had no substantive contact with Brecht until 1942, when the composer was supporting himself as a labourer at a chicken farm in New Jersey. Brecht noted in his diary that Dessau was 'much less developed and set in his ways than Hanns Eisler', and in order to remain in close contact Brecht convinced him to move to Hollywood, and five years later, to East Berlin.[11] Indeed, Dessau described his contact with Brecht and his ideas as decisive; they immediately began work on three large-scale projects that were never finished, including a huge oratorio, the *Deutsches Miserere*. Beginning in 1946, Dessau wrote new incidental music for *Mother Courage and Her Children* and, a year later, *The Good Person of Szechwan*. After returning to Europe, he composed scores for productions of *The Exception and the Rule* (1948), *Mr Puntila and his Man Matti* (1949), *Man is Man* (1951), *The Caucasian Chalk Circle* (1954), as well as several cantatas and the opera *The Condemnation of Lucullus* (1949). Believing that opera is 'the most powerfully expressive genre with which to highlight artistically the social issues of our time', Dessau continued after Brecht's death to set his texts, including an operatic treatment of *Puntila* (1957–9). Maintaining a more deferential attitude toward Brecht than had Eisler, not to mention Weill, Dessau consistently provided what Brecht asked for. Today, however, after the dissolution of the GDR, Dessau has achieved little independent identity.[12] Theatres now routinely substitute newly composed music for his incidental scores, a practice almost inconceivable for Brecht's joint musico-dramatic ventures with Weill and Eisler.

No other composer achieved the *Mitarbeiter* (co-worker) status Brecht reserved for only Weill and Eisler, who not only supplied music but also contributed to the overall conception and actual text of their collaborative works. At the time each began working with Brecht, he had already rejected the aesthetic assumptions and hierarchies which modernism had inherited from romanticism and left largely unaltered. At approximately the same time, both composers ended studies with their formidable teachers – Weill with Ferruccio Busoni, Eisler with Arnold Schoenberg – and set off in new directions on their own, each seeking in his own way to transcend the self-preoccupation, subjectivity and ultimately isolation of the New Music and to forge new contacts with mass culture and mass audiences for a socially engaged musical art. In collaborations with Georg Kaiser (*Der Protagonist*, 1924–5) and Iwan Goll (*Der neue Orpheus*, 1925), Weill had decisively rejected both musical and literary expressionism and embraced popular idioms. Eisler's musical reorientation, evident in the *Zeitungsausschnitte*, op. 11 (1925–7), preceded his first discussions and collaboration with Brecht by at least four years; in 1926 he had shocked his teacher by declaring: 'I am bored by modern music, it is of no interest to me; much of it I even hate and despise.' Yet, as David Drew observed, 'neither the power nor the extraordinary durability of his collaboration with Brecht would have been attainable but for the self-awareness and the mastery he had first achieved within Schoenberg's orbit and then developed on the tangential path he took in 1927'.[13] By then Eisler was a committed Marxist in both theory and practice: as music critic for the communist *Die rote Fahne*, composer of militant workers' choruses and marching songs, and leader of the study group Dialectical Materialism in Music.

Whereas Weill's lifelong commitment to a renewal of the musical theatre rested on socialist sociological premises, Eisler's political agenda rendered any theatrical ambitions incidental. Yet aesthetically and technically they had more in common than just Brecht:

> For many years the parallactic view of Brecht's musical collaborators that rendered them figuratively and even functionally indistinguishable from Brecht himself was supposed to justify the idea that resemblances between (for instance) the music of Weill and Eisler were simply attributable to the influence of Brecht. Today it is perhaps permissible to suggest that Weill was one of the means whereby Eisler temporarily freed himself from Vienna. Of all the composers who were to a greater or lesser extent struck by Weill's deeply paradoxical achievement he was the only one at that time who had both the technical equipment and the strength of mind and musical character to turn to his own advantage a wide range of possibilities ... The influence was mutual – there are traces of Eisler in Weill's music until as late as 1938.[14]

While Brecht considered Eisler's settings to be 'the tests of his poems, what productions were to his plays', he credited Weill with 'first providing what [he] had needed for the stage'.[15] The four years of his nearly continuous collaboration with Weill were transitional ones for Brecht; he concentrated on Marxist studies begun in 1926, published his first collection of poetry, and completed only those dramatic works in which music was essential rather than incidental. Creatively at a disadvantage in that he had no experience of working with a composer of stature, he found himself perilously close to performing the normal functions of a librettist.[16] Yet it was in these pieces of socially engaged music-theatre that the montage techniques which have become fixed in public consciousness as 'Brechtian' were developed and the dramaturgical foundations of 'epic' drama laid. The four cornerstones of that new theatre comprised an unsentimental, repertorial, *sachlich* mode of presentation; development of new didactic genres for production outside the state-subsidised system; adaptation of cinematic techniques; and radical separation of the elements. With the latter Brecht tried to avoid the detested muddle of the Wagnerian *Gesamtkunstwerk*, where the various constituents are fused and consequently degraded. He hoped to bypass altogether what he called 'the great struggle for supremacy between words, music, and production – which always brings up the question "which is the pretext for what?": is the music the pretext for the events on the stage, or are these the pretext for the music?' (*BT*, p. 37).

Weill recognised Brecht's dilemma and in 1929 confided to a friend his strategy for dealing with it:

> Music has more impact than words. Brecht knows it and he knows that I know. But we never talk about it. If it came out in the open, we couldn't work with each other any more. Brecht asks for complete submission. He doesn't get it from me, but he knows that I'm good and that I understand him artistically, so he pretends that I'm utterly under his spell. I don't have to do anything to create that impression. He does it all himself.[17]

Brecht indeed later claimed that he 'had whistled things for Weill bar by bar and above all performed them for him'.[18] This familiar account of Brecht's ventriloquism (and single-handed rescue of his 'dummy' from Schrekerian 'atonal psychological operas') has been obliquely substantiated by a frequently cited essay published under Lotte Lenya's name but written by her second husband, George Davis: 'Sometimes Brecht impressed on Kurt his own ideas for a song, picking out chords on his guitar. Kurt noted these ideas with his grave little smile and invariably said yes, he would try to work them in.' The original typescript includes another sentence suppressed in publication: 'Naturally they were forgotten at once.'[19] With two or three celebrated exceptions, Weill proved an unwilling mouthpiece for Brecht's melodies. He was as aggressive as the poet when it came to defending his territorial imperative; in a recently rediscovered interview from 1934, when the interviewer commented on the dominant role Brecht had played in their collaboration, Weill answered him sharply:

It almost sounds as if you think Brecht wrote my music ... Brecht is one of modern Germany's greatest literary talents; but being a great poet doesn't necessarily mean he's also a good composer ... Brecht is a genius, but for the music in our joint works, I alone am responsible.[20]

Although Brecht and Weill always remained wary of one another and retained the formal mode of address, what permitted them to pursue common goals, while gradually realising that aesthetic and sociological premises were insufficiently shared, was the mediating concept of *Gestus*, a term introduced into print by Weill in December 1928.[21] Within the dramaturgy of a music-theatre which strove to illuminate social relationships between characters rather than internal psychological states, Weill and Brecht both conceived *Gestus* as a means of making manifest on stage the behaviour and attitudes of human beings toward one another.[22] They agreed that music was indispensable in communicating the fundamental *Gestus* of a theatrical situation. A new 'gestic' language, combining dramatic, lyric and epic modes of poetry, would require a 'gestic' music in which musical autonomy and expressivity would yield before dramatic and sociopolitical purposes. In their respective prescriptive essays, Weill and Brecht borrowed terminology and exchanged examples as each groped toward a working definition of both *Gestus* and *gestische Musik* based on his own reading of their evolving practice.

For Brecht, *Gestus* was but one of several strategies for 'epicisation' of interpretation, presentation and reception of his dramatic works. Although he progressively referred to *Gestus* in less behaviourist and more Marxist terms (characters' social relationships must be presented as determined by economic and political factors), initially it seems to have served primarily as a means to reserve space within the song for his own poetic voice/persona and to dictate readings of his texts by both composer and performer. He claimed 'to be thinking always of actual delivery', how his authorial voice would be mediated by the performer for the spectator.[23] Recognising that the 'text' of music-theatre is fully assembled and experienced only in performance, Brecht adhered to the 'inflexible rule that the proof of the pudding is in the eating'. By fixing the rhythm, stress, pitch, timbre, pauses, phrasing, dynamics, tempos and intonation of his poetry in a musical setting, Brecht hoped to make his works virtually performer-proof and ensure a 'drug-free' effect on their audiences. Because he realised that 'the effectiveness of this music depends largely on the way in which it is performed', it is not accidental that the concept of *Gestus* emerged only after he had stopped writing and publicly singing his own songs, when he himself could no longer entirely control the reading of his poems (*BT*, p. 88).

Although Weill's theoretical formulations were equally inconsistent and undeveloped, the practical significance of the concept was very different for him. He described *Gestus* almost exclusively as a technical tool of the composer, with historical precedents in the music of Bach, Mozart, Beethoven, Offenbach and Bizet. He assumed that *Gestus* would enable music to regain a privileged position in the overall structure of musical theatre works, 'right down to the execution of the smallest details'. *Gestus* could channel and focus music's communicative capacities and free it from its traditional parallelism to the text, as well as its descriptive and psychological functions, thereby granting wider melodic, formal and harmonic latitude. Gestic music could articulate that which the text does not make explicit and thereby provide a subtext ready-made for the performer. The resulting 'play' between the music and the lyric – particularly frustrating expectations and subverting conventions – could convey complicated layers of meaning and contradictory attitudes.

When Brecht wrote that 'Weill's music for [the opera *Mahagonny*] is not purely gestic', he called attention to the discrepancies in both theory and practice inherent to their respective gestic formulas (*BT*, p. 87). Fixing the *Gestus* and separating the ingredients according to various recipes had failed to settle the 'great struggle for supremacy' between text and music. Perhaps the unresolved dissonance between Weill's and Brecht's non-unison voices is best heard at the climactic clash over Ernst-Josef Aufricht's Berlin production of the full-length *Rise and Fall of the City of Mahagonny* at the Theater am Kurfürstendamm in December 1931. Although it had been cast largely with singing actors rather than the originally intended opera singers (necessitating certain cuts and simplifications to which Weill had reluctantly acquiesced) and accompanied by a reduced orchestra of less than forty players, during rehearsals Brecht bemoaned that 'all is washed out by the music'. In a scene worthy of *Capriccio*, he publicly denounced Weill as a 'phoney Richard Strauss'. Lawyers threatened to stop rehearsals, and in a last-ditch effort to salvage his production, Aufricht convinced Brecht to bow out. Leaving *Mahagonny* to Weill and designer Caspar Neher (who had already written the libretto for *Die Bürgschaft* with Weill), Brecht instead staged *The Mother*, his adaptation of Gorky's novel, in the theatre's basement, with his wife Helene Weigel, Ernst Busch, Theo Lingen and Margarete Steffin among the cast.

The move downstairs was decisive, irreversible and symbolic of a much larger shift: Brecht left behind opera, the commercial theatre and Weill; thereafter Brecht would hail *The Mother* – with Eisler's nine songs, ballads and choruses – as the classic model for politically mature epic theatre:

> Far more deliberately than in any other play of the epic theatre, the music in
> *The Mother* was designed to induce in the spectator a critical approach.

Eisler's music can by no means be called simple. Qua music it is relatively complicated, and I cannot think of any that is more serious. In a remarkable manner it makes possible a certain simplification of the toughest political problems. (*BT*, p. 88)

With what Ernst Bloch labelled the 'radical monotony' of his music, Eisler succeeded in refunctioning the *Song* – Weill and Brecht's concoction, combining aspects of the *Lied*, the American popular song and the opera aria, that first had taken the stage in a role central to epic dramaturgy in the *Songspiel Mahagonny* and then had achieved worldwide recognition in *The Threepenny Opera*. 'Lob des Lernens' (In Praise of Learning), 'Lob des Kommunismus' (In Praise of Communism), and 'Grabrede über einen Genossen' (Funeral Oration for a Comrade) were in no danger of being 'misunderstood', of embarrassing the playwright as had the *Schlager* (hit-tunes) of *The Threepenny Opera* – 'the light music of 1930', for which, T. W. Adorno claimed, the public had mistaken them. The concurrent productions of *Mahagonny* and *The Mother* evinced how far Weill and Brecht's paths had diverged; the critic of *Die rote Fahne* compared Eisler's score to Weill's:

> Here there's no monstrous orchestra as on the Kurfürstendamm for Weill's score for Brecht's *Mahagonny*; no intoxicating violins, bloated wind sonorities, flowing harmonies, but rather a very small ensemble of a couple of brass players, percussion, and piano. But here there is sharp, clear voice-leading, brittle march rhythms, proletarian songs that grip you tensely from the first to the last note. In the incidental music for *The Mother*, Eisler's ability to bind words, sentences, slogans into a unified structure of striking effect through music reveals itself anew in a transcendent way.[24]

Eisler himself suggested much later that Weill had never really understood Brecht's ideas: 'he saw only the innovative effects, not what was really going on'. The reverse, of course, was equally true. And with their popularity undiminished, the products of the Brecht–Weill collaboration continued to pose problems for Brecht long after their premières. His retrospective dissatisfaction with them is most vividly demonstrated by the fact that he either repudiated or unilaterally revised each of them, eventually republishing all but one in literary versions incompatible with Weill's music. In two cases Brecht paralleled these revisions with commentary reinterpreting or correcting, from his maturing Marxist perspective, the 'misunderstandings' engendered by the originals. In his and Peter Suhrkamp's lengthy notes to *Mahagonny* published in 1930, Brecht acknowledged that in the eating, the opera had turned out to be 'culinary through and through'. *Mahagonny* had demonstrated that opera could not be reformed; it must be demolished and replaced:

The opera *Mahagonny* was written three years ago, in 1927 [*recte* 1927–30]. In subsequent works attempts were made to emphasise the didactic more and more at the expense of the culinary element. And so to develop the means of pleasure into an object of instruction, and to convert certain institutions from places of entertainment into organs of mass communication. (*BT*, pp. 41–2)[25]

If Brecht's notes to *Mahagonny* set forth theoretically an aesthetic and political agenda for epic theatre that the opera itself had failed to address, much less accomplish, the notes to *The Threepenny Opera* were intended as a corrective to the performance practice that had accounted for its unexpected success, which Brecht (and his Marxist critics) now viewed as 'mistaken'. In an interview with himself dating from about 1933, Brecht answered the question, 'What, in your opinion, accounted for the success of *The Threepenny Opera*? I'm afraid it was everything that didn't matter to me: the romantic plot, the love story, the music.'[26] His revisions to the text and the new notes reflect what he would have liked the play to have been, in the light of the dire post-première changes in political and economic circumstances and his subsequent experiments with didactic modes of music-theatre, principally with Eisler. Informing subsequent readings of the play with tropes on the original seemed Brecht's best bet for bringing out a clear socio-political message absent or diffused in the text of the 'comic literary operetta' (then still being staged around the world), which *Die rote Fahne* had dismissed as an 'entertaining mishmash without a trace of modern social or political satire'.

Brecht's *Threepenny Opera* notes were intended to be corrective rather than descriptive in yet another sense: several sections are barely camouflaged attempts to reverse text–music relationships inherent in the original. If the text had lost round one in the struggle for supremacy, Brecht was not inclined to concede the bout. (In 1933 Weill informed his publisher that he would have to attend the New York première of *The Threepenny Opera* because 'Brecht wants to go, which means that the music would be pushed completely into the background'.)[27] Brecht would simply change strategies: the composer's need not be the last nor necessarily the decisive reading of a poetic text. An audience's reading will be based to a large degree on that of the director and performers, who give empirical voice to the personae of poet, composer and dramatic characters and modulate those with their own. Thus, in the section of *The Threepenny Opera* notes entitled 'About the singing of the songs', Brecht admonishes actors not 'to follow the melody blindly'. 'There's a way of speaking against the music which can be very effective just because of an obstinate matter-of-factness, independent of and incorruptible by the music and rhythm.' He also stipulates that 'the actor must not only sing but show a man singing' (*BT*, pp. 44–5).

In these three suggestive sentences Brecht set forth the underpinnings of what thereafter would be taken at face value to be the essence of authentic 'Brechtian' performance practice. By calling for uncultivated voices that have resisted training in classical technique and by reminding his actors that they need not sing all the time, the aesthetic distraction of the 'voice-object' is minimised, and the scope of the performer's (and consequently also the composer's) voice restricted. Leaving the melody 'unsung' at crucial moments simultaneously muffles the composer's and mutes the character's virtual voice to allow the poetic persona to be heard without competition, clearly enunciating the text while the singing voice retreats. The composer is banished to the orchestral pit, but Brecht offers him compensation for loss of his voice. Invoking the *lyrisches Ich*, in German literary criticism a construct roughly analogous to 'persona', Brecht suggests that

> In the orchestra, no matter how small, lies your chance as a musician . . . Your orchestra is your troupe, your gang, your constant. True, it has to supply supports for the aforementioned non-musicians; otherwise he [the actor] will collapse, but every instrument that you can wrestle free from this duty is won for you, for the music, sir! . . . Instruments don't speak per 'I' but rather per 'he' and 'she'. What forces you to share the feeling of the 'I' on stage? Where are your own feelings? You are entitled to adopt your own position to the song's theme. Even the support you give can serve other arguments![28]

Requiring that the actor 'not only sing but show a man singing' can be read as a parallel effort to ensure that the poetic persona also shares the stage with the protagonist. Brecht distances the performer from the performed and differentiates the presence of the character from that of the performer. With characteristic dialectics, Brecht requires the actor to depict her or his character's reality and yet stand outside it observing as an eyewitness: 'The singer becomes a reporter, whose private feelings must remain a private affair' (*BT*, p. 38).[29] The poet thereby forges an alliance with the performer, who then stands in for him as narrator and commentator, displacing the protagonist as author of the words being sung. Thus even a solo performance is a type of montage, a combination of mimetic immediacy and diegetic distancing, a composite of dissected realities. Although intended to seem 'naive' to an audience, it is anything but simple for the performers, who must demonstrate awareness of their own presence in the performance.

When used sparingly for narrative passages of speech-like declamation by singing actors consciously holding additional vocal resources in reserve, and not out of necessity, 'theory' proved itself effective in the practice of the *ad hoc* company of actors, operetta singers and cabaret artists who had gathered around Brecht: Peter Lorre, Oskar Homolka, Carola Neher, Helene Weigel, Ernst Busch, Kurt Gerron, Harald Paulsen, Theo Lingen,

Kate Kühl, and, of course, Lotte Lenya. Most were indeed actors first, with razor-edged diction, but almost all of them could also really sing; the theatrical system required such versatility, and the customary training of actors had nurtured it. Paulsen, for example, took over Tauber's roles in Lehar, and Weill chose Ernst Busch for the *Heldentenor* role in Weill's *Der Silbersee*. Carola Neher and the young Lenya were both soprano songbirds with voices aptly described by Ernst Bloch's characterisation of Lenya's – 'sweet, high, light, dangerous, cool, with the radiance of the crescent moon'. *The Threepenny Opera*'s sensational popularity had propelled many members of that loose collective into the recording studio: the songs appeared on more than forty discs with twenty different labels. A large selection of these shellac recordings have now been re-released (Capriccio CD 10346 and 10347); that is as close as we can come to sampling the original pudding, a bit of *echt* Brechtian performance practice.

But in the wake of posthumous interpreters of Brecht ranging from the composers Cerha, Henze and Berio to singers as diverse as David Bowie, Robyn Archer, Dietrich Fischer-Dieskau, Dagmar Krause, Teresa Stratas, Tom Waits and Sting, 'Brechtian' has now come to mean something very different from what would have been recognised as such in performances of the Weimar period. A 'performance tradition' based on theory post-dating the works in question, with precepts from a later period of Brecht's career misapplied to works from an earlier, is now routinely invoked as a standard for the entire Brecht canon and, because of his paradigmatic stature, beyond. Whereas 'Brechtian' originally denoted an unsentimental, 'cool', repertorial, *sachlich* presentation, closely allied to the matter-of-fact directness of popular singers and cabaret artists, it was nonetheless musically accurate. Now, however, by privileging *ex post facto* theory over the musical demands of the works themselves, a 'Brechtian' approach has been extended to repertoire, most notably to some of the Weill–Brecht pieces, which barely survive such treatment. The common practice of transposing songs down to actresses' speaking registers produces the now *de rigueur* Brechtian bark reminiscent of Brecht's widow Weigel. High notes are frequently replaced or rendered as *Sprechstimme*, musical subtleties ignored, the youthful vulnerability that once balanced textual toughness lost. Rearranging scores for smaller ensembles has eliminated much of the play among personas and inhibited the music's counterpoint to the lyric; the text may seem to win, but the song certainly loses.

The enforced orthodoxy of prevailing 'Brechtian' performance practice has diminished the poet as much as 'his' composers, for Brecht's inimitable voice is never truer, more telling or more powerful than when competing for cohabitation with worthy music sung by performers capable of meeting the particular challenges it presents. Only when the wide range of music associated with Brecht has been performed and recorded accurately will it be possible to 'prove the pudding', to test theory against practice and assess fairly the full impact of Brecht's contradictory musical impulses and ideas.

NOTES

The most comprehensive surveys of 'Brecht and Music' have appeared in the German language: Joachim Lucchesi and Ronald K. Shull's *Musik bei Brecht* comprises a long introductory overview of Brecht's involvement with music, his known writings about music, a catalogue of compositions dating from his lifetime and a discography. An English translation is scheduled for publication by Pendragon Press in 1993. Less useful but nonetheless exhaustive are Albrecht Dümling's 736-page critical survey, *Lasst euch nicht verführen: Brecht und die Musik* (Kindler: Munich, 1985) and Fritz Hennenberg's 3-volume *Das grosse Brecht-Liederbuch* (Suhrkamp: Frankfurt, 1984). In English, the best short survey remains John Willett's 'Brecht and the Musicians' in *Brecht in Context*. Though essentially uncritical despite its subtitle, Michael John T. Gilbert's *Bertolt Brecht's Striving for Reason, Even in Music: A Critical Assessment* is a serviceable chronicle of Brecht's musical collaborations and writings about music. For in-depth treatment of individual works, students might begin with single-composer overviews such as David Drew's *Kurt Weill: A Handbook* and Albrecht Betz, *Hanns Eisler: Political Musician*, as well as articles in music periodicals. The 65-page monograph of Kenneth Fowler, *Received Truths: Bertolt Brecht and the Problem of Gestus and Musical Meaning*, explores reasons for the dearth of genuine musical criticism of music associated with Brecht as opposed to a plethora of 'uncritical applications of Brechtian theory resulting in dogmatic demonstrations of the fulfilment of its propositions'. Although all of the Brecht–Weill collaborations have been published and recorded, only *The Threepenny Opera* and *Happy End* are available for study in full score. Publication and recording of Eisler and Dessau are less complete, while much of the music composed for original productions remains inaccessible.

1 Mersmann, 'Die neue Musik und ihre Texte', *Melos* 10 (May/June 1931), p. 171.
2 Brecht, *Arbeitsjournal*, vol. I, 3 August 1938.
3 Quoted by Willett, in *Brecht in Context*, p. 152.
4 *Ibid.*
5 Brecht, *Tagebuch*, 26 August 1920; quoted in *Musik bei Brecht*, ed. Lucchesi and Shull, p. 97.
6 *Berlin Börsen-Courier*, 9 December 1923; quoted and translated by Fuegi, *Bertolt Brecht: Chaos, According to Plan*, p. 15.
7 Eisler's comment was recorded by Hans Bunge, *Fragen Sie mehr über Brecht: Hanns Eisler im Gespräch* (Rogner and Bernhard: Munich, 1970), p. 210.
8 Brecht, 'Texte für Musik', GW, XIX, p. 406; reprinted in Lucchesi and Shull, *Musik bei Brecht*, pp. 150–1.
9 Edward T. Cone, *The Composer's Voice* (University of California Press: Berkeley, 1974), p. 45.
10 Eisler, 'Bertolt Brecht und die Musik', *Sinn und Form* (1957), pp. 439–41; trans.

by Marjorie Meyer in *A Rebel in Music: Selected Writings*, ed. Manfred Grabs (International: New York, 1978), pp. 173–4.

11 *Arbeitsjournal*, vol. I, 6 November 1944.

12 The most comprehensive (if ideologically distorted) consideration of Dessau's collaboration with Brecht is Fritz Hennenberg's *Dessau-Brecht: musikalische Arbeiten* (Henschel: Berlin, 1963).

13 David Drew, 'Eisler and Austrian music', *Tempo*, 161/162 (June and September 1987), pp. 28–9.

14 *Ibid.*, p. 28.

15 Brecht's comment about Eisler is quoted in Willett, *Brecht in Context*, p. 162; his appraisal of Weill appears in the *Arbeitsjournal*, vol. I, 7 October 1940. Other than the two 'cantatas', *Vom Tod im Wald* and *Das Berliner Requiem*, outside the theatre Weill composed only two songs with texts by Brecht. Eisler, in contrast, was a prolific composer of self-standing *Lieder*, many with texts by Brecht.

16 *The New Grove's Dictionary of Music and Musicians*, s.v. 'Brecht, Bertolt', by David Drew.

17 Felix Jackson, 'Portrait of a quiet man: Kurt Weill, his life and his times', unpublished biography (photocopy in Weill–Lenya Research Center, New York), p. 110.

18 *Arbeitsjournal*, vol. I, 16 October 1940.

19 'That was a time!', *Theatre Arts* (May 1956); reprinted as 'August 28, 1928', in *The Threepenny Opera*, trans. Eric Bentley and Desmond Vesey (Grove Press: New York, 1964), p. ix. George Davis derived the essay from interviews with Lenya and Elisabeth Hauptmann; the transcripts of those interviews and the typescript of the essay are now in the Weill–Lenya Research Center. The nature and extent of the few documented musical 'borrowings' by Weill from Brecht are discussed by David Drew in *Kurt Weill*, pp. 201–5.

20 Ole Winding, 'Kurt Weill i Exil', *Aften-Avisen* (Copenhagen), 21 June 1934; German trans. in Weill, *Musik und Theater: gesammelte Schriften*, ed. Jürgen Schebera and Stephen Hinton (Henschel: Berlin, 1990), pp. 314–17.

21 'Der Musiker Weill', *Berliner Tageblatt*, 25 December 1928; reprinted in Weill, *Musik und Theater*, pp. 52–4.

22 For specific insight into *gestische Musik*, see Michael Morley, 'Suiting the action to the word: some observations on *Gestus* and *gestische Musik*', in Kim H. Kowalke, ed., *A New Orpheus* (Yale University Press: New Haven, 1986), pp. 183–201.

23 Brecht, 'Über reimlose Lyrik mit unregelmässigen Rhythmen', *Das Wort* 3 (March 1939); reprinted in *GW*, XIX, pp. 395–403.

24 Quoted in Albrecht Dümling, *Lasst euch nicht verführen: Brecht und die Musik* (Kindler: Munich, 1985), pp. 354–5.

25 For a comparison of Weill's and Brecht's comments on *Mahagonny*, see Stephen Hinton, 'The concept of Epic Opera: theoretical anomalies in the Brecht–Weill partnership', in *Festschrift Carl Dahlhaus* (Laaber: Laaber, 1988), pp. 285–94.

26 See Kim H. Kowalke, 'Accounting for success: misunderstanding *Die Dreigroschenoper*', *The Opera Quarterly* 6 (Spring 1989), pp. 18–38; also Stephen Hinton, 'Misunderstanding *The Threepenny Opera*' in *Kurt Weill: The Threepenny Opera*, pp. 181–92.

27 Weill to Universal Edition, 6 February 1933.

28 *Arbeitsjournal*, vol. I, 2 February 1941. In his notes to *Mahagonny*, Brecht had asserted that 'the orchestral apparatus needs to be cut down to thirty specialists or less'.

29 Because often the performer is 'reporting' rather than experiencing first-hand, many of Brecht's songs may be sung interchangeably by various characters within a given play or even in different plays. Thus, at different times in the run of the original production of *The Threepenny Opera*, Polly and Lucy each sang the 'Barbara-Song', and in later years Lenya appropriated 'Pirate Jenny' for Jenny's role.

17

CHRISTOPHER BAUGH

Brecht and stage design: the *Bühnenbildner* and the *Bühnenbauer*

'The Friends'

The war separated
Me, the writer of plays, from my friend the stage designer.
The cities where he worked are no longer there.
When I walk through the cities that still are
At times I say: that blue piece of washing
My friend would have placed it better.   (*Poems*, p. 415)

The contribution of Brecht to the scenography of the twentieth century goes far beyond important changes in the appearance of the stage. In his writing and in his practice, he deconstructs the human complexity of the 'director–designer relationship' and offers a mode of creating theatre which, in an organic way, links not only the end products of dramaturgy and scenography, but also centralises within this process the working practices of dramatist, director and scenographer. We have to consider therefore the relationship between Brecht's political and philosophical view of theatre and his expectations of scenography; the way in which these expectations developed in the collaboration with Caspar Neher; and finally the reverberant effects which these ideas and practices have had, and still have, upon contemporary theatre.

Throughout his stage career, Brecht worked with three scenographers: Caspar Neher,[1] Teo Otto and Karl von Appen. Whilst von Appen was an important and influential successor to Neher at the Berliner Ensemble, both he and Otto may, from one point of view, be considered as substitutes at times of Neher's unavailability. Of Brecht's many collaborations, that with Neher was the most durable. They had been classmates at school, although Neher was a year older, and their friendship survived the separation enforced initially by Neher's horrific war service. Long conversations reinforced a shared vision of the artist and the world (a vision partly caught in Neher's drawings of short combative men with bared teeth), and the friendship developed into one of the most crucial associations in twentieth-century theatre. It was a partnership based on the actively pleasurable (*lustig*) involvement in devising theatre. Neher had as great a commitment to writing and devising theatre as Brecht had to visual imagery, stage furnishings and effects; neither would contemplate a stage aesthetic which was separate from the political rationale for theatre.

As students, both were based in Munich: Brecht at the University and Neher at the Academy where he studied illustration and later painting. During the period from 1919 to 1922, Brecht was writing *Baal*, *Drums in the Night*, *Galgei* (an early version of *Man is Man*), working on film scripts, and writing and singing in cabaret. Neher shared this creativity; preparing visual propositions which extended as well as illustrated ideas and which constantly led to revision and development. In spite of their collaboration on *Drums in the Night*, Neher's drawings were rejected by the Munich Kammerspiele in September 1922, where he was an assistant, and the work given to Otto Reigbert, the more pictorially coherent resident designer. But by the following year Brecht had developed authority (favourable notices and the Kleist Prize) and Neher had acquired sufficient theatrical credibility by designing Kleist's *Kätchen von Heilbronn* at the Staatstheater in Berlin for managements actively to encourage their collaboration. This began in May 1923 with the production of *In the Jungle* at the Munich Residenz-Theater, directed by Erich Engel, the most successful of Brecht's predecessors as director of his plays. Neher worked with Brecht on his adaptation of *Edward II* at the Kammerspiele and moved as a contracted designer, with Brecht as junior director, to the Deutsches Theater in Berlin where *In the Jungle* opened at the end of October, and work on the adaptation of *Coriolanus* began.

Neher's style at this time grows away from the typical pictorial 'effects' of expressionist art: harsh, distorted, angular lines and tightly focussed, steeply angled light sources and their inevitable play with dramatic shadows. He appears to be trying to find a theatre equivalent of the sketch: a way of bestowing wood, canvas and stage paint with a softness of definition similar to the undogmatic, thought-provoking effects achieved by drawing with ink upon damp watercolour washes, a favoured medium at this time. Neher's habit of sketching characters from a play while Brecht was working on it, as author or director, provided material for debate between the various collaborators. These were not costume designs but, perhaps uniquely in the European theatre, visual quests for the appropriate dramatis personae.

This early activity culminates in the major collaboration involved in staging *The Threepenny Opera* at the Theater am Schiffbauerdamm during the summer of 1928. This was the first production in which the idea of an

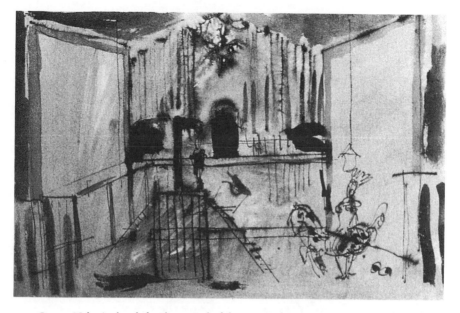

11.   Caspar Neher's sketch for the arrival of the mounted messenger to save Macheath from the gallows.

entire staging achieved the status of a 'model'[2] – not only from a personal sense of pride (and copyright) but in the important sense that the setting could exist as a layer of meaning within the text; a layer which is as contributive, and therefore perhaps as inappropriate to separate from future productions as the dialogue and Kurt Weill's musical score.[3]

A more significant 'culmination' of the Weimar period for Brecht's theory and practice as it relates to scenography was what is usually considered as either a dramaturgical caesura (if you follow a biographical 'growth and development' approach) or alternatively, the arrival at the absolute centre of Brechtian thinking. The *Lehrstücke* were experiments in audience/performer redefinition which pared down scenic material to a minimum. Visual statement develops from an illustration of an action or argument, to action (and therefore argument) itself. The theoretical basis of these plays expresses the central relationship between Brecht's view of theatre and what inevitably follows as his expectation of scenography and the scenographer.

Lehrstücktheater is radically one without an audience, since the act of theatre is seen as a dialectic: an active process in which the audience take upon themselves the role of interpretation and in effect become actors. This contrasts with traditional views of practitioners and theoreticians, which suggest that theatre has, as its base procedure, a series of strategies designed to manipulate its audience in a variety of predetermined, 'getting the

12. Production photograph from the 1928 *Threepenny Opera* at the Theater am Schiffbauerdamm, showing a section of Neher's stage just before the arrival of the mounted messenger.

message across' ways. The question 'what is my job and responsibility as a theatre practitioner?' is consequently of more fundamental importance than the actuality of stage aesthetics. Right at the heart of this there is the problem of names.

Designer or scenographer, *Bühnenbildner* or *Bühnenbauer*?[4] The distinction was very important to Brecht and Neher and must be of more than pedantic interest today. It goes to the heart of Brecht's consistent and unified understanding of the stage as *Lehrtheater* stemming from clear political philosophy:

> Marxism posits certain methods of looking, certain criteria. These lead it to make certain judgements of phenomena, certain predictions and suggestions for practical action. It teaches a combination of thinking and active intervention as a means of dealing with reality in so far as social intervention is able to deal with it. It is a doctrine that criticises human action and expects in turn to be criticised by it. A true *Weltanschauung*, however, is a picture of the world, a hypothetical knowledge of the way in which things happen, mostly moulded in accordance with some ideal of harmony.[5]

The object of the *Bühnenbildner*, the whole stage picture, suggests such a harmoniously composed knowledge of the world as this; it offers an interpretational viewpoint, if not necessarily a wholly coherent outlook, upon a play's topic and theme. Whereas the scenographer as *Bühnenbauer* is forced to consider that the job in hand is to create or build a scene as an integral component of a play's dramaturgy and which therefore should be considered an act of performance: as 'a combination of thinking and active intervention'. The scenographer will be responsible with others for the building of theatre 'gests' involving a combination of variable performance elements. This is a significantly different attitude from that which aims for a composed stage picture, with its assumption that the designer is responsible for the 'setting' which stands on the stage and which provides a sympathetic and appropriate environment in and on which performance can occur.

This distinction helps to clarify and make further sense of Brecht's ultimate rejection of those pillars of leftist revolutionary theatre of the period such as Piscator and Meyerhold, and designers like Georg Grosz whose stage 'pictures' firmly defined a world view:

> This theatre is in reality anti-revolutionary, because it is passive and reproductive. It has to rely on pure reproduction of existing – that is prevailing – types, and will have to wait for the political revolution to get its own archetypes. It is the ultimate form of the bourgeois naturalistic theatre.[6]

Theatre 'reality' still engaged director and scenographer as they resumed their collaboration after the Second World War, when Neher considered the term *Bühnenbild* to be a 'Nazi' term, since it pretended to offer as being 'real' a coherent view of the world:

> A picture is never realistic, the stage is always realistic. That's why I maintain that the 'realistic stage picture' is a nonsense.[7]

13. 'Neher's scenographic sketch for a scene from Brecht's unfinished play,
The Breadshop (1929–30). 'The scenographer will be responsible with others for the
building of theatre "gests".'

The performances of the *Lehrstücke* offer some of Brecht's most radical
scenographic exploration: the rejection of traditional theatre architecture
and its proscenium arch; the presence of a large choir of singers who, in *The
Flight over the Ocean* and *The Baden-Baden Cantata of Acquiescence* (1929)
defined and became the narrative process; and such powerful constructions
as the use of a boxing-ring for the singers of the 'zonks' in the *Songspiel
Mahagonny* (1927). There were projections by Neher and direct exhortations to the audience ('follow the words in your programmes and sing
along loudly!') which must have created, even within the context of a Festival of New Music in Baden-Baden, a remarkably discordant atmosphere.
Teo Otto designed *The Measures Taken* at the Grosses Schauspielhaus in
Berlin in 1930 with a workers' choir beneath the projection screen and with
the actors and choir lit by low-hanging industrial lamps.[8]

For *The Baden-Baden Cantata* a large, roughly 3-metre high grotesque
figure was constructed, which effectively 'animated' its design. Two
'clowns', in order to theatricalise the inhumanity of man, grotesquely saw
off the figure's limbs, all of which takes place in front of and amongst the
choir.[9] These *Lehrtheater* experiments should not be seen only as short-
lived particularised attempts to create didactic, Marxist theatre, but in terms
of understanding the nature of Brecht's theatre they should be seen equally
as providing the operational basis for the future development of his theory
and practice.

The closest possible creative collaboration between writer, director and scenographer was central, not only for the development of a stage aesthetic and a working practice, but for the development of Brecht's dramaturgy; which in turn was inseparable from a philosophy which redefined or 'refunctioned' (*umfunktioniert*) theatre. In consequence, it is inappropriate and impossible to isolate the designs and consider the stage aesthetic which they represent without seeing them as merely the most tangible remains (apart from production photographs) of a complex and still revolutionary mode of giving effective form to a philosophy which understands theatre as the logical annotation of life.

Close to the very heart of their collaboration lies the fundamental ability for director, writer and designer democratically to consider *all* aspects of theatre without following an etiquette of prescribed 'areas of responsibility' established by a tradition of professional practice. The inseparability of creative contribution was essential in creating a theatre which relished diversity and a conscious separation of scenographic elements. Neither Brecht nor Neher served any form of established apprenticeship, so neither acquired 'professional' practices and skills which might temper their un- tutored passion and joy in shared creativity. Close to the end of their work together, Egon Monk describes them rehearsing *The Tutor* in the spring of 1950:

> Brecht and Neher sitting next each other at rehearsal. Both of them leaning back, their knees pressed against the seats in front. Brecht appreciatively studying his cigar; Neher, his eyebrows exaggeratedly raised or exaggeratedly frowning over his glasses, more severe ... They are rehearsing 'by interjec- tions'. Each interjection is prefaced by Neher or Brecht naming its originator. 'Neher thinks ... ', 'Besson thinks ... ', 'Brecht thinks ... ', 'Monk thinks ... '. The interjection is listened to, then tested. If a detail works, then Brecht giggles with pleasure and Neher gives him a look of amusement ... This lasts a long time.[10]

The logical progression from a theory formulated in the *Lehrtheater* which united political and theatrical ideology to a practical grappling with rehearsal was inevitable. This is an aspect of the 'text' of Brecht which deserves constant re-examination. His descriptions of the 'problems' of traditional practice are recognisable and evident within contemporary theatre:

> Normally the sets are determined before the actors' rehearsals have begun, 'so that they can start', and the main thing is that they evoke an atmosphere, give some kind of expression, [and] illustrate a location; and the process by which this is brought about is observed with as little attention as the choosing of a

postcard on holiday. If at all, it is considered with regard to creating a space with some good possibilities for performance . . . It seems very strange that set designers [*Bühnenbildner*], who feel and claim that they are artists with a 'vision' which they must realise, seldom reckon with the actors, maintaining that set designers can work just as well, or even better, without actors.[11]

The working model for an alternative to this still common attitude is spelt out just as clearly:

> The good scene designer [*Bühnenbauer*] proceeds slowly and experimentally. A working hypothesis is based on a precise reading of the text, and substantial conversations with other members of the theatre, especially on the social aims of the play and the concerns of the performance, are useful to him. However, his basic performance ideas must still be general and flexible. He will test them constantly and revise them on the basis of results in rehearsals with the actors. The wishes and opinions of the actors are wells of discovery for him. He studies to what extent their strengths are adequate and intervenes . . .
>
> This is how a good stage designer [*Bühnenbauer*] works. Now ahead of the actor, now behind him, always together with him. Step by step he builds up the performance area, just as experimentally as the actor.[12]

Building the imagery of the stage is as much a rehearsed process as that of building the performances of actors. By this possibility, Brecht and Neher enfranchised scenography, empowering it with potential for comment, criticism, humour and disruption. Brecht writes about the *Songspiel Mahagonny* (Baden-Baden, 1927):

> so long as the arts are supposed to be 'fused' together, the various elements will all be equally degraded, and each will act as a mere feed to the rest. . . . Showing independent works of art as part of a theatrical performance is a new departure. Neher's projections adopt an attitude towards the events on stage; as when the real glutton sits in front of the glutton whom Neher has drawn. These projections of Neher's are quite as much an independent component of the opera as are Weill's music and the text.   (*BT*, pp. 37–8)

Scenography happens in time, working alongside and in conjunction with the actors, their movement and their groupings, and inevitably requires its own rehearsal. The few wooden poles and simple plank door (*The Caucasian Chalk Circle*, scenography by Karl von Appen, 1954) have scant architectural and no theatrical significance until they are bursting at the seams with wedding guests whilst the wedding bed lies, not quite empty, to the side. The final result, originating from the placement of people who define the spaces, creates a stage beauty of haunting significance:

> the *Neher principle* of building the set according to the requirements established at the actors' rehearsals allowed the designer to profit by the actors'

performance and influence it in turn. The playwright could work out his experiments in uninterrupted collaboration with actor and stage-designer; he could influence and be influenced. At the same time the painter and the composer regained their independence, and were able to express their view of the theme by their own artistic means.   (*BT*, p. 134)

For both Neher and von Appen, the constant notation of actors' groupings and relationships, with often only faintly sketched-in backgrounds, was not only an appropriate beginning but also lay at the core of their working method within the overall collaboration. From the perception of performance 'shapes' created by these groupings the scenographer can construct a stage which in its precise sizing and format can physically exemplify the anatomy of action. These sketches, moreover, were not simply a scenographer's transcription of dramatic text into visual text *en route* to becoming theatre text; for Brecht, they were a constant part of rehearsal methodology. Far from being exclusive to the scenographer, they drew strength from the actors, were fed back to them and served as models for stage blocking and textual development. Egon Monk's description of the rehearsals for *The Tutor* again:

> They [Neher's sketches] always lay ready to hand on the director's table, with the scene currently being rehearsed on top. Nearly all the blocking of the Berliner Ensemble derived directly from Neher's sketches. If there was a particular scene, or a particular moment within a scene – a 'nodal point' as Brecht and Neher would call it – that had no sketch, or if Neher for once was not there (a rare occurrence in the first years of the Berliner Ensemble), then that rehearsal might well be broken off. As for instance when the last scene but one of *The Tutor* was being rehearsed: 'Engagement in a Snowstorm'. This had to appear as an idyll, amiable at first but gradually undermined by malice.
>
> On stage, a large number of actors, glasses in their hands, drinking a toast (yes, but how?). Projected behind them, falling snow. Brecht rehearsed somewhat indecisively, asked first one then another of his aides to try blocking the scene, looking helplessly at the actors on stage, who looked equally helplessly down on him, then finally said: 'It's no use, we'll have to wait till Cas gets here.'[13]

This is more than a reliance upon a comrade in rehearsal, it is scenography standing side by side with dramaturgy. As the theatre text emerges, 'self-supporting' energies of meaning are constantly created by confrontations between actors and scenic material in ways which cannot be thought of as three-dimensional literature. Monk continues:

> Friedrich Maurer as Wenzeslaus the Schoolmaster ... One hand holding Neher's sketch, the other holding the long quill pen with which the sketch

14.   A sketch by Neher towards a working model for the staging of *The Tutor* by the
Berliner Ensemble (1950).

shows him driving Count Vermuth and the Major's armed domestics from the
room. A most impressive moment, clarifying the scene as no subsequent performance could do.[14]

The movement of the theatre process is the energy which transforms a
long quill pen into scenography. In a similar way, old wicker hampers and
skips become a nineteenth-century stage-coach in the Royal Shakespeare
Company's *Nicholas Nickleby* (1981) and a suspended assortment of old
metal domestic objects (cheese-graters, egg whisks, oil lamps etc.) are transformed into the starry firmament in William Dudley's scenography for *The
Mysteries* (1985) at the National Theatre. The actor is the catalyst for this
energy, the 'chemistry' is that of the scenographer and it is the audience who
read the 'formula' and offer any resolution. Properties and furniture,
however beautifully researched and crafted, have no value in themselves –
they can only exist in relationship to the value which is created by their role
within performance. Scenic 'material' thereby acquires its place within the
dialectic of theatre.

> Too little attention is paid these days to the life of reality. The things we put
> on stage are dead, never mind how real they are, if they have no function – if
> they are not used by actors or used on their behalf.[15]

However, Brecht was no harsh utilitarian when it came to the appearance
of properties and stage furnishings. Much is made of statements describing

his love of old objects which 'recount' by their appearance the conditions of their use and imply a 'sociology' of prop-making; and this is right. But from his earliest statements on theatre language to the last examples of his practice, there is also a demand for the energy and beauty which is the product of artistry. The beauty of a well-used copper saucepan, certainly, but also the beauty of an object or a piece of stage architecture joyfully chosen and designed so that it might rightfully take its individual place and not just 'service' the action with appropriate size, location and finish. The joy and the self-referential beauty of Brecht's and Neher's theatre, with its constant reminders of illusion (and inevitable mutability) invite its audience to engage with the theatrical in their own lives. This is a central tenet of the 'refunctioning' of stage language which is not well served by the dour, utility Brecht of many post-Brecht revivals.

It is neither clear nor indeed especially relevant to an assessment of theatrical ideas whether the 'break' which took place between Brecht and Neher over the winter of 1952–3 was intended to be both practically and emotionally final. However, Neher seems to have made his professional position clear when he chose to become a regular designer at the Volksbühne in West Berlin, and in 1954 accepted the appointment as head of design at the Munich Kammerspiele. Significantly, in December of that year, Brecht received the Stalin Peace Prize and Neher was appointed to the Board of the Salzburg Festival. The increasing rate of production at the Ensemble needed a fully resident scenographer.

Karl von Appen had a considerable theatre career behind him when Brecht first invited him to design for the Ensemble in the spring of 1953. Barred from working during the Nazi period, he spent the final years of the war in a concentration camp. He worked in Dresden at the Sächsischen Staatstheater until his invitation to the Ensemble, where his first scenography was for *Katzgraben* by Erwin Strittmatter, directed by Brecht and Manfred Wekwerth. Von Appen records in his notebook what might well have been his job interview with Brecht:

BRECHT: How do you visualize it?
APPEN: I can offer nothing more specific than a certain aversion, but this might actually prove fruitful.
          The only thing I'm quite sure about is that theatre must be created for actors.
BRECHT: That's what you feel – as a designer? By the way, I agree with you ...
APPEN: ... as a playwright? Your colleague Shakespeare didn't have these worries – but even in those days technical innovations could be

> created for each play. Molière had *his* own solutions – and remember that the Chinese performed in front of a carpet for centuries! All these difficulties only seem to have started with the coming of complex machinery.
>
> BRECHT: What – you're a machine wrecker?
>
> APPEN: I am if the machines are only meant to create even greater illusions of external reality. And that's what's happening.[16]

When the Ensemble moved into the renovated Theater am Schiffbauerdamm in the spring of 1954, von Appen was appointed principal designer and collaborated on the first production of *The Caucasian Chalk Circle* later that year. Ironically, it is the scenography of von Appen and Teo Otto which travelled the world and established the image of the 'Brechtian' stage. *Mother Courage*, arguably the most scenically influential of the Ensemble's productions, toured in what was essentially the original scenography created by Otto for the première production at the Zurich Schauspielhaus in 1941, rather than the staging which Neher prepared for the Zurich revival of April 1946.[17] Paradoxically, therefore, Neher's work was not represented at all when the company visited London shortly after Brecht's death in August 1956.[18]

Although he was clearly indebted to Neher, there is a distinct change of attitude apparent in von Appen's work. If teeth are still bared, then they are shown with an artistic skill which sometimes prevents the eye going below the surface to engage in a dialectic. The scenographies seem to offer visual unities: the coherence of a 'world-view' with pre-interpreted, and therefore closed, ideologies.[19] Evidently the battle with definitions of stage reality which had taxed Neher and Brecht as root 'problems' could not be engaged in Stalinist East Germany during the 1950s other than by offering completed 'solutions': 'realism within a utopian horizon'.[20]

> Nevertheless, a common factor can be established: within the variety of individual methods we have developed a realistic style in the theatrical work of our Republic. In this theatrical work socialist realism is a method aimed at selecting the socially fruitful means out of the whole wealth of means at the stage designer's disposal, and at always discovering new ones.[21]

But in practice the working methodology continued: von Appen was constantly in rehearsal, producing copious drawings and sketches of the actors and their groupings which created 'storyboard' outlines of the movement of plays:

> Arrangements [*Arrangementskizzen*] fix the movement on the stage. They determine the position of groups and decide on how they are changed. It is their task to elucidate the plot. Finding arrangements should be the starting point of any rehearsal work.[22]

15. Karl von Appen's *Arrangementskizzen* for *Turandot*.

Von Appen usually read Brecht's *Bühnenbauer* as scene-builder; and he acknowledges the direct link with Brecht's dramaturgy:

> To my mind an arrangement outline is part and parcel of optical dramaturgy, and should form the basis of all further work. I start by trying to narrate a play optically, and it is only after this has been done that the shaping of the actor's environment begins.

This sounds easy and is appreciated by many of our colleagues, also by those from abroad. But in reality they adhere to the old decorative conceptions because it is more convenient to do so. We in the GDR too, do not yet attach enough attention to this aspect of basing the work of scene designing on the arrangement.[23]

Von Appen was therefore the agent whereby Brecht's and Neher's collaborative theatre-building became enshrined into the practice of the Berliner Ensemble, but whilst he constantly emphasises his ideological debt to Brecht, he rarely refers to Neher or his work. The Ensemble's influence spread to a larger audience through training programmes and the OISTT (International Organisation of Scenographers and Theatre Technicians). This was dominated by the heavily funded theatre institutions of Eastern Europe and their related training schools which organised the major design exhibitions during the 1970s and 1980s. Throughout most Western theatre, therefore, the prevailing theatrical preference is for the Brecht–Neher, and more accessible von Appen solutions, to be preserved in a well-meaning, but reverential struggle to stage 'authentic Brecht'.

Of course, 'solutions' have a disarming way of disassociating themselves from their theoretical context and becoming *the* object of study and theatrical imitation. The early reception of Brecht outside Germany suffered considerably from a 'fetishisation' of the Berliner Ensemble's appearance and its effects. Unfamiliarity with the language and ignorance of the plays resulted, especially in Britain, in a thorough distortion by directors and designers of Brecht's theatre.[24] This was an objectification of his theatre which Brecht clearly recognised:

> When studying the following remarks, consisting of a number of thoughts and ideas conceived while rehearsing a play, one should – when faced with certain solutions to problems – recognise primarily the problems.[25]

But whilst acknowledging this, it is still tempting to try to present a play which is 'true' to Brecht scenographically, since he is the rare dramatist who has written copiously and clearly about designing his plays. The performance imagery attains the power of dramatic utterance: harsh white lighting from exposed lighting instruments, stripped bare stage, undyed or 'earth' coloured hessian and canvas costumes, half stage-height curtains running on horizontal strainer wires across the stage and terse, combative 'literary' captions painted or projected onto screens which straddle the stage. Kenneth Tynan reports the potent physicality of this scenography at the Palace Theatre, London, in 1956:

> Let me instance the peasant wedding in *The Caucasian Chalk Circle*, a scene more brilliantly directed than any other in London. A tiny cell of a room, ten

16.   Von Appen's drawing for the peasant wedding in *The Caucasian Chalk Circle*. Such
drawings are ideas for staging.

by ten, is cumulatively jammed with about two dozen neighbours and a sot-
tish monk. The chances for broad farce are obvious, but they are all rejected.
Reality is preferred, reality of a memorable and sculptured ruggedness. I defy
anyone to forget Brecht's stage pictures. No steps or rostra encumber the
platform; the dominant colours are browns and greys; and against a high,
encircling, off-white backcloth we see nothing but solid, selected objects – the
twin gates in *The Caucasian Chalk Circle* or Mother Courage's covered
wagon. The beauty of Brechtian settings is not of the dazzling kind that begs
for applause. It is the more durable beauty of *use*.[26]

These were, of course, the artistic solutions to the problems generated by
the historical collision of play, production team, theatrical and political
context. Admiration for solutions must not dominate attempts to understand the attitudes towards theatre which Brecht writes about and which
his practice exemplified. There is nothing in any way Brechtian in re-
constructing the performance conditions of the plays' original productions,
beyond the nostalgic or the historicist.

Nevertheless, to stage *Mother Courage* and ignore Teo Otto's sparse
screens, the bleached revolving stage and the early drawings for Courage's
wagon seems tantamount to ignoring or re-writing the spoken text. But
there is a problem: if indeed the scenography is as central to Brecht's theatre

as the written text, then surely we *should* endow the original scenography with a similar 'textual' status. An original staging by Brecht, Neher, Otto or von Appen, therefore, can only be thought of in terms of 'the model'. In the *Courage-Modell 1949* Brecht offers such a resolution by offering an idea of the model which resists permanence in *any* aspect of theatre:

> Provisional structures must be erected, and there is the danger that they may become permanent. Art reflects all this; ways of thinking are part and parcel of ways of life. As far as the theatre is concerned, we throw our Models into the gap ... And the Models will be misused by those who accept them and have not learnt how to handle them. Intended to make things easier, they are not easy to handle. Moreover, they are not made to exclude thought, but to inspire thought; they are not made to replace artistic creativity, but to compel it.[27]

Within such Brechtian parameters, it would be reckless to dismiss, on principle, the models offered by historical stage iconography.

But in addition we must also remember that much of Neher's work gained its power as performance by virtue of its contrast with prevailing theatre styles and audience expectations. 'Reconstructions' presume a timelessness in our sense of theatre, but we have already assimilated so much of their practice that any sense of disturbance of expectations, let alone shock, is unlikely. A contemporary audience is prepared for the separation and dislocation of dramatic and scenic elements, for a narrative borne along by differing media, for a wide variety of 'effects' designed to jolt us out of any tendency to believe that what we see is any other than the product of art. The humblest West End and Broadway musical of recent years can usually offer its audience a whole catalogue of genuine 'Brechtian' techniques.

Brecht's refunctioning of stage practice signifies a major shift in theatrical philosophy – from an essentially romantic aesthetic founded upon the principle of the 'absorption' of the spectator in the product of art towards a theatre of rhetorical gesture and process. An Aristotelian catharsis is often cited as the arch-villain in Brechtian theatre, but the scenic 'world' of accurate topographical verisimilitude, advocated by naturalist theory and its practitioners of the late nineteenth century, presents an equally significant combatant. There are important ways in which contemporary theatre has learnt from and extended Brecht's fundamental concept of scenography as active performance; extensions and developments which are, perhaps, more truly 'Brechtian' than the revival of the plays.

It is not usual to see the ideas of Gordon Craig 'bracketed' with Brecht's, since Craig is usually evaluated on his aesthetic and non-political consideration of the stage. But both looked to, and were enriched by, past scenographies: the rhetorical narrative stage of the Renaissance, a theatre constructed from the skills of performance in *commedia dell'arte* and oriental forms where 'reality' is a combined generation of the actor and scenographic rhetoric. Both Craig and Brecht clearly envisioned a theatre which was a creative and active process – matched at its reception by a similarly engaged and active audience:

> To-day they *impersonate* and interpret; to-morrow they must *represent* and interpret; and the third day they must create.[28]

In many important ways, Brechtian heirs and successors are to be found on 'the third day': especially in the theatre of performance art where interpretation is banished from the stage and the audience become participants in endowing meaning and significance to performance. Important attitudes of *Lehrtheater* and Brechtian theatre-building continue in the work of companies such as Théâtre de Complicité, Cheek by Jowl, Théâtre du Soleil and Steppenwolf, and are developed in performance art and the dance theatre of Pina Bausch. Heiner Müller has written of his collaboration with the 'operas' of Robert Wilson:

> There's a text and it's delivered, but it is not evaluated and not coloured and not interpreted either, it's just there. Then there's noise, and that's there too and is also not interpreted. I regard this as important. It's a democratic concept of theatre. Interpretation is the work of the spectator and is not to take place on the stage. The spectator must not be absolved from this work. That's consumerism ... capitalist theatre.[29]

Wilson believes that confrontation and absorption create a fascist theatre: 'I like a great deal of space and I want the spectator to have sufficient space to have his own thoughts and ideas, inner impressions that are analogous to the outer ones on the stage.'[30] It is possible that performance strategies of postmodern theatre may well serve as the most appropriate model for practical Brechtian research today.

Brecht's scenographic ideas offer political and aesthetic 'space' for both the theatre artist and the audience whose integration into a theory of theatre establishes the dialectic nature of performance. The writings and the accounts of his collaborative practice are extensive and sometimes confusing, but in the last analysis they are a coherent and lucid source of ideas: ideas which demand the constant reassessment of personal practice and responsibility, and therefore the endless 'refunctioning' of theatre.

NOTES

1 Willett's *Caspar Neher: Brecht's Designer* is the only critical biography in English and, although short, its catalogue format (Arts Council Touring Exhibition, 1986) permits it to offer a great deal of basic and reliable information.

2 Although their collaborative work on the adaptation of *Antigone* was the first to be formally prepared as a model in the *Antigonemodell 1948*.

3 Collaboration with Weill introduced Neher to opera which dominated his work after the separation from Brecht in 1933.

4 *Bühnenbildner* is someone concerned with creating stage pictures for which, in this context, I use the term 'designer'. 'Stage', or 'scene' builder is of course a more correct translation of *Bühnenbauer*. However, within contemporary practice in Europe and in North America, the word 'scenography' is understood to represent a collaborative and integrated approach to the stage and its relevant practitioners. This is precisely the point which Brecht's and Neher's semantic distinction initiates.

5 *The Messingkauf Dialogues*, p. 36.

6 Cited in Völker, *Brecht: A Biography*, p. 116.

7 Neher to Brecht, *c.* 1951, cited in Willett, *Caspar Neher*, p. 75.

8 After study in Kassel and Paris, Otto had taught at the Bauhausschule in Weimar in 1926 and was an assistant at the Berlin Staatsoper in 1928. He always maintained a commitment to painting and exhibited at the Berlin Exhibition in 1930. Shortly after *The Measures Taken*, as the Nazis seized power, Otto returned to his native Switzerland and began his 25-year residency at the Zurich Schauspielhaus.

9 Fuegi (*Bertolt Brecht*, p. 34) considers this giant figure in some detail and examines contemporary audience response, which in some cases seems to have bordered on the hysterical. The contemporary reports which he cites, however, do not indicate whether the depth of feeling was generated by a heightened awareness of man's inhumanity to man, or merely by the gruesomeness of the immediate theatrical effect.

10 Cited in Willett, *Caspar Neher*, p. 111.

11 *Gesammelte Werke*, vol. xv, pp. 442–3. All translations from *GW* are by Juliette Prodhan and myself.

12 *Ibid.*, pp. 443–4.

13 Cited in Willett, *Caspar Neher*, p. 109.

14 *Ibid.*, p. 109.

15 Neher to Brecht, *c.* 1951, cited in *ibid.*, p. 76.

16 Quoted by Friedrich Dieckmann in *Théâtre International*, nos. 3–4 (1981), pp. 10–11; an obituary assessment of von Appen's work.

17 Otto's scenography was adapted by Heinrich Kilger when Brecht directed the play at the Deutsches Theater in 1949.

18 Neher's opera designs had been seen at Glyndebourne in 1952, and a Brecht–Neher scenography in Sam Wanamaker's production of *The Threepenny Opera* at the Royal Court Theatre in February 1956.

19 Neher had already expressed qualms about some of the scenic tendencies at the Ensemble, which he had sensed in the 'realistic' conventionalism of John Heartfield's designs for *Kremlin Chimes* in 1952.

20 This is the title of Dieckmann's essay on von Appen in *Théâtre International*, nos. 3–4 (1981).

21 'Introduction to the GDR contribution to the Prague Quadrennial, 1971' – possibly written by von Appen himself – in 'Stage Design in the German Democratic Republic', unpublished conference papers (in an anonymous translation prepared for the International Quadrennial of Scenography, Prague, 1971).

22 Von Appen, 'On arrangement sketches', in *ibid.*, p. 11.

23 *Ibid.*, p. 15.

24 See a particularly clear survey of this theme in Maro Germanou, 'Brecht and the English theatre', in *Brecht in Perspective*, ed. G. Bartram and A. Waine, pp. 208–24. Jocelyn Herbert's scenography for the English Stage Company at the Royal Court during the 1960s and her relationship with new writing clearly benefited from the Ensemble's example. John Bury's work at the Royal Shakespeare Company – especially for *The Wars of The Roses* (1964–5) – attempted to define an English scenographic attitude in line with Brecht's and Neher's ideas.

25 *Courage-Modell 1949* (Henschel: Berlin, 1958), trans. Eric Bentley and Hugo Schmidt, reprinted in *Encore* 12, no. 3 (May–June 1965), p. 6.

26 Kenneth Tynan, *Tynan on Theatre* (Penguin: Harmondsworth, 1964), p. 241.

27 *Courage-Modell 1949*, in *Encore*, p. 5.

28 See Edward Gordon Craig, 'The actor and the Über-marionette' in *On the Art of the Theatre* (Heinemann Mercury: London, 1962), p. 61.

29 Heiner Müller and Olivier Ortolani, 'Die Form entsteht aus dem Maskieren', *Theater 1985*, p. 91; quoted and trans. by Wright, *Postmodern Brecht*, p. 129–30.

30 From an interview with Peter Friedl in *Theater 1981*, pp. 77–82, cited in Wright, *Postmodern Brecht*, p. 129.

18

MARGARET EDDERSHAW

Actors on Brecht

One of Brecht's favourite sayings was: 'The proof of the pudding is in the eating.' Although his essays, poems and plays tell us a great deal about both his aesthetics and his dramatic theories, it is to his practice (and to that of others engaged in performing his work) that we must turn for meaningful insight into Brechtian performance. The aim of this essay is to examine the implications of Brechtian theory and practice for the performer. This will be done by means of a brief discussion of Brecht's ideas on acting, followed by a fuller consideration of the views and experiences of actors who have played major roles in Brecht's plays.

Brecht was first and foremost a man of the theatre, a playwright who also directed, so that one might well suppose that without his sixteen years in exile, during which time the practice of his directorial skills was necessarily limited, the world would have received many fewer words about his dramatic theory. Certainly as a director Brecht seems to have referred very little even to the most famous of his theoretical ideas. As Lotte Lenya, the great actress who worked with Brecht, amusingly puts it in her description of rehearsing the song 'Surabaya Johnny' with him after the war:

> Right in the middle of it, I stopped for a second and said: 'Brecht, you know your theory of epic theatre – maybe you don't want me just to sing it the way I sang it – as emotional as "Surabaya Johnny" has to be done?' ... He said: 'Lenya, darling, whatever you do is epic enough for me.'[1]

Brecht's notions of what constituted an appropriate mode of performance for his epic theatre were, of course, evolved in opposition to the style of acting he observed in Germany in the 1920s and early 1930s. His objections to the over-emotional, self-indulgent 'romanticism', which he associated – not altogether correctly – with Stanislavskian 'naturalism', are most clearly

The abbreviation *BT* refers to *Brecht on Theatre*. Unattributed quotations from Janet Suzman, Michael Gambon, Glenda Jackson and Antony Sher are from interviews with the author.

expressed in his unfinished work *The Messingkauf Dialogues*. Here Brecht pours scorn on Stanislavsky's idea that an actor should and can convince an audience that he or she really is the character, by drawing on a 'system' of exercises that aid the expression of the inner feelings of the role. Brecht not only doubted the efficacy of such a technique but was antagonistic to and critical of the intent to 'deceive', and to lure the audience into an emotional proximity with the character portrayed. The plays that Brecht wrote for his epic theatre were intended to serve a socio-political function and therefore, he argued, required a different kind of performance style. From his very early days as a writer/director he wanted to reduce – not eliminate – the audience's empathy with the characters on stage in order to aid their intellectual understanding of the events presented. This intention led Brecht to his theory of *Verfremdungseffekt* (which is better translated as 'distancing' than 'alienation' effect). This 'distancing' or 'making the familiar strange' was not an original aesthetic idea, but Brecht's application of it to theatre and the resultant dramaturgical effects were new.

The significant implication of the V-effect for the actor was that he or she was not supposed to pretend to be the character: 'To achieve the V-effect the actor must give up his complete conversion into the stage character. He *shows* the character, he *quotes* his lines, he *repeats* a real-life incident.'[2] This meant, according to Brecht, that, while not eliminating emotion altogether in his or her performance, the actor would stimulate the audience to feel emotions that were not the same as those 'felt' by the character. For example, if the character were 'sad', the audience might experience 'anger' at the circumstances which made the character feel that way. It is probably this demand by Brecht that actors should 'demonstrate' their roles and remain to some extent 'detached' from their character that has caused most misunderstanding among actors. In fact, it was a plea for a more restrained, clear style of acting, not for 'less' acting. In any case, Brecht built into his plays many V-effect techniques – episodic scenes, direct narration, songs, unusual linguistic structures – so that the actor does not need to work hard at 'distancing'. It becomes largely the responsibility of the writer and/or director.

The main impact for the actor, perhaps, is a shift in balance, a refocussing, whereby the emphasis in Brechtian performance is placed more on the collective story-telling than on the significance of the individual characters. Nonetheless, a Brechtian actor still has to understand the behaviour of the character he or she is playing; that behaviour has to be fully observed, selectively detailed. But the emphasis is ultimately on the sociological rather than the psychological motivation of character. The function and the social attitude of the character are thus more highlighted than the emotions. This idea is best encapsulated in Brecht's term *Gestus*, which he used to describe a combination of physical gesture and social attitude. Effective use of *Gestus* by the actor enables the audience to perceive and understand the socio-political implications of the events on stage. For Brecht, the *Gestus* of a key moment in a play had to be so clearly expressed by the actors that it would be possible for it to be understood through a sheet of glass, or like a still from a film. The semiotics of a particular *Gestus* are also dependent on accurate costuming, carefully chosen and handled props and an understanding by the actor of the effects of life's experiences on a character's physical expression (such as the toll exacted by the character's job). All these elements contribute to the audience's understanding of the character's social significance within the play.

While wanting his theatre to be socially significant, Brecht also thought it should be entertaining. It had to be both functional and fun. It was to be intellectual yet retain the naïve quality of children. He believed strongly in their 'unspoiled and unprejudiced observation'.[3] Brecht also appreciated the naïve in art; in particular he admired what he perceived as V-effects in the work of Brueghel: he 'manages to balance his contrasts, he never merges them into one another, nor does he practise the separation of comic and tragic; his tragedy contains a comic element and his comedy a tragic one' (*BT*, p. 157). The same description could very aptly be applied to Brecht's plays, and certainly this notion of 'contradiction' was important to his understanding of how an actor should approach the playing of an epic role. In contrast to the Stanislavskian system, which implied that the actor should find a consistency of character, a 'through-line' that made all the actions seem coherent, Brecht insisted that the actor should emphasise the contrasts, the contradictory behaviour of the character. In this way the changes in a character's social behaviour, brought about by the behaviour of others or by particular social circumstances, are highlighted for the audience. This 'contradictory' approach is, therefore, significant in showing the spectator that humans are alterable, their behaviour is not fixed or inevitable. They can behave differently, they have an alternative. In the latter years of his life Brecht came to see this 'alternative' possibility as the most important aspect of his work and he replaced the term 'epic' theatre with that of 'dialectical' theatre. He developed techniques with his company, the Berliner Ensemble, aimed at helping the actors make it clear to the audience that characters, at key moments in the story, could have made other, alternative decisions. These moments of decision, or nodal points as Brecht called them, were highlighted by the actors through the use of pauses, small gestures or vocal changes. Such physical separation of one moment from the next also enabled the undercutting of emotion and the insertion of the necessary 'distance'. The subtlety and detail of Brecht's work with his actors on moments such as these indicate the importance he placed on precision and clarity in performance. An observer of Brecht's rehearsals for *Antigone* in 1948 wrote: 'The directorial method was based on investigation and varied experimentation that could extend to the smallest gesture – eyes, fingers ... Brecht worked like a sculptor on and with the actor.'[4]

Within this last remark lies another crucial aspect of Brecht's ideas about acting: that it must be a collaborative, collective process, working towards a common goal and that the specific intention and style of performance should be allowed to emerge during this interactive rehearsal process in which the whole company participates. This approach was unusual in Brecht's day and is still too often impeded by the hierarchical structure within theatre companies and the unequal power relationship between actor and director.

Brecht also had some unusual views on the physical attributes of actors, believing that there was an unhelpful emphasis on the necessity for 'good looks': 'Parts are allocated wrongly and thoughtlessly. As if all cooks were fat, all peasants were phlegmatic, all statesmen stately ... As if all who love and are loved are beautiful.'[5] Indeed, the kind of actors Brecht chose to work with and/or admired reveals a great deal about his ideas on acting.

ACTORS BRECHT ADMIRED

During his time in Berlin before the Hitler *putsch*, Brecht came to admire a number of performers for their acting style, comic talent and ability to make contact with an audience. One of his favourites was Karl Valentin, a popular Munich slapstick comedian, whose act contained songs, dialogues and comic mime, conveying the naïve wisdom and proverbial pathos of the 'little man'. In a programme note for the Munich Kammerspiele in 1922, Brecht praised Valentin for his 'virtually complete rejection of mimicry and cheap psychology',[6] comparing him favourably with the film actor Charlie Chaplin. Brecht had seen the latter's film *The Face on the Bar-Room Floor* in 1921, noting in his diary that it was 'the most profoundly moving thing I've ever seen in the cinema: utterly simple ... it's unadulterated art ... of a quite alarming objectivity and sadness'.[7] For Brecht, Chaplin had a 'gestic way of performing',[8] by which he meant that through his silent gestures Chaplin conveyed the character's attitudes towards others. In this respect and in his 'demonstration' of character Brecht thought Chaplin would 'come closer to the epic than to the dramatic theatre's requirements' (*BT*, p. 56). Chaplin added weight to Brecht's view by stating in his auto-

biography: 'I abhor dramatic schools that indulge in reflections and intro-
spections to evoke the right emotion. The mere fact that a student must be
mentally operated upon is sufficient proof that he should give up acting.'[9]

Two other actors particularly admired by Brecht were Oskar Homolka
and Peter Lorre, both of whom worked with him in Germany during the
1920s and 1930s and were then part of the group of German exiles who
welcomed Brecht to the United States in the 1940s. Homolka, described as 'a
burly, ambitious, temperamental Viennese',[10] displeased Brecht during their
first production together (*Edward II* in 1924), by getting drunk during the
opening performance and as a consequence gesticulating too much.
However, Brecht's admiration for Homolka's strong style of performance
overcame this inauspicious start and they subsequently co-directed *Baal*, in
which the actor also played the lead. Later, when in exile, Brecht was to
conceive both Azdak in *The Caucasian Chalk Circle* and Galileo with
Homolka in mind. He even wondered (in a letter to Piscator) about asking
him to consider playing Arturo Ui.[11]

Brecht first worked with the Hungarian-born Peter Lorre in 1929 on a
production of Marieluise Fleisser's *The Pioneers of Ingolstadt* in Berlin. One
day the theatre manager, Aufricht, 'found a small actor waiting patiently for
an interview. He told the man that he looked like a tadpole, but he could go
down to the stage and ask Brecht to cast him as the village idiot. He was
given the part and Brecht soon afterwards advised Aufricht to offer him a
three-year contract. His name was Peter Lorre.'[12] Lorre's most successful
pre-war Brechtian role was that of Galy Gay in *Man is Man*, for which
Brecht asked him to speak in a broken and disjointed manner in order to
convey the character's contradictions. While this seems to have puzzled
some critics and audience members, Brecht commented: 'This way of acting
was perfectly right from the new point of view, exemplary even' (*BT*, p. 53).
On the other hand, Lorre's instinctive way of performing was more realistic,
which led to his success in the cinema. It was said that, in his playing of the
central role in Fritz Lang's film *M*, 'in appearance, voice and expression,
Lorre captured the inner torment of the perverted killer'.[13]

Even this short list of actors whom Brecht admired indicates clearly that
his ideas on what constituted a good performer were not fixed or limited
and, despite his consistent opposition to 'naturalism', he did not rule out the
actor's use of emotions. This is nowhere more abundantly substantiated
than in Brecht's open admiration for Charles Laughton, with whom he
worked in America. This great stage and film actor was best known at the
time for his large, powerful and emotional (even excessively emotional) style
of performance, but Brecht was attracted by what he perceived as Laughton's ability to act with realism and a lack of sentimentality. It is true that

17.   Charles Laughton as Galileo (1947). The back-projection shows one of the instruments
of torture that might have been used on him if he had not recanted.

the actor himself seems to have had a simple and direct attitude to his job.
Once, when asked why he acted, Laughton replied: 'Because people don't
know what they're like and I think I can show them' (*BT*, p. 164). Brecht's
view of the proper outcome of good acting was similar: 'It is less a matter of
the artist's temperament than of the notions of reality which he has and
communicates, less a matter of his vitality than of the observations which
underlie his portraits and can be derived from them' (*BT*, p. 164). Equally,
Laughton thought Brecht had an extraordinary talent, and in 1943 he agreed
to help the writer prepare an English version of *Life of Galileo* (which
Brecht had completed in 1938).

Laughton spoke no German and Brecht's English was uncertain, but they
established an immediate and effective *rapport*. With the aid of dictionaries,
they acted, demonstrated the text for each other until the meaning satisfied
both. As Brecht put it:

This system of performance-and-repetition had one immense advantage in
that psychological discussions were almost entirely avoided. Even the most
fundamental gests, such as Galileo's way of observing, or his craze for pleasure, were established in three dimensions by actual performance . . . We were
forced to do what better equipped translators should do, too: to translate

gests. For language is theatrical in so far as it primarily expresses the mutual attitude of the speakers.   (*BT*, p. 165)

Laughton's biographer claims that the actor was very much responsible for making the character of Galileo more human, 'making him touchingly and harshly a real man instead of a saintly martyr'.[14] And Brecht admitted that Laughton was so anxious 'to show things as they really are that, despite all his indifference (indeed timidity) in political matters he suggested and even demanded that not a few of the play's points should be made sharper' (*BT*, p. 164). When it came to the production, however, Laughton claimed he did not understand what Brecht was talking about and 'he just went on stage and acted'.[15] Nonetheless, Laughton was so concerned about the possible effects of the prevailing heatwave at the time of the production that he proposed that trucks filled with ice should be parked by the walls of the theatre 'so that the audience can think' (*BT*, p. 168).

ACTORS OF THE BERLINER ENSEMBLE ON BRECHT

When Brecht returned to Germany after the Second World War and formed the Berliner Ensemble, he collected about him some actors of previous acquaintance, like Ernst Busch, and some new, but all were strong, physical, unsentimental performers with a commitment to an open, exploratory method of work that put every idea to the practical test. Carl Weber, who joined the Ensemble, describes a company rehearsal – which initially he had assumed to be a break:

> It was typical of the loose way Brecht worked, of his experimental approach and of the teamwork the Ensemble was used to ... The actors also took an experimental attitude. They would suggest a way of doing something and if they started to explain it, Brecht would say that he wanted no discussion in rehearsal – it would have to be tried.[16]

Actors in the Ensemble were well aware that Brecht never cared how they worked or by what means they achieved a performance, he was only concerned with the end results. Equally, he did not begin rehearsals with preconceived ideas on the style for a particular production. Weber again: 'He began with a long exploration of the intricate social relationships of the characters and the behaviour resulting from them.'[17]

Brecht's and the company's mainstay was, of course, Helene Weigel, Brecht's actress wife. In addition to playing major roles, she organised and managed the company, leaving Brecht to concentrate on the artistic direction of the productions. Weigel's own comments on performing Brechtian characters were always direct and matter-of-fact. For example, when asked

18. Ernst Busch as the nearly blind Galileo in the production on which Brecht was working shortly before his death. It was eventually staged in 1957, with Erich Engel as the named director.

about the famous V-effect by the British actor/director, Bernard Miles, she is said to have replied that it simply 'grew out of Brecht's efforts to deal with difficult actors'.[18] She was scathing about non-Brechtian approaches to performance, declaring that 'the psychology generally used in the theatre is very inferior, old-fashioned and useless'.[19] She did, however, stress the importance to the actor of imagination and observation and the interaction of the two: 'Often I observe something and know for sure, that's a point I can use in a particular role. But mostly you don't know where the ideas come from. Observation and imagination often complement each other.'[20] Weigel also made it clear that, like Brecht, she saw a character's action in terms of function, so that when asked why Coriolanus fought bravely, she answered: 'It was his job.'[21] On the issue of the Brechtian actor's separation from the role, her attitude was equally straightforward:

> How, for example, am I as Courage at the end of the play, when my business dealings have cost me the last of my children, to deliver the sentence: 'I have to get back into business', if I am *not* personally shattered by the fact that this person I am playing does not possess the capacity to learn?[22]

And when asked about the Berliner Ensemble's method of work, she stressed that there was very little concern with theory, saying simply: 'We tell the story.'[23]

Brecht's lack of interest in promoting or referring to his own theoretical ideas in rehearsal and the company's concern with the telling of the story are recurring themes in the comments on Brecht's work from Ensemble actors. Angelika Hurwicz, the first actress to play Grusha in *The Caucasian Chalk Circle*, claims that she only heard Brecht use the term *Verfremdung* once during months of rehearsal for that production. This was when working on the scene between Grusha, her brother and the sister-in-law, which struck Brecht as too emotional, so 'he made the actors rehearse with interpolations of "said the man" or "said the woman"'.[24]

To Hurwicz, playing epic theatre quite simply means telling the story clearly in order to show how people behave in certain situations: 'All the work is subordinated to this end . . . He demonstrates persons as the product of the conditions in which they live, and capable of change through the circumstances which they experience.'[25] She is also clearsighted about both the differences and the similarities between Brecht and Stanislavsky. She told Brecht that on reading Stanislavsky's first book about his acting 'system', *An Actor Prepares*, she discovered 'parts which appeared quite important, which I have made use of for years now'.[26] And she goes on to argue that these two great directors were not really in opposition, that (despite *The Messingkauf Dialogues*) Brecht was not 'hostile to drama exercises aimed at ensuring the truth to life and the warmth of the presentation of the role; in fact, he regards them as a pre-requisite'.

Hurwicz points out, too, that Brecht started with what Stanislavsky called the super-objective of the actor, and, in effect, required the actor to go a stage further, to move beyond the realistic portrayal that Stanislavsky sought, to add a socio-critical dimension to that 'real' character. She is aware of the problems caused by the misunderstanding of Brecht's theoretical writings and gives a useful perspective on the main issue of the relationship between actor and character:

> All that he [Brecht] said in the *Small Organon* [*sic*] against the possession of the actor by his role, which has caused so much confusion and indignation, is aimed against actors who forget about their super-task, who only see their own parts, and who offend against the content of the play as a whole, even when they give their parts interesting details and great acting ability.

Hurwicz also offers some pertinent information on Brecht's methods as a director, confirming others' views of his extraordinarily precise and detailed work in rehearsal to assist actors in highlighting significant moments, while retaining an overview of the play:

19. Ekkehard Schall as the vigorous Galileo of the early scenes (with Renate Richter as Frau Sarti). This production, directed by Manfred Wekwerth and Joachim Tenschert in 1978, remained in the repertoire of the Berliner Ensemble into the 1990s.

With actors who fail to produce a certain nuance necessary at a key-point in the plot, Brecht takes all possible measures to achieve his ends. He replaces emphasis by gesture, gesture by a pause, a look by a throat-clearing, and so on. In this way Brecht trains actors to be exact, to be responsible with regard to their parts and the whole play, without forcing them.[27]

But Hurwicz is also aware that on occasion it is necessary for the detailed portrayal of a particular character to be put aside in favour of the more general, social meaning of the play. To her, this points to the essential difference between the surface reality of 'naturalism' and the more significant, deeper reality of 'social realism'. Her understanding of this grew out of playing Mother Courage's dumb daughter, Kattrin:

Working on this role I learnt the difference between realism and naturalism. If I'd played the dumbness as the result of an injury done to the tongue ... my expression could very easily have become rather idiotic. It would have been quite wrong to give an impression of retarded development. What was important was to show that intelligent people, born to happiness, can be crippled by war. Precision in portraying an individual case had to be sacrificed for this general truth.[28]

Hurwicz's views on the Brechtian actor's approach to developing a character are confirmed by Ekkehard Schall, who also worked under Brecht's direction and, in the years since the playwright's death, has become a leading performer with the Berliner Ensemble. He stresses the importance of social behaviour in creating a role: 'You can't approach any part with blinkers of moral preconceptions, nor with the preconception of "character". You also can't play a certain "character", rather you've got to play a sum of ways of behaviour in various situations.' Schall does not rule out 'psychology' altogether but insists that it does not provide the fundamental basis of a part:

> I like to add psychological touches – virtues or vices – to the roles I play, but they are not useful in making basic judgments about the characters. Furthermore, such judgments are made not during rehearsal by the character and director, but at an earlier stage in the production, on the dramaturgical level, when discussions take place about what is happening in the play, what the fable is, and what the characterizations have to show.[29]

Schall is particularly clear about the role of the emotions in Brecht's theatre and the way he himself uses them as a performer:

> I am not at all a distancing, distanced actor. I am a passionate, a very passionate actor. But I'm not an actor who gives out pure emotions; emotions want to impress but not to disturb. To disturb, that's more important to me ... I don't act emotions, I present them as ways of behaviour. Brecht's term here would be *Gestus*. And when you fill behaviour with emotion, that's when you get passionate, or intense or vital.

Schall confirms the previously expressed views that Brecht avoided theory when working with his actors: 'During rehearsals he was only a practitioner. Actually he only gave explanations which helped the actors to present something in a vital manner.' There was one theoretical expression that, according to Schall, Brecht did use in rehearsal – 'to epicise' (*episieren*) – and this specially invented Brechtian verb brings us back to story-telling: 'It's very simple, you just tell the scene, the text and everything that's happening – that's epicising. He'd say: "Just tell me the scene."' And again Schall agrees with other Ensemble actors about Brecht's exploratory approach to the style of each production: 'A Brecht production does not start with a style; the style emerges during rehearsals in the sequence of situations, in which attitudes are assumed and then played.'[30]

BRITISH ACTORS ON BRECHT

Despite Brecht's reportedly open approach to the style of a production, it was the perception of a Berliner Ensemble 'style' that had an impact on other theatre practitioners. This was particularly true in Britain, where most people who saw the performances by the company on its first visit to London in 1956 could not understand German. It was, therefore, inevitable that it was the staging and the overall visual style that contributed most significantly to the impact. Nonetheless, the acting of the Ensemble was also greatly appreciated. George Devine, the actor/director who, in 1956, was running the Royal Court Theatre in London, remarked: 'Although the actors seemed to be like children playing, they gave the impression that they worked because they liked and believed in what they had to portray. Such devotion changes everything that comes off the stage. There was none of the affected, clichéd acting which is current in our theatre.'[31]

Yet when Brecht first established the Berliner Ensemble he had advised all the young actors in the company to go and see the performances of two well-known British actors – John Gielgud and Peggy Ashcroft – who were playing in Berlin in *Much Ado About Nothing* at that time (1948). Gielgud, however, did not reciprocate. He was dismissive of what he knew of Brechtian theatre (drawn from the odd article by Brecht). In a piece entitled 'Actors reply to Brecht' Gielgud, along with his fellow British actor, Alec Guinness, was antagonistic to Brecht's theories: 'I hardly feel it is very informative to be told of the influence of the Chinese theatre and the experimental German theatre on his [Brecht's] work ... The theatre only lives before an audience, and the less that audience knows how the miracle occurs the better.' Guinness, too, opposed what he perceived as a purely intellectual approach to acting on Brecht's part: 'I feel his theories cut right across the very nature of the actor, substituting some cerebral process for the instinctive and traditional accumulation of centuries ... I believe in the mystery and illusion of the theatre which Brecht seems to despise.'[32]

Peggy Ashcroft, on the other hand, took a much more open and pragmatic approach to Brecht when she became the first British actress to play the eponymous role in *The Good Person of Szechwan* (in 1956). She maintained that for her the approach to all parts was the same and decided that Brecht himself took responsibility for 'alienation' in the writing of the play. Helene Weigel, who attended some of the rehearsals for this production, agreed with Ashcroft's idea that the Brechtian actor has 'to realize the character that he plays just as fully as any other character, and so the actor has to make his effect with great economy of means, but the realization must be complete'.[33] Ashcroft also aptly made comparisons with her experience of playing Shakespeare, in particular the history plays, where the impact resulted 'from the story and the theme rather than the depth and detail of character'.[34] She went on to acknowledge, however, that the actors performing in the production of *The Good Person of Szechwan* found it difficult to achieve an appropriate playing style.

Twenty years later the acting style was less of an issue; the political implications of *The Good Person* were more to the fore. Janet Suzman, the South African-born actress, who played Shen Te/Shui Ta in London in 1978 underlines the significance for her of the socio-political purpose of the play: 'It is nonsense to ignore the politics of the play – they are at the heart of it ... My own personal commitment, my South African background was very important to my understanding of the play.' Notwithstanding, she believes that the social relationships within a play are of primary importance: 'Whatever play one does ... it's not so much the politics that take precedence as the behaviour of the people in their specific situation.'[35] Thus it was agreed by the cast that the poor characters in the play must not be patronised or 'guyed', for as Suzman says: 'They are real and unpleasant and we have to understand why.' This did not, however, lead them to neglect the comedy of the piece, which relied in this production on a collaborative approach in rehearsal and ensemble playing in performance. Even with the support of an ensemble, however, Suzman finds Brecht challenging: 'Like all apparently simple texts it's actually very difficult. You are naked out there, nothing to lean on. It requires a strong inner sense of what you're doing as an actor, so you can be relaxed, have a lightness of touch.'

The importance of relaxation and a light touch is echoed by other actors who have appeared in 'British Brecht'. Michael Gambon has performed in two productions at the National Theatre: in *Mother Courage and Her Children* (1965) and *Life of Galileo* (1979). As Eilif in the first, he had felt himself to be miscast and was unhappy with the extrovert aspect of the character, in particular in the scene in which Eilif sings and dances. Gambon explains: 'I realised later that I had been working too hard at the scene, trying too much. Later I met Ekkehard Schall at the Berliner Ensemble. He did Eilif's dance for me. He didn't move his arms. They just hung by his side. It was so simple, so easy, relaxed. Perfect.' Gambon did, however, enjoy playing Galileo. The part allowed him to exploit his large physique and rich voice – both so reminiscent of Charles Laughton – and to draw on his established 'physical' approach to a role: 'I am a very physical actor. Finding walks. I get an image. I look back and see this person standing there. I've got a big voice. Vocal changes ... I relish all that. *Galileo* is a massive, epic play, how else should I do it?' In addition, he already had a reputation as a comic actor (having starred in a number of plays by Alan Ayckbourn), and he responded instinctively to Brecht's humour: 'It was my responsibility to find the comedy within the play. It enriches the audience's experience if in the same evening – even in the same scene – they can laugh and also be hit by the message.' Gambon's success in finding a broad, comic style of performance in *Galileo* is borne out by Jim Hiley: 'It was Brechtian in its relish. Gambon

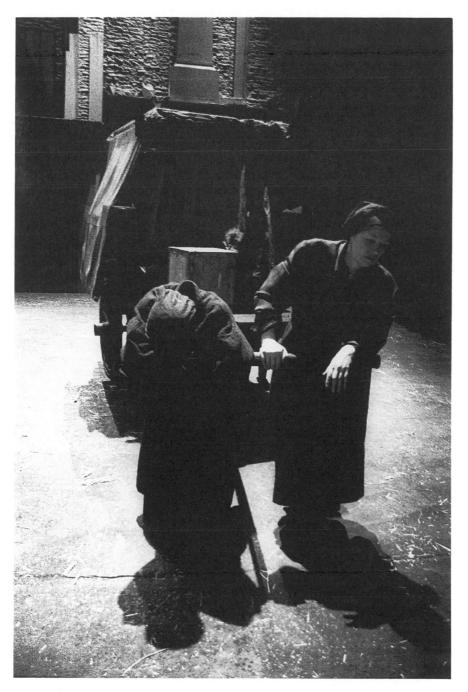

20.   Glenda Jackson as Mother Courage at the Glasgow Citizens Theatre (1990). 'She
doesn't see herself as a victim – ever!'

seized the part with both hands, and like Galileo at his goose, devoured it greedily.'[36] The one aspect of the production that failed to satisfy Gambon was the lack of a company spirit; there was, he claimed, no real sense of ensemble playing. He blamed this on a somewhat dictatorial director (John Dexter), the hierarchical structure and organisation of the National Theatre and the lack of personal involvement by the actors in the day-to-day decisions in the theatre. The general political background to this production was, in Gambon's view, unhelpful.

A similar awareness of the importance of the ensemble, of giving scope for Brecht's humour and finding a broad style of playing was expressed by Glenda Jackson, when she was preparing to take the lead in *Mother Courage* (Citizens Theatre, 1990). Her starting-point for the role drew on her memory of being told by Lotte Lenya that Weigel regarded Ethel Merman, the American entertainer, as the archetype for Courage. This makes total sense to Jackson:

> That up-front, bravado, energy – brooks no argument; you take it or leave it. It's a world seen absolutely on her terms. And if you don't like it, tough! So it was the idea of this big, big woman who believes she is in charge of her own destiny, which I found most helpful. She doesn't see herself as a victim – ever!

In preparing the part Jackson avoided reading any Brechtian theory, regarding it as 'an excessive kind of baggage' and preferring instead to work directly from the text itself. She found that Brecht gave her a 'huge sub-text' but recognised that 'what he's particular about is that you have to use it truthfully and live moment by moment'. She decided that in order to achieve a Brechtian kind of truth she needed 'the simplicity, the immediacy and totality of a child. That kind of simple, immediate response was what I was working for. That's exactly what Brecht is about, it seems to me.' (And, of course, he would have agreed.) She accepts that the idea of a through-line from the individual character's point of view is irrelevant in Brecht. But for an actress whose predominant experience is in 'realism', this 'living the moment at the moment' was, Jackson admitted, hard to achieve. She recalls rehearsing the scene in which Mother Courage first appears after the death of her son, Swiss Cheese:

> For a long time I thought to myself, how am I going to bring in, how am I going to show Swiss Cheese's death? And then I thought that's precisely what you haven't got to do because the memory of Swiss Cheese's death doesn't come up till Kattrin's been attacked – and then all that suddenly comes up to the surface. You don't have to bring anything because that's the antithesis of what Brecht's writing. For every character there is no past, no future, there's only now.

Like Peggy Ashcroft, Jackson finds similarities here between Brecht and Shakespeare: 'Inasmuch that every scene is a new beginning, I find this play quite similar to Shakespeare. Shakespeare does exactly the same thing. You receive all you need to know from a variety of sources, you're not beholden to one person to tell you the whole play; it's beholden to one person to play their character, to take their share of the story.'

Antony Sher, when working on the role of Arturo Ui (National Theatre, 1991), also saw story-telling as important in Brechtian acting. But he deviated from the idea of 'living in the moment' as expressed by Glenda Jackson, by pointing out his wish to trace the character's 'journey' through the play. He tried to show Ui's transition from street thug to Chicago boss, seeing the famous 'Actor' scene, in which Ui learns how to speak and move in public from a 'ham' actor, as a scene of transformation. To Sher this signals more than a physical change in Ui: 'I thought that the Actor's scene could change Ui quite completely. He doesn't just learn a few Hitler gestures. He transforms.' This idea might still be accommodated within Brecht's notion that to study a role is to study the narrative. The play is the story of Ui's 'Resistible Rise' and that scene is a pivotal, 'nodal' point in the story. Sher did, however, approach the role in the same way as he approaches any other, admitting he

> wouldn't know how to play a character in an alienated way. I don't know what that means. The same rules apply, as far as I'm concerned, to whatever you're acting. You've got to get in there and find out as much as possible about the character. Then either the production or the play itself will create a kind of style.

Despite this evident resistance to theory, Sher is known as an 'intellectual' actor, someone who prepares himself and the background to a part very thoroughly – in this case he read *Mein Kampf* and several biographies of Hitler. But, like Michael Gambon, he also stresses the importance for him of the physical image in creating Ui. Since Sher is a trained artist, he worked on this image by making sketches of the character during the rehearsal period, following (unwittingly) in the footsteps of Brecht's designer, Caspar Neher. One of Sher's ideas was that Ui had to be very awkward: 'A street thug in the way the National Socialists were. People that literally fight with their fists. And then we were specifically taking it into the Scorsese, Capone, Mafia world. Sketches started about how to be Italian.' There was considerable acclaim for Sher's performance, but he found the experience of playing Ui less than satisfactory. He puts this down to two things: what he saw as some structural weaknesses in the play, and the company's over-reverence towards the text, which he thought hindered their search for an appropriate

21. Antony Sher as Arturo Ui at the National Theatre, London (1991): 'A street thug in the way the National Socialists were.'

performance style. Of the play, he said: 'It feels like early writing, like first draft writing. Brecht never got the chance to go back and sort it out. I'm sure if the play had been done in his lifetime and he'd had a chance to see it, it would all have been simplified, much less plot.' He remembers being told about Schall's performance of Ui at the Berliner Ensemble (after Brecht's death), in which he was described not only as being 'Chaplinesque' but also as including sequences of acrobatics. Sher had originally found this description puzzling, but after the opening night, he told a friend: 'Tonight I understood why Schall did acrobatics – because the play doesn't. Brecht promises us "criminal history as pantomime" but doesn't deliver that.' During the subsequent run of the National Theatre production, Sher came to the conclusion that they should have gone further towards a 'living cartoon', making the performance not only lighter and funnier but more grotesque, too:

> I would cut the play more so you could do it very fast ... punchier ... more fun ... It's got to work as impact theatre. It can't hang about. That way one could score comic points *and* show the terror more dynamically than we did.

SUMMARY

The consensus of actor-opinion on Brecht's ideas and the challenges of performing his plays can be summarised simply. In working on a character, the Brechtian performer, while not avoiding psychology, places more emphasis on the role's social interaction and behaviour. The characterisation is usually still 'complete' in terms of detailed observation, but the actor is required to make the attitudes of the character clear, to be economical in playing the emotions and to find ways of highlighting key moments of decision in order to emphasise their social truth and to undercut potential sentimentality.

Overall, actors perceive a shift in balance in performing Brecht from character to plot, from role to story-telling, and see the importance of comedy in Brechtian roles and scenes, not only as a distancing device but as a way of making the message entertaining and accessible.

Finally the consensus places great significance on the theatre company as an 'ensemble'. This assumes the possibility of not only a common (sociopolitical) purpose but also a collaborative approach to theatrical aesthetics. In addition it allows for an experimental attitude in which all ideas can be tried and tested in rehearsal and performance, thus placing practice before theory. For, as Brecht said: 'There is no purely theoretical access to our manner of acting.'[37]

NOTES

1 *The Listener*, 24 May 1979, p. 709.
2 *The Messingkauf Dialogues*, p. 104.
3 Carl Weber, 'Brecht as director', *Tulane Drama Review* 12, no. 1 (1967), p. 106.

4 'Brecht and the contradictory actor', *Theatre Journal* 36, no. 1 (1984), p. 31.
5 *The Messingkauf Dialogues*, p. 87.
6 Quoted in Willett, *Brecht in Context*, p. 111.
7 Brecht, *Diaries 1920–1922*, pp. 140–1.
8 Ewen, *Bertolt Brecht*, p. 232.
9 Chaplin, *My Autobiography* (Bodley Head: London, 1964), p. 227.
10 Hayman, *Brecht: A Biography*, p. 103.
11 *Letters 1913–1956*, p. 341.
12 Hayman, *Brecht: A Biography*, p. 138.
13 F. W. Ott, *The Films of Fritz Lang* (Citadel Press: New Jersey, 1979), p. 156.
14 Charles Higham, *Charles Laughton* (W. H. Allen: London, 1976), p. 135.
15 Eric Bentley, 'Portrait of the critic as a young Brechtian', *Theatre Quarterly* 6, no. 21 (1976), p. 6.
16 Weber, 'Brecht as director', p. 103.
17 *Ibid.*, p. 105.
18 *The Times Educational Supplement*, 8 January 1982.
19 'Dialogue: Berliner Ensemble', *Tulane Drama Review* 12, no. 1 (1967), p. 112.
20 Ronald Hayman, *Techniques of Acting* (Methuen: London, 1969), p. 54.
21 *The Observer*, 22 August 1965.
22 'Notes on Stanislavsky', *Tulane Drama Review* 9, no. 2 (1964), p. 163.
23 E. Capon, 'Brecht in Britain', *Encore* 10, no. 2 (1963), p. 28.
24 Hayman, *Brecht: A Biography*, p. 380.
25 H. Witt, ed., *Brecht As They Knew Him*, p. 133.
26 'Notes on Stanislavsky', p. 161.
27 This and the previous two quotations are from Witt, *Brecht As They Knew Him*, pp. 132–3.
28 Hayman, *Techniques of Acting*, p. 52.
29 'Dialogue: Berliner Ensemble', p. 117. Other quotations are from 'An interview with Ekkehard Schall', *Theater Magazine* (New Haven, Spring 1986).
30 Pia Kleber, *Exceptions and Rules*, p. 84.
31 *The Encore Reader*, ed. C. Marowitz, T. Milne, D. Hale (Methuen: London, 1965), p. 15.
32 *New Theatre* 5, no. 10 (April 1949), p. 15.
33 Hal Burton, *Great Acting* (BBC: London, 1967), p. 95.
34 *Ibid.*, p. 95.
35 *Plays and Players*, August 1977, p. 12.
36 Hiley, *Theatre At Work*, p. 211.
37 P. Demetz, ed., *Brecht: A Collection of Critical Essays*, p. 112.

19

MICHAEL PATTERSON

Brecht's legacy

For playwrights or theatre practitioners to have their names turned into adjectives is a somewhat dubious accolade that is rarely accorded: in the last hundred years we have acquired Chekhovian, Shavian, Stanislavskian, Artaudian, even Beckettian and Pinteresque, but not Reinhardtian, Piscatorian, Brookian or Genetesque. But the one adjective that lifts most easily off the tongue, the one that sounds least like an Armenian exile, is undoubtedly 'Brechtian'. Alone among Germans (except for the somewhat arcane 'Schillerian'), Brecht enjoys, both as writer and director, a privilege which can be misleading and misappropriated: 'Brechtian' can legitimise; it can also limit; it can certainly distort.

Writing in the 'Sacred Cows' series, published in *The Sunday Times Magazine* in 1977, Sheridan Morley complained:

> 'Brechtian' has become one of those critical hold-alls, now bursting at the seams but still used to describe everything from a stage on which the designer has failed to place enough chairs to an acting company loosely dedicated to a political ideal somewhere faintly to the left of Mrs Thatcher.[1]

It is small wonder that Brecht's ideas have not been well understood in the English-speaking world. Until the year of Brecht's death only a few scattered and unsuccessful productions acquainted an unenthusiastic public with Brecht's work: for example, *The Threepenny Opera* on Broadway in 1933; *Anna Anna* (*The Seven Deadly Sins*) at the Savoy Theatre, London, in 1933; a BBC broadcast of *The Tuppenny-ha'penny Opera* (*sic*) in 1935; *The Mother* at the Theatre Union, New York, in 1935; *The Rifles of Señora Carrar* at the Unity Theatre Club, London, in 1938; and, most notably, Joseph Losey's production of *Galileo* in 1947, with Charles Laughton in the title role, which ran for only twelve performances in Los Angeles and for six in New York. Only a 1954 off-Broadway production of *The Threepenny Opera*, starring Lotte Lenya, enjoyed any degree of success.

Then, in 1956 the Berliner Ensemble paid their famous visit to the Palace

Theatre in London with productions of *Mother Courage, The Caucasian Chalk Circle* and *Trumpets and Drums*. Championed especially by Kenneth Tynan, Brecht had arrived in the British theatre. With the plays performed in a language unfamiliar to the majority of the audience, the greatest impact was made by the simple but visually satisfying sets, the worn and grimy costumes and props of *Mother Courage* and the rich and fluid patterns of movement of the actors.

Unfortunately, more time passed before English-speakers had access to Brecht's theories. Occasional pieces in translation appeared, especially in the journal *Encounter*. In 1959 Martin Esslin published his pioneering but silly book *Brecht: A Choice of Evils*, in which, in the words of Maro Germanou, Esslin argued that 'Brecht's plays are good, despite Brecht, his theory and his politics.'[2] In the United States the translations and essays of Eric Bentley and the competent chapter on Brecht by David Grossvogel in *Four Playwrights and a Postscript* (1962) were assisting in making Brecht familiar, but it was John Willett, first in *The Theatre of Bertolt Brecht* in 1959 and then in the compilation of Brecht's own writings in *Brecht on Theatre* of 1964, who first allowed the non-German-speaker proper access to these new theories. Unfortunately, one of Brecht's key words, *Verfremdung*, probably best rendered in English by the ugly word 'distanciation', was translated by Willett as 'alienation', the equivalent of the Hegelian/Marxist *Entfremdung*. This is not a mere linguistic quibble; for the word 'alienation' implies that audiences should become either antagonised by the performance or detached from the stage action to the point of boredom. As Peter Brooker points out, what Brecht in fact pursued was 'de-alienation'.[3] However, many political theatre groups, emboldened with an apparent seal of approval from a socialist intellectual leader, could subject their audiences to harangue, tedium and often both, congratulating themselves on their success in 'alienating' their 'bourgeois' audience. I recall in the early 1970s enduring an extremely wearisome West End production of *The Threepenny Opera* which was lifeless, underlit and whose main feature was the clown-white make-up of all the performers. The offence against Brecht was further compounded by a leading critic who wrote in the following Sunday's *Observer* that 'it was perhaps not gloomy enough for Brecht fans'.

Paying unreasoning homage to Brecht can be as destructive as perverting his methods, even though, as Eric Bentley says, 'It is understandable ... that people who wish to pay tribute to Brecht should cite his influence.'[4] In the United States many progressive groups have acknowledged a debt to Brecht. The San Francisco Mime Troupe, founded in 1959, has staged *The Exception and the Rule* (1964), *Turandot* (1969) and *The Mother* (1973) and speaks of the importance of Brechtian ideas for their work:

We posited that all action on the platform was fake, masked, indicated, enlarged show biz, while everything offstage was real.[5]

Similarly, Luis Valdez of the Teatro Campesino, founded in 1965, asserted: 'I am a very strong advocate of the alienation effect ... It's there, consciously or unconsciously, in all of my work.'[6] Even The Performance Group (later The Wooster Group)[7] and The Living Theatre[8] both claim Brecht as one of their progenitors. With such diverse and frequently suspiciously irrational forms of theatre waving a Brechtian banner, one begins to wonder whether the word 'Brechtian' can indeed have any real content, especially when Judith Malina can write of the arrest of Julian Beck and herself during rehearsals for *The Brig* as follows:

> They took us out of the theatrical prison and put us into the wagon and drove us into the real prison and locked the real prison door. And it was an Artaudian experience, it was a Brechtian experience, it was a life experience.[9]

It is not clear what she means, perhaps some disturbing juxtaposition of stage fiction and reality, perhaps some identification with Brecht as a victim of political repression (something in fact that Brecht was fairly skilful at avoiding). The truth is that Brecht's name is often invoked to lend a spurious legitimacy to theatrical work that would have been anathema to the man who sought to create theatre 'for the scientific age'; as Eric Bentley says, 'Brechtian' is often not so much a literary or theatrical term as an exercise in public relations.[10]

Turning to Germany, where for obvious reasons, Brechtian concepts have been better understood, one nevertheless finds that his true legacy has been all too frequently obscured by misguided theatre practice and the prevailing political climate. Sadly, one of the worst offenders has been the Berliner Ensemble itself, where until 1989 it was very difficult to take a fresh look at Brecht's work. Each production tended faithfully to follow the staging of the appropriate *Modellbuch*, although Brecht had always insisted that these were to be used as a record of his discoveries, like the write-up of an experiment, not as the blueprint to be copied slavishly by later directors. Brecht's work was ossified as a series of classics, a lifeless homage to socialism rather than as a challenge to the audience to reflect on their own situation. If such challenges came at the Berliner Ensemble, they seemed to have little to do with Brecht. In 1986 a Chilean guest director staged an adventurous dramatisation of Saint-Exupéry's *The Little Prince*, prefaced by a 20-minute sequence set in East Berlin's main station, the Bahnhof Friedrichstrasse. This 'Prologue', suggesting the desert in which the Little Prince would find himself, consisted of a well-observed series of entrances and exits of several dozen typical figures of this urban milieu, all performed with considerable virtuosity by a handful of actors. It was clever and theatrical, but was studied with almost disturbing intensity by the audience present. When one of the cast was asked why the reaction to this bravura piece was so muted, he replied that one had to understand that this was the first time for years that Berliners had seen their own environment accurately represented on stage, and that this necessarily provided a shock. It is alarming to think that it was in Brecht's own theatre that it was such a rarity for 'the familiar to be seen as unfamiliar'.

Predictably, since the 1989 'revolution' East German theatres have tended to reject the compulsory diet on which they were fed under communism and now perform Brecht in a way that has often characterised his treatment in the West.

The Western approach to Brecht has generally consisted of a grudging acknowledgement that he is a fine playwright *in spite of* his Marxist beliefs. Despite the efforts of directors like Harry Buckwitz, who defied public protests to stage Brecht in Frankfurt, there was a strong antipathy towards his work during the Cold War of the 1950s. This 'Brecht boycott' intensified after Brecht's apparent acquiescence in the suppression of the workers' uprising in East Germany in 1953, documented by Günter Grass in *The Plebeians Rehearse the Uprising* (1965), and intensified again after the Hungarian Revolution in 1956 and the building of the Berlin Wall in 1961. The change in Brecht's fortunes occurred with the swing to the left after the student uprisings of 1968 and in the wake of the questioning of 'imperialist' policies in Vietnam and Africa: 'the Brecht-boycott of the fifties gave way to a regular Brecht-boom', as Schneider writes.[11] This boom, however, became something of a passing fashion, and by the late 1970s had been replaced by what Werner Mittenzwei called 'Brecht-weariness' (*Brecht-Müdigkeit*),[12] not least because the stranglehold of the Brecht estate on his copyright prevented any theatrical experimentation with his plays. Brecht is still frequently performed in the new united Germany, but one could not claim that productions of his own works are trend-setting for the German theatre of the last decade of this century.

Given then the widespread misunderstanding of Brecht outside Germany and the lack of consistency and freshness in approaching him within Germany, can one claim that Brecht's legacy is anything more than a matter of employing a more or less fashionable label to enhance theatre work ranging from performance art to agitprop? Is there, for example, any substance to Ronald Hayman's claim that 'He has exerted more influence than anyone else not only on playwriting, design and style in production, but on our whole approach to theatre'?[13]

When considering playwriting, we immediately encounter the difficulty that some writers who acknowledge Brecht as an influence are patently not writing in a Brechtian mode, while other considerably more Brechtian play-wrights understandably wish to establish their own originality by denying a debt to Brecht. A case of the former is Robert Bolt, who declared in his Preface to *A Man For All Seasons* (1960): 'The style I eventually used was a bastardised version of the one most recently associated with Bertolt Brecht.'[14] Yet his piece is thoroughly un-Brechtian, inviting, as it does, our sympathy with the travails of the noble central figure, Sir Thomas More. A contrasting case is Edward Bond, whose political perspective and distanced epic treatment, especially in a piece like *Narrow Road to the Deep North* (1968, rewritten as *The Bundle*, 1977), mark him out as a 'Brechtian' play-wright, while he has insisted: 'I don't think I'm influenced by Brecht at all.'[15] Reference back to Brecht can indeed be crippling for a dramatist. As Martin Walser said in 1966 at a writers' conference: 'Als Dramatiker hat mich Brecht kaputt gemacht!'.[16]

On a more positive note it is clear that Brecht has had a profound effect on several playwrights who, through their acquaintance with his work, devel-oped in ways that might otherwise not have occurred. This effect on playwrit-ing might be summarised as follows: first, a means of portraying dramatic characters not as unchanging and circumscribed entities but as contradictory, alterable beings, their 'individuality' a function of their social situation; secondly, the resulting primacy of interest in that social situation rather than in the emotions or psychology of the individual; thirdly, a willingness to forgo suspense about the outcome of the plot to focus attention on the way the plot develops, inviting a consideration of other possible outcomes ('epic' method); fourthly, an encouragement to write plays that are vigorously theatrical, using the visual quality of 'gestic' action, employing songs, using the stage to represent exotic locations that are distant in geographical or his-torical terms, above all, rediscovering the 'fun' (*Spass*) of the theatrical event; finally, for German playwrights, the discovery of a stage language, sometimes called *Brechtsch*, which avoided the high-flown artificiality of High German without resorting to dialect that is unintelligible outside its own region.

One can easily list post-war playwrights who reveal strong traces of Brechtian influence: in Germany Peter Hacks, Volker Braun, Martin Walser, Peter Weiss, Tankred Dorst, Heiner Müller; outside Germany John Arden, Edward Bond, Howard Brenton, David Hare (especially in *Fanshen*, 1975), Armand Gatti, Dario Fo, *et al*. One could cite many acknowledgements of the effects of Brecht's legacy: for example, Peter Weiss's early plays, influ-enced by Kafka and Strindberg, were full of dream-like symbolism, *The Tower* (*Der Turm*, 1948), *Night With Guests* (*Nacht mit Gästen*, 1962). Then he began to acquaint himself with Brecht:

Brecht influenced me as a dramatist. I learnt most from Brecht. I learnt clarity from him, the necessity of making clear the social question in a play. I learnt from him lightness. He is never heavy in the psychological German way.[17]

The result of this 'conversion' was a play that was so theatrically adventurous that it may justifiably be regarded as the most exciting piece of political theatre since Brecht, *The Marat/Sade*, 1964.

A clear demonstration of the impact of Brecht on British playwriting is provided by a comparison of two political plays performed within months of each other at the Royal Court Theatre, London, in 1959: Arnold Wesker's *Roots* and John Arden's *Serjeant Musgrave's Dance*. It would appear that Wesker was unfamiliar with Brecht's theories, while Arden declared that *Mother Courage* was the play he would most have liked to have written.[18] Wesker's play is broadly naturalistic, with contemporary interior realistic settings; Arden's is, according to his own description, 'poetic', using a variety of simply defined historical locations; *Roots* explores the development of the character of Beatie, the central figure; Serjeant Musgrave is enigmatic, the emphasis is on his 'mission' not on his individuality; Wesker's dialogue imitates everyday speech patterns; Arden's is consciously poetic; the one song in *Roots* arises naturally out of a realistic situation; many of the songs in *Musgrave* are, to use the Brechtian phrase, 'separated from the rest'; above all, *Roots* depends on verbal exchange, *Musgrave* is full of 'gestic' action.

Here the case for acknowledging Brecht's influence seems incontrovertible, and yet in 1966 Arden said:

I don't copy Brecht; I don't use him as a model. After I had started writing plays I decided that Brecht was inspired by the same sort of early drama that was interesting me: the rather conventionalised plays of the European Middle Ages, the Elizabethan writers and various exotic styles such as the Japanese and Chinese theatre.[19]

Clearly, many of the impulses that came from Brecht were not invented by him. Psychology and sociology had undermined idealistic concepts of the individual long before Brecht, and classical Greek and medieval theatre had managed well without strong individual characterisation; the Elizabethan and Jacobean stage had obvious 'epic' qualities, employed songs and music, was strongly visual and thoroughly theatrical, and anyway all these elements had been a part of the theatrical revolution of the German expressionists. But to acknowledge that Brecht was himself drawing on theatrical traditions is not to negate his achievement. Any epigone can copy what has gone before; it takes an original mind to transform it into something usable in the present.

But how usable are Brecht's methods by playwrights in the last decade of the twentieth century, especially in the wake of the collapse of communism in Eastern Europe? Some of Brecht's writings for the theatre appear hopelessly dated. The optimistic portrayal of Soviet collective farming in the Prologue of *The Caucasian Chalk Circle* must seem a cynical piece of propaganda to those who were intimidated and dispossessed in the name of Stalinist collectivisation and whose children are facing starvation because of the collapse of this policy. The *Lehrstücke* confront us with terrible choices, apparently resolved in favour of Stalinist brutality.[20] If one wishes to use the theatre as a museum, then there is little harm in portraying Brecht's hopes for a radical renewal of Soviet society after the devastation of the Second World War nor in presenting his understandably extreme response to the growing power of fascism. What one could assert with some authority is that it is unthinkable that Brecht, were he alive today, would perform *The Caucasian Chalk Circle* with its original Prologue or would not insist – yet again – on rewriting *The Measures Taken* to take account of the changes in political thinking over more than half a century. As Heiner Müller said in 1980: 'Using Brecht without being critical of him is a form of betrayal',[21] or as Peter Hacks wrote in 1972:

> Brecht's reality was the reality of the first half of the twentieth century. But our reality is different; our methods must appear to be different from Brecht, if they are to be Brechtian. Like every achievement of the human mind, Brecht's achievement is historical. It is both transitory and permanent. It can be developed only by negating it not by prolonging it.[22]

As with playwriting, much of Brecht's legacy to theatrical practice may be in need of modification and anyway his techniques may ultimately derive from much older theatrical traditions. So-called Brechtian staging principles are now widely applied in the area of stage design, are often considered in the directing of plays, but, in English-speaking countries anyway, are least well understood in acting.

The minimal, functional and flexible sets that we now associate with Brecht are a reversion to a style of theatre used for generations, until the nineteenth century began to develop its obsession with realism. Besides, designers like Craig and Appia, and the experiments of the German expressionists, most notably Leopold Jessner's productions in Berlin in the early 1920s, had already paved the way for the regular use of a permanent set which underwent minor changes to suggest shift of location. The bare stage, with, say, a throne to denote a palace, a banner to identify an army or a tent to suggest a camp on the battlefield, dates back to at least the Elizabethan stage and has remained a commonplace of Asian theatre. The enthusiasm with which post-war designers have embraced this style of staging may in part testify to the importance of Brecht's legacy, but it may also have other more potent reasons.

The first of these is economic. Even the best subsidised companies would be hard pressed financially to provide authentically realistic sets for a Shakespearian production, and such décor is now normally only seen in plays set in an Ibsenite single domestic interior. Secondly, cinema and television have made a major impact on theatrical design. Since it is almost impossible for the stage to compete with these modern media in presenting elaborately authentic milieux, the theatre has mercifully returned to creating visual images which stimulate the imagination of the audience rather than feed them with literal depiction. This is a negative influence, a pressure on the theatre to reassert one of its major strengths. By contrast, the pace of narrative of television and the cinema has had a positive influence in forcing the theatre to develop a fluency of presentation that requires sets to be sufficiently flexible to allow of very rapid change.

When Brecht then insists that the stage should be like a building-site with its sign 'No access to anyone not having business here',[23] the advice will accord well with contemporary theatre practice. It may seem to constitute a strong element in his influence, but in this, as in many other respects, it would be true to say that Brecht's influence came, as all successful influences do, when the time was anyway right for it.

Some of Brecht's other proposals regarding staging have become so much a part of standard stage practice that it is difficult to determine whether they actually result from his influence. When present-day theatregoers lift their heads and see rows of lights hanging above them in the auditorium or witness a scene change without the front curtain being drawn, then it is doubtful whether this is a part of Brecht's legacy, although it precisely follows his recommendations. What one can say is that these practices contribute, as Brecht intended they should, to the demystification of the theatrical process, the abandonment of the 'magic of theatre' in favour of a more rational and 'scientific' approach to the stage.

In terms of his influence on the director, Brecht helped to show how Marxist principles could be introduced to the realisation of a text in performance. Despite the rejection in Eastern Europe of a system based on so-called 'Marxist-Leninist' principles, the importance and continuing relevance of Marx as a social philosopher cannot be denied. In its simplest formulation Marx argued that 'social being determines consciousness', and this standpoint has profound implications for the theatre, implications that were first fully explored by Brecht. By examining humankind in its social function and by challenging the primacy of human individuality, Brecht, more decisively than any dramatist before him, continued the assault, begun by the naturalists, on the autonomy of the will of the dramatic protagonist, the basis of all traditional tragedy (idealism), and instead posited a view of the individual as created by social and economic, and therefore changeable factors (materialism).

Since theatre has conventionally focussed on the individual, the Marxist approach to theatre produces a productive tension between the central figure, who must remain sufficiently active to maintain our interest, and the historical, social and economic context in which this activity takes place. Thus, in Brecht's schematic treatment of this problem in *The Good Person of Szechwan*, Shen Te can pursue her own individual inclination towards generosity by inventing the *alter ego* of Shui Ta, a fiction created by the capitalist context and one that enables Shen Te to continue functioning as 'a good woman' in a world of greed and exploitation. Similarly, Mother Courage and Galileo, two of the most clearly defined 'characters' of twentieth-century drama, can be properly evaluated only in relation to the historical period in which they live.

The major implication for directorial practice lies in a new approach to texts that places an emphasis on the 'social being' instead of on the individual 'consciousness'. This change of focus is not confined to theatre, but has informed literary criticism as well, as in the rejection of Bradleyan character-based readings of Shakespeare in favour of a more sophisticated, less idealistic model. We no doubt all recall the examination question of the type: 'Give a character sketch of either Horatio or Gertrude or Polonius', as though each of these characters were self-sufficient entities with an existence independent of each other. Now both in critical and theatrical practice the interest is, for example, not so much in the disturbed psychological make-up of Hamlet as in the situation of a reasonably normal and enlightened young man reacting with understandable passion to the duplicity of the court and to the outmoded code of revenge by which he is obliged to live. In fact, the rediscovery has been made, as Michael Bogdanov regularly assured viewers in his Channel Four television series, that 'Shakespeare is a political playwright'. It is now rare for a director to approach Shakespeare with the intention of portraying 'the human condition' or 'universal truths' without giving consideration to the historical situation, both the situation depicted in the play and that in which Shakespeare lived and which therefore informed his writing. Indeed, traditionalists often feel that things have gone too far. So, for instance, Terry Hands's production of *King Lear* in 1977, in which beggars banging empty food tins crossed the stage between scenes and Donald Sinden's Lear was uniformed like the Grand Duke of a small pre-First World War republic, invested so much in the need to see the play as history that it failed to present it as myth.

This Brechtian approach to directing a text insists that the director should be well informed about the piece to be worked on but should not arrive at rehearsal with preconceived notions about the end product. Director and actors should engage in a series of experiments, which, as in the natural sciences, will be evaluated according to how well they correspond with known truths. Brecht himself would constantly challenge his own results in the course of rehearsal and would never allow a scene to be played a certain way only because this was what had been agreed upon in the past. This scientific approach, in which the director works most productively by asking questions rather than by supplying answers, now characterises the methods of most leading European directors today, for example, Peter Brook, Roger Planchon, Giorgio Strehler, Peter Stein – 'beginning from zero', as Stein calls it.[24]

The functional quality of Brechtian set design is reflected also in the visual composition of scenes. The tendency of the naturalist production to introduce 'business', either to reinforce verisimilitude or simply to introduce variety, is replaced by the 'gestic' principle, that each scene is making a statement and that each figure on stage is contributing to that statement in their positioning and moves. This does not mean that the Brechtian director favours static stage pictures or seeks symbolic effects, but that what is seen issues a specific message about the content of the scene and clarifies, as it were, the caption that might be written to define the scene's function in the play. The risk here is that, if the insistence on visual clarity is applied too rigorously, such directorial methods can remove the ambiguity of theatrical images and thus undermine the dialectical tensions which Brecht himself favoured. As Elizabeth Wright persuasively argues in *Postmodern Brecht*, the work of Pina Bausch, Robert Wilson and Heiner Müller in presenting powerful and multi-layered images may more truly represent Brecht's legacy than dated forms of conventional political theatre. However, this once again runs into the danger of allowing Brecht's name to be the rallying cry for all that is exciting and experimental in contemporary theatre. In a world where all progressive forms of theatre are 'Brechtian', none is.

When Brechtian methods are applied to acting, we encounter, in America and Britain at least, considerable resistance to the application of the *Verfremdungseffekt*. There are many reasons for this. First, given the dire economic situation of most actors, there is tremendous pressure on them to assure themselves of popularity and so further their careers by charming their audiences: they have to project their individuality as a saleable commodity – in a thoroughly un-Brechtian fashion. Secondly, most British and

American drama schools are imbued with a Stanislavskian ethos, where an actor's identification with the role is taught by staff and sought by students, the major crime being to 'come out of role', that is, to acquire the very distance that Brechtian theory demands. The predominance of Stanislavskian methods is not just a historical accident and further testimony to the slow response to Brechtian ideas we have already noted, but is also perpetuated by the fact that Stanislavsky's methods tend to be much more satisfying to the individual performer. To be told on receiving a minor part that one is contributing to the 'gest' of a scene is not nearly as encouraging as to be asked to create a biography for one's character, flesh this out with detail and be reassured that there are 'no small parts, only small actors'. Similarly, it is far easier to discover the through-line of motivation and explore the emotions of a well-written role than to try to seek out the contradictions of a character and to try to present these in all their complexity. Thirdly, the close-up of television and film, which now provides most of our experience of acting, militates against the boldly stated performance (what the Germans call 'plakativ' – like a wall poster). The greatest fear of most students of acting in Britain today is not that they may be boring but that they may be 'overacting'; the lift of the eyebrow or the curl of the lip become the high points of emotional expression – certainly they are the techniques which will be in demand in the best-paid acting engagements.

One therefore tends to encounter Brechtian acting only in the stable ensembles of German municipal theatres or in theatre collectives and student groups in Britain and America. One meets it also traditionally in comedy: without ever having heard of Brecht, Oliver Hardy could create a moment of pure 'alienation' by turning from a gibbering Stan Laurel to look into the camera, eyebrows raised, and share an unspoken reaction with the spectator. One also finds 'Brechtian' elements in almost all outstanding performances, because an ingredient of effective acting is to reveal cross-currents and contradictions, to explore a dialectic. Helene Weigel's silent scream over the corpse of Swiss Cheese is not only good Brecht; it is good theatre.

Is there then any clearly distinguishable Brechtian legacy in the field of acting? In Britain one can point (as Ronald Hayman does[25]) to the newfound acceptance of regional accents even in classical roles, or one might compare Laurence Olivier's regal and sensitive film portrayal of Henry V in 1944 with the robust, almost plebeian performance of Kenneth Branagh in the same role nearly half a century later. But it would be a Brechtian insight to acknowledge the process of democratisation in the post-war period and the resultant changes in social values which have no doubt affected attitudes far more profoundly than could the aesthetic programme of a single individual.

Perhaps the most truly revolutionary legacy of Brecht is his effect on our understanding of the relationship between performer and spectator. Here one can distinguish, on the one hand, between his attempt to reform existing bourgeois theatre by negotiating a new relationship with the audience, and, on the other, a truly revolutionary theatre in which the division between actor and spectator is removed. As we learn from Steinweg's work on the *Lehrstück* in 1972,[26] a fragment in the Brecht archives describes these two approaches as the Minor Pedagogy and the Major Pedagogy (*kleine Pädagogik* and *grosse Pädagogik*). The Minor Pedagogy encourages the audience to adopt a more productive attitude in their reception of a theatrical performance. Instead of being passive spectators, only engaging empathetically in the action, they are invited by Brecht through the use of 'alienation' – the challenge to view things with fresh eyes – to engage in a critical dialogue with stage action. However, this dialogue can only be mental and silent. It would be inappropriate for the spectator of a Brecht play to shout out comments, much less to climb onto the stage to save Kattrin or block Mother Courage's path as she trudges off towards the war yet again.

Even the director has little opportunity to enter into a critical relationship with Brecht's mature plays. One may productively take freedoms with Shakespeare; it would be a nonsense to transfer *Galileo* or *Mother Courage* to another period or to play them in an abstract setting, and little would be gained from an un-Brechtian experimental approach to the text. These plays are models of epic theatre, which can and should be reworked in each production but which are not susceptible of radical change.

By contrast, the Major Pedagogy envisages a theatre which has change as its fundamental principle. Already the *Lehrstück*, which Brecht said of all his work most pointed forward to the future of theatre,[27] represented a new form of theatre, not intended for performance to non-participatory spectators, but as a means of learning for the actors. So, for example, when *The Measures Taken* was premièred in Berlin in 1930, the 'role' of the Control Chorus was taken by the 3,000 workers present. Properly understood, the *Lehrstück* would need to be rewritten each time a committed cast works on it. Far from being ejected from the theatre for challenging the content of the piece, the actor/spectator is invited to do so as an essential part of the learning process.

Brecht never lived to see this Major Pedagogy at work, but it has formed the basis of the practice of Augusto Boal in his 'Forum' theatre. An account of his work on a recent visit to Bradford in Yorkshire is provided by Albert Hunt:

> Boal worked for a week with a group of 18, which included artists from Mind the Gap, social workers, and physically and mentally handicapped people. They prepared a demonstration of Forum Theatre before an invited audience. Boal first explained what would happen. The group had prepared four scenes.

In each of them someone was oppressed. After they had performed the scenes we would choose two of them to explore. We would suggest ways in which the oppressed person might act ... In the mother scene, Boal challenged men – the oppressors – to offer solutions for the women. At first the men held back – it was a woman who wrote out a shopping list, gave it to her husband and then went out to a party. When a man eventually dared to take the mother's apron, he sat at the table doing nothing. If the family wanted dinner, he said, they would have to make it themselves.

(Boal, by the way, is flying back to Brazil to stand as a candidate in an election in which he will invite Forum theatre audiences to create his political programme.)[28]

It is doubtful, in Europe anyway, how successful Boal's application of the Major Pedagogy could be in a wider context. It is significant that the audience for the Bradford experiment was 'invited', since theatre audiences would normally need to be alerted to this form of participation. There is also a great risk in this form of spontaneous theatre-making that the participants merely create their own stereotypes (as here, the victimised woman, the selfish male). Nevertheless, it is clear that in terms of reassessing the relationship between stage and spectator – in a way that is also immediately transferable to the world of practical politics – Boal has shown himself to be one of Brecht's major legatees.

Whether in playwriting, theatre practice or in the relationship between stage and audience, Brecht's 'scientific' methods are still of considerable importance, but only when it is remembered that these *are* methods; for as Maarten van Dijk reminds us, the main reason why attempts to be 'Brechtian' have so frequently failed is due to 'the overwhelming tendency to see Brecht's theory and practice as a style rather than as a *method*'.[29]

Despite misunderstanding and misappropriation Brecht's name will deservedly continue to be used as an adjective and condition the way we think about theatre for many decades to come; for to see the world with fresh eyes, as Brecht urged us to, is a benefit to anyone; for the playwright, director and actor, it is essential.

NOTES

1 Sheridan Morley, 'Playing with words', *The Sunday Times Magazine*, 28 August 1977, p. 70.
2 Maro Germanou, 'Brecht and the English theatre', in *Brecht in Perspective*, ed. Bartram and Waine, p. 213.
3 Peter Brooker, *Bertolt Brecht: Dialectics, Poetry, Politics*, p. 79.
4 Eric Bentley, 'The influence of Brecht', in *Re-interpreting Brecht*, ed. P. Kleber and C. Visser, p. 192.

5 R. G. Davis, *The San Francisco Mime Troupe: The First Ten Years* (Ramparts Press: Forestville, 1975), pp. 34–5.

6 Yolanda Julia Broyles, 'Brecht: the intellectual tramp. An interview with Luis Valdez', *Communications from the Brecht Society* 12, no. 2 (April 1983), p. 40.

7 Richard Schechner, who founded The Performance Group in 1967, staged *Mother Courage* in 1975 (see Paul Ryder Kyan, 'The Performance Group in *Mother Courage*', *Tulane Drama Review*, 19, no. 2 (1975), pp. 79–93).

8 See Julian Beck, *Life of the Theatre* (Limelight Editions: New York, 1986), esp. p. 68.

9 *Material der Berliner Filmfestspiele* for the film *Signals Through the Flames* by Sheldon Rochlin and Maxine Harris, 1984.

10 See Bentley, 'The influence of Brecht', esp. p. 186.

11 M. Schneider, 'Bertolt Brecht – ein abgebrochener Riese. Zur ästhetischen Emanzipation von einem Klassiker', *Literaturmagazin 10: Vorbilder* (Rowohlt: Reinbek, 1979), p. 27.

12 Werner Mittenzwei, *Wer war Brecht?* (Aufbau: Berlin, 1977), p. 100.

13 Ronald Hayman, 'Brecht in the English theatre', in *The German Theatre*, ed. Hayman (Wolff: London, 1975), p. 201.

14 Bolt, *A Man For All Seasons* (Heinemann Educational: London, 1979), p. xvii.

15 'A discussion with Edward Bond', *Gambit* 5, no. 17 (1970), p. 39. Bond later modified his position, e.g.: 'I have worked consciously – starting with Brecht but not ending there', Edward Bond, 'On Brecht: a letter to Peter Holland', *Theatre Quarterly* 8, no. 30 (Summer 1978), p. 35.

16 'As a dramatist Brecht has destroyed me.' Cited by Anthony Waine, 'The legacy for German-speaking playwrights', in *Brecht in Perspective*, ed. Bartram and Waine, p. 197.

17 'Playwright of many interests', *The Times*, 19 August 1964.

18 In *Distinctions* (Jonathan Cape: London, 1985), pp. 20–2, Wesker makes no mention of Brecht. Arden's statement about *Mother Courage*, which he had seen in London in 1956, is cited by Frances Gray, *John Arden* (Macmillan: London, 1982), p. 8.

19 Walter Wager, 'Who's for a revolution? Two interviews with John Arden', *Tulane Drama Review* 11, no. 2 (1966), p. 46.

20 See Michael Patterson, 'Aspects of terrorism in the work of Piscator and Brecht', in *Terrorism and Modern Drama*, ed. John Orr and Dragan Klaic (Edinburgh University Press: 1990), pp. 90–3.

21 Müller, *Theater 1980*, p. 134.

22 Peter Hacks, *Das Poetische* (Suhrkamp: Frankfurt, 1972), p. 45.

23 'Unbefugten ist der Zutritt verboten.' See 'Das Nötigste ist genug', *Schriften zum Theater*, vol. III, ed. W. Hecht (Suhrkamp: Frankfurt, 1963), p. 240.

24 See Michael Patterson, *Peter Stein* (Cambridge University Press: 1981), p. 4 and pp. 162f.

25 Hayman, 'Brecht in the English theatre', p. 204.

26 Reiner Steinweg, *Das Lehrstück*. See Wright, *Postmodern Brecht*, pp. 12f. and 23, n. 8.

27 'I asked Brecht, who did not like questions fired at him like pistol-shots: "Brecht, name a piece which you consider to possess the form of the future." And like a pistol-shot came the reply: "*The Measures Taken*".' Manfred Wekwerth, 'Die

letzten Gespräche', in Brecht, *Die Massnahme*, Kritische Ausgabe, ed. Reiner Steinweg (Suhrkamp: Frankfurt, 1972), p. 265.
28 Hunt, 'Augusto Boal', *The Guardian*, 19 May 1992.
29 M. van Dijk, 'Blocking Brecht', in *Re-interpreting Brecht*, ed. Kleber and Visser, pp. 121 and 204, n. 14.

BIBLIOGRAPHY

This bibliography is a selected list of works by and about Brecht, chosen with particular reference to the topics covered in this volume. With a few exceptions, it is confined to works in English.

WORKS BY BRECHT

Plays

Collected Plays volumes I to VIII, annotated and ed. John Willett and Ralph Manheim (Eyre Methuen, London: 1970 and continuing). The same editors are responsible for the American publication of the *Collected Plays*. There are unresolved disparities between the English and American collections; the following list of contents refers only to the volumes already published, or announced for publication, in England:

Vol. I: *Baal*; *Drums in the Night*; *In the Jungle of Cities*; *The Life of Edward II of England*; *A Respectable Wedding*; *The Beggar*; *Driving out the Devil*; *Lux in Tenebris*; *The Catch*

Vol. I (i): *Baal*

Vol. I (ii): *A Respectable Wedding* and other one-act plays

Vol. I (iii): *Drums in the Night*

Vol. I (iv): *In the Jungle of Cities*

Vol. II (i): *Man equals Man*; *The Elephant Calf*

Vol. II (ii): *The Threepenny Opera*

Vol. II (iii): *The Rise and Fall of the City of Mahagonny*; *The Seven Deadly Sins*

Vol. III (i): *Saint Joan of the Stockyards*

Vol. III (ii): *The Baden-Baden Cantata*; *The Flight over the Ocean*; *He Who Said Yes*; *He Who Said No*; *The Measures Taken*

Vol. IV (i): *The Mother*; *The Exception and the Rule*; *The Horatii and the Curiatii*

Vol. IV (ii): *Round Heads and Pointed Heads*

Vol. IV (iii): *Fear and Misery of the Third Reich*; *Señora Carrar's Rifles*

Vol. V (i): *Life of Galileo*

Vol. V (ii): *Mother Courage and Her Children*

Vol. V (iii): *The Trial of Lucullus*; *Dansen*; *What's the Price of Iron?*

Vol. VI (i): *The Good Person of Szechwan*

Vol. VI (ii): *The Resistible Rise of Arturo Ui*

Vol. VI (iii): *Mr Puntila and his Man Matti*
Vol. VII: *The Visions of Simone Machard; Schweyk in the Second World War; The Caucasian Chalk Circle; The Duchess of Malfi*
Vol. VIII (i): *The Days of the Commune*
Vol. VIII (ii): *Turandot; Report from Herrnburg*
Vol. VIII (iii): *Downfall of the Egoist Johann Fatzer; The Life of Confucius; The Breadshop; The Salzburg Dance of Death*

Poetry

Poems 1913–1956, trans. & ed. J. Willett and R. Manheim (Methuen: London and New York, 1976, 1979, revised paperback edition 1987). An extensive selection of poems by Brecht, arranged chronologically, with index of titles in German. Includes notes by Brecht on different groups of poems, as well as editorial notes on individual poems and on collections. Approximately 500 poems; 627 pages.

Selected Poems, trans. and introduced by H. R. Hays (Reynal and Hitchcock: New York, 1947; Grove Press: New York and Calder: London, 1959). First selection of Brecht's poems to be translated into English. Fifty poems translated by Hays, and chosen in consultation with Brecht.

Prose

Arbeitsjournal 1938–1955 Volume I: 1938–42, volume II: 1942–55, ed. Werner Hecht (Suhrkamp: Frankfurt, 1973).

Diaries 1920–1922, ed. Herta Ramthun (Eyre Methuen: London, 1979; Methuen Paperback: London, 1987).

Gesammelte Werke – sometimes abbreviated to *GW* – (Suhrkamp: Frankfurt, 1967). Published in two editions; one edition in seven volumes and the other in twenty volumes, both by the same publisher, using the same pagination.

Letters 1913–1956, trans. Ralph Manheim and ed. with commentaries and notes by John Willett (Methuen: London, 1990).

Short Stories 1921–1946, ed. John Willett and Ralph Manheim (Methuen: London, 1983).

Theory and practice of theatre

Brecht on Theatre – sometimes abbreviated to *BT* – trans. and ed. John Willett (Methuen: London, 1964, 1974). The immense influence on the English-speaking world of Willett's selection of material in this volume can hardly be overstated. For some time, the volume offered the only opportunity for English-speakers to read Brecht's critical and theoretical writings. Consequently, the inclusion or exclusion of specific essays has had a major effect in shaping our understanding of Brecht's views on theatre and aesthetics. It includes, for example, *A Short Organum for the Theatre*, but doesn't include *The Messingkauf Dialogues*; as a result, the former remains better known to students of Brecht than the latter.

The Messingkauf Dialogues, trans. and ed. John Willett (Methuen: London, 1965).

Theaterarbeit, ed. Ruth Berlau, Brecht, *et al.* (Dresdner: Dresden, 1952). Collection of photographic material, essays, notes and documents on the early work of the

Berliner Ensemble, including extracts from some of the *Modellbücher*. Untranslated.

Films

The Threepenny Opera (Nero-Film: 1931).
Kuhle Wampe (Praesens-Film: 1932).
Murderers are on Their Way (Combined Studio: 1942), never released.
Hangmen Also Die (United Artists: 1942).

WORKS ABOUT BRECHT AND HIS IMMEDIATE ASSOCIATES

Bartram, G. and Waine, A., eds., *Brecht in Perspective* (Longman: London, 1982).

Benjamin, Walter, *Understanding Brecht* (NLB: London, 1973).

Bentley, Eric, *The Brecht Commentaries* (Grove Press and Eyre Methuen: New York and London, 1981). Collection of articles, many of them introductions to specific plays, and some correspondence between Brecht and Bentley.

    The Brecht Memoir (PAJ Publications: New York, 1985). An 'eye-witness' account of Brecht from 1942, when Bentley first met him, to 1956. Includes anecdotes, images, impressions, meetings and correspondence from and to Auden, Laughton, Otto, Wilder – and, of course, between Brecht and Bentley. Gives as strong a personal impression of Bentley as it does of this period of Brecht's life.

Berlau, Ruth, *Living for Brecht*, ed. Hans Bunge (Fromm IPC: New York, 1987).

Betz, Albrecht, *Hanns Eisler: Political Musician*, trans. Bill Hopkins (Cambridge University Press: 1982).

Brooker, Peter, *Bertolt Brecht: Dialectics, Poetry, Politics* (Croom Helm: London, 1988).

Demetz, P., ed., *Brecht: A Collection of Critical Essays* (Prentice Hall, Inc.: Englewood Cliffs, NJ, 1962).

Dickson, Keith, *Towards Utopia: A Study of Brecht* (Clarendon Press: Oxford, 1978).

Drew, David, *Kurt Weill: A Handbook* (Faber: London, 1987).

Esslin, Martin, *Brecht: A Choice of Evils* (revised paperback edition, Methuen: London and New York, 1984).

Ewen, Frederic, *Bertolt Brecht, His Life, His Art and His Times* (Citadel Press: New York, 1967).

Fowler, Kenneth, *Received Truths: Bertolt Brecht and the Problem of Gestus and Musical Meaning* (AMS Press: New York, 1991). A 65-page monograph.

Fuegi, John, *Bertolt Brecht: Chaos, According to Plan* (Cambridge University Press, 1987). Focusses on how Brecht worked in the theatre: 'Treating theory in much the way Brecht treated it (for him it had a valuable place outside of the theatre but almost none in actual day-to-day staging practice)', Fuegi examines Brecht's 'practical problem-solving' in staging and directing theatre. Chapter 6, 'Diary of a production: *The Caucasian Chalk Circle*', builds a vivid picture of the process of Brecht's rehearsals, interaction with actors and theatrical battles and solutions.

    Brecht & Co.: An Archaeology of Voices (forthcoming 1993).

    The Essential Brecht (Hennessy & Ingalls, Inc.: Los Angeles, 1972). Includes chapters on *Edward II*, *The Mother*, *Antigone*, *Mother Courage*, *Schweyk*, *The Good Person*, *Chalk Circle*, *Galileo*.

Gilbert, Michael, *Bertolt Brecht's Striving for Reason, Even in Music: A Critical Assessment* (Peter Lang Verlag: New York, 1988).

Gray, Ronald, *Brecht the Dramatist* (Cambridge University Press: 1976).

Hayman, Ronald, *Brecht: A Biography* (Weidenfeld & Nicolson: London, 1983).

Hiley, Jim, *Theatre at Work: the Story of the National Theatre's Production of Brecht's Galileo* (Routledge & Kegan Paul: London, Boston, 1981).

Hinton, Stephen, ed., *Kurt Weill: The Threepenny Opera* (Cambridge Opera Handbooks, Cambridge University Press: 1990).

Jacobs, N. and Ohlsen, P., eds., *Bertolt Brecht in Britain* (Irat Services Ltd./TQ Publications: London, 1977). Introduction by John Willett.

Kleber, P., *Exceptions and Rules: Brecht, Planchon and The Good Person of Setzuan* (Peter Lang Verlag: New York, 1987).

Kleber, P. and Visser, C., eds., *Re-interpreting Brecht: His Influence on Contemporary Drama and Film* (Cambridge University Press: 1990).

Lucchesi, J. and Shull, R., *Musik bei Brecht* (Henschel: Berlin, 1988).

Lyon, James K., *Bertolt Brecht in America* (Princeton University Press: 1980; Methuen Paperback: London, 1982). An account of the six years of Brecht's exile in America (1941–7). Includes material from interviews with those who worked with or knew Brecht during this period. Draws on documents such as unpublished letters, contracts, newspaper articles and released FBI files on Brecht.

Bertolt Brecht and Rudyard Kipling (Mouton: Paris and The Hague, 1975).

Mews, Siegfried, ed., *Critical Essays on Bertolt Brecht* (G. K. Hall & Co.: Boston, 1989).

Mews, S. and Knust, H., eds., *Essays on Brecht: Theater and Politics* (University of North Carolina Press: Chapel Hill, 1974).

Mueller, Roswitha, *Bertolt Brecht and the Theory of Media* (University of Nebraska Press: Lincoln, Nebraska and London, 1989).

Needle, J. and Thomson, P., *Brecht* (Basil Blackwell: Oxford, 1981). Concentrates on the staging of plays, and considers Brecht's theoretical writings, politics and response to Hitler and contemporary events as part of the context for the plays. Chapter 7, '*Mother Courage*: Brecht's staging', analyses specific key moments of Brecht's production and is particularly useful in revealing the crafting of stage moments in Brecht's play.

Patterson, Michael, *The Revolution in German Theatre 1900–1933* (Routledge: London, 1981).

Pike, David, *Lukács and Brecht* (University of North Carolina Press: Chapel Hill, 1985).

Sanders, Ronald, *The Days Grow Short: The Life and Music of Kurt Weill* (Holt, Rinehart & Winston: New York, 1980).

Schechter, Joel, *Durov's Pig: Clowns, Politics and Theatre* (Theater Communications Group: New York, 1985).

Speirs, Ronald, *Brecht's Early Plays* (Macmillan Press: London, 1982). Chapters on *Baal*, *Drums*, *In the Jungle*, *Edward II*, *Man is Man*, the Operas and the *Lehrstücke*.

Steinweg, Reiner, *Das Lehrstück. Brechts Theorie einer ästhetischen Erziehung* (J. B. Metzler: Stuttgart 1972).

Suvin, Darko, *To Brecht and Beyond: Soundings in Modern Dramaturgy* (The Harvester Press and Barnes and Noble Books: Sussex and New Jersey, 1984).

Tatlow, Antony, *The Mask of Evil: Brecht's Response to the Poetry, Theatre and Thought of China and Japan: A Comparative and Critical Evaluation* (Peter Lang: Berne, 1977).

Thomson, Philip, *The Poetry of Brecht* (University of North Carolina Press: Chapel Hill, 1989).

Völker, Klaus, *Brecht: A Biography*, trans. John Nowell (Marion Boyars: London and Boston, 1979).

Brecht Chronicle, trans. Fred Wieck (Seabury Press: New York, 1975).

Weber, Betty Nance and Heinen, Hubert, eds., *Bertolt Brecht: Political Theory and Literary Practice* (University of Manchester Press: 1980).

Whitaker, Peter, *Brecht's Poetry* (Oxford University Press: 1985). The problem with this book, for the non-German speaker, is that all the poems are quoted in German, as are the titles, which makes the study less accessible than it might be.

Willett, John, *Brecht in Context: Comparative Approaches* (Methuen: London and New York, 1984).

Caspar Neher: Brecht's Designer (Arts Council/Methuen: London, 1986).

The Theatre of Bertolt Brecht: A Study from Eight Aspects, revised paperback edition (Methuen: London, 1977). Includes brief factual analysis of all the stage and radio plays, as well as chapters on the subject-matter; the language; theatrical influences; the music; theatrical practice; the theory; politics; the English aspect.

Witt, Hubert, ed., *Brecht As They Knew Him*, trans. John Peet (Lawrence & Wishart: London, 1975). A wonderful collection of 34 recollections by writers, actors, collaborators, musicians and friends who worked with Brecht. Includes contributions from Lenya, Hauptmann, Berlau, Eisler, Hurwicz, Dessau, Neher.

Wright, Elizabeth, *Postmodern Brecht: A Re-presentation* (Routledge: London, 1989).

INDEX OF WORKS BY BRECHT

GENERAL INDEX